EDWARD
THE
CONFESSOR

EDWARD THE CONFESSOR

Frank Barlow
Fellow of the British Academy
Emeritus Professor in the University of Exeter

EYRE METHUEN

LONDON

First published 1970
Reprinted 1979; first paperback edition 1979
© 1970 Frank Barlow
Printed in Great Britain for
Eyre Methuen Ltd
11 New Fetter Lane, London EC4P 4EE
by Richard Clay (The Chaucer Press) Ltd,
Bungay, Suffolk

ISBN 0 413 27830 1 (hardback)
ISBN 0 413 45950 0 (paperback)

I wondered what other men – in addition to Stringham – had been 'in her life', as Mrs Erdleigh would have said; what, for that matter, had been Miss Weedon's true relationship with Stringham. One passes through the world knowing few, if any, of the important things about even the people with whom one has been from time to time in the closest intimacy.

ANTHONY POWELL, *The Kindly Ones*

CONTENTS

ILLUSTRATIONS

The author and publishers offer thanks to owners and trustees for permission to reproduce the items listed above. Acknowledgements to the sources appear with the captions to the plates.

MAPS AND TABLES

MAPS

GENEALOGICAL TABLES
folding pages at the end of the book

PREFACE

It was reading the *Vita Ædwardi Regis*, about ten years ago, when I was writing a book on the English Church before the Norman Conquest, which first made me specially interested in Edward. Since then I have often thought about this enigmatic king and made several attempts to elucidate his behaviour. I was, therefore, delighted when Professor David Douglas invited me to contribute a book on Edward to the English Monarchs series he was editing. I was also very touched by the generosity of the offer, for I knew that Douglas had once thought of writing this book himself and I knew also that he was aware that my interpretation would not be his – indeed, in its coolness towards the Norman party might even cause him pain. I accepted without hesitation. One writes one's own book. My Edward could not be his or anyone else's.

Although I have as far as possible made my own path, I have not shunned company. I have tried out most of my ideas on my pupils. The work when completed was read in manuscript by Mr David R. Bates, Professor David Douglas, Mr G. W. Greenaway, Mr L. J. Lloyd, and Miss Mary Anne O'Donovan, besides the publishers. From all these I accepted criticism and advice while stubbornly keeping my basic positions intact. I have had kind services from Miss Marion M. Archibald, Dr Pierre Chaplais, Professor F. W. Clayton, Mrs Audrey Erskine, Miss Ann Hamlin, Professor H. R. Loyn, Miss Catherine Morton, Miss Hope Muntz, and Mr Peter Sawyer. The enterprise almost from the beginning has been under the interested care of my secretary, Marjorie Bowen. To all who have helped me I offer my most grateful thanks. It is even possible that St Edward the Confessor may look graciously upon them, his servants.

FRANK BARLOW

The University of Exeter
8 June 1970

PREFACE TO SECOND EDITION

The reprinting has allowed me to correct such errors as I have found and to take some, though necessarily limited, account of work published since 1970. Nothing that I have read has led me to think that my view of the reign was unreasonable or misguided. Kathryn Y. Wallace sent me a useful reference, and I am grateful to all those who have helped me with criticism or advice.

FRANK BARLOW

Middle Court Hall, Kenton, Exeter
4 October 1978

ABBREVIATED REFERENCES

Adam of Bremen	*Magistri Adam Bremensis Gesta Hamma-burgensis ecclesiae pontificum*, ed. Bernhard Schmeidler (Scriptores rerum Germani-carum in usum scholarum, 3rd ed., Han-nover and Leipzig, 1917)
Barlow, *English Church*	Frank Barlow, *The English Church 1000–1066* (1963, reprinted 1966)
Chron.	*The Anglo-Saxon Chronicle*, ed. Dorothy Whitelock with David C. Douglas and Susie I. Tucker (*EHD*, vol. i, and inde-pendently 1961)
Chron. Abingdon	*Chronicon Monasterii de Abingdon*, ed. J. Stevenson (Rolls ser. 1858)
DB	*Domesday Book*
Eadmer, *Historia Novorum*	Eadmer, *Historia Novorum in Anglia*, ed. M. Rule (Rolls ser. 1884)
EHD	*English Historical Documents*, ed. D. C. Douglas: i (1955) ed. Dorothy Whitelock
EHR	*The English Historical Review*
Encomium Emmae	*Encomium Emmae Reginae*, ed. Alistair Campbell, Royal Hist. Soc., Camden 3rd ser., lxxii (1949)
Florence	Florence of Worcester, *Chronicon ex chronicis*, ed. B. Thorpe (Eng. Hist. Soc., 1848–9)
Freeman, *NC*	E. A. Freeman, *The History of the Norman Conquest of England* (i, ii, 2nd ed. 1870; iii–v, 1st ed. 1869–75)
Harmer, *Writs*	F. E. Harmer, *Anglo-Saxon Writs* (1952)
HCY	*The Historians of the Church of York and its Archbishops*, ed. J. Raine (Rolls ser. 1879–94)
Jumièges	Guillaume de Jumièges, *Gesta Norman-norum Ducum*, ed. Jean Marx (Rouen and Paris, 1914)

KCD
J. M. Kemble, *Codex Diplomaticus Aevi Saxonici* (Eng. Hist. Soc., vols. iii, iv, vi, 1845, 1846, 1848)

Körner, *Battle of Hastings*
Sten Körner, *The Battle of Hastings, England and Europe 1035–1066* (Lund, 1964)

Liber Eliensis
Liber Eliensis, ed. E. O. Blake, Royal Hist. Soc., Camden 3rd ser., xcii (1962)

Liebermann, *Die Gesetze*
F. Liebermann, *Die Gesetze der Angelsachsen* (Halle, 1903)

Maitland, *DB and Beyond*
F. W. Maitland, *Domesday Book and Beyond* (1897); refs. are to the reissue, Fontana Library (1960), which has, unfortunately, a different pagination

Malmesbury, *GP*
William of Malmesbury, *De Gestis Pontificum Anglorum*, ed. N. E. S. A. Hamilton (Rolls ser. 1870)

Malmesbury, *GR*
William of Malmesbury, *De Gestis Regum Anglorum*, ed. W. Stubbs (Rolls ser. 1887–1889)

Migne, *PL*
J. P. Migne, *Patrologiae cursus completus: Patrologia latina* (1844 ff.)

Oleson, *Witenagemot*
Tryggvi J. Oleson, *The Witenagemot in the reign of Edward the Confessor* (1955)

Ordericus Vitalis
Historia Ecclesiastica libri tredecim, ed. A. le Prévost (Paris, 1838–55)
The Ecclesiastical History, ii–vi (Bks III–XIII), ed. and trans. Marjorie Chibnall (1969–78)

Plummer, *Two Chronicles*
C. Plummer and J. Earle, *Two of the Saxon Chronicles parallel*, vol. ii, Plummer's introduction, notes, and index (1899)

Poitiers
William of Poitiers, *Gesta Guillelmi*, ed. and trans. Raymonde Foreville (Les classiques de l'histoire de France au moyen age, Paris, 1952)

Robertson, *Charters*
Anglo-Saxon Charters, ed. and trans. A. J. Robertson (Cambridge Studies in English Legal History, 1956)

Robertson, *Laws*   *Laws of the Kings of England from Edmund to Henry I*, ed. and trans. A. J. Robertson (1925)

Rolls ser.   Chronicles and Memorials of Great Britain and Ireland during the Middle Ages, publ. under the direction of the Master of the Rolls

Sawyer   P. H. Sawyer, *Anglo-Saxon Charters: an annotated List and Bibliography* (Royal Hist. Soc., 1968)

Symeon, *HDE*   *Symeonis Monachi Opera Omnia: Historia Ecclesiae Dunhelmensis*, ed. T. Arnold (Rolls ser. 1882)

Symeon, *HR*   *Symeonis Monachi Opera Omnia: Historia Regum*, ed. T. Arnold (Rolls ser. 1885)

VCH   *The Victoria History of the counties of England* (1900 ff.)

VEdR   *Vita Ædwardi Regis* (*The Life of King Edward*), ed. and trans. Frank Barlow (Nelson's Medieval Texts, 1962)

Vita Wulfstani   *The Vita Wulfstani of William of Malmesbury*, ed. R. R. Darlington, Royal Hist. Soc., Camden 3rd ser., xl (1928)

Whitelock, *Wills*   *Anglo-Saxon Wills*, ed. and trans. Dorothy Whitelock (Cambridge Studies in English Legal History, 1930)

Addition

Carmen   *The Carmen de Hastingae Proelio of Guy bishop of Amiens*, ed. and trans. Catherine Morton and Hope Muntz (Oxford Medieval Texts, 1972)

INTRODUCTION

In general Saints' Lives offer little difficulty to the modern historian, and royal saints are the least taboo. No aura of sanctity has condensed to protect Charlemagne,[1] Edward the Martyr (the Confessor's half-uncle), Olaf Helgi of Norway, Cnut II of Denmark, Henry II of Germany, or Louis IX of France from critical scrutiny. It is tacitly accepted that the canonization of a king is part of the history of the man's posthumous reputation, that it is related to the social and religious atmosphere which led to belief in his sanctity and to the political events which nurtured and gave authority to the belief. Although a judgment on the past, canonization rarely sheds much light on the person it honours. Even though it may sometimes confirm a sound traditional belief in the man's Christian life and benevolence towards the church, occasionally it appears completely irrelevant to, or even at variance with, the man's true historical character. The posthumous fame of Edward the Martyr is a case in point.

Edward the Confessor's canonization by Pope Alexander III on 7 February 1161,[2] although but tenuously connected with events which occurred before 1066 and almost exclusively related to the history of the mid-twelfth century, has, however, had some influence on later, even modern, interpretations of the king's character and behaviour. Because Edward's actions were rarely of outstanding interest at the time, and contemporary accounts of his reign are meagre, it is tempting to pad out his biography, or explain its shadowiness, by his religion. Edward ruled England for almost a quarter of a century; his reign led to, or at least preceded, the Norman Conquest; and historians have

---

[1] Charlemagne, admittedly, was canonized (on 29 December 1165) by the Anti-pope Paschal III for the Emperor Frederick I. R. Folz, 'La chancellerie de Frédéric Ier et la canonisation de Charlemagne', *Le Moyen âge*, lxx (1964), 13–31.

[2] See below, p. 280. He is pronounced a confessor in the papal bull, below, p. 324. In the early church confessors were those who suffered for confessing the Christian faith, but short of martyrdom. Later, the idea was more that the confessor had demonstrated his religion in the face of the temptations of the world. Edward was regularly called 'the Confessor' presumably in order to distinguish him from his half-uncle, King Edward the Martyr, whose feast day was 18 March. See Barlow, *VEdR*, pp. 124–5.

usually felt that the man and his reign deserve detailed attention. The tradition of sanctity, whether it was accepted as accurate or, as was common with Protestant historians, regarded as an inflation of negative characteristics, gave an easy clue to a story of which the end was known.

Although later observers may be better placed to form a true appreciation of the life of an historical character, it is unreasonable to base our interpretation of Edward on twelfth-century views. Writers like William of Malmesbury and Osbert of Clare, despite the research they undertook, were men of a new age, involved in new interests. The one wrote under the shadow of the Norman Conquest and was disturbed by the problem of the justice of the expropriation. The other was committed to the cause of proving that Edward was a saint. Neither could go behind the literary sources available to them; their only new material was the traditions which had formed since Edward's death and the evidence of Edward's continuing life in Heaven, his posthumous miracles. Twelfth-century views have to be noted and considered, in the same way as all later interpretations have to be reviewed, in order to see whether they help. But the basic task of the modern historian is to try to reconstruct Edward in his contemporary setting, from a superior position to make sense of the earliest reactions. Especially his task is to uncover the Edward who existed before the Norman Conquest took place. It needs careful detachment, rejection of all hindsight, to avoid treating Edward's reign as the prelude to the Conquest and giving undue attention to incidents and acts which lead causally in that direction. Yet, unless it is believed that Edward was committed from first to last, unhesitatingly, without deviation, to the succession of William – and there have been historians who have held this opinion – it must be recognized that most of Edward's actions, most of the events of the reign, lay outside this single concatenation. We should not trace a receding perspective of the Norman Conquest back and back until it encloses so small a sector of the past that our prospect of it becomes gravely contracted.[1]

The problem of recreating the living Edward is made difficult by the nature of the sources for his life; and an evaluation of these is a fundamental duty.

The lantern which William of Malmesbury used to guide his steps when he was writing his *History of the English Kings*[2] was the Anglo-

[1] Cf. J. E. A. Jolliffe, *Angevin Kingship* (1955), Introduction, p. 1.
[2] Malmesbury, *GP*, p. 4.

Saxon Chronicle, annals written in Old-English; and it remains the
surest guide. It is particularly valuable, because the first draft, at least,
of that part of the Chronicle which covers most of Edward's reign was
put together before the king's death,[1] a circumstance which ensured
that the events recorded were not chosen so as to explain either the
Norman Conquest or Edward's reputation for sanctity. For our period
the Chronicle has survived in four manuscripts (the C, D, E, and F
Annals), and, in translation, was also incorporated into twelfth-
century Latin chronicles, such as those written by 'Florence of
Worcester', Simeon of Durham, and Henry of Huntingdon. Annal C
was probably written at Abingdon abbey. Annal D is the northern
version written at Worcester or, more probably, at York. Annal E is a
St Augustine's, Canterbury, version, subsequently revised at Peterborough abbey. Annal F is an almost straight copy of this made for
Christ Church, Canterbury, and so without interest to us. The Latin
versions seem to be based on one or more of the extant vernacular
annals and, in so far as they are derivative, have no independent
authority.[2] Occasionally, however, the Latin chronicler offers us
information which he has obtained from elsewhere, sometimes from
annals or historical material preserved in his own church, sometimes, one
suspects, from his historical imagination. Hence William of Malmesbury,
'Florence', and several of the other twelfth-century historians can be
viewed as the earliest commentators on the Chronicle history.

All these sets of annals are for this period synoptic. They are clearly
derived, directly or indirectly, from some basic version, which no
longer exists: the entries for each year usually contain much common
material presented in nearly identical language. But, as the existing
versions are re-editions, produced in different monasteries, each with
its own interests and political sympathies, all have their variants.
Items are omitted, new items are introduced; the order in the entries is
sometimes disturbed; years are lost, sometimes with an accumulative
effect; occasionally the editor modifies an entry in order to give it a
different political tone or to incorporate local information. All the
same, although the several versions of the Chronicle can be regarded as
independent chronicles, and recently have been printed in a way
which accepts that they are,[3] they are really only marginally independent. The bulk of the material that they contain derives from the

[1] Körner, *Battle of Hastings*, pp. 14 ff.   [2] *Ibid.*, pp. 24 ff.
[3] Ed. Dorothy Whitelock with David C. Douglas and Susie I. Tucker (1961).

common source. Therefore the several annals, when they agree, do not corroborate each other. It is only when they disagree that we have more than a single witness.

We do not know in which monastic house the common source was written, nor the exact date when the section which covers Edward's reign was assembled. We may be sure, however, that it was written in a monastery in the south of England, and, as the entries are most detailed for the period 1049–58, it is likely that it was during this time that the annalist first collected his materials together. After 1058 the entries become short and scrappy, the effect possibly of a haphazard continuation of an existing work. The entry for 1066 was certainly written after the close of that year.

Even more uncertain are the dates when the existing versions were composed in the several monasteries. Chronicle *C* ends in 1066 and the manuscript is written in mid-eleventh-century scripts; and as the other versions reveal a continuing interest in the politics of Edward's reign, it is unlikely that they were made long after Edward's death. Each has its characteristic bias. The *C*, Abingdon, version is royalist; the *E* version, written at St Augustine's, Canterbury, is Godwinist. The northern version, *D*, is politically neutral; its special feature is the attention it gives to Welsh and Scandinavian affairs. Yet, although the occasional loaded word or expression, the spasmodic refashioning of an entry, reveal the feelings of the chronicler, the product remains basically annalistic. Obits are regularly entered, usually without comment; events are mentioned without explanation. There is no continuity of theme, no thesis, little causality. For men who had lived through Edward's reign the Chronicle would have recalled vivid memories; for us it draws attention to largely inexplicable happenings.[1]

Associated with the Chronicle, but entirely different in method, is the *Vita Ædwardi Regis*, written about the time of the king's death by a foreign monk associated with Edward's queen, Edith.[2] Although it gives us few facts which are not to be found in the Chronicle, and the author probably made use of the *E* version or its prototype, it is an historical pamphlet with a purpose and a distinct point of view. Its aim is to glorify the family of Earl Godwin and especially three of the elder children, Queen Edith and Earls Harold and Tostig. Its theme is that when the king was governed by the house of Godwin, and while that

[1] Cf. J. H. Round, *Feudal England* (1895), pp. 317–18, 'the arid entries in our jejune native chronicle'.   [2] See below, Appendix A.

family remained united of purpose, the kingdom was prosperous and Edward ruled like another Solomon, giving the country peace. Presages of Edward's sanctity appear in the later pages of the book – and the *Vita Ædwardi Regis* is in fact the foundation on which the hagiographical legend was built – but the book itself is not a saint's life. It is the earliest and most interesting history of a section of Edward's court. It has to be used with caution. The author was not only writing for a purpose but also, as a foreigner by birth and a visitor to England only late in the reign, he must have had a very superficial knowledge of English history. Nevertheless, it is the earliest attempt to give a pattern to the events.

The one other early explanation of Edward's reign is what can be called the Norman tradition. This did not take literary form until after the Conquest had occurred, and appears in its most developed form in William of Poitiers' *Gesta Guillelmi*, written after 1073 or perhaps 1076. As the archdeacon of Lisieux's main purpose was to praise William the Conqueror and justify his actions, his view of Edward's reign is simple. Edward, because of the benefits he had received from the counts of Normandy, wished William to succeed him as king.[1] Consequently those men whom the archdeacon considered – rightly or wrongly – to have opposed or obstructed the king's wishes, notably Godwin and Harold, are vilified. The theme determined the archdeacon's selection of events, and his presentation of these arbitrarily selected events may be misleading; but we are at least given the history of a diplomacy which is not recorded elsewhere and a useful corrective to the eulogy of the house of Godwin presented by the *Vita Ædwardi Regis*.

The first Anglo-Norman to consider Edward and his reign was William, precentor and librarian of Malmesbury abbey, who wrote the first edition of his *Gesta Regum Anglorum* in 1118–25. William was a fair man, interested in the kingdom's past, and technically well equipped as an historian. He read the Chronicle, and for Edward's reign the *Vita Ædwardi Regis* and the *Gesta Guillelmi*. Although he may have been able to draw on an oral tradition that was not quite dead, and was more aware than his predecessors of the nascent cult of the saint, it is obvious that he had no written sources which are not available to us. What is more, he was unable to solve the problem that they presented. Faced with discordant views, he did not know which to accept or how to reconcile them. He took the honest, if unenterprising, course of recording

[1] Poitiers, pp. 28–32. For the date, see Chibnall, Orderic Vitalis, ii. App. III.

the different interpretations, almost without comment. He made no attempt to give the reign a pattern. For once he failed to write history.

Before William of Malmesbury was dead, the first Life of Edward as a saint had been written. Osbert of Clare, prior of Westminster, where Edward was buried, a man engaged in restoring the abbey's muniments by reconstituting or forging its charters, became equally committed to promoting Edward's claims to sanctity.[1] By 1138 he had written his *Vita beati regis Eadwardi*, a free adaptation of suitable parts of the *Vita Ædwardi Regis*. Osbert rejected his source's main theme, the contribution of the house of Godwin to Edward's and England's glory, and omitted almost all the history, replacing it with legends and accounts of the miracles which had begun to occur at the royal tomb. Osbert's Life was rewritten by Ailred of Rievaulx in 1163, in time for the translation of Edward's body to a new tomb in the abbey after the papal canonization, and is therefore the archetype of all later versions of the ecclesiastical legend.[2] From this literary genealogy it will have become clear that the hagiographical tradition can be disregarded as an historical source for Edward's earthly career. The few historical elements which it conserved are drawn from literary works, all of which have survived independently and are more profitably studied in the original.

The rather sparse and somewhat enigmatic accounts of Edward's *conversatio* and *res gestae* presented by the several versions of the Anglo-Saxon Chronicle and the *Vita Ædwardi Regis* can be supplemented, of course, by notices in the other English monastic chronicles. These were usually drawn up in the twelfth century in order to justify and explain a monastery's claims to lands and privilege. For the early period they are, either overtly or covertly, charter-chronicles, that is to say they either rehearse the charters which their benefactors are alleged to have granted, sometimes with a commentary, or attempt to digest the charter material. From such sources we occasionally get interesting anecdotes about the men and women of the period, although the veracity is always doubtful. We are in the domain of the forged charter, the anachronistic claim, and it is always hard to decide whether a commentary on a forgery is worth serious attention.

Foreign observers showed little interest in England and were almost invariably ill-informed. There is no contemporary Norman reference to English affairs. A few scraps can be collected from other French sources; but they do not amount to much. Scandinavia and its fringe,

[1] See below, pp. 272 ff.   [2] Barlow, *VEdR*, p. xxxvii.

however, make a small, but interesting contribution. All the Scandinavian kings were pretenders to the English throne; and the sagas, although they were hardly committed to writing before the thirteenth century, preserve some contemporary skaldic verses. The prose in which the poetry is embedded is hardly the stuff out of which sober history can be made; but the Viking view of Edward, as a typical character of that warlike age,[1] is at least interesting. Finally, we have the *Gesta Hammaburgensis ecclesiae pontificum*, written before 1076 by Adam, master of the cathedral school at Bremen, who was personally acquainted with Svein Ulfsson or Estrithson, king of Denmark, Edward's nephew by marriage. Adam gives us glimpses of England as seen by the Scandinavian courts.[2]

No less scrappy and recalcitrant are the governmental records which have survived. The eleventh century lies before the period of systematic archives. The ecclesiastical records of Edward's reign are minimal. The actions of the royal government have left only a fitful trace. Edward seems to have issued no new laws: no further revision was made after Cnut's two great codes issued about 1020. From ecclesiastical chronicles, cartularies, and archives have been collected a substantial number of charters and writs, ostensibly issued by the king. The charters,[3] however, were mostly composed by the beneficiaries to record the royal grant, and – a more serious defect – have seldom been transmitted in their original form. They range from the very rare parchment of the period, through copies, increasingly revised, to the out-and-out forgery, usually of the twelfth century. All but the complete fabrication – interesting only for the period when it was made – are best regarded as literary accounts of the royal action and criticized as such. Writs,[4] most of

---

[1] See below, pp. 6–8.   [2] Cf. Körner, *Battle of Hastings*, pp. 138 ff.

[3] For charters, see Sawyer; Harmer, *Writs*, pp. 38–41; Galbraith, *Studies in the Public Records* (1948), pp. 31–5; Eric John, 'Some Latin Charters of the Tenth Century Reformation in England', *Revue Bénédictine*, lxx (1960), 334–5, 340n., 357; Barlow, *English Church*, pp. 124–9; P. Chaplais, 'The Origin and Authenticity of the Royal Anglo-Saxon Diploma', *Journal of the Soc. of Archivists*, iii (1965), 48–61, 'The Authenticity of the Royal Anglo-Saxon Diplomas of Exeter', *Bulletin of the Institute of Historical Research*, xxxix (1966), 1–34; H. P. R. Finberg, 'Some Crediton Documents Re-examined with some Observations on the Criticism of Anglo-Saxon Charters', *The Antiquaries Journal*, xlviii (1968), 84–6. The British Academy has commissioned a new edition, beginning with *Charters of Rochester*, ed. A. Campbell (1973). See also below, pl. 7.

[4] For writs, see Harmer, *Writs*; V. H. Galbraith, *Studies in the Public Records*, pp. 35–6; T. A. M. Bishop and P. Chaplais, *Facsimiles of English Writs to A.D. 1100* (1957); P. Chaplais, 'The Anglo-Saxon Chancery: from the Diploma to the Writ', *Journal of the Soc. of Archivists*, iii (1966), 160–76. See also below, pll. 5 and 6.

which were probably written by royal clerks, are easier to judge, for they can more easily be tested by the criteria of diplomatic. They are, however, less informative than the charters. The product of Edward's government which has survived in the largest quantity is the coinage, the silver pennies.[1] For us coins are metallic documents. They carry inscriptions and images and were, besides a means of exchange, vehicles for royal propaganda. Foreign archives do not supplement the English; and among the few papal instruments referring to England in this period even fewer have any serious claim to authenticity.

One great public record, however, throws some light on the reign: Domesday Book, compiled in 1086.[2] The royal clerks not only attempted to record the names of those who held landed estates in 1066 and their value at that time, but also occasionally allowed some incidental information about the men or their estates to slip through into the penultimate and even the final draft. Domesday statistics have been shown to be inaccurate, misleading, and sometimes fanciful;[3] and the pre-Conquest data is likely to be the least reliable. Domesday Book is not only dense, but also full of riddles. Brave indeed is the man who walks confidently through the maze. Nevertheless it should not be neglected because of its difficulty. F. W. Maitland, who was both brave and imaginative, reconstructed a vanished society from its pages.

Perhaps most disappointing of all is the almost complete lack of literary compositions. We have seen that annals were written in some monasteries. If homilies, saints' lives, treatises on law or theology, and poetry were also written, almost none has survived. Some, especially those written in the vernacular, may well have disappeared. But the great tenth-century reformation in the English church, which had led

[1] For coins, see G. C. Brooke, *English Coins* (3rd ed. 1950); *Sylloge of Coins of the British Isles* (British Academy, 1958 ff.); J. J. North, *English Hammered Coinage*, i (Spink & Son, 1963). Among articles the following are of special importance: R. H. M. Dolley and D. M. Metcalf, 'The Reform of the English Coinage under Eadgar', *Anglo-Saxon Coins: Studies presented to F. M. Stenton* (1961), pp. 136–68; H. R. Loyn, 'Boroughs and Mints, A.D. 900–1066', *ibid.*, pp. 122–35; Peter Seaby, 'The sequence of Anglo-Saxon coin types, 1030–1050', *British Numismatic Journal*, xxviii (1958), 111–46; R. H. M. Dolley, 'New light on the order of the early issues of Edward the Confessor', *ibid.*, xxix (1960), 289–92. The sequence of the types is not now in dispute, but the dates for the various issues are less certain. See also below, pll. 9 and 10.

[2] See, especially, Maitland, *DB and Beyond*; V. H. Galbraith, *The Making of Domesday Book* (1961); R. Welldon Finn, *The Domesday Inquest* (1961), *An Introduction to Domesday Book* (1962), *The Liber Exoniensis* (1964), *The Eastern Counties* (1967).

[3] Cf. my review of Finn, *The Liber Exoniensis*, in *History*, clxix (1965), 213.

to a considerable literary renaissance in the early eleventh century, was almost spent. Men seem to have been content with what had been written; and it was not until the end of Edward's reign that the first harbingers of what could have been a new literary revival – Goscelin and Folcard from St Bertin's monastery at St Omer – visited England apparently to undertake literary commissions.[1] The welcome which these strangers received in English monasteries of good tradition and repute proves that the Latin culture of the English church was at a low ebb.

To write the history of Edward and his reign we have to scrape the barrel with care: every scrap of information is precious. We have also to use the most exact techniques and rely much on our understanding of contemporary society in other countries. Any historical reconstruction must be a personal creation, and the scarcer and more untrustworthy the evidence the greater the artifice. The facts simply do not speak for themselves. Nor can the facts and the historian's contribution be separated. A history is not made of bricks and mortar. The historian does his best and writes in good faith. He meets uncertainty at every point and offers his solution. Sometimes the only course that he can honestly follow is to offer several equally plausible possibilities, between which he cannot decide. He has to steer between bland assurance, for which he has no warrant, and complete scepticism, which denies his craft. Above all, he has to withstand the temptation to squeeze his sources too hard. A few clear drops of information are better than a larger but more turbid yield.

The most detailed account of the reign is in volume ii of E. A. Freeman's *The History of the Norman Conquest of England, its causes and its results,* first published in 1868. Of this Charles Plummer wrote in 1899, 'I may perhaps be allowed to say generally that the second volume of Mr Freeman's great work, while based, like everything he wrote, on a wide and careful comparison of the original authorities, seems to me in *tone* both tedious and untrustworthy, owing to the author's extravagant admiration of Godwine and Harold and his almost childish detestation of everything Norman and French.'[2] This is a merciful judgment. No one, of course, can neglect Freeman's book: it is a mine of miscellaneous information. But I have not thought it necessary to refute his views, to indicate where and why I differ from him, or to correct his errors. And,

[1] *VEdR*, pp. xliv ff. For recent ascriptions of MSS to the mid eleventh century, see Barlow, *English Church* (2nd edn., 1979), App. 2.
[2] Plummer, *Two Chronicles*, pp. 225–6.

although I have read with profit most later accounts of Edward's reign, here, too, I have considered it otiose to record my agreement or disagreement with them. I would not, however, be thought ungrateful. Even if I in my turn have gone back to the earliest authorities, and even though I have tried always to look at them with fresh eyes, I must accept that much of my attitude has been formed (if sometimes by reaction) by the opinions of my predecessors in this field. To them my homage and thanks.

EDWARD
THE
CONFESSOR

Chapter 1

EDWARD'S BACKGROUND

The world into which Edward, King Æthelred's son, was born was a world deeply disturbed by Viking raids, conquests, and settlements. The 'royal' charter, dated 1005, in which Edward makes his first appearance as a witness, refers to them in its preamble:[1]

> I, Æthelred, in the company of the priests of God and our counsellors, contemplating with the pacific gaze of a religious mind and with good will the anger of God raging with ever increasing savagery against us, have decreed that he shall be appeased with the unremitting performance of good works and that there shall be no desisting from his praises. And since in our days we suffer the fires of war and the plundering of our riches, and from the cruel depredations of barbarian enemies engaged in ravaging our country and from the manifold sufferings inflicted on us by pagan races threatening us with extermination we perceive that we live in perilous times . . . it greatly behoves us . . . to give the utmost care and attention to the profit of our souls.

In 1005 Æthelred was about thirty-five, having reigned for twenty-seven years and still to reign for another eleven. This long and mostly inglorious reign ended in disaster. In it loyalty to the dynasty was weakened, the ruling classes seem to have lost confidence in themselves, and there was a general deterioration in the standards of behaviour. Æthelred's father, Edgar, had ruled over a great empire in Britain, thus crowning the military exploits of the West-Saxon kings since Alfred; but, unlike them, Edgar did not have to fight wars in order to achieve and maintain his imperial position. Besides establishing peace and prosperity, he also patronized a radical reform of the English church; and, after his premature death in 975, at the age of thirty-two, his reputation continued to grow, for, seen in retrospect, his reign was a golden age. The astonishing collapse of royal power which followed his death was due to the accession of children to the throne and the resumption of Viking attacks on the kingdom. Æthelred's difficulties

[1] *KCD*, no. 714.

were also increased by the way in which he gained the crown. His elder step-brother, Edward, was murdered by members of Æthelred's household in 978; and the people's detestation of this crime is proved by the way in which they transformed an unpleasant youth into Edward 'king and martyr' and flocked to his shrine at Shaftesbury.

Although Æthelred has little claim to a great reputation, it is clear that posterity, which treated his father so generously, treated him with less than justice. The account of his reign as it now appears in the Anglo-Saxon Chronicle was written after his death, after his final humiliation,[1] and is coloured throughout by the ending. Although Æthelred was a most active prince, a vigorous soldier, fertile in schemes for victory, often experimenting, always trying, never giving up hope, the plans, we are told, always went awry, the efforts always came to nought. Especially we learn of the repeated, blatant, inexplicable treachery of Eadric Streona, the villain who deserted whenever the king was about to win, yet was always restored to a position of trust. There is also the mystery of Æthelred and his council. During his minority he was served by the *witan*, the counsellors, of his father; and in two important sources for his reign his acts are normally ascribed to him and his *witan*. The Anglo-Saxon Chronicle goes out of its way to deny autocratic government to the king. 'Then the king and all his *witan* decreed that all the ships that were any use should be assembled at London' (992). 'Then the king and his *witan* determined to . . . promise them tribute and provisions, on condition that they should cease from harrying' (994). 'Then all the *witan* were summoned to the king in order to consider how this country should be defended' (1010). Similarly Æthelred's laws were all enacted by the king and his *witan*.

Yet the chronicler writes of the *un-raed*,[2] the lack of counsel and decision, and how all things were *raed-leas*,[3] done ill-advisedly, phrases which suggest that men were making a play on the king's name (noble counsel), and calling him *un-raed*, 'no counsel'. The likeliest meaning of the nickname is that Æthelred himself was incapable of giving good counsel: he lacked wisdom and was an unlucky king. It is also clear that his counsellors were no less unwise and that there was much difference of opinion. The chronicler tries to spare the king by blaming his counsellors and favourites for the country's misfortunes. But later chroniclers[4]

[1] Cf. Körner, *Battle of Hastings*, pp. 7–10.
[2] *Chron. s.a.* 1011; cf. 1016. [3] *Chron. s.a.* 1009.
[4] Malmesbury, *GR*, i. 185–91, 207–15, is hostile and severe. But, pp. 190–1, he confesses that he does not entirely understand the cause of the disasters.

and historians were less charitable, and the mis-translation of *un-raed* as 'unready' hardly helped Æthelred's reputation. He may have been without good advice, he may have behaved with consistent stupidity and lack of judgment, but he was no sluggard.

England, already in part a Danish country as a result of the ninth-century invasions and colonization, in Æthelred's reign was again deeply influenced by the north. Scandinavian adventurers regarded the British Isles as a convenient area for raiding and settlement and Scandinavian kings aimed at conquest. The political ambitions of Kings Svein Forkbeard and his son, Cnut, made this period of Scandinavian aggression different from the earlier phase which Alfred had tamed. Also these invaders were even more dangerous. Harald Gormsson, or Bluetooth, Svein's father, had organized professional military units, the Jóms-vikings, which were probably superior to anything which an English king could put into the field. From 980, when Viking raids on England began again, until 1017, when Cnut was generally accepted as king, there were few years in which there was no fighting in England. In 991 the great Viking hero, Olaf Tryggvason, defeated the Ealdorman Brihtnoth at the battle of Maldon. But there were not many battles: usually the invaders were bought off. In 1012 a famous Jóms-viking, Thorkell Hávi, changed sides and entered Æthelred's service with forty-five ships, probably because he was disgusted by the killing of Ælfheah, archbishop of Canterbury, by his drunken soldiers; and in 1013, Svein of Denmark, using Thorkell's desertion as an excuse, invaded. He had conquered all England and forced Æthelred and most of his family to flee to Normandy when he died on 3 February 1014. Æthelred was able to return and this was the time when English forces should have been victorious. Svein's son, Cnut, was young and inexperienced, and withdrew from England for part of the years 1014–15; but Æthelred died on 23 April 1016 and his son and successor, Edmund Ironside, on 30 November, leaving Cnut without a serious rival.

The Viking way of life had an attraction even for a Christian king like Edgar. In the flattering notice, composed or inspired by Bishop Wulfstan,[1] inserted in the Chronicle under 959, the year of Edgar's accession, appears this reservation, 'Yet he did one ill-deed too greatly: he loved evil foreign customs and brought too firmly heathen manners

[1] K. Jost, 'Wulfstan und die angelsächsische Chronik', *Anglia*, xlvii (1923), 105–23.

5

within this land, and attracted hither foreigners and enticed harmful people to this country.' In Æthelred's reign, as Wulfstan tells us,[1] some Englishmen joined the invading armies, and perhaps renounced Christ for Thor, Odin, and Frey. Æthelred recruited in 1012 Thorkell Hávi into his service and in 1014 made use of Olaf Haraldsson, the future saint.[2] Although he had not the renown of these captains, or of that other hero, Olaf Tryggvason,[3] he was fully at home in the Viking world and was given an honourable place in Norwegian saga, which generally had an anti-Danish bias.

We learn from the Saga of Gunnlaug, 'Serpent's Tooth', that Gunnlaug, the Icelandic poet, visited Æthelred's court twice, apparently in 1001 and 1003–4.[4] On the first occasion he and his companions disembarked at London quay in late autumn. 'At that time there ruled over England, King Æthelred, Edgar's son, and he was a good prince.' Gunnlaug obtained an audience, told the king that he had written a poem about him, and asked leave to recite it. Then 'Gunnlaug recited the lay well and boldly; and in it is this refrain: All the host of the generous and dauntless prince fears England's lord as a god, and the sons of men do homage to Æthelred.' The king thanked the poet and gave him in return a scarlet cloak lined with the finest skins and hemmed with lace. He also made him his retainer (*hirthmann*) and kept him with him over winter. In the spring, when the shipping season started again, Gunnlaug asked leave to depart, and received as parting gift a gold ring weighing six ounces and a very warm invitation to return. Æthelred's correct and generous behaviour is contrasted with King Sihtric's provincial and ignorant manners at Dublin.

Æthelred was probably shown as a sophisticated northern prince because of his association with the three greatest Viking heroes of the time. In the saga of Olaf Tryggvason we are told that Æthelred was a great friend of Olaf's and we read in the Anglo-Saxon Chronicle that in 994 Olaf was confirmed at Andover by Bishop Ælfheah with Æthelred as sponsor, and that the treaty made between the two leaders was honourably observed. In Norway it was also believed that Olaf was one

[1] Wulfstan, *Sermo Lupi ad Anglos* (1014). *EHD*, i. 855–8.

[2] For Thorkell and Olaf, see Campbell, *Encomium Emmae*, pp. 73 ff. For Thorkell, see also Barlow, *English Church*, pp. 273–4.

[3] For Olaf Tryggvason, see Margaret Ashdown, *English and Norse Documents relating to the reign of Ethelred the Unready* (1930), p. 286; *Olafsdrapa, ibid.*, pp. 126 ff., *Olafs Saga Tryggvasonar, ibid.*, p. 152; Campbell, *Encomium Emmae*, p. 68.

[4] *Gunnlaugs Saga Ormstungu*, caps. 8–15 (ed. Ashdown, pp. 190–5).

of Edward the Confessor's heroes.[1] Equally important was Æthelred's association with Olaf Haraldsson. According to this man's saga,[2] when Æthelred returned from France to England in 1014, he summoned to him all those men who wanted to win a reward by helping him to recover his kingdom. A great army joined him 'and there came to his aid King Olaf with a force of Norwegians.' In the fighting which followed, it was Olaf's advice, resourcefulness, and heroism which gave victory to the English king, but Æthelred is depicted as a doughty warrior, and the verses of a contemporary poet, Ottar the Black, are quoted, 'You (Olaf) came to the land, . . . and, mighty in your strength, assured his realm to Æthelred. The true friend of warriors was thus your debtor.'

Æthelred's position in this northern world was also helped by his marriage in 1002 to Emma, daughter of Richard I, count of Normandy (942–96), and sister to the ruling count, Richard II.[3] The Scandinavians in north-west France were by this time mostly Christian and were rapidly becoming French; but their origins were well known, and Norman ports were available to Viking raiders on England. A Norman alliance was one of the keys to English security. In 991 Æthelred and Richard of Normandy made a treaty of amity under papal supervision[4] and the marriage in 1002 provided a stronger bond. Henceforth the counts of Normandy had an abiding interest in the English crown. Their ambition at first was that a child of Emma should succeed to the throne.[5] But although two sons of Emma did rule in turn, Harthacnut and Edward, both were childless, and Norman ambition had to take another form.

Involvement in the Scandinavian world gave England and her rulers wide horizons. The poet Gunnlaug visited Eric, earl of Hlathir in Norway,[6] a man who married Svein of Denmark's daughter and became an English earl under his wife's brother, Cnut; Sigurth, earl of the Orkneys; Sihtric Silkeskegg, king of Dublin; and Olaf, king of Sweden. A common language, *Norsk* (Old-Icelandic), facilitated political and

[1] *Olafs Saga Tryggvasonar*, cap. 286 (ed. Ashdown, p. 152).
[2] *Olafs Saga Helga*, caps. 12–15 (ed. Ashdown, pp. 155–61); see also Campbell, *Encomium Emmae*, pp. 77–8, 99.
[3] For Emma, see Campbell, *Encomium Emmae*, pp. xl ff.
[4] *Memorials of St Dunstan*, ed. W. Stubbs (Rolls ser. 1874), pp. 397–8; *EHD*, i. 823–4.
[5] Cf. F. Barlow, *Edward the Confessor and the Norman Conquest* (The Hastings and Bexhill Branch of the Historical Association, 1966), p. 7.
[6] For whom, see Campbell, *Encomium Emmae*, pp. 66 ff.

cultural exchange, and English was sufficiently close to have made it possible for Æthelred, with an effort, to understand Gunnlaug's poem. Travellers were welcomed not only for their wares, whether poetical or material, but also for the news they brought. As he travelled around, Gunnlaug must have picked up information ranging from Greenland to the Scandinavian empire in Russia and so to Byzantium, where Vikings formed the Varangian regiment of the Imperial Guard.

This was one of the worlds into which Edward was born. The other was the Christian church, a society which regarded the Vikings with fear and loathing, preferring always to look south and east. The English monastic reform of the tenth century had been greatly influenced by Ghent in Flanders and Fleury (St Benoît-sur-Loire); and if we plot English religious associations on the map, for example the foreign saints commemorated in the ecclesiastical calendars, we find that they mark the pilgrim routes to Rome. An equilateral triangle formed by joining Mont St Michel, Utrecht, and the Great St Bernard Pass in the Alps, encloses most of these places.[1] Archbishop Sigeric's tours of Rome in 990 and the stages by which he returned from the Holy City after obtaining the pallium from the pope were carefully recorded,[2] perhaps to help his successors. English men and women were enthusiastic travellers and pilgrims, and followed the roads to Rome and even to Byzantium and Jerusalem.[3] On these journeys they could see all the marvels of the classical and Christian civilizations and learn something of Muslim culture too. They could also exchange English wares for foreign goods and services. Pavia was one of the great markets on the route, famous for its traffic in relics,[4] and perhaps already known for the pleasures which later the archpoet was to immortalize.[5] The main exchange was probably between the home-spun products of the north and the trumperies of the south; but occasionally there were more valuable transfers. English manuscripts were sometimes lost or sold on the way, and fine works of art, such as the cameos which Æthelred gave to St Albans,[6] brought back.

[1] See map, Barlow, *English Church*, pp. 12–13.

[2] *Ibid.*, pp. 292–3.   [3] *Ibid.*, pp. 20–1, 290–1.

[4] Cf. Plummer, *Two Chronicles*, p. 204.

[5] 'Quis in igne positus igne non uratur? / Quis Papiae demorans castus habeatur', etc., *Die Gedichte des Archipoeta*, ed. Max Manitius (Münchener Texte, nr. 6, 2nd ed. 1929), poem III, verse 8.

[6] *Gesta abbatum monasterii S. Albani*, ed. H. T. Riley, i (Rolls ser. 1867), 83–4; cf. Barlow, *English Church*, p. 20.

This world was as real as the other to Æthelred and Emma. The queen became an ardent collector of relics, and the king was told by his bishops and priests, and believed, that the disasters experienced by the kingdom were God's punishment for the sins of his people. In the preamble to the charter of 1005 Æthelred expresses this point of view. The contradictory advice given by his *witan* – some urging military action, some fasting and prayer – may well have added to the king's difficulties. And the use of semi-heathen Vikings to fight against their fellow countrymen probably blurred Æthelred's image.[1] Alfred had fought against, not with, the heathen invader. Æthelred's reign started with a foul crime and finished in confusion with the king himself a Viking.

In 1005, the year in which Edward may have been born, Ælfric 'the Homilist' became abbot of Eynsham and so brought to an end his most productive period as a writer of ecclesiastical manuals.[2] Ælfric, the pupil of St Æthelwold, bishop of Winchester, was both aware that he lived in a degenerate age and also anxious to reform it. Like many exposed to danger, he found comfort and strength in the Old Testament, and translated some of the historical books for the benefit of the nobility, hoping especially that 'Judith' would inspire the thegns to defend their country by force of arms against the invaders.[3] Yet, although there were few years in Æthelred's reign completely free from Viking incursions, and after 991 these became larger and wider ranging, Ælfric himself seems never to have been seriously inconvenienced. Years later Abingdon abbey remembered that the community, protected by the mercy of God and under the abbot's watchful care, had suffered no damage at all, although both to the right and the left the Danes had destroyed everything or, when in a good mood, allowed the people to ransom themselves.[4] It is, indeed, difficult to estimate what was the direct effect of the raids on English society and individuals. The Anglo-Saxon Chronicle tells of ravaging and burning and of the collection of booty. Sometimes we are also told that men and cattle

---

[1] Æthelred had Scandinavian mercenaries under his command before 1001, when Pallig, Svein of Denmark's brother-in-law, deserted him (*Chron. A*). The 'St Brice's Day massacre' of Danes at Oxford in the following year was possibly of disloyal mercenaries.

[2] Barlow, *English Church*, pp. 68–70, 280 ff.

[3] *The Old English Version of the Heptateuch, Ælfric's Treatise on the Old and New Testament, and his Preface to Genesis*, ed. S. J. Crawford (Early Eng. Text Soc. 160, 1922), p. 48.   [4] *Chron. Abingdon*, i. 432.

were slaughtered. The cattle, no doubt, were killed for food and the men because they resisted the foraging parties. The ravaging and burning were to induce the people and their governors to buy the marauders off.[1] The usual aim of the Vikings was to collect loot at the least cost to themselves. Yet we cannot simply dismiss as unlikely the violence referred to by Wulfstan in his Sermon to the English (1014),[2] for this aspect of ravaging was probably taken for granted. And to Wulfstan even more shameful than the ignominy inflicted by the heathen on the Christians, by the pirates and their slaves on the English nobility, was the acceptance of these insults by the English: thegns watching their own women-folk being raped, sometimes by a dozen soldiers one after the other; people watching two or three seamen driving droves of Christians to their ships to be sold as slaves.[3]

The sea-rovers normally fought only if brought to battle and offered no escape. When a band, which in 991 had ravaged Folkestone, Sandwich, and Ipswich, was intercepted at Maldon by Brihtnoth, ealdorman of Essex, the invaders asked to be bought off: 'If you are rich enough, there is no need for us to destroy each other. In return for gold we are ready to make a truce. . . . We will take the treasure back to our ships, put out to sea, and keep faith with you.'[4] It was because Ælfheah, archbishop of Canterbury, refused to pay tribute or be ransomed that he was martyred on 19 April 1012 by Thorkell's army.[5] This casual violence at Greenwich shocked not only the English but some Danes as well, and was probably the reason why Thorkell entered Æthelred's service. But the Vikings, even if clean fighters, were hardly honourable bandits. The one thing which reduced the physical impact was the smallness of the invading armies[6] and the limited area that they could pillage. The stories of the atrocities, however, would have lost nothing in the telling, and the rumours which radiated from the stricken areas caused widespread alarm in England.

Wulfstan thought that 'the English have been for a long time now completely defeated and too greatly disheartened through God's anger; and the pirates so strong with God's consent that often in battle one

[1] *Chron.* s.a. 991; *The Battle of Maldon*, ll. 25-40 (*English and Norse Docs*, ed. Ashdown, p. 22); II Atr. (Robertson, *Laws*, pp. 56-61).

[2] *EHD*, i. 854 ff.; cf. also II Atr. 6 (Robertson, *Laws*, p. 59).

[3] *EHD*, i. 857-8; cf. VI Atr. 9 (Robertson, *Laws*, p. 95).

[4] *Maldon*, ll. 25-41.

[5] *Chron.* s.a. 1012; *Vita S. Elphegi, Anglia Sacra*, ed. H. Wharton, ii (1691), 140.

[6] P. H. Sawyer, 'The density of the Danish Settlement in England', *University of Birmingham Historical Journal*, vi (1957-8), 3-7.

puts to flight ten, sometimes less, sometimes more, all because of our sins.'[1] It is, however, possible to exaggerate the military shame of the English. It was by no means easy for a commander to intercept and bring to bay mobile raiders anxious to get back with the booty to their ships. The whining tone of the moralists and of the chronicler must also be discounted. Whereas it seems that the Chronicle in its earliest annals records only the victories of English kings, there is reason to suspect that for Æthelred's reign the chronicler lists only the defeats, or counts any battle in which there were English losses as a defeat, for it is unbelievable that the English commanders never won an engagement. Ulfkell, an East-Anglian noble, resolutely defended what the Norse remembered as 'Ulfkell's land', yet all his recorded battles are shown as lost. In 1004, according to the Chronicle, he attacked Svein of Denmark at Thetford, 'and many fell dead on both sides. There the flower of the East-Anglian army (folc) was killed. But if they had been there in full strength, the Danes would never have got back to their ships; they themselves said that they never met harder fighting in England than Ulfkell dealt to them.' In 1010 Ulfkell fought against Thorkell Hávi and Olaf Haraldsson at Ringmere – and many leaders 'and many good thegns and a countless mass of the army (folc)' were killed.[2] In 1016 he brushed with Eric Hakonarson west of London.[3] A stanza from Thorthr's *Eriksdrapa* has survived: 'The lord used to handling gold (Eric) stirred up strife to the west of London. The thunderer of the horse of the sea (Eric) strove for possession of lands. Ulfkell, bold in the rain of Rokkvi's house (under his shield), met with deadly blows when grey swords shook above the thingmen (soldiers).' In 1016 in Edmund Ironside's fifth great battle, at *Assandun*, Ulfkell 'and all the nobility of England were destroyed.'[4]

The church met this challenge for the most part with despondency and moralizing. Wulfstan opened his famous sermon in 1014 with the words, 'Beloved men, realize what is true: this world is in haste and the end approaches; and therefore in the world things go from bad to worse, and so it must of necessity deteriorate greatly on account of the people's sins before the coming of Antichrist, and indeed it will then be

---

[1] *Sermo Lupi ad Anglos*, EHD, i. 857.

[2] *Chron. s.a.* 1010; cf. Campbell, *Encomium Emmae*, p. 77.

[3] *Olafs Saga Helga*, cap. 25 (k) (ed. Ashdown, p. 164); cf. Campbell, *Encomium Emmae*, pp. 70-1.

[4] *Chron. s.a.* 1016. Cyril Hart, 'The site of Assandun', *History Studies*, i (1968), 1-12, would locate the battle at Ashdon rather than at Ashingdon.

dreadful and terrible far and wide throughout the world.' At one point he quotes Alcuin, who refers to Gildas. All moralists agreed that the disasters were due to sin. These sins Wulfstan lists and exemplifies. He contrasts the reverence of the heathen towards their gods and priests with Christian negligence. He regards society as almost in dissolution, with men buying and selling women, fathers selling their sons, sons their mothers, and brothers their brothers. 'In short', he writes, 'God's laws are hated and his precepts despised.' Especially Wulfstan denounces the disloyalty and treachery, the abandonment of honourable standards. He points to the most infamous examples in his own times: 'Edward [the Martyr] was betrayed, and then killed, and afterwards burnt, and Æthelred was driven out of his country.' The only escape that Wulfstan offers is through repentance and atonement; and we can see that in his heart of hearts he does not believe that this opportunity will be taken, except by individuals who may save their own souls.

These themes appear also in the laws of Æthelred which were written or inspired by Wulfstan:[1] 'If the law of God shall henceforth be zealously cherished both in word and in deed, God will forthwith have mercy upon this nation.' (V Atr. 26.) And so the duties of the clergy and the duties of the laity towards God and the church were defined. Church taxes were to be paid, festivals and fasts observed, and the moral laws kept. Even gluttony and drunkenness were condemned (V Atr. 25). Evil doers – wizards, sorcerers, magicians, prostitutes, secret killers, and perjurers – were to be expelled so as to purify the land (VI Atr. 7). Once a national penance was decreed (VII Atr.); and the proclamation of the festival of St Edward (V Atr. 16) may have been designed to exorcize that crime. In 1014, when Æthelred had been restored to the throne after making promises of good government, he issued laws defining the rights of the church (VIII Atr.). There were also enactments against treachery (V Atr. 30; VI Atr. 37). More positive were the laws enjoining loyalty to the king (V Atr. 35; VI, 1; VIII, 44) and those ordering the proper performance of military duties (V Atr. 26–8; VI, 32–5). For example, the people were reminded that, 'it is a wise precaution to have warships ready every year soon after Easter.' (VI Atr. 33; cf. V, 26.)

There were, however, still some Englishmen who did not have to be coached in their duties, soldiers who proclaimed the traditional military virtues. As Brihtwold, the old retainer, cried in the final

[1] Robertson, *Laws*, pp. 47 ff.

moments of the battle of Maldon, 'Thoughts must be the braver, hearts the more valiant, courage the greater, as our strength grows less.'[1] The warfare may, indeed, have encouraged a new output of heroic poetry, of which one example, the poem on Ealdorman Brihtnoth's battle at Maldon (991), has survived. In this poem the heroic virtues are displayed for imitation. The ealdorman scornfully rejects the Vikings' suggestion that he should pay tribute: 'Take back this message, messenger of the seamen [whom we know, from the Chronicle, to have been commanded by Olaf Tryggvason]. Say ... that there stands here with his army an earl of unstained renown, ready to guard this realm, the home of Æthelred, my lord, this people and land. It is the heathen who will fall in battle.' But Brihtnoth is imprudent and in the fighting is mortally wounded by a spear. He is immediately avenged by one of his men, who in his turn is struck down. We are not, however, in an ideal world. After the fall of 'the army's commander, Æthelred's earl', some of his retainers and thegns flee. But others scorn to return home 'lordless men', and like Offa, who 'lay, as befits a thegn, at his lord's side', die with their leader. The words of these brave men, and their deeds, are a reproach to the cowardly. But, all the same, the battle of Maldon was a defeat for the English.

The great heroes of the world in which Edward's boyhood was spent were the Vikings Thorkell Hávi, Eric Hakonarson, Olaf Haraldsson, and Olaf Tryggvason, and in England Ulfkell (with a Scandinavian name) and Edward's elder brother, Edmund Ironside. Unless Edward was an unusual boy, some of these must have been his heroes too. It is, however, unlikely that he could include his own father in this circle, especially as he could hardly have avoided hearing criticism of him.[2] By the time Edward became king almost all direct ties with his boyhood had been broken, and he showed no friendliness towards the kin of these men. Even Edmund's son, Edward 'the Exile', died in England

---

[1] *Maldon*, ll. 312–13.

[2] There are few references to Æthelred in Edward's charters and writs, but probably because the position under Cnut was taken as the norm. In his last years, however (1061–6), Edward granted land at Wedmore (Som) for the maintenance of the clerks of St Andrew's, Wells, for the sake of his own soul, his father's soul, and the souls of all his ancestors who had established the episcopal see. Harmer, *Writs*, no. 68. It should be noticed that Æthelred's eldest son, Æthelstan, who died just before his father, clearly respected, perhaps loved him, and in his will left him 'the silver-hilted sword which belonged to Ulfkell' – possibly the East Anglian warrior, although he was still alive at the time the will was made. Whitelock, *Wills*, no. XX.

before he met the king. This later indifference, perhaps even hostility, towards associations with his youth does not mean that his boyhood experiences were unimportant – rather that they were remembered without pleasure, probably with pain. Hence the rootlessness which Edward showed when he returned to England in his middle age.

As we see from *The Battle of Maldon*, one of the best ways of getting under the surface of the eleventh-century world is through poetry.[1] But this medium, because it is poetry, because we have only a small, possibly quite unrepresentative selection, and because it is difficult to know how archaically it sounded in Edward's reign, is not easy material to use. The last is the most serious problem. There would be little profit today in explaining the feelings of men and women in Queen Victoria's reign by means of Elizabethan and Augustan poetry, although this was collected, read, and appreciated at that time. Yet even if great social changes occurred between Offa's reign in the eighth century (when the poem *Widsith* was probably written), Alfred's reign at the end of the ninth century (when, it is thought, much of the other extant poetry was composed), and the middle of the eleventh century, society was relatively unchanging, and, viewed from this distance, had over long periods many basic features, more important than the superficial changes which we can barely discern.[2] And although it is easy to get the impression that Edward and his French friends would not have been sympathetic to northern poets, there is no good evidence for this: it is possibly a mistaken impression derived from the *Vita Ædwardi Regis*, from the Norman apologists who try to divorce Edward from his natural setting, and especially from the worthless later Latin and French Lives. We know that Æthelred's court harboured the traditional culture;[3] most of the secular poetry that has survived was copied into the Exeter Book about 960–90,[4] presumably not for purely anti-

[1] The relatively small corpus of Anglo-Saxon poetry is conveniently collected in *Bibliothek der Angelsächsischen Poesie*, ed. Christian W. M. Grein and Richard Paul Wülcker (1883–98), to which most of the following notes refer, and individual poems have been frequently re-edited in modern times, mainly for student use. Less satisfactory is the position with regard to translations. R. K. Gordon, *Anglo-Saxon Poetry* (Everyman, 1926) is serviceable. Some more spirited, poetical renderings are in Michael Alexander, *The Earliest English Poems* (Penguin Classics, 1966).

[2] The modern tendency is to stress the changes which occurred; cf. D. A. Bullough, 'Anglo-Saxon Institutions and Early English Society', *Annali della Fondazione italiana per la storia amministrativa* (Milan), ii (1965), 647–59. But we can still think that the period had a distinctive culture.

[3] See above, pp. 6–8.

[4] *The Exeter Book*, ed. G. P. Krapp and E. van Kirk Dobbie (1936), pp. xiii–xiv.

quarian reasons; our one manuscript of *Beowulf* dates from about 1000; Edward, like most of his French friends, was of Viking descent; and the majority of his earls[1] and several of his bishops were completely at home in the Anglo-Scandinavian setting. It is not unreasonable to think, therefore, that the old poetry was still heard and appreciated in Edward's reign. Moreover, although the author of the *Vita* claimed that the poets were silent and he was the first to sing about King Edward,[2] it is likely that poems were still being made. There is no reason why there should have been a complete silence between the poem on the Battle of Maldon (991) and that on Edward's death inserted in the Annals. The Latin poem in the *Vita* which describes the campaigns of Harold and Tostig could easily have had a vernacular model.[3] The other problems which poetry poses are familiar and cause no real trouble.

Because the literary recorders of Anglo-Saxon verse were monks, much of what remains is religious poetry. This includes only one piece of highly original composition – *The Dream of the Rood* – and tells us little about the people that we cannot learn from non-poetical sources. Much more interesting is the latent pagan pessimism in some of the poems. All men knew that the church gave glad tidings and that for Christians the life after death was more real than the life on this earth; and yet some, even in the eleventh century, must occasionally have had the misgivings which a few or many of the poets (we cannot tell how many) had expressed. In the *Gnomic Verses*, proverbs or sententious sayings, we are told that, 'the Lord multiplies children; but early sickness takes them away, so that there is established on earth a fixed number of the race of men. There would be no limit to progeny on earth if He who created this world did not reduce their number.'[4] And in *The Fates of Men*, also from the Exeter Book, are listed mostly unfortunate endings: death in youth, devoured by a wolf, from hunger, tempest, war; death after blindness and maiming; death by falling from a high tree, death on the broad gallows and on the pyre; death in a drunken brawl on the mead-bench, suicide when drunk. Few shall overcome the misery of youth and become happy in old age.[5]

---

[1] The one who is known to have retained an Icelandic court poet is Waltheof Siwardsson, who patronised Thorkel Skallason: cf. *King Harald's Saga*, caps. 96–7.

[2] *VEdR*, p. 3. His, 'Vatibus exclusis, cessantibus atque poetis', may, of course, refer merely to the position immediately after 1066.

[3] *VEdR*, pp. 57–9. [4] Grein and Wülcker, 1, 343, ll. 31–4.

[5] Grein and Wülcker, 3, 1, 148–51.

Moreover, the life to come is uncertain. The *Gnomic Verses* conclude with, 'The future state is secret and hidden; the Lord alone knows, the Father who saves. No one returns hither under our roofs who may truly tell men here on earth what is the Lord's decree, the abodes of those who have triumphed, where He himself abides.' In the penitential poems, *Seafarer* and *Wanderer*, which are concerned with punishment and exile,[1] there is bitter despair, outwardly Christian but rooted in older attitudes.

In *Seafarer*:[2]

> Kings are not now, kaisers are not,
> there are no gold-givers like the gone masters
> who between them framed the first deeds in the world,
> in their lives lordly, in the lays renowned.
> That chivalry is changed, cheer is gone away,
> it is a weaker kind who wields earth now,
> sweats for its bread. Brave men are fewer,
> all excellence on earth grows old and sere
> as now does every man over the world.

In *Wanderer*:[3]

> The wine-halls crumble; their wielders lie
> bereft of bliss, the band all fallen
> proud by the wall. War took off some,
> carried them on their course hence; one a bird bore
> over the high sea; one the hoar wolf
> dealt to death;[4] one his drear-cheeked
> earl[5] stretched in an earthen trench.

There may have been gaiety when men played and laboured together, much joy in the meeting of men and women; there may have

---

[1] Dorothy Whitelock, 'The Interpretation of *The Seafarer*', *The Early Cultures of North-West Europe* (H. M. Chadwick Memorial Studies), ed. Sir Cyril Fox and Bruce Dickins (1950), pp. 261–72; E. G. Stanley, 'Old-English poetic diction and the interpretation of the Wanderer, the Seafarer, and the Penitent's Prayer', *Anglia*, lxxiii (1955–6); P. L. Henry, *The Early English and Celtic Lyric* (1966).

[2] Grein and Wülcker, 1, 293–4, ll. 82–90. Translation by Michael Alexander.

[3] *Ibid.*, 1, 287–8, ll. 78–84. Translation by Michael Alexander.

[4] Presumably Odin's beasts, the raven and the wolf, the scavengers of the battle-field.

[5] *eorl* is regularly used in the poetry in the sense of 'noble warrior' or 'hero'; but here it probably refers to a superior.

been plenty of merriment on the benches in the wine-halls; but always round the corner lurked the shadows, the unhappiness felt by men haunted by insecurity. The poetry is distinctly sad.[1] But although the hazards of existence, the deterioration of the world, and the transitoriness of this life were themes common to all kinds of writing, the consolations offered to the unfortunate were various. The message of the poem *Deor* is that just as other griefs had faded, so too in time will present sorrow disappear: 'That passed, so may this.' Man must stick it out: an answer which Alfred found in Boethius.[2] The church taught that man should prepare on earth for unearthly, everlasting life. But the old pagan view was that immortality was fame in this world: that man should perform memorable deeds so that poets would recite his feats for ever. And most memorable deeds were acts of bravery and of military conquest. To quote again from *Seafarer:*[3]

> I do not believe
> earthly estate is everlasting:
> three things all ways threaten a man's peace
> and one before the end shall overthrow his mind;
> either illness or age or the edge of vengeance
> shall draw out the breath from the doom-shadowed.
> Wherefore, for earl whatsoever, it is afterword,
> the praise of livers-on, that, lasting, is best:
> won in the world before wayfaring,
> forged, framed here, in the face of enmity,
> in the Devil's spite: deeds, achievements.

It was not impossible, as the phrase 'in the Devil's spite' shows, to qualify for both commemorative rolls. The great northern saint of the period is King Olaf Haraldsson, the Viking killed by his rebel Norwegians at Stiklestad in 1030. The saga of Olaf is also a saint's life. Another Norwegian king, Harald Sigurdsson (Hardrada), Olaf's half-brother – who at the age of fifteen escaped from the disaster at Stiklestad with nothing worse than a wound and died in England shortly after Edward, but, unlike the English king, in battle – won

---

[1] Although cf. Jean I. Young, 'Ungloomy Aspects of Anglo-Saxon Poetry', *The Early Cultures of North-West Europe* (H. M. Chadwick Memorial Studies), ed. Sir Cyril Fox and Bruce Dickins (1950), pp. 275–87.

[2] Murray F. Markland, 'Boethius, Alfred, and Deor', *Modern Philology*, lxvi (1968), 1–4.

[3] Grein and Wülcker, 1, 293, ll. 66–76. Translation by Michael Alexander.

only secular fame. And he made sure of this by encouraging the poets. As his favourite poet, Thjodolf Arnorsson, declaimed:[1]

> Norway's liberal sea-king
> Gave me gold for my poetry;
> His royal favours are always
> determined only by merit.

Snorri Sturluson, the late-twelfth-century Icelandic historian, reports Halldor Brynjolfsson's view – the opinion of a man who was intimately acquainted with the half-brothers – that they were in fact remarkably alike:[2]

They were both highly intelligent and extremely brave in battle, hungry for wealth and power, imperious and haughty, able rulers and ruthless in punishment. King Olaf forced the people to adopt Christianity and the true faith, and cruelly punished those who were slow to obey him. The chieftains would not endure his just and rightful rule and raised an army against him, and killed him in his own kingdom. For that reason he was made a saint. But King Harald went to war for fame and power, and he forced everyone he could into submission; and so he was killed in another king's land.

Both earned and deserved fame everlasting.

It was the abundance of court poetry composed in honour of the tenth- and eleventh-century Norwegian heroes which enabled Snorri Sturluson to write in the early thirteenth century the great series of sagas which together composed his *Heimskringla*. He was able to turn old poetry, still remembered, into history. As Widsith declared:[3]

> The poet's fate is to be a wanderer:
> the poets of mankind go through the many countries,
> speak their needs, say their thanks.
> Always they meet with someone, in the south lands or the north,
> who understands their art, an open-handed man

---

[1] *King Harald's Saga*, cap. 99. Translation by Magnus Magnusson and Hermann Pálsson.

[2] *King Harald's Saga*, cap. 100. Translation by the same.

[3] Grein and Wülcker, 1, 6, ll. 135–43. Translation by Michael Alexander, slightly adapted.

who would not have his fame fail among the guard
nor rest from an earl's deeds before the end cuts off
light and life together. Lasting honour shall be his,
a name that shall never die beneath the heavens.

The position in England was very different. Although Edward and
his earls had all been educated to believe that while life is short fame
endures for ever, and a few scraps of the verses written in honour of
Æthelred have survived,[1] there are no court poems or sagas about the
men of the next generation. This is understandable. Æthelred attracted
poets and enjoyed their sycophantic praise, but performed no really
memorable deeds. Edward Æthelredsson did nothing worthy of a court
poet's attention. Indeed the contrast between the careers of Harald
Sigurdsson, forced into exile at fifteen, and of Edward, driven abroad a
little younger, is remarkable. While Harald was campaigning in Russia
against Poland and later with the Varangian regiment of the Imperial
Guard in the Greek Islands, Asia Minor, and Sicily, amassing out of his
booty a great fortune which he banked in Russia, playing dirty for high
stakes, up to the neck in imperial intrigues, winning women as well as
cities and battles, Edward was living quietly in France. Harald,
probably an unpleasant man, who later was called *Hardradi*, the
Ruthless, must have despised Edward utterly.

The one thing that Edward and Harald had in common was a period
of exile from their homeland; and banishment we know from the
political history of the period was a common fate. For the adventurous
and resourceful it was not a crushing penalty. The Viking world was
large and varied. A banished man could seek his fortune in Norway,
Sweden, Denmark, Iceland, the Orkneys, Ireland, England, Normandy,
Russia, and Constantinople. If he was famous or well-connected he
would find friends or kinsmen wherever he travelled within this area.
Edward was taken to his uncle's court in Normandy, Malcolm of
Scotland to his uncle's court at York; Tostig went twice to his brother-
in-law's court in Flanders. Outstanding men found new lords. Harald
Sigurdsson was welcomed by Jaroslav, ruler of Russia, and eventually
married his daughter, Elizabeth. Edward 'the Exile', Edmund Ironside's
son, made his way at the Magyar court, married Agatha, a German or
Hungarian princess, and when he was invited back to England, returned with great treasure. Some, like the subject of the poem, *The*

---

[1] See above, pp. 6–7.

Husband's Message, settled down among strangers, prospered, and decided to make their home there, sending back for their womenfolk:[1]

> The man has now
> laid his sorrows, lacks no gladdeners;
> he has a hoard and horses and hall-carousing
> and would have everything within an earl's having
> had he my lady with him.

Others had the credit to raise troops abroad and return home by force of arms, like Svein Estrithson in Sweden, Harold Godwinsson in Ireland, and Ælfgar Leofricson in Wales. But there were also many who were unable to re-establish themselves, men like Osgot Clapa and Swegn Godwinsson. We learn from *Wanderer* and *Seafarer* what misery divorce from kin and lord could cause. The *wraecca*, the lordless man, had been expelled from a tightly-knit society, in which he had huddled for safety; and his one desire was to find a new lord. As we read in *Wanderer:*[2]

> Wretched I went thence,
> winter-wearied, over the waves' bound;
> dreary I sought hall of a gold-giver,
> where far or near I might find
> him who in meadhall might take heed of me,
> furnish comfort to a man friendless,
> win me with cheer.

>   *   *   *

> Remembered kinsmen press through his mind;
> he singeth out gladly, scanneth eagerly
> men from the same hearth. They swim away.
> Sailors' ghosts bring not many
> known songs there.

It was terrible to be an outlaw, to wear the wolf's head; but the exile, the man performing penance among strangers, with no kin or lord to protect him, was in a state almost as desperate.

In some obvious ways this northern society had a very masculine culture. There is no romantic love interest in the sagas and probably there was little in the lives of the heroes. Much of their time was spent

---

[1] Grein and Wülcker, 1, 310, ll. 42–6. The staff, on which the message is carved, is speaking. Translation by Michael Alexander.

[2] Grein and Wülcker, 1, 285, 286, ll. 23–9, 51–5. Translation by Michael Alexander.

without the company of women; their ideals and code of behaviour were created by comrades-in-arms in the face of danger. Nevertheless, most of the Viking leaders found time to contract marriages with the daughters of kings and earls and beget children. And, since there was much remarriage, all the noble families in the Scandinavian world were related to each other.[1] As we would expect, it is not in theory a promiscuous society. The integrity of the individual is a cardinal right. Rape is a crime. And among the five great misfortunes of the Old Germanic heroic tradition listed in the poem *Deor*, two are rapes: the forcing of Beadohild by Wayland and of Maethhild by the Geat: 'their bitter love banished sleep.'[2]

Marriages, we know, were usually arranged by a girl's parents; and usually, it may be assumed, a girl married the man chosen for her. But in this northern society a woman was far from being a chattel and on many occasions her wishes were consulted. About 1050 when King Harald Sigurdsson of Norway tried to make peace with Hakon Ivarsson, who had inherited a feud against him, Hakon stipulated marriage with Ragnhild, the granddaughter of St Olaf, and a suitable dowry.[3] Harald agreed, with the reservation that Ragnhild must give her consent; and when Ragnhild, a king's daughter, refused to marry a simple farmer, and Harald refused to make him an earl, the treaty fell through, Hakon taking refuge in Denmark. Later, when it suited Harald, Hakon was appointed earl and the marriage took place. Here, as so often, the woman was 'the peace-weaver', the cementer of friendship between kins, tribes, and nations.[4] Widsith travelled with 'the fair Ealhhild', daughter of Eadwine, king of the Lombards, to her marriage with Eormanric, king of the Ostrogoths. In legend the great Eormanric was a tyrant, probably because of his treatment of his wife. A maiden handed over to weave a peace did not always obtain the love of her husband. But there is plenty of evidence that there were men who regarded their wives as something more than the mother of their children. At least a wife gave a man more kin, more points of reference, a bigger stake in the world.

[1] See Table 2 below, and the charts in M. Ashdown, *English and Norse Documents*, p. 214, showing the connexions between the families in Norway, Wendland, Denmark, and Sweden; and see chart in Barlow, *English Church*, p. 172, for a Northumbrian genealogy.

[2] The meaning of the latter episode, unknown from other sources, is, however, uncertain. [3] *King Harald's Saga*, caps. 45–50.

[4] Cf. *Beowulf*, l. 1942; translation by David Wright (Penguin Classics, 1957), p. 73.

Some of these situations are illustrated in the verse. In the poem *The Wife's Complaint*, we read of one whose life from girlhood was a succession of sorrows and afflictions. Her husband went overseas; his kinsmen schemed to break up the marriage; and finally her husband forced her to live in an earthen den dug under a tree:[1]

> Here the grief bred
> by lordlack preys on me. Some lovers in this world
> live dear to each other, lie warm together
> at day's beginning; I go by myself
> about these earth caves under the oak tree.
>
>   * * *
>
> May grief and bitterness blast the mind
> of that young man! May his mind ache
> behind his smiling face! May a flock of sorrows
> choke his chest! He would change his tune
> If he lived alone in a land of exile
> far from his folk.

A married woman could indeed be a woman in exile, outside the protection of her kin, at the mercy of a lord who may have found little joy or profit in the union. It was not unusual in the Anglo-Scandinavian world for a man to have a concubine. King Harald Sigurdsson, after his marriage to Elizabeth, daughter of King Jaroslav of Novgorod, who bore him two daughters, married Thora, Thorberg's daughter; and it was their two sons, Magnus and Olaf, who succeeded Harald in Norway. In 1062, when Harald defeated Svein of Denmark at the battle of the Nissa, he had Thora with him. In 1066, when he sailed to his death in England, he left Thora and Magnus at home and took with him Elizabeth, the two daughters, and Olaf, disembarking the women in Orkney.[2] These arrangements suggest domestic harmony. But probably it was not always so.

We have as well in the poetry scenes of marital faithfulness and love. In the poem *The Husband's Message* we read:[3]

> The carver of this token entreats a lady
> clad in clear stones to call to mind
> and hold in her wit words pledged

[1] Grein and Wülcker, 1, 304, ll. 32–6, 42–7. Translation by Michael Alexander.

[2] *King Harald's Saga*, caps. 33, 66, 82–3.

[3] Grein and Wülcker, 1, 309, 310, ll. 12–18, 29–35. Translation by Michael Alexander.

often between the two in earlier days:
then he would hand you through hall and yard
lord of his lands, and you might live together,
forge your love.

* * *

He does not conceive, he said to me,
that a greater happiness could be his in this world
than that all-wielding God should grant you both
days when together you may give out rings
among followers and fellows, free-handed deal
the nailed armbands. Of which he has enough,
of inlaid gold.

A simple scene of domestic happiness is pictured in the *Gnomic Verses*:[1]

But how loving the welcome
of the Frisian wife
when floats offshore
the keel come home again!
She calls him within walls,
her own husband
– hull's at anchor! –
washes salt-stains
from his stiff shirt
brings out clothes
clean and fresh
for her lord on land again.
Love's need is met.

There is even some romantic poetry. In the Old-English version of the story of Walter of Aquitaine, *Waldere*, one of the themes is the love of Waldere and his betrothed, Hildeguth princess of Burgundy, both hostages at the court of Attila, king of the Huns. They escape together, protect and cherish each other through great dangers, and in the end are able to marry. In the poem *Wulf and Eadwacer* the theme is probably adulterous love. A woman remembers her absent lover:[2]

It was rainy weather, and I wept by the hearth,
thinking of my Wulf's far wanderings;
one of the captains caught me in his arms.
It gladdened me then; but it grieved me too.

[1] Grein and Wülcker, 1, 346, ll. 95-100. Translation by Michael Alexander.
[2] *Ibid.*, 3, 1, 183-4, ll. 9-14. Translation by Michael Alexander.

Wulf, my Wulf, it was wanting you
that made me sick, your seldom coming,
the hollowness at heart; not the hunger I spoke of.

Here we have one of the rare hints of sophisticated sexual attitudes. But there is remarkably little suggestion in the poetry of sensual pleasure.[1] Comradeship, security, trust, warmth of feeling, sorrow in absence, all these feelings are conveyed; but physical passion was presumably outside the conventions of this aristocratic poetry. No doubt there were more vulgar songs; it is not to be thought that English men and women were cold. A hint of a coarser tone is sometimes to be found in the riddles.[2] The answer to:

I'm the world's wonder, for I make women happy.

* * *

I am set well up, stand in a bed,
have a roughish root. Rarely (though it happens)
a churl's daughter more daring than the rest
– and lovelier! – lays hold of me,
rushes my red top, wrenches at my head,
and lays me in the larder. She learns soon enough,
the curly-haired creature who clamps me so,
of my meeting with her: moist is her eye!

is, of course, an onion.[3]

And in asking the riddle which should be answered 'Oxhide', the contriver included:[4]

Or, far from her Wales,
a dark-headed girl grabs and squeezes me,
silly with drink, and in the dark night
wets me with water, or warms me up
before the fire. Fetched between breasts
by her hot hand, while she heaves about
I must stroke her brown part.

[1] There is a reference to pleasure to be obtained from women in *Seafarer*, l. 45.
[2] It is generally conceded that Riddles 25 (onion), 44 (key), 45 (dough), 55 (scabbard), and 63 (beaker) are obscene, deliberately constructed as *double entendres*. In early editions these numbers are all advanced by one because the poem *Wulf* is presented as the first riddle.
[3] Riddle no. 25, Grein and Wülcker, 3, 1, 198. Translation by Michael Alexander.
[4] Riddle no. 12, *ibid.*, 3, 1, 191–2 (no. 13). Translation by Michael Alexander, slightly modified.

There is sufficient erotic poetry to suggest that men took a healthy interest in women, and enough portrayal of the domestic scene to show the important place held by women in society. While the lord was away on his adventures the wife ruled his hall, his family, and his estate. In the eighth-century poem, *Beowulf*, Wealtheow, queen of Hrothgar, king of the Danes, plays a significant role in the banqueting hall.[1] Nobly attired and ornamented with gold, she offers a jewelled goblet and words of welcome to the guests. She also counsels her husband ' "Take this cup, my lord and king. Enjoy yourself, generous friend of men, and, as is proper, speak cordially with the Geats. Be open-handed to them remembering the gifts which have come to you from the ends of the world. . . . O protector of the Danes, I know my good Hrothulf [their nephew] well enough to be sure he will take honourable care of our sons if you die before him. . . ." With this she turned to the bench where her children sat among a group of youths, all sons of chieftains.' Also in the poem we read of Hygd, 'youthful, wise, and accomplished', the queen of the Geats, quite different from 'that imperious [fourth-century] princess Thryth, who practised unspeakable atrocities. No one of her court except her future husband was so bold that he dared look her directly in the face.' But she was tamed by her husband, Offa of Angel, and 'on his throne she became celebrated for her goodness. . . . She greatly loved the king, who, they say, was the best of men the wide world over.'[2] Nor does it seem that the status of women deteriorated between the eighth and the eleventh centuries. In England women held land and made wills, distributing their wealth among their relatives, retainers and friends, and the church. No one could doubt that Edward's mother, Emma, was a dominating woman; and Cnut's sister, Estrith, must have been considered more important than her husband, for their children were generally called Estrithson rather than Ulfsson.

Edward's own relationship with women forms one of the most difficult and controversial areas of his biography. Perhaps here we should merely note that it is possible that both his mother and his wife were domineering. Counsel pushed too hard, attempts at petticoat rule, would explain some of Edward's apparent peevishness towards Emma and Edith.

The world into which Edward was born was thought to be approach-

---

[1] *Beowulf*, ll. 612 ff., 1168–91; translation by David Wright, pp. 41–2, 54–5.
[2] *Beowulf*, ll. 1926–57; translation by David Wright, pp. 72–3.

ing its end, so evil were the times, so hopeless the outlook. It was no place for the weak or faint-hearted. Neither was it a place for the English hero. Edmund Ironside was as ineffective as his father. Brihtnoth and Ulfkell did no better than Eadric Streona. So irresistible were the pressures that the strongest were broken. In the end it was necessary to bow before the storm; and the qualities which ensure survival under adversity are not the heroic virtues. Two who survived the calamities were Emma and Edward, following different paths towards a peaceful death at a ripe old age. If Emma was the more successful, she was probably also the more resourceful, and, perhaps, the better endowed, although women have special advantages in this kind of race. But Edward's emergence after a long eclipse, even if not by his own efforts alone, is in a way more remarkable than Emma's success in always keeping near the limelight. When Edward in 1043, at last secure on his throne, turned to punish his mother for her neglect of his interests, Emma may well have reflected that her son after all was not completely unworthy of his mother.

It is, however, when we come to consider the physical characteristics which Edward inherited from his parents that we realize how inadequate our information is. Edward's environment can be reconstructed in broad outline, but his heredity can only be surmised. All the same, an investigation of it is worth while, if only because the findings discourage the adoption of some of the simpler views that have been held of Edward's nature.

Edward could trace his ancestry through the paternal line to Cerdic, founder of the kingdom of the West Saxons in the first half of the sixth century. Judging by the names of the men, the family must have been Anglo-Welsh; but, as most kings married into the English nobility, the British strain was probably quickly bred out. This royal line was the one survivor out of many similar Anglo-Saxon dynasties, and, although luck undoubtedly played a part, its survival is a testimonial to its vigour. Indeed, its record for courage and intelligence is extremely good, the dynasty being particularly distinguished in the tenth century. There may, however, have been some physical weakness in the family. Although we need not believe Asser's stories of Alfred's bad health, he and his descendants were rather short lived. Between Alfred who reached fifty and Æthelred about forty-eight, Edward the Elder and Athelstan ruled fifteen years apiece and Eadred nine; Eadwig died at sixteen and Edgar at thirty-two; and Edward the Martyr was murdered at seventeen and Edmund at twenty-five. Early death had an effect on fertility. The direct line occasionally failed: neither Athelstan nor Eadred married and Eadwig died childless. Despite multiple marriages, only Edward the Elder and Æthelred were prolific, Edward having at least thirteen children from three marriages and Æthelred probably even more from his two. The West-Saxon royal line cannot on this evidence be considered degenerate. There were inexplicable dead ends from causes unknown and Edward could not have expected to live into his sixth decade. But these features were characteristic of the period.

Edward's mother, Emma, was the great-granddaughter of Rolf, or Rollo, a Norwegian, the first count of Normandy. This family was probably longer lived than the English: Rolf ruled for forty-two years, William Longsword for fifteen, and Richard I, Emma's father, for fifty-four. Her brother, Count Richard II, ruled for thirty years. As far as we know, all the males were fertile, and Emma was one of a large family. Her youthful marriage with Æthelred was completely exo-gamous, uniting two stocks which, whatever their weaknesses, were vigorous enough; and it could be expected to produce healthy children. To some extent, however, it may have fallen short of expectation. As it happened, only one, Edward, of Emma's three sons from her two marriages took a wife, and none is known to have had children. Alfred was murdered when in his twenties, Harthacnut died of natural causes (apparently a stroke) at about twenty-four. But her two daughters, one by each husband, were fertile.

It does not seem that any theory can be based on these few facts. There is no obvious pattern. All that we can say is that Edward was Anglo-Scandinavian, half a Viking, by birth, with an almost completely favourable background. We can point to nothing in his heredity which might cause him to be physically weak, unadventurous, degenerate, or sterile. We can see no reason why Æthelred and Emma should not have produced, if not another Alfred, Edward the Elder, or Edgar, at least another Æthelred. In fact Edward lived into his sixth decade, was vigorous until his fatal stroke, and is not known to have suffered from ill health. It seems that Edward was a normal child of healthy parents.

Chapter 2

EDWARD ÆTHELING

Æthelred was thirty-four and the father of mar · children when he married Emma, Edward's mother, in the spring of 1002.[1] A charter of that year[2] lists among the witnesses his six sons: Æthelstan, Egbert, Edmund, Eadred, Eadwig, and Edgar. These names (except Egbert, which is out of series) repeat in historical order Æthelred's forerunners on the throne, omitting only his immediate predecessor, Edward the Martyr.[3] The mother of these sons and perhaps also of four or five daughters[4] was, it seems, Ælfgifu, daughter of an English ealdorman, or earl.[5] Her union with Æthelred was clearly of long standing, and it must have started in the king's youth; but, although it was probably a legal marriage, it may not have been blessed by the church and

[1] *Chron. CDE.*

[2] *KCD*, no. 707 (Sawyer, no. 904), for Wherwell.

[3] It is interesting to see how Æthelred's great-granddaughter, St Margaret, named her first four children by Malcolm III, king of Scots, Edward, Edmund, Æthelred, and Edgar, thus tracing back her ancestry in the direct male line, probably as far as she could conveniently go. It may have been uncertainty about Edgar's predecessors which caused her then to shift to Alexander and David.

[4] Edith, who married (1) Earl Eadric Streona and (2) possibly Earl Thorkell Hávi; Ælfgifu, who married Earl Uchtred of Northumbria; ? Wulfhild, who married Ulfkell, earl of East Anglia; one who became abbess of Wherwell; and possibly others. The names Edith and Wulfhild are associated with King Edgar: St Edith was Æthelred's step-sister. Ælfthryth and Wulfthryth, the names of Æthelred's half-aunt and mother, would be expected in this list.

[5] According to a royal genealogy in Florence, i. 275, Æthelred had from his wife Ælfgifu, daughter of Earl Æthelberht, three sons, Edmund, Eadwig, and Æthelstan, and a daughter, Edith, and from his wife Emma, Alfred and Edward. According to Ailred of Rievaulx, *Genealogia regum Angliae et regis David Scotiae* (written in 1153-4), *Historiae Anglicanae scriptores X*, ed. R. Twysden (1652), p. 362b, Ælfgifu was the daughter of Earl Thored. Preference is usually given to Florence on the grounds that he is the earlier source; but the real point is who recorded the sounder authority. Florence's list of children is most unsatisfactory: it is incomplete and each set is given in the wrong order. We cannot, therefore, put much trust in Earl Æthelberht, who is, except for his witness to *KCD*, no. 629 (Sawyer, no. 838), dated 981, otherwise unknown. Earl Thored of Northumbria, however, was one of Æthelred's captains in 992 (*Chron. CDE*); and, although Ailred gives us a very incomplete list of Æthelred's children, he makes no positive error there.

Ælfgifu may not have been anointed queen. After 988, when Æthelred was twenty, the only survivor of the bishops who had been powerful in his father's reign and his own minority was Oswald, bishop of Worcester and archbishop of York, probably a tolerant man. But the names given to the sons suggest that Æthelred regarded them as king-worthy and legitimate. If so, it is likely that by 1002 Æthelred was a widower,[1] although fifteen years later, when Emma married Cnut, she did not insist on completely vacant possession.

The first recorded child of Æthelred's second marriage, Edward, was born at Islip in Oxfordshire, a place which his mother gave him as a birthday gift.[2] The earliest date at which a child could have been born is Christmas 1002; and the first mention of Edward's existence is in two charters dated 1005, and earlier than 16 November,[3] where Edward is listed as the seventh prince. His witness is followed by the entry, 'Ego Ælfgifu regina', thought to be his mother in her new English style. No charters dated 1003 have survived; but as Edward is not listed among the princes in three charters dated 1004,[4] there is a *prima facie* case that he was born in 1005. Yet in charters of the reign Edward is only recorded in 1005, 1007, 1008, 1011, 1013, 1014, and 1015,[5] and the poor

---

[1] Strangely enough Æthelstan, the eldest son of Æthelred and his first wife, in his will which he made *c.* 1013 (Whitelock, *Wills*, no. XX) makes no mention of his mother or her soul, a pointed omission because he has much to say of his father and refers to his grandmother, who brought him up, and his foster-mother.

[2] Harmer, *Writs*, no. 104, and pp. 334 ff. The writ has some unsatisfactory features, but an authentic document probably lies behind it. It is unlikely that the information about Edward's birth was invented.

[3] *KCD*, no. 714 (Sawyer, no. 911), for Eynsham, and no. 1301 (Sawyer, no. 910), for a thegn; the witness lists are consistent with 1002 × 16 Nov. 1005 (death of Ælfric of Canterbury). The witness list of no. 672 (Sawyer, no. 912), for St Albans, dated 990, where Edward also occurs, can be compared. If we regard Æthelsi as a mistake for Æthelric (of Sherborne), this list contains eight of the larger number of bishops who appear in the others, and would seem to be of the same date (1002 × 5).

[4] *KCD*, nos. 709–11 (Sawyer, nos. 909, 906–7). No. 1300 (Sawyer, no. 908) is spurious.

[5] *KCD*, nos. 1303 (Sawyer, no. 915), dated 1007; 1305 (Sawyer, no. 918), dated 1008; Nat. Lib. Wales, Peniarth MS 390, pp. 364–5 (Sawyer, no. 923), dated 1011; *KCD*, nos. 1308 (Sawyer, no. 931), dated 1013; 1309 (Sawyer, no. 933), dated 1014; 1310 (Sawyer, no. 934), dated 1015. Edward does not witness the other Æthelred charters in Peniarth 390, Sawyer, nos. 920, 922, 924, 928–30, dated 1008, 1009, 1011, 1012. Sawyer, no. 923 bridges what was an awkward gap. It is a sale by Æthelred of 2 hides at Hallam (Derbys) to his thegn Ælfmod. There is nothing suspicious about the charter, which is witnessed by Æthelred, 'rex totius Brittannice telluris'; Ælfheah, archbishop of Canterbury; Wulfstan, archbishop of York; Ælfgyvu, 'collaterana eiusdem regis'; the *clytones*, Æthelstan, Eadmund, Eadred, Eadwig, Eadweard;

recording of Alfred, the second son,[1] is cautionary. Westminster abbey preserved the tradition, or invented the story, that Leofrun, 'the wife of Earl Tostig', was Edward's foster-mother;[2] but who she was we cannot say. The third child of the marriage to survive was a daughter, Godgifu, whose place in the order cannot be determined. As she was able to make such a good marriage, to Eustace, count of Boulogne, after the death of her first husband, Drogo, count of the Vexin, in 1035, she may have been the youngest child.

By naming the boy Edward, Æthelred completed the series from Æthelstan, and the king may well have been thinking of his murdered half-brother. Yet, as the next son was called Alfred, it is equally possible that Æthelred had reverted to Edward the Elder and was proposing to continue backwards to Egbert. In neither case was Æthelred making a break with his earlier practice. Just as he seems to have called Emma by the name of his first wife, Ælfgifu, so he incorporated the children of the second marriage into the single family. It is possible that as a result of his own experiences as a child Æthelred was symbolically denying that there was a division in his house.

Of the six sons of the first marriage only two, Edmund Ironside and Eadwig, survived their father. In the witness lists to charters Egbert disappears after 1005, Edgar after 1008, and Eadred and Æthelstan after 1012. On the charter evidence Æthelstan, until his death, would appear to be his father's heir.[3] He always heads the list

---

bishops Ælfhun [of London], Æthelwold [of Winchester], Lyvingc [of Wells], Æthelric [of Sherborne], Ælfwold [of Crediton], Athulf [of Hereford], Godwine [of Lichfield or Rochester], Eadnoth [of Dorchester], Ælfmaer [of Selsey]; six unnamed abbots; four unnamed *duces*; and 23 unnamed *ministri*. See below, p. 328.

[1] Cf. Alistair Campbell, *Encomium Emmae*, p. xlii. Alfred witnesses only an obviously manufactured charter, *KCD*, no. 1308 (Sawyer, no. 931), dated 1013, with a witness list which cannot be later than 1012 if Æthulf stands for Æthelwulf of Hereford, and *KCD*, no. 1309 (Sawyer, no. 933), dated 1014, a rather doubtful and irregular charter, with four princes witnessing after the bishops and earls, and with a witness list to be dated 1013.

[2] Harmer, *Writs*, no. 93; the authenticity of the writ is discussed, pp. 303-6.

[3] It is not clear exactly when Æthelstan died. He is omitted from *KCD*, no. 1309 (Sawyer, no. 933), dated 1014, and seems to play no part in the events of 1013-16. But Miss Whitelock, *Wills*, p. 167, dates his will 1015, accepting the late endorsement. Bishop Ælfsige [of Winchester] is a witness to both documents. The date of his consecration is usually placed between 1012 and 1014; but he in fact witnesses an unpublished charter dated 1011 and probably another dated 1012 (Sawyer, nos. 924, 929); but even if he were consecrated in 1014, the will could be of that year — after midsummer, as appears from internal evidence. All the same, Æthelstan's witness is omitted from the charter dated 1014; and there is reason to think that this should be

of sons (indeed the order of precedence among the brothers is consistently recorded) and occasionally is the only son named. On this evidence Edward started seventh in the line of succession and in 1016, when his father died, had advanced to third. By 1017, when Edmund Ironside was dead and Eadwig executed, Edward and Alfred were the sole surviving sons. It is possible that some of the sons of the first marriage had left children; but the only one we know to have done so is Edmund Ironside, who was survived by two infants, Edmund and Edward ('the Exile'). There is no need, however, to determine the law of succession, for in that same year Emma married Cnut and the claims of Æthelred's descendants passed into abeyance.

Clearly Edward had been advancing closer to the throne owing to the elimination of his half-brothers. It is not, however, in those terms that his claim is described in the *Vita Ædwardi Regis*, which omits all reference to Æthelred's first family. When Emma was pregnant with Edward all men swore that if she bore a son they would recognize him as their future lord and king. Thus Edward's tardy accession in 1042 was miraculous, the will of God. Both God and the people had chosen him as king before the day of his birth, and God postponed the event only in order to punish the people for their sins.[1]

We can easily believe that Edward's eventual succession to his father's throne struck men as miraculous; but the portent cited as evidence is a very secular ceremony and one which is capable of historical explanation. In 1017, according to Emma's encomiast,[2] she refused to marry Cnut unless he would take an oath that, if God should grant her a son by him, he would never appoint the son of any other wife as his successor. For it was said that Cnut had sons by another woman, and she wanted to provide wisely for her own children and make arrangements prudently in advance. Shortly after William of Normandy married Matilda of Flanders (about 1052), his barons took oaths of allegiance to him and also to his offspring as yet unborn.[3] Although William, so far as we know, had no previous wife *more danico* or bastard children, Matilda's family was securing that no children by other women could rightly claim the inheritance; and provision for

---

corrected to 1013. After the witness of Archbishop Wulfstan [of York] appears Bishop Lyfing, presumably the bishop of Wells who was translated to Canterbury in 1013. There seems no good reason why the will should not be dated 1012 in accordance with the available evidence.

[1] *VEdR*, pp. 7–9, 60.   [2] *Encomium Emmae*, pp. 32–3.   [3] Poitiers, p. 44.

such a ceremony may have been usual in princely marriage contracts. It is, therefore, possible that in 1002 Count Richard II proposed these terms when Æthelred asked for his sister. But there is little to suggest that Æthelred, even if he accepted them, honoured the contract or paid any attention to the consequences. In the religious houses where the charters were written the birth of Edward was given no special significance. The new aetheling or *clito* was simply added at the bottom of the list of princes. Moreover, in 1041–2 Emma herself was apparently denying that the ceremony had taken place.[1] The denial, however, proves that claims based on oaths were being advanced by pretenders to the English throne, probably by supporters of Edward; and even if the story in the *Vita* is based only on 'legitimist' propaganda, the propaganda may not have been without foundation. We notice that whereas Æthelred's first wife never appears among the witnesses to charters, Emma, like the queen mother, Edgar's widow, received this honour; and the title of queen which she was sometimes awarded strongly suggests that she had been crowned and anointed after the marriage.[2] In this way, perhaps, a cautious distinction was made between the two broods.

Nor would it be the first time that unusual arrangements had been made in the West-Saxon royal family. Æthelwulf, when he had at least four healthy sons, sent the youngest, Alfred, at the age of four to Rome for a 'coronation' by the pope.[3] Thus Alfred's accession – after his brothers and despite nephews – in 871 was almost as miraculous as Edward's and preordained by a ceremony even stranger. We cannot doubt that, when Edward was born, his mother ardently hoped that one day he would become king and did everything possible to help this come true.

A story in the twelfth-century chronicle of Ely abbey, that Æthelred and Emma gave Edward as a child to the monastery so that he could be educated as a monk,[4] is, therefore, surprising. It is the first of several anecdotes relating to Edward's religious life which lack sound authority and also plausibility.[5] This story, however, differs from the others in

---

[1] *Encomium Emmae*, p. 48. Her encomiast, no doubt instructed by her, makes Edward deny that the English nobles had taken an oath to him.

[2] Cf. A. Campbell, 'The status of Queen Emma and her predecessors', *Encomium Emmae*, pp. 62 ff.   [3] Cf. Eric John, *Orbis Britanniae* (Leicester, 1966), pp. 37 ff.

[4] *Liber Eliensis*, II, c. 91, pp. 160–1.

[5] Osbert of Clare, who wrote Edward's life in 1138 (below, p. 274), was exiled to Ely after 1121, *The Letters of Osbert of Clare*, ed. E. W. Williamson (1929), pp. 47,

that it is independent of the hagiographical tradition. It was unknown to the author of the *Vita Ædwardi Regis* and so was not incorporated into the saint's life. The anecdote was used at Ely to explain two completely unrelated objects:[1] an embroidered pall, which the monks showed to visitors as the one in which Edward was wrapped when his parents offered him to St Ætheldreda, and a charter of privileges, which, they alleged, Edward had given them after he became king in gratitude for the hospitality he had received. But the pall does not seem to be a relic of Æthelred's reign. The charter is linked with a papal privilege, and both documents are, if not complete forgeries, at least interpolated and revised. Moreover, the long historical preamble in the royal charter makes no reference to Edward's special ties with Ely. The problem is whether there is a grain of truth in all the falsity.

Since Edward did not become a monk, there could have been fairly general suppression of an episode which monks would have regarded as damaging to his reputation. The story of a spoiled monk was not good material for a saint's life, although, with a little refashioning, the episode could easily have been used to show how a short sojourn at Ely implanted in Edward's mind a lasting love of God. But English kings did not put their sons into the church and it is inconceivable that Emma should have sacrificed her first-born in this way.[2] English princes, however, often received some of their education from an abbot or bishop. King Edgar had studied as a youth under St Æthelwold at Abingdon and he entrusted his son, Edward the Martyr, to Bishop Sideman of Crediton.[3] The difficulties in Edward's case are that it was unusual to be put to letters at so tender an age and the choice of Ely, rather than a West-Saxon monastery, is inexplicable.

The one remaining possibility is that Edward was hidden away for a time in this island fortress,[4] from which he could have been carried to

---

156–7; cf. 116 ff. But, although he collected *Edwardiana* assiduously and had no critical sense, he did not incorporate this story into his work. It could, of course, be said that Osbert would not wish to share Westminster's treasure with Ely.

[1] Cf. F. Barlow, 'Edward the Confessor's Early Life, Character and Attitudes', *EHR*, lxxx (1965), 227 ff.

[2] Strong evidence against Ely's story that Edward was an oblate is that the abbey recorded no free gifts of land by Æthelred or Emma and never claimed Islip, which would, presumably, have been given with Edward.

[3] Eric John, 'The King and the Monks in the Tenth-century Reformation', *Orbis Britanniae*, pp. 159–60; *Vita S. Oswaldi*, *HCY*, i. 449.

[4] For Ely's reputation for invulnerability – and it was in fact immune in this period – see *Gesta abbatum monasterii S. Albani*, ed. H. T. Riley, i (Rolls ser. 1867), 34.

Normandy by water. In 1006 a great Danish fleet based on the Isle of Wight ravaged the mainland until it was bought off in the following year. Between 1008 and 1012 Thorkell's army raided most of the country east of Southampton Water and south of the Wash. During these years the king and queen must have paid some attention to the safety of their younger children, although a refuge in the far West rather than in the path of the Danes would seem more suitable. All the same, Edward's name never disappears for long from the witness lists to royal charters; and its occurrence in 1007, 1008, 1011, and 1013 is conclusive evidence that Edward was neither a monastic oblate nor completely removed from the political scene. In 1013 the king of Denmark himself, Svein Forkbeard, accompanied by his younger son, Cnut, arrived for the kill; and in the autumn Emma, Edward, and Alfred were in London, protected by the fleet which Æthelred had recruited from the invaders of 1008–12. It was, apparently, Emma who first fled to Normandy, taking with her the abbot of Peterborough. The king then sent the two princes under the care of the bishop of London to join her; and he himself followed by way of the Isle of Wight. But hardly had he arrived when he heard that Svein was dead (3 February 1014).[1]

The rapid changes in the political scene between Svein's death and Cnut's acquisition of the whole kingdom in November 1016 throw some light on the attitudes and ambitions of the main characters. In the first place it is clear that the royal family was divided, and not only physically, into at least two parties. There is no evidence that any of the surviving sons of the first marriage took refuge abroad. About this time, possibly in 1012, certainly no later than 1015, Æthelred's eldest son, Æthelstan, made his will, apparently when dying.[2] He was a warrior prince with a great collection of swords, some famous, and a number of prized horses. His sword-sharpener and stag huntsman received bequests. He was unmarried and made no provision for children. He dispersed his estates and possessions among churches and 'good causes', kinsmen, friends, and servants. He referred most appreciatively to his father and to his grandmother, Ælfthryth, who had brought him up.[3] He also left money to St Edward at Shaftesbury, his murdered half-uncle. He left a good estate to his foster-mother, Ælfswith. He remem-

---

[1] *Chron. CDE.*   [2] Whitelock, *Wills*, no. XX. See also above, p. 30, *n.* 3.
[3] According to Malmesbury, *GR*, i. 184, Ælfthryth lived a life of penance for Edward's murder in the nunnery at Wherwell.

bered his two surviving full brothers. One of these, Edmund Ironside, witnessed the will. Not only did he receive estates and war gear, but he also got the most precious of Æthelstan's swords, the one which had belonged to King Offa – perhaps of Mercia – or could it have been the fourth-century King Offa of Angel? The other brother, Eadwig, was given only a silver-hilted sword. But neither his mother nor the half-kin, his step-mother and the aethelings, Edward and Alfred, are mentioned. Among the many bequests is one to Godwin, Wulfnoth's son, possibly the future Earl Godwin, and one to Sigeferth, possibly the East-Anglian thegn who, with his brother, Morkere, was murdered in 1015 and whose widow Edmund Ironside then married. It looks as though the royal family was in some disarray.

Æthelred had not necessarily capitulated to Emma's ambition for her children. But in the spring of 1014, when he dispatched ambassadors to England to negotiate for his return to the throne, he sent Edward with them, presumably as a seal and pledge for his promise of good government.[1] He must, therefore, have regarded Edward – and expected others to regard the prince – as at least a possible heir to the throne. Shortly after Æthelred's return to England, Edmund Ironside began to act independently of his father. Whereupon, it seems, Emma transferred her support to him. In the *Encomium Emmae Reginae*, which she commissioned, Æthelred is not only omitted, his very existence is suppressed.[2] Emma would not have chosen to forget him because of his infidelities, as William of Malmesbury alleges;[3] it was surely because of his failure. He had let her down. In the same work Edmund is regarded as a hero. After Æthelred's death (23 April 1016), until his own death seven months later, Edmund occupied the throne and withstood Cnut. According to Scandinavian tradition Edward fought at his brother's side, and distinguished himself by almost carving Cnut in two.[4] Edward could not have been more than thirteen and was

---

[1] Cf. Pierre Chaplais, 'The Anglo-Saxon Chancery: from the Diploma to the Writ', *Journal of the Society of Archivists*, iii (1966), 172.

[2] Cf. Campbell, *Encomium Emmae*, pp. xliii, xlvi.   [3] *GR*, i. 191; cf. p. 237.

[4] Edmund and Edward were regarded as co-kings: cf. *Olafs Saga Helga (Hk.)*, cap. 16, 'Now the third spring King *Athalrathr* died and his sons *Eathmundr* and *Eathvathr* succeeded to the kingdom'. Margaret Ashdown, *English and Norse Documents relating to the Reign of Ethelred the Unready* (1930), p. 161. They are described jointly fighting against Cnut, *ibid.*, cap. 26 (p. 165) and *Olafs Saga ins Helga (Fl.)*, cap. 20 (pp. 177–8), where the dramatic, and unlikely episode, in which Edward almost kills Cnut, appears: 'Earl Thorkell the Tall went to help King Cnut win the other part of London town, and as luck would have it just saved his life, for Edward, King

probably only eleven. But the tradition that Emma had sent Edward to serve Edmund, even if only by helping to reunite different factions, is probably sound. This opportunism may be considered typical of her. Edward was too young to have stood a chance on his own. Her only hope of recovering her estates and an honourable position in England rested on Edmund. She must have liked and trusted her step-son. The claims of her own children could wait, would have to wait.

On 30 November 1016 Edmund died and Cnut, already in possession of the Danelaw and Mercia, received the submission of Wessex. On Christmas Day Edward, 'when deprived of his father's kingdom and visiting the abodes of the saints in search of pardon for his sins and of restoration to his ancestral realm by their aid', promised the monastery of St Peter at Ghent the restoration of its English possessions when he became king.[1] Edward was presumably travelling back from England to Normandy by way of Flanders. Too much can be made of this charter. It must have been drawn up by the monastery, and it was in the monks' interest to get a grant from any English aetheling who might one day become king. We cannot assume that on Edmund's death Edward immediately claimed the throne. Indeed it is possible, even likely, that Cnut inherited by virtue of the terms of the treaty he had made with Edmund in the summer, when they had divided England between them.[2] Edward was simply an English prince going into exile, a prince with poor prospects of ever making a victorious return.[3]

Æthelred's son, struck at that time a blow which men have held in memory in after days. Thorkell thrust Cnut off his horse, but Edward smote asunder the saddle and the horse's back.'

[1] A. Van Lokeren, *Chartes et documents de l'abbaye de Saint-Pierre au Mont-Blandin à Gand*, i. (Ghent, 1869), no. 96, pp. 72–3; *Messager des sciences historiques de Belgique* (1842), p. 238; J. H. Round, *Calendar of Documents preserved in France*, i. (1899), no. 1374. Campbell, *Encomium Emmae*, p. lxiv, *n*. 3, throws doubt on the authenticity of this charter, but for historical reasons which seem unsound. Edward's second charter to Ghent, dated 1044 (*KCD*, no. 771; Sawyer, no. 1002), is certainly a forgery. See Pierre Chaplais, *A Medieval Miscellany for Doris Mary Stenton*, Pipe Roll Soc. lxxvi (1962), 92–3.

[2] It is stated explicitly in *Olafs Saga ins Helga* (*Fl.*), cap. 21 (ed. Ashdown, p. 179), 'After this battle Edmund and Cnut came to terms and divided England between them, and were both kings, and if one should die before the other, he who survived should be sole king over united England.' Cf. *Historia Norwegiae* in *Monumenta Historica Norvegiae*, ed. Gustav Storm (Christiania, 1880), p. 123. Florence (i. 179) reports, on unknown authority, that in December the English nobles falsely told Cnut that Edmund had appointed him his heir. *Chron. CDE, s.a.* 1016, is non-committal.

[3] In *Olafs Saga Helga (Hk.)*, caps. 27–28 (ed. Ashdown, pp. 165–7), Æthelred's sons (unnamed) are described as continuing the fight in alliance with Olaf Haralds-

Since the English royal family could no longer provide a champion to fight against Cnut, Emma lost no time in coming to terms with the conqueror. In July 1017 she crossed to England for her marriage to her husband's supplanter. Such a marriage was not unusual at the time, and it is doubtful whether Emma attracted much blame, either from the nobility or the church.[1] There were advantages to both the contracting parties. Cnut obtained the important Norman alliance and some control over the aethelings in exile, as well as Emma's political experience. Emma recovered her position as queen, and by leaving her children in Normandy did not return defenceless to England. Cnut apparently did not abandon the union that he had recently formed with Ælfgifu of Northampton and clearly retained the right to make proper endowment for their children. But it must also have been stipulated in Emma's marriage contract that at least England and Denmark would go in the first instance to the children she would have from Cnut.[2] There seems no reason to think that Emma could at this time have extorted something for Edward and Alfred; she could only make provision for a family as yet unborn.

It is difficult to imagine how Edward viewed his mother's behaviour. He was being left in the cold. But we do not know whether he was regarded as the one and only true legal heir, or, if so, whether Emma exerted herself on his behalf before deciding that there was nothing she could do. On the whole it is unlikely that much attention was paid to legal niceties when a man was out of possession and unable to raise military forces. Whatever may have been the terms on which Emma married Æthelred, much was changed since then and Emma's interests had altered. The theoretical problem was difficult, for among the elder brothers at least one, Edmund Ironside, who had possessed the throne, had left children; but what damned Edward in the eyes of his kinsmen was his youth. We have to remember the case of Edgar Ætheling in 1066. Edward also may have been without great ambition, or may have been unable to inspire confidence in others. Emma chose the

---

son. They join up with Olaf at Rouen during the winter and make a treaty by which, if they recovered England, Olaf should have Northumbria. In the autumn (?1016) Olaf sent his foster-father, Hrani, to England in order to recruit supporters, and in the spring (?1017) Olaf and Æthelred's sons invaded England at 'Jungufurtha', a town which they stormed. But Cnut came up with superior forces and the invaders withdrew and separated, the sons back to Rouen, Olaf to Northumbria.

[1] Later, William of Malmesbury, *GR*, i. 218, considered it disgraceful.
[2] *Encomium Emmae*, pp. 32–3.

easier course, but also possibly the only one. Presumably her brother, Count Richard II of Normandy, was unwilling to attempt to replace the fugitives by force of arms. Edward could have complained that his mother abandoned his cause too quickly; but it is doubtful whether (leaving sentiment out of account) he could have complained of more; and Emma could have replied that her quick action had salvaged for each of them something out of the disaster.

Some twenty years later the relationship between mother and son was cold. Not only the long separation after 1017, but also the separations during childhood may have been responsible. And even if Edward felt no bitterness in 1017, there was time for bitterness to grow. It is unreasonable to suppose that Edward was complaisant and felt nothing but gratitude towards his mother and her kin for having protected his life: that he punished Emma for her neglect as soon as he was crowned king proves the long grudge. Edward always behaved like one who had been deprived of love.

From 1017 until his death on 12 November 1035 Cnut ruled England in complete security. As the master of a Scandinavian empire, which included at times, besides Denmark, Norway and parts of Sweden, the Viking colonies in the Isle of Man, the Scottish isles and Ireland, and also comprised lordship over the king of Scots, Cnut commanded the respect of his neighbours. His ostentatious pilgrimage to Rome in 1027 in order to attend the coronation of the Emperor Conrad II set the seal on his diplomatic recognition as one of the great powers.[1] The Norman chronicler, William of Jumièges, has the story that Count Robert of Normandy (1027–35), in order to put pressure on Cnut in the interests of Edward, prepared and dispatched a naval expedition from Fécamp; but the fleet was hindered by bad weather and Robert employed it against Brittany.[2] Even if the chronicler has not confused Britain and Brittany, nothing came of this gesture. Cnut seems to have been in no real danger from across the Channel.

Cnut also appeared to be establishing his dynasty. By his concubine, Ælfgifu of Northampton, he had a son whom he named after his father, Svein, and whom he appointed nominal regent of Norway, and another

[1] F. Barlow, 'Two Notes: Cnut's Second Pilgrimage and Queen Emma's Disgrace in 1043', *EHR*, lxxiii (1958), 650–1.

[2] Jumièges, pp. 109–11. *Carmen* ll. 330–4, where the king is urged to repeat the great deeds of his ancestors: 'Normannos proavus superavit, avusque Britannos; Anglorum genitor sub juga colla dedit.' Cf. R. H. C. Davis, 'The Carmen de Hastingae Proelio', *EHR*, xciii (1978), 258.

boy, Harold 'Harefoot', whose parentage was later disputed. Emma gave birth to a son and a daughter, Harthacnut and Gunnhildr. In these circumstances Edward and Alfred, although they did not lose all diplomatic importance, were reduced to pawns.

If Edward had been intended for the church, or had a monk's vocation, he now had the opportunity to resume his interrupted pupilage. Even if it was in the Norman interest to keep the claims of this line alive, Alfred could represent it. The only information we have about Edward's religious life at this time is the parenthetical statement in the *Vita Ædwardi Regis*, in connexion with Edward's miracles, that some Normans (*Franci*) testified that Edward had performed similar cures as a young man in Normandy.[1] This statement is so devoid of authority and probability that no time need be wasted on it. We also learn from the same source that Edward on his deathbed had a vision in which he met two monks whom he had known in Normandy.[2] Edward's friendship with Robert, abbot of Jumièges, is well known, and cannot be used as an argument that he had been a monk or a sort of monk. Nor are the gifts which Edward made during his reign to Norman monasteries, especially Fécamp,[3] evidence that he had once lived in them. William Calculus, monk of Jumièges, states categorically that Edward and Alfred were educated in the ducal hall, a statement repeated by William of Poitiers, archdeacon of Lisieux.[4] Although both these writers were drawing attention to Edward's indebtedness to the Norman dukes, we cannot doubt that if Edward had lived for a time in Jumièges or any other Norman monastery, they would not have suppressed the fact.

Indeed it is clear that the exiles in Normandy were educated as nobles. Godgifu was found a husband, apparently as soon as possible; and Edward and Alfred – to judge by their later interests and actions – were brought up as knights. In the eyes of contemporaries Edward

---

[1] *VEdR*, p. 62.   [2] *Ibid.*, p. 75.

[3] *DB*, i. 17 a ii. Montagu Burrows, *Historic Towns: Cinque Ports* (1888), pp. 26–9; J. H. Round, *Feudal England*, pp. 319, 567–9; Round and L. F. Salzmann, *VCH Sussex*, i. 375; Donald Matthew, *The Norman Monasteries and their English Possessions* (1962), pp. 19–26.

[4] 'Ii [*sc.* Edwardus atque Alvredus] enim intra Normannorum ducum aulam educati', Jumièges, v, 7 (p. 81), 8 (p. 82), vi, 9 (p. 109); 'Exules adhuc manebant in curia propinqui sui, Guillelmi principis, Edwardus ac Alveradus, qui olim, pueri ne jugularentur, ad avunculos in Normanniam effugerant', Poitiers, I, 1 (p. 2). Cf. *VEdR*, p. 8, 'puer defertur ad avos suos in Franciam, ut cum eis ablactionis suae transigat infantiam.'

always had a martial air. And that neither Edward nor Alfred married while in exile is no argument to the contrary. Few of their contemporaries married young, except for reasons of state;[1] and we know nothing about the aethelings' estate. William of Poitiers places in the mouth of William the Conqueror a speech in which he claims that Edward bequeathed him the crown in return for the great honours and many benefits (or benefices) that he and his ancestors had granted to Edward and Alfred and their men.[2] But *honores* and *beneficia* are ambiguous words, which can cover everything from marks of respect and kindness to real estate, and are for that reason most useful to the pleader. Neither William of Jumièges nor William of Poitiers writes explicitly that the exiles were given landed estates or fiefs. And if the princes had not a prince's estate they could not expect to marry a social equal. Whether they were clean-living young men is quite another matter, which, as we are completely without reliable evidence, cannot be profitably discussed.

Equally obscure is where the exiles lived. We know that they started their new life in the ducal household, and Edward appears as a witness to a few of the later charters of Duke Robert and one of William the Bastard.[3] But as he is twice described as 'king' the evidence is not entirely convincing. Also, although Edward's brother-in-law, Count Drogo of the Vexin, accompanied Robert on his pilgrimage to Jerusalem in 1034, and like him did not survive the adventure, neither Edward nor Alfred was moved to go. It is unlikely, in view of the silence of the Norman chroniclers, that the English princes were left behind in order to safeguard the ducal interests and heir, and we can only conclude that Edward was not as intimate with Robert as the Norman apologists for the conquest of England liked to maintain. However that may be, Edward was through his mother plentifully endowed with other kinsmen in the area. Even if we confine our attention to uncles and first cousins, there was a string of these from Brittany to Flanders: Alan III, count of Brittany; Eon de Porhoët, count of Penthièvre; Gilbert, count of Brionne; Robert, archbishop of Rouen and count of

[1] Cf. Barlow, 'Edward the Confessor's Early Life', p. 234.

[2] 'ob maximos honores et plurima beneficia quae illi et fratri suo necnon hominibus eorum ego et majores mei impendimus', Poitiers, II, 12 (p. 174); cf. I, 14 (p. 30).

[3] *Recueil des Actes des Ducs de Normandie de 911 à 1066*, ed. Marie Fauroux (Société des Antiquaires de Normandie, 1961), nos. 69, 70, 85 (dated 1031/5), nos. 69 and 70 are also witnessed by Alfred; no. 111 (dated 1035/48). The aethelings are never high on the witness list and on no. 69 (April 1033) are last but one on a long list.

1. Queen Aelfgyfu (Emma) and King Cnut placing a gold cross on an altar in New Minster, Winchester, afterwards Hyde abbey. Above is Christ in Majesty with the Virgin on his right and St Peter on his left. Below are monks of the monastery. The drawing, in the Winchester style, can be dated about 1020. *Liber Vitae* of New Minster. (*Reproduced by courtesy of the Trustees of the British Museum,* Stowe MS. 944, fo. 6.)

2. Queen Emma, King Harthacnut, and Prince Edward, with the author of the *Encomium Emmae* kneeling in front. Frontispiece (damaged by two holes) from a mid-eleventh-century MS. of the *Encomium.* (*Reproduced by courtesy of the Trustees of the British Museum,* Additional MS. 33241, fo. 1ᵛ.)

Evreux; William, count of Eu; Mauger, count of Corbeil; Aelis, married to the count of Burgundy; and Eleanor, married to the count of Flanders. Edward's sister, Godgifu, was until 1035 countess of Mantes and later countess of Boulogne. The king of France was his own lord's direct feudal superior.[1]

If Edward's foreign friends from the period after 1041 are any guide, he had not been stationary in Normandy. Robert of Jumièges is an obvious link with Rouen, or possibly Brionne. That Edward took his sister's son with him to England (or welcomed him later) proves that he had kept in close touch with her at Mantes.[2] He gave land in England to Bretons.[3] We find him once at Bruges[4] and he returned to England with two clerks who had been educated in Lorraine.[5] He certainly knew Henry I of France, and in 1043 Henry was one of those who congratulated Edward on his accession.[6] There is also evidence, although admittedly of a doubtful nature, that Edward had visited the French royal court.[7] The *Vita Ædwardi Regis* in a rhetorical passage, but one which makes sense, describes the many congratulatory embassies received by Edward after his coronation, and mentions those sent by foreign dukes and princes. Moreover, it maintains that in return Edward made to the Frankish princes gifts, which seem to have included money fiefs and grants of land in perpetuity.[8] If there is any truth in this statement, Edward was not simply making conventional counter-gifts but sharing the spoils with those who had a claim on his gratitude. The evidence, such as it is, suggests that Edward had divided his time between several courts; and it is easy to believe that after an exile of more than a quarter of a century he had many debts to repay,

[1] See genealogical chart in Barlow, 'Edward the Confessor's Early Life', p. 232.
[2] See below, p. 50.
[3] Alan III, count of Brittany (1008–40), and Eon de Porhoët, count of Penthièvre, were Edward's first cousins; and there were several Bretons at Edward's court: Ralf, the staller, and Robert fitzWimarch (? Norman-Breton). See further J. H. Round, *Feudal England*, p. 327; F. M. Stenton, *Anglo-Saxon England*, pp. 419–20.
[4] See below, p. 47.   [5] See below, p. 50.
[6] Jumièges, pp. 104–5; Round, *Calendar*, no. 1422; Fauroux, *Recueil*, no. 69; *VEdR*, p. 10.
[7] According to the tradition reported in *Leges Edwardi Confessoris* (? 1130–5), cap. 37, *De usurariis*, Edward banished usurers from his kingdom: 'Hoc autem dicebat sepe se audisse in curia regis Francorum, dum ibi moratus esset, nec immerito usura enim summa radix omnium viciorum interpretatur', Liebermann, *Die Gesetze*, i. 668.
[8] 'Ædwardus facit eisdem Francorum principibus [regalia munera] vel annua vel continua', *VEdR*, p. 11.

obligations which the creditors would not be slow in bringing to his royal attention.

In 1035, when Robert of Normandy and Cnut died, Edward was at least thirty years old, young enough to take advantage of opportunities which could now appear, even if too old to take risks with abandon. Although Edward was probably not an adventurer, not even, perhaps, adventurous, he was always prepared to take his chance. He must also have been well equipped to exploit each opportunity. From living in such rough society he cannot have been without military training and experience. We can be sure from his successful survival in a not altogether friendly world that he was tenacious, resilient, accustomed to shifts in fortune, prepared to be used by others in the hope of turning it to his advantage, quick to find an opening, quick to escape from a situation which threatened his interests. Exile is rarely the school for heroic virtues, but, as we see from the behaviour of most kings who succeeded after years in the wilderness, it teaches more useful qualities: opportunism and flexibility, patience, caution, a grasp of the oblique approach. Moreover, from ill-treatment and ill-fortune men gain an understanding of the secrets of human behaviour, of the true motives behind the appearance, and learn how to exploit men's fear and greed. There is every reason to think that Edward, too, had learned worldly wisdom, and, disillusioned, cynical, without great hopes or great ambition, was prepared to accept whatever fate had in store.

Cnut died at Shaftesbury on 12 November 1035 aged about forty.[1] His death seems to have been unexpected and there is nothing to show that careful provision had been made for the succession to the English throne. Cnut's elder son by Ælfgifu of Northampton, Svein, was with his mother in Norway attempting to rule that turbulent kingdom. He died in the following year[2] and seems to have taken no part in the English drama. Cnut's son by Emma, Harthacnut, was ruling Denmark; but the queen had remained in England and on Cnut's death claimed England for her son.[3] Also in England was Svein's younger brother, Harold Harefoot, aged about eighteen, who, on the basis of three kingdoms and three sons, thought that England should go to him.[4]

[1] The following narrative is based on *Chron.* and Florence. See Plummer, *Two Chronicles*, pp. 208–10.

[2] Adam of Bremen, II, lxxvii, p. 135.

[3] According to *Encomium Emmae*, pp. 6, 32–4, Cnut had always been of a mind that Harthacnut should succeed to England as well as Denmark.

[4] According to Adam of Bremen, II, lxxiv, p. 134, Cnut had willed that his empire

The political situation which developed cannot be fully understood because we know so little about the politics of Cnut's reign. The Anglo-Saxon Chronicle is based merely on jottings. What happened is that shortly after Cnut's burial in the Old Minster at Winchester all the counsellors (*witan*) met at Oxford and split into two parties. Earl Leofric of Mercia, at the head of almost all the thegns north of the Thames and the naval crews of London, favoured Harold; Earl Godwin of Wessex, representing the queen and the nobility of the south, including the archbishop of Canterbury,[1] supported the absent Harthacnut.

Clearly Oxford was the frontier town between two hostile regions, roughly the Danelaw and the English part. Yet the two candidates and their champions reverse the position. Harold Harefoot was probably considered a native of Northampton[2] and Earl Leofric was a member of an old and distinguished Mercian family.[3] On the other side Harthacnut was the Dane, ruling in Denmark, and Earl Godwin, although of English birth, was married to Gytha, the sister of earls Ulf and Eilifr, the sister-in-law of Cnut.[4] Godwin was, moreover, a creation of Cnut and probably completely identified with the interests of his royal master. It would seem, therefore, that the movement in favour of Harold was inspired by a reaction against Cnut's attitude and policies and to some extent represented established Anglo-Danish interests against a court party relying on the loyalty of Wessex to the crown. As it appears that the church was opposed to Harold – the Chronicle doubts his paternity and his maternity[5] – it may be that Harold was supported by men who thought that Cnut had been too generous to the church; and since a pillar of the old order like Leofric backed this doubtful claimant it is likely that there was still rivalry between Mercia and Wessex, personal rivalry between Leofric and Godwin, and much rancour left behind by Cnut's patronage of new men.

should be divided in this way, in accordance with the custom, prevalent among barbarians, of treating legitimate and illegitimate children alike.

[1] The story in *Encomium Emmae*, p. 41, that Archbishop Æthelnoth refused to crown Harold, makes explicit what is implicit in the *Chron.*

[2] His mother, Ælfgifu, was the daughter of Earl Ælfhelm and Wulfrun, *Chron. E, s.a.* 1035; Florence, i. 190.

[3] Harmer, *Writs*, pp. 565–6; Robertson, *Charters*, p. 396.

[4] Barlow, *VEdR*, pp. lxiv–lxv, 4; Campbell, *Encomium Emmae*, pp. 82 ff.

[5] *Chron. CDE, s.a.* 1035. Florence, i. 190, elaborates: Ælfgifu was barren; Svein was really the son of a priest, Harold the son of a cobbler. Cf. *Encomium Emmae*, p. 41, *VEdR*, p. 20.

Indeed, such was the unpopularity of the court party that Harold's faction was dominant from the start and continued to prosper.

Although Emma seems immediately to have seized the royal treasure and regalia at Winchester, presumably in the name of her son, Harold was able to take them from her;[1] and it was probably in order to avoid civil war that Emma was left at Winchester on her dower lands while the chief men of the kingdom met at Oxford to discuss the situation. The settlement which Harold and his supporters imposed took more account of the actual balance of power than of legality. Harold was made protector of the whole of England for himself and his absent half-brother; Emma and Godwin with the royal bodyguard were to hold Wessex for Harthacnut. The position of Emma and her son was gravely compromised by this treaty; but all was not lost provided that Harthacnut returned with all haste from Denmark. He would be able to take over Wessex as a base and either negotiate new terms or make war on Harold.

Harthacnut, however, did not return to England until 1040, after Harold's death. He was detained in Denmark by war, but obviously showed a greater interest in Denmark than in England, an attitude which may well explain why so many preferred to have Harold as king. It must have been as soon as Emma realized that Harthacnut was going to let her down that she turned to her sons in Normandy. Her hatred of Harold was intense. She repeated the scurrilous rumour that he was not even the son of Cnut's concubine, but the child of a servant placed secretly in Ælfgifu's bed.[2] She also maintained that Harold, in order to lure her Norman sons to their death, forged a letter in her name to Edward and Alfred, in which she complained about Harold's behaviour and invited them to visit her so as to make plans for the future; and this letter, she claimed, brought Alfred, with Edward's approval, to his martyrdom in England.[3]

All these accusations are the inventions of an unscrupulous woman. The truth would seem to be that both sons in turn, and presumably at Emma's instigation, crossed to England in 1036.[4] Although the story

---

[1] The order of events is not clear from *Chron.*, for *C* and *D* tell of the treasure and *E* of the council of Oxford. Florence, however, places the spoliation of Emma before the division of the kingdom.

[2] *Encomium Emmae*, p. 41; cf. above, p. 43, note 5.

[3] *Encomium Emmae*, pp. 41–3.

[4] Ely commemorated Alfred's death on 5 February, B. Dickins, 'The day of Byrhtnoth's death and other obits from a twelfth-century Ely Kalendar', *Leeds*

of Edward's adventure is only told a generation later by the Norman apologists, is uncorroborated by the Anglo-Saxon Chronicle, and is tainted by the Norman wish to portray Edward as the debtor of the Norman court, it is plausible, and one that William of Jumièges, followed by William of Poitiers, is unlikely to have invented.[1] The Norman tale is that Edward, presumably sailing direct from Normandy, invaded England in the Southampton area, fought a successful battle, which, however, he was unable to exploit, and returned to Normandy with rich booty. If we accept the basic truth of this tradition, we can see that Edward, intending to join his mother at Winchester, was repulsed soon after landing – indeed, may well have been treated like a Viking raider – and gave up. We do not have to believe that Edward was commanding a large-scale military invasion, and we can easily understand why, except among the Normans, this fiasco was allowed to remain unchronicled.

Alfred's visit to England, because of its fatal ending, is well recorded.[2] Learning perhaps from his brother's failure, he and his escort travelled overland to Flanders and sailed from Wissant or Boulogne.[3] His ships escaped from the English naval forces which tried to capture them and made a safe landing.[4] But he and his men were intercepted by Earl Godwin's troops and taken to Guildford. Although Edward's and Alfred's incursions cannot have taken place very long after the treaty of Oxford, and both princes landed in Wessex, where their mother was supposed to be in control, we see that they had few, if any, friends in England. It is difficult to envisage the exact purpose of the expeditions. We can only accept William of Poitiers' view that each brother had as

---

Studies in English and Kindred Languages, vi (1937), 19. It is more likely to be February 1037 than 1036.

[1] Jumièges, pp. 120–1; Poitiers, pp. 4–6. Florence, i. 191–2, possibly attempting to harmonize several sources, makes Alfred and Edward cross together to England. Edward reaches his mother at Winchester; Alfred, however, is invited to a parley with Harold at London and is captured by Godwin. When news comes through of Alfred's death, Emma sends Edward back to Normandy. The falseness of Florence's account is shown by the way it presupposes that Alfred is the elder brother.

[2] *Chron. CD, s.a.* 1036; Florence, i. 191–2; *Encomium Emmae*, pp. 41–7; *VEdR*, pp. 20–1; Jumièges, pp. 121–2; Poitiers, pp. 7–13; Plummer, *Two Chronicles*, pp. 221 ff.

[3] *Encomium Emmae*, p. 43. This is evidence that his widowed sister, Godgifu, had just married, or was about to marry, Count Eustace.

[4] *Ibid.* According to Jumièges, Alfred sailed from Wissant, which Poitiers renders as *portus Icius*. According to Poitiers, Alfred reached *Dorobernia*, which Professor Raymonde Foreville translates 'Canterbury', but which probably represents Dover. In 1051 and 1067 Eustace of Boulogne crossed to Dover.

his objective the throne,[1] if we think it possible that they could have been so misinformed about the situation. It seems more likely that Emma, in desperation because her position was crumbling, called them to her side without having considered fully what they could do when they arrived.

A further difficulty in understanding this episode is the different interpretations of Earl Godwin's behaviour. The *Encomium Emmae* exculpates the earl: Harold's men took the captives out of Godwin's custody and were responsible for the atrocities.[2] And, although the original Anglo-Saxon annal for 1036 probably blamed the earl, one version of the Chronicle tries to obscure this and another omits the whole entry.[3] For obvious reasons, the English sources tried to avoid an outright condemnation of Godwin. The Normans, on the other hand, attributed the whole responsibility to him and even justified William's killing of Harold in 1066 as punishment for Godwin's murder of Alfred thirty years before.[4] The author of the *Vita Ædwardi Regis* did not know what to believe.[5] The account in the *C* version of the Chronicle would seem to be nearest to the truth: that Godwin and the other leading men in Wessex were coming to the conclusion that they would have to accept Harold as king. They would, therefore, regard the intervention of Emma's 'Norman' sons as a tiresome irrelevance and be ready to curry favour with Harold by handing over the captives. During Harthacnut's reign, we are told,[6] Godwin cleared himself of the charges brought against him by swearing that in 1036 he was simply acting on Harold's orders. This was probably more or less the truth. Anyhow, most of Alfred's companions were executed at Guildford and Alfred was taken to Ely where he was blinded so carelessly by the king's servants that he soon died. The monks buried him in the south chapel at the west end of their church, and there appeared signs to suggest that Alfred was a saint and martyr.[7]

---

[1] 'Sceptrum et ipse [Alveradus] paternum requirebat', p. 6. Similarly *VEdR*, p. 20, 'superque patrio regno adipiscendo cum ageret incautius'.

[2] *Encomium Emmae*, pp. 42–3.

[3] *Chron. C* baldly records Godwin's hostile acts and Florence agrees; *D* suppresses his name; *E* has no entry for 1036.

[4] Jumièges, pp. 135–6; Poitiers, pp. 10–13.   [5] *VEdR*, p. 20.

[6] Florence, i. 195: 'Insuper etiam non sui consilii nec suae voluntatis fuisse quod frater ejus caecatus fuisset, sed dominum suum regem Haroldum illum facere quod fecit jussisse, cum totius fere Angliae principibus et ministris dignioribus regi juravit.' Cf. *VEdR*, p. 20.

[7] *Encomium Emmae*, pp. 46–7. The account in *Liber Eliensis*, pp. 158–60, is based on

In the year following the invasions, 1037, Harold was recognized by all men as king, and Emma, expelled from England, in the late autumn took refuge at Bruges.[1] Her whole surviving family was now on the Continent. Emma remained indomitable. She sojourned at Bruges presumably because it was her chosen rendezvous with Harthacnut and also a place to which she could summon aid from Normandy. Indeed, according to her own story,[2] as soon as she was settled she called Edward to her and asked for his help. But Edward, while sympathetic, declined to act. The English nobles, he explained, had taken no oaths to him; and he advised Emma to turn to his brother (Harthacnut). He then returned to Normandy. It is very likely that Edward did go to meet Emma in Flanders in 1038 and that they discussed the future. We cannot believe, however, that the queen, who was entirely familiar with the situation in England, seriously thought that she could be immediately restored by force or that Edward would be able to organize a large-scale invasion. Her great-nephew, William of Normandy, was only ten years old and in his unquiet minority, so that no ducal expedition could be organized; and she can hardly have expected Edward, especially if he had been routed in England two years before, to show enthusiasm for a hopeless adventure. There is reason to think that the *Encomium Emmae*, written during Harthacnut's reign, was intended, among other things, to discredit Edward's claim to the throne, and, if so, this was the second piece of recent evidence produced to this end: just as Edward in 1036 sent Alfred to England in his place, so now he proposed that Harthacnut should act in his stead.

There can really be no doubt that Emma was at Bruges primarily to wait for Harthacnut and that he was the only one who could restore the family fortune. He was after all king of Denmark and, once free of his war with Magnus of Norway, could use the Danish navy against England. Although Emma may sometimes have lost patience with her son, Harthacnut showed sound judgment in refusing to leave Denmark at the mercy of Magnus while he embarked on a risky campaign against Harold. Emma was forced to wait. In 1039, however, Harthacnut

---

Florence and Poitiers. The ending, however, is independent of all sources: 'Quo in loco mire et pulchre visiones luminum et virtutum sepe contigerunt.' According to marginal notes the body was moved to near the altar of St Alban and then near to the altar of St Edmund and St Thomas.

[1] *Chron. CD*; Florence, i. 192. All the versions agree that she was driven out. Her own story was that she diplomatically withdrew, *Encomium Emmae*, pp. 46–9.

[2] *Encomium Emmae*, pp. 48–9.

by some means freed his hands. His cousin, Svein Estrithson, claimed in later years that he had acted as Harthacnut's military lieutenant in Denmark.[1] There was also in circulation the story that Harthacnut made a peace treaty with Magnus, by which, if either died childless, the other was to succeed to both the northern kingdoms.[2] Be that as it may, Harthacnut sailed with ten ships for Bruges.[3] On 17 March 1040 Harold Harefoot died; there was much coming and going between England and Flanders; and just before midsummer Harthacnut and Emma crossed with the sixty ships they had recruited for a military expedition to a peaceful reception at Sandwich.[4]

One of Harthacnut's first acts after his belated accession to his father's throne was to have Harold's body ejected from Westminster abbey and thrown into a fen.[5] In the following year his other half-brother, Edward, came to England. This family reunion in 1041 was a turning point in Edward's life, but we know nothing of what lay behind it and little about the motives of the parties. The Anglo-Saxon Chronicle merely records that Edward returned to England, was 'sworn in as king', and remained at court until Harthacnut died.[6] The *Encomium Emmae*, which was written almost immediately after Edward's return, is more forthcoming: Harthacnut, inspired by brotherly love, invited Edward

---

[1] Adam of Bremen, II, lxxvii, p. 135.

[2] 'tali proposita conditione, ut uter regum sine certo herede – hoc est, prole ventris sui – prior humanis rebus abscesserit, residuus utrumque regnum obtineat sine ulla contradictione', *Theodrici monachi historia de antiquitate regum Norwagiensium*, in *Monumenta Historica Norvegiae*, ed. Gustav Storm (Christiana, 1880), p. 46. 'Tunc Hartheknud et Magnus rex Norwegiae talem conditionem inter se fecerunt, et super reliquias cum juramento firmaverunt, ut, qui diutius viveret, superstes regnum defuncti acciperet, duoque regna quasi hereditario jure possideret.', *Anonymi Roskildensis Chronicon Danicum*, in *Scriptores Rerum Danicarum Medii Ævi*, ed. Jacobus Langebek, i (Copenhagen, 1772), 377. 'iureiurando pactus, eius, qui prior decederet, superstiti regnum esse cessurum', *Saxonis Grammatici Gesta Danorum*, ed. Alfred Holder (Strassburg, 1886), p. 360. Cf. Snorre Sturlason, *Heimskringla*, Magnus the Good, caps. 6, 37–8, translated by Erling Monsen and A. H. Smith (1932), pp. 479–80, 502–3. Theoderic, the Anonymous, and Saxo Grammaticus clearly believed that the treaty applied only to Norway and Denmark. England, of course, was not in Harthacnut's possession at the time. But Snorre has Magnus claiming England under its terms. See also Körner, *Battle of Hastings*, pp. 145 ff.

[3] *Encomium Emmae*, pp. 48–51; *Chron. C*; Florence, i. 193.

[4] *Encomium Emmae*, pp. 50–3; *Chron. CDE*; Florence, i. 193–4; Poitiers, p. 12; *Chronicon abbatiae de Evesham*, ed. W. D. Macray (Rolls ser. 1863), pp. 36–7.

[5] *Chron. CD*; Florence, i. 194, elaborates.

[6] *Chron. CD*; *E* merely records his arrival and genealogy. Florence, i. 196, lies between: 'Eadweardus . . . venit Angliam, et a fratre suo Heardecanuto rege susceptus honorifice, in curia sua mansit.'

to come and hold the kingdom with him. Edward obeyed the summons, and, as a result, 'Emma and her two sons, among whom there is true loyalty, amicably share the kingdom's revenues.'[1] William of Poitiers, although probably not independently, also regarded Harthacnut as Edward's benefactor, but chose to believe that William of Normandy (then aged thirteen) in some way helped the returning exile.[2]

Edward could not have returned uninvited, although the initiative could have been his. It is not impossible that a family settlement was made while Emma waited at Bruges, all three agreeing to sink their differences and share any reward. Or Harthacnut and Emma could have found themselves so unpopular in England that they thought it advisable to associate Edward with the government. Or Harthacnut may have been anxious to resume his war against Magnus of Norway and wanted Edward to act as his regent in England.[3] It is doubtful whether the recall of Edward was contrary to the treaty which Harthacnut is supposed to have made with Magnus, and the scheme would seem to be his rather than Emma's. In the *Encomium Emmae* she goes out of her way to show that Edward's claim to the English throne was weaker than Harthacnut's and that Harthacnut made this provision for his brother merely out of love. A quite different sort of explanation was advanced by William of Poitiers:[4] Harthacnut was a dying man, with God before his eyes, and for this reason summoned Edward to his side. But there is nothing else to suggest that Harthacnut was living under the shadow of death, and we may well have here a false deduction from Harthacnut's death in the following year. Clearly no firm explanation of the motives can be based on the evidence

[1] *Encomium Emmae*, pp. 52–3, the closing passage; Körner, *Battle of Hastings*, pp. 64–7. In one of the two writs which have survived from Harthacnut's reign (in Latin translation) Ælfgifu (Emma) is associated with her son, Harmer, *Writs*, no. 57. Edward, when he confirmed that grant (between 1043 and 1049), referred to the writ of 'his brother and mother', *ibid.*, no. 58; and in a writ of 1042/3 for Bury St Edmunds Edward again referred to Harthacnut as his brother, *ibid.*, no. 8. The encomiast's view of the family set-up is illustrated in the frontispiece to MS London, British Museum, Add. 33241, written in the eleventh century, probably early in Edward's reign, and, at least later, in the possession of St Augustine's abbey, Canterbury. Campbell, *Encomium Emmae*, p. xii; N. R. Ker, *Medieval Libraries of Great Britain* (R. Hist. Soc., 1964), p. 42. Emma, enthroned, accepts a copy of the book from the author, while two young men, presumably Harthacnut and Edward, watch from the side. The subordination of the sons to the mother is most marked. See plate 2.

[2] Poitiers, pp. 12, 28–31.

[3] It seems from Svein Estrithson's story (below, p. 52) that Magnus continued to threaten Denmark.   [4] Poitiers, p. 12.

available to us. But one is left with the feeling that this family reunion was dictated by convenience, not love, that it was a pooling of resources and claims demanded by weaknesses in the position of each, a closing of ranks which had been sadly thinned.[1]

Later writers believed, probably correctly, that Edward was accompanied to England by a household. William of Poitiers, who thought that Edward owed his restitution to Norman threats, imagined that he was escorted by a troop of Norman knights.[2] This may have been so; but the information is provided only in order to strengthen the case that Edward was William's debtor. Other sources provide us with four names: the clerks Leofric and Herman;[3] Robert Champart, abbot of Jumièges;[4] and Edward's nephew, Ralf, a son of his sister, Godgifu, and Drogo, count of the Vexin.[5] Although the last two do not witness charters before 1046 and 1050 respectively,[6] this information may be correct. These four are presumably those of Edward's early household who obtained important offices in England. Abbot Robert was probably the oldest of the group and the most intimate with Edward. Ralf, a younger son, was looking for an estate in England. Harder to account for are the clerks. Leofric, an Englishman educated in Lotharingia, and Herman, a native of those parts, may have been friends; but when, where, and why Edward recruited them is unknown. It is possible that Leofric, wishing to return to England, attached himself to Edward in Flanders at some time between 1035 and 1041, and brought Herman with him. Obviously it would be unwise to generalize too freely from this short list. It is inconceivable that Edward's household was predominantly clerical, although it may have been for the most part masculine. It may be an accident that only one Norman was named. But the list is a warning against giving Edward an exclusively monastic

---

[1] Such was the view of Saxo Grammaticus, *Gesta Danorum*, ed. Alfred Holder (Strassburg, 1886), pp. 360-1: 'Eduardum fratrem . . . in regni societatem adsciscit, non quod fraterno illum affectu coleret, sed ut eius ambicionem munificencia ac liberalitate precurreret, regnique parte potitum totum cupere prohiberet. Itaque non tam veneracione carum, quam popularium ambicione paternique generis auctoritate suspectum, consortem imperii facit.'

[2] Poitiers, p. 30. Cf. *VEdR*, p. 17, 'Cum predictus sanctae memoriae Ædwardus rex repatriaret a Francia, ex eadem gente comitati sunt quam plures non ignobiles viri'.

[3] *KCD*, nos. 762, 767; *Ordnance Survey Facsimiles*, ii, Exeter charters, no. 12 (Sawyer, nos. 993, 999, 1003).

[4] *VEdR*, pp. 17 ff.

[5] *Chronicon abbatiae Rameseiensis*, ed. W. D. Macray (Rolls ser. 1886), p. 171.

[6] See below, pp. 79, 89.

and Norman environment. It is also evidence that Edward was not accompanied to England by a very distinguished court; and we may think that even if he gave adequate rewards to those who shared his adventure, he did not introduce enough new blood seriously to disturb the established order.

In 1057 Edward 'the Exile' returned with obvious reluctance from the Magyar court to England. There is nothing to suggest that in 1041 the elder Edward had to take time to consider his reply. Although he could not have known Harthacnut well, indeed it is unlikely that they had ever met, and we know that by 1043 Edward had grievances against his mother, he seems to have joined them in England with alacrity, obviously anxious to improve his situation. It is true that Normandy cannot have been very comfortable since 1035 and Edward's position there may have deteriorated since the death of his cousin, Count Robert I, but clearly he returned from exile as soon as he could. It can hardly be doubted that the thesis of the Norman apologists that Edward loved Duke William as a brother or son, that he was always conscious of the great debt he owed the Norman court, being especially grateful for the efforts it had made to restore him to the English throne,[1] contains exaggerations if not untruths. In 1041 William was thirteen and Edward at least thirty-six. They must have known each other, for Edward witnessed one of William's charters;[2] but their kinship was not very close, and no one remembered any incident linking the two, any way in which Edward was involved in the perils of William's boyhood. There is no convincing evidence that there had ever been a tender relationship between Edward and William; and, even if there had been, the two did not meet again for at least ten years. Nor is there much concrete evidence of Edward's gratitude to the Norman court and his mother's kin. William of Poitiers may have noticed the discrepancy between the sense of gratitude he was describing and the sparse manifestations of it, for he implicitly explained the difficulty away. The English, he wrote, allowed Edward to return with only a small Norman escort.[3]

It would seem just as possible, perhaps more likely, that Edward had a grievance against the Norman court. It would have been a little unfair, but hardly unexpected, if he had claimed that his Norman

[1] Poitiers, pp. 28–33, 174–6.
[2] *Recueil des Actes*, ed. Fauroux, no. 111. But see above, p. 40.
[3] Poitiers, p. 30.

51

relations had kept him out of his ancestral inheritance. The charges which Edward brought against his mother in 1043 he could equally have levelled against other members of her family. Obviously this is why William of Poitiers claims that William demanded Edward's restoration in 1041, was prepared to restore his cousin by force of arms, and that the English, terrified by this threat, welcomed Edward home.[1] But the story cannot be true. As late as 1047 William had to flee to the court of his overlord, the king of France, to beg him to return with him and quell a serious rebellion. It is possible that William wrote on behalf of Edward in 1041 and helped him all he could; but obviously he was in no position to do much.

Another kinsman of Harthacnut, who was to play an intermittent but important part in English affairs, came to England about this time, his cousin, Svein junior, Estrith's son, a man who could claim to be Harthacnut's heir presumptive, at least to Denmark. Svein was also related to Godwin, earl of Wessex, who had married Svein's aunt, Gytha. Svein, we learn,[2] had been soldiering in Sweden under King Anund, and on his way to England was captured while devastating the lands of the archbishop of Bremen. According to Svein's own story, Harthacnut put him in command of a fleet and sent him to Denmark to fight against Magnus of Norway, a task too great for Svein's resources. If there was discussion in England about the future, Svein would have been recognized as the heir to Denmark and informed that Edward was the heir to England.[3] A repartition of the empire between the closest claimants would be in accordance with recent practice. Svein had two younger brothers, Beorn and Osbeorn, who also came to England, but possibly a little later, as suitors for a share of the family fortune.

Of Edward's life in England between his arrival and Harthacnut's death we know almost nothing. It appears that in some way he was associated with the kingship; but this would not seem to mean that he

---

[1] Poitiers, pp. 28–30.

[2] Adam of Bremen, II, lxxiii, lxxv, lxxvii, pp. 134–6.

[3] Although, according to Saxo Grammaticus, *Gesta Danorum*, ed. Alfred Holder (Strassburg, 1886), p. 361, Svein, when he sailed for Denmark, expected to succeed Harthacnut in England. He left behind garrisons and put his trust not only in the sons of Godwin, to whom he was related, but also in the stupidity and lack of enterprise of the co-king, Edward. In the event he was defrauded by perfidious Albion (*Anglica perfidia*), especially by Harold Godwinesson, who massacred his garrisons, p. 362. These are wild embroideries. See also below, p. 101.

was crowned king.[1] One charter,[2] with an unexceptionable witness list, recording a grant to Abingdon abbey and dated 1042 at Sutton in Berkshire, is witnessed by King Harthacnut, Ælfgifu, the king's mother, and Edward, the king's brother, in that order and with those styles. Among the clerks are Herman and Leofric; but if there are Edward's men also among the thegns they cannot be identified. There are no obviously Norman names. Other charters dated 1042 do not list Edward;[3] and such evidence as there is indicates that he was very much the junior partner. On 8 June 1042, however, Harthacnut died at Lambeth, apparently while drinking at the wedding feast of Gytha, daughter of Osgot Clapa, and Tofig the Proud,[4] two thegns who witness the charter, 'signed' also by Edward. No doubt among the guests was Edward, well placed to take advantage of his brother's death.[5]

[1] We are not told explicitly that Harold or Harthacnut was consecrated king. The expression in *Chron. CD*, 'theh waes to cinge gesworen', does, however, suggest that Edward was recognized in some ceremony.

[2] *KCD*, no. 762 (Sawyer, no. 993). There are several anachronistic expressions in the charter, which has certainly been revised; but the witness list is sound.

[3] *KCD*, no. 761 (Sawyer, no. 995) (with an unsatisfactory witness list) and 764 (Sawyer, no. 1396) (a charter of Bishop Lyfing of Worcester).

[4] *Chron. CDE*; Florence, i. 196, elaborates.

[5] All the Chronicle versions imply, although they do not state, that Edward was in London at the time. *VEdR*, pp. 9–10, copied by Richard of Cirencester, *Speculum Historiale de Gestis Regum Angliae*, ed. J. E. B. Mayor (Rolls ser. 1869), ii. 207–8, has another story to tell. After the English were at last freed by God from the Danish bondage, Godwin took the lead in urging Edward's claim and so carried the royal counsellors with him that earls and bishops were sent to bring the aetheling back (apparently from the Continent). Edward was given a warm welcome in England and was crowned king. The *Vita* is not a good authority for the beginning of the reign; and this account seems to be an ignorant compression of the events of 1041–3, designed to demonstrate Edward's indebtedness to Godwin. See further, Plummer, *Two Chronicles*, pp. 221–2. The author of the *Quadripartitus*, a lawbook written in 1114, recorded the tradition that Edward was recalled at the instigation of Bishop Ælfwine of Winchester and Earl Godwin, and that at a council of all the barons called to Horsted (Sussex) he was accepted as king after he had taken an oath to preserve the laws of Cnut and his sons: Liebermann, *Die Gesetze*, i. 533.

Chapter 3

THE ANOINTED KING

Although the reigns of Old-English kings were short, the procedure for recognizing a new king had never been firmly established, and after 955, because of disputed successions, military conquests, and the rival claims of the English and Danish royal lines, it had become increasingly confused. An orderly, generally accepted, and efficient practice was no longer observed. The traditional components in a lawful, as opposed to a violent, accession were eligibility by birth, designation by the late king, election or recognition by the secular and ecclesiastical magnates, and consecration by the church.[1] The most orderly procedure was when the king's eldest son was named by his father as his heir, acclaimed by the nobility of the whole kingdom after his father's death, and then crowned and anointed by the archbishop of Canterbury in a public ceremony. But so deranged had English politics become, that a king might easily at different times nominate different men as his heir, the various regions or interests in England could make rival elections, and consecration by the church could sometimes be dispensed with.[2]

Edward had some obvious advantages over his rivals in June 1042, when Harthacnut died; but his position was not unassailable and he had to push his claim. He was certainly qualified by birth, and in this particular was pre-eminent, for no other son of Æthelred or Cnut was still alive, no other descendant of Æthelred and Edgar was in a position to advance a claim. Moreover, although Svein Estrithson, the grandson of Svein Forkbeard, probably with justice regarded himself as Cnut's heir-general, with a claim to England as well as to Denmark, even the Scandinavians in England may have acknowledged that Edward represented the senior and more illustrious royal line. The English royal

---

[1] Cf. Karl Schnith, 'Die Wende der englischen Geschichte im 11. Jahrhundert', *Historisches Jahrbuch*, 86 (1966), 4 ff.

[2] *Chron.* does not mention the consecration of Kings Cnut, Harold, and Harthacnut, although it records Æthelred's and Edward's coronation. This may be prejudice; but the *Encomium Emmae*, although referring to Harold's vain request for a coronation (pp. 40–1), never states that Cnut or Harthacnut was consecrated.

house was, in fact, the most distinguished in Europe. In France and Germany were parvenu dynasties. Kingship in Scandinavia was relatively new and in southern Europe the kingdoms were small or ephemeral. According to the historical traditions preserved in the Anglo-Saxon Chronicle Edward was the seventeenth from Cerdic, who with his son Cynric came to Britain with five ships probably in 514 and who in 519 succeeded to the kingdom of the West Saxons; and Cerdic was the ninth from Woden.[1] A genealogy covering some eight centuries and historically authentic for at least five-and-a-half was a legitimate cause for pride and helps to explain the respect in which Edward was held by other kings.

Edward not only had a 'natural right' to the throne,[2] a right by birth, he was also his predecessor's designated heir. Moreover Harthacnut, by sending his cousin, Svein, to Denmark to fight against Magnus, had indicated an equitable division of the empire between his rival kinsmen.

Yet we can easily exaggerate the loyalty and sentiment aroused by Edward's distinguished lineage among the nobility in England or the respect inspired by Harthacnut's nomination. Heroic poetry is full of true and loyal vassals and servants, men who put their lord's life and safety before their own, men who observe the highest principles of honour. But there is reason to think that the qualities which are stressed in this ideal world are those which were in short supply in everyday affairs. Edward's great-grandfather, Edmund, was killed in 946 by an outlaw, and his father, Æthelred, gained the crown as a result of the murder of Edward 'the Martyr' in 979. In Æthelred's reign there had been much treachery and the events since 1013 must have weakened patriotism and reverence for the old dynasty. That there was a fund of good will and sentiment on which Edward could draw is undoubted. But it was not unlimited, and it is possible that the laity contributed the least to it. The bishops and earls were becoming accustomed to choosing the king, and, although they had not yet gone outside candidates presented to them by birth or conquest, they clearly believed that they had a part to play. In 1042 Edward had to rally support. Unfortunately we have little information about the state of the parties. We are told that

---

[1] *Chron.*, preface to *A*, pp. 3–4; cf. p. 11.

[2] 'swa him gecynde waes', *CD*; cf. 'in nativi iuris sui throno', *VEdR*, p. 9; 'heres scilicet legitimus', *Encomium Emmae* (MS. P), p. 52 *n.*; 'hereditarius rex', 'Heremanni archidiaconi miracula S. Eadmundi', F. Liebermann, *Ungedruckte Anglo-Normannische Geschichtsquellen* (Strassburg, 1879), p. 238.

the leaders of Edward's faction were Godwin, earl of Wessex, and Lyfing, bishop of Devon, Cornwall and Worcester,[1] and that the Londoners acclaimed Edward as king.[2] It appears, therefore, that Edward was the choice of the southern English; and this is what we would expect.

Yet Godwin's championship of Edward is surprising. He owed everything to Cnut; in 1035 he had supported Harthacnut; he was Svein Estrithson's uncle; and he was to back Svein strongly in Denmark. Both he and Lyfing had been punished by Harthacnut for coming to terms with Harold; both knew, therefore, how important it was to back the right candidate; and in 1042, we must assume, both decided that Edward was the candidate who would rally the most support. Once Wessex and London had made their choice, Edward would have looked to Mercia and Northumbria. We do not know whether Leofric, earl of Mercia, and Siward, earl of Northumbria, were at court when Harthacnut died or whether they took part in the acclamation of Edward at London; but in any case they may have considered it prudent to return to their provinces and sound the opinion of the local nobility. Not a few kings in the tenth century had been recognized by the several provinces in turn, or, in the case of a military conqueror, by the regions through which he progressed. Edward probably expected Leofric to acknowledge him and bring over the midland thegns. The earl's father, Leofwine, had served Edward's father, and in 1035 Leofric had favoured the more native candidate, Harold, against Harthacnut. He was married to an Englishwoman, Godgifu or Godiva, and, although no English patriot, was a man of honour, religious and loyal.[3] He may have taken his time in coming to a decision in 1042; but this was the prudence of a man who had no wish to be a turncoat. He may also have been aware that his decision would be decisive, for, although Northumbria had a tradition of independence, more recently, whenever there had been a split between the regions, Northumbria had paired with Mercia.[4] Siward, a

<hr>

[1] Florence, i. 196–7. *VEdR*, p. 9, attributes Edward's recognition to Godwin. Malmesbury, *GP*, p. 34, names Eadsige, archbishop of Canterbury, as the earl's ally; but this is probably an inference from the coronation.

[2] 'all the people chose / received Edward as king', *Chron.*, and *E* adds, 'in London'. Cf. Florence, i. 197, 'Lundoniae levatur in regem'. According to (some MSS of) Malmesbury, *GR*, i. 238, Godwin got Edward recognized as king in a council held at Gillingham.

[3] Cf. Barlow, *English Church*, pp. 56–7.

[4] In 957 only Wessex remained loyal to Eadwig; in 1016 Edmund held Wessex; in 1035 Mercia and Northumbria declared for Harold; and in 1065, when the North-

Dane promoted by Cnut, had married into the Northumbrian aristo-cracy,[1] and so like Godwin, although the position was reversed, represented both nations. With territorial ambitions in Scotland, he wanted no trouble in his rear. He may well have been content to take Leofric's advice about a king, or to follow his lead.

It would be normal for the great men to do homage as vassals to the new king and make him gifts. Edward, in return, would confirm them in their honours and estates and promise them his favour.[2] According to the *Vita Ædwardi Regis* the greatest gift of all was from Godwin, a warship, manned and splendidly fitted out,[3] similar to the one he had given Harthacnut two years before.[4] As he was certainly the richest earl, an upstart, probably in possession of many estates received from Cnut on a precarious tenure, he might be expected to curry favour.

Leofric and Siward were probably won over from a position of benevolent or prudent neutrality. We are not told who Edward's opponents were; but those whom he punished after his coronation had probably incurred his displeasure in 1041–3. Strangely enough, the most prominent of his victims were women. In 1044 Edward banished Gunn-hildr, the daughter of Cnut's sister and Wyrtgeorn, king of the Wends, who had been married to Earl Harald, the son of Thorkell Hávi. Her husband had been murdered on 13 November 1042, when returning from a pilgrimage to Rome, at the instigation of Magnus of Norway, apparently because of the claim he could have made to Denmark.[5] Gunnhildr, with her sons, Hemming and Thorkell, represented the highest Danish nobility, and her father-in-law had been Æthelred's naval commander.

Even more scandalous was the breach between Edward and his

umbrians rebelled against Tostig, they chose the brother of the earl of Mercia as their leader (below, p. 236). In the tenth and eleventh centuries the boundary on the Thames may have been even more important than that on the Humber.

[1] For Siward, see Harmer, *Writs*, p. 572.

[2] In 1042 × 3 Edward confirmed to the old Abbot Ufi of Bury St Edmunds all the rights granted to the abbey by King Cnut and King Harthacnut, 'my brother', Harmer, *Writs*, no. 8; about the same time he confirmed to his men in the gild of the English *cnihtas* in London the good laws that they had enjoyed under Edgar, his father [Æthelred], and Cnut, and promised to augment its benefits, *ibid.*, no. 51; cf. *ibid.* no. 54 for St Paul's minster and nos. 109–10 for Winchester.

[3] *VEdR*, pp. 13–14.

[4] Florence, i. 195.

[5] *Chron. D*; Florence, i. 199, cf. 184; Adam of Bremen, II, lxxix, pp. 136–7; Camp-bell, *Encomium Emmae*, pp. 84–5. Malmesbury, *GP*, p. 34, thought that the opposition to Edward came from the Danish party.

mother. Emma, by now past her middle fifties and much bereaved, may have been embittered by recent events and temporarily unbalanced. It was remembered half a century later at St Augustine's, Canterbury, in connexion with a miracle of St Mildred, that she was accused of inciting Magnus of Norway to invade England.[1] Although it is likely that she was indeed accused of treachery, even of conspiring with Magnus, there was probably little or nothing in the charge. Magnus, the son of St Olaf by a concubine, was summoned by the Norwegian nobles from Russia, about three years after Olaf's death at the battle of Stiklestad in 1030, in order to liberate the country from Danish rule. After the death of Cnût's son, Svein, who had been regent in Norway, Magnus invaded Denmark and so kept Harthacnut there.[2] In 1042 Magnus was about nineteen years old, a boy whom Emma could never have met and in whom she had no conceivable interest.[3] Even if Harthacnut had made a treaty with Magnus by which the survivor was to inherit the other's kingdom, this did not refer to England; and we can no more believe that Emma wanted to compensate Magnus in England because her nephew, Svein Estrithson, was trying to prevent him from inheriting Denmark, than that Magnus at this moment aimed at England rather than Denmark.

Svein's own account of these events is that, after his unsuccessful expedition for Harthacnut against Magnus, he returned to England, only to find Harthacnut dead and Edward elected in his place. Edward feared his claim to England and made a treaty with him appointing him his immediate successor, even if he (Edward) should beget sons. Whereupon Svein returned to Denmark and continued the struggle with Magnus until forced to flee to the court of Anund of Sweden.[4]

Svein's story, although throwing no direct light on Emma's attitude,

[1] F. Barlow, 'Two Notes: Cnut's Second Pilgrimage and Queen Emma's Disgrace in 1043', *EHR*, lxxiii (1958), 649 ff. For a possible confirmation of Emma's close connexion with St Augustine's, see above, p. 49, *n.* 1.

[2] *Theodrici monachi Historia de antiquitate Regum Norwagiensium*, pp. 39–48; *Anonymi Roskildensis Chronicon Danicum*, pp. 376–7.

[3] There was a story, however, that Magnus's mother was English. William of Malmesbury has a romantic tale of Ælfilda, captured by Norwegian raiders, raped first by her owner, a Norwegian jarl, then coveted and raped by King Olaf, with Magnus as the result. Later, apparently after Magnus's death (1047), Ælfilda returned to England, and after further adventures became a nun and was buried at Malmesbury. Hence the English monk's knowledge. Malmesbury, *GP*, pp. 412–15.

[4] Adam of Bremen, II, lxxvii, lxxviii, pp. 135–6. Cf. Körner, *Battle of Hastings*, pp. 154–7.

at least suggests that the Scandinavian princes were still interested in the English throne; and Emma may have been regarded, and may even have regarded herself, as the natural leader of the Scandinavian cause. It could well be that foreign claimants got in touch with her – and that her behaviour was equivocal. In 1035 she had held on to her husband's treasure and bodyguard in the name of her absent son. She had worked and suffered for Harthacnut's succession, and his premature death must have been a great shock and disappointment to her, while Edward's advance must have seemed a cruel jest of fate. She, therefore, in 1042–3 clung to Harthacnut's treasure, and may have flirted, although not in real earnest, with northern pretenders in order to spite Edward. Her counsellor, we are told, was Stigand,[1] who had been one of Cnut's clerks, a man with a Norwegian name from East Anglia, perhaps Norwich.[2] What Stigand counselled we do not know. In his subsequent career he showed himself an adroit political realist, and he is not likely to have engaged in absurd conspiracies in 1042. The distraught woman may possibly have said foolish things which were repeated and perhaps exaggerated; but it is most unlikely that she and Stigand would ever have seriously plotted a Norwegian invasion in order to keep Edward off the throne.

Stigand's dubious behaviour was probably exceptional. Although among the bishops only two of Æthelred's appointments, Æthelstan of Hereford and Beorhtweald of Ramsbury, were still in office, those promoted by Cnut and his sons were almost all English by blood, and nine of the fifteen bishops were monks. The abbots, too, were recruited from the nobility of the south of England. The devotion of the church to the monarchy, and to the West-Saxon dynasty in particular, was remarkable. Since Alfred the kings had built up a credit which neither Æthelred's carelessness nor Cnut's withdrawals could exhaust. What the church wanted was a second Edgar; and the Danes were still remembered as heathen Vikings. Beorhtweald, who had been monk and abbot of Glastonbury before his promotion to Ramsbury in 995 or 1005, was reaching the end of his long life, but had survived to see the first demonstration of the truth of a vision he had experienced while in retreat at Glastonbury during Danish rule.[3] Once, after long and tearful prayers in the church for the return of the exiled native royalty, he had fallen asleep, and in a dream had seen St Peter consecrate a dignified

[1] Chron. C, s.a. 1043.   [2] Cf. Barlow, English Church, pp. 77–81.
[3] VEdR, pp. 8–9, 85–7.

man as king, then assign to him the life of a bachelor and determine the number of years he was to reign. And when the king asked, 'Who then will succeed me in the kingdom?', the saint replied, 'The kingdom of the English is the kingdom of God, and God has been pleased to make provision for its future.' This vision could not be fully interpreted before 1067[1] and some of its enigmatic detail may be accretions intended to make it more wonderful. But when Edward recovered his father's kingdom many prayers would be answered at last, many prophecies fulfilled.

The *Vita Ædwardi Regis*, inspired by clerical sentiment, describes Edward's return and succession as a joyful jubilee, God's mercy to the people after his punishment of them for their sins, a time of general rejoicing. 'Everywhere Edward was acclaimed with loyal undertakings of submission and obedience.'[2] And in a poem, 'A rosy light shining from Heaven on the new king ushered in the dawn for the English, released the pain from their hearts.'[3] This is an idealized picture. Although Edward was proclaimed king in London before Harthacnut's burial, he was not crowned until Easter 1043, almost ten months later. The delay must have been caused in part by negotiations with Mercia and Northumbria and perhaps with Scandinavian princes. But step by step the fullest procedure for the making of a king was observed. Edward had hardly been fortune's darling, but in 1041–3 he advanced with determination into his complete inheritance. Political reasons may have delayed his coronation; but it is also possible that the church suggested waiting until the greatest Christian festival for this religious ceremony.

Since the church wanted a second Edgar, the royal monasteries and those bishops who were at least distant heirs of the tenth-century reformation were ready to remind the king of his duties. The most spectacular reminder was the king's ordination. The early history of the coronation ceremony is the story of a fruitful collaboration between church and king.[4] The king sought added splendour and sanctions; the

---

[1] Apart from the inability to know the length of Edward's reign and identify his successor, there was the problem of Edward's *caelebs vita*. In 1042, no doubt, this meant that Edward was unmarried. But after Edward's marriage in 1045 it had to be re-interpreted.

[2] *VEdR*, pp. 8–10. [3] *VEdR*, p. 13.

[4] Cf. P. E. Schramm, 'Die Krönung bei den Westfranken und Angelsächsen von 878 bis um 1000', *Zeitschrift der Savigny-Stiftung für Rechtsgeschichte*, liv, kan. abt. xxiii (Weimar, 1934), 117–242; Schramm, *Herrschaftszeichen und Staatssymbolik* (Schriften der Monumenta Germaniae historica, 1954–6); Eric John, *Orbis Britanniae* (1966), pp. 27 ff.

church was well content to create a sacramental kingship. The church contributed the anointing with holy oil, the assimilation of the coronation to the ordination of a bishop, the infusion of new meanings into the ceremonies of election and investiture with the regalia, and, above all, the impression that the king was an ecclesiastical person. All this the church was willing to do because it wanted the king to be its true lord, benefactor, and protector. And if in the coronation *ordines* that it developed the church conferred great honour on the king, it also used the opportunity to teach him his duties towards the church. In 'the announcement of the king's estate', which followed the delivery of the insignia, occurred these words, 'And as you see the clergy stand nearer to the altar, so remember that in places convenient you give them greater honour, that the mediator of God and man may establish you in this kingly throne to be the mediator betwixt the clergy and the laity.'[1]

The coronation ceremony was a national anthem. Although it incorporated and perpetuated features which put limits and conditions on the king, although it stressed the idea that the king was a servant of God and the church and had assumed important Christian duties, it also rallied loyalty to his person and to the office. The claimant had been put in possession of the crown, throne, and kingdom as securely and as publicly as the wit of man could devise. His power had been legitimized. *Potestas* was converted into *auctoritas*. He had also been given a new character. He was now different from other men.

Edward was crowned at Winchester on Easter Day (3 April) 1043 'with great ceremony' by Archbishops Eadsige of Canterbury and Ælfric Puttoc of York.[2] Both these prelates were Cnut's men; but, although Eadsige's connexion with the tenth-century reformers was probably slight, Ælfric had been provost of Winchester before his promotion to York in 1023[3] and must have been well acquainted with the Winchester liturgical tradition. The last coronation for which we know that a special *ordo* was composed was Edgar's in 973; and it is thought that this was used, suitably revised, throughout the eleventh century.[4]

---

[1] 'Edgar' *ordo*, 973, cap. 21; Schramm, 'Die Krönung', p. 228; Leopold G. Wickham Legg, *English Coronation Records* (1901), pp. 20–1.

[2] *Chron. CD*; Florence, i. 197. According to *VEdR*, pp. 9–10, Edward was consecrated king ('consecratur christus dei') in Christ Church, Canterbury. Some MSS of Malmesbury, *GR*, i. 239, place the coronation at London. The pictures of Harold's coronation on the Bayeux Tapestry should be held in mind.

[3] Barlow, *English Church*, pp. 72–4.

[4] Schramm, 'Die Krönung', pp. 167–82, 221 ff.; L. G. Wickham Legg, pp. 14 ff. Cf.

In 1043 all concerned with Edward's coronation must have wanted to stress continuity. In any case the English *ordo* had been developed from West-Frankish and German models, and there were no novelties on the Continent that Edward and his foreign clerks or monks could have wished to introduce. Easter Day was probably deliberately chosen so as to give the maximum religious dignity to the ceremony. Winchester may have seemed the most auspicious city, for, although Æthelred had been crowned at Kingston and buried in London, at Winchester were buried both Cnut and Harthacnut, and it was old Germanic custom to take an inheritance on the grave of the predecessor. Also the two archbishops would meet not only on neutral ground but in a church which had been the real centre of the reform movement.

By the late tenth century the development of the royal coronation ceremony was in its essentials complete. One of the least developed features, however, was the opening scene, the procession to the church. Two bishops, possibly the two archbishops, led the king by the hand in an almost exclusively ecclesiastical procession, the choir singing the anthem: *Let thy hand be strengthened and thy right hand be exalted. Let justice and judgment be the preparation of thy seat and mercy and truth go before thy face.* (Ps. lxxxviii. 14–15.) In contrast to later practice the king probably wore his crown.[1] When the procession reached the high altar, the king took off his crown and he and the bishops prostrated themselves. It was probably after this abasement that one or two of the bishops asked the clergy and people if they would accept Edward as their king, for this procedure appears in the Continental *ordines* on which the English *ordo* was based,[2] is implied by a subsequent reference to the 'king who has been elected by the clergy and people', and is logically completed by the singing of the hymn *Te deum laudamus*. This ceremony of acclamation was observed in 1066 and cannot have been omitted in 1043: it was at the centre of the secular right. Next the king was asked by the bishops to take the triple oath. It is possible that, as in 975 or 978, Edward made his promises in the vernacular, reading from a schedule

also H. G. Richardson, 'The English Coronation Oath', *Speculum*, xxiv (1949), 43–6; 'The coronation in medieval England', *Traditio*, xvi (1960).

[1] *Vita Sancti Oswaldi*, by a monk of Ramsey, Schramm, 'Die Krönung', pp. 231–2, *HCY*, i. 436.

[2] 'Erdmann' *ordo*, *c.* 900, cap. 3, Schramm, 'Die Krönung', p. 203; 'Mainz' *ordo*, *c.* 961, cap. 8, Schramm, 'Die Krönung in Deutschland bis zum Beginn des Salischen Hauses (1028)', *Zeitschrift der Savigny-Stiftung für Rechtsgeschichte*, lv, kan. abt. xxiv (Weimar, 1935), 312.

given him by the archbishop and then placing it on the altar.[1] According to the Chronicle, Archbishop Eadsige gave Edward 'good instruction before all the people and admonished him well for his own sake and for the sake of all the people.' Edward, like his predecessors and successors, promised that the church of God and the whole Christian people within his dominion would keep true peace; that he would forbid rapine and wrongful acts to men of every degree; and that he would ordain that justice and mercy should be observed in all legal judgments, so that merciful God should have mercy on him and on them all.[2]

These were preliminaries. At the heart of the religious ceremony was the unction. After prayers with the theme of the Christian life and its reward in Heaven, and Christian kingship with its duties of defending and instructing the church, defending and bringing peace to the people, and terrifying the infidel, the king was anointed on the crown of his head while the anthem *They Anointed Solomon* (1 Chron. xxxix. 22) was sung. It is likely that chrism, the holiest oil known to the church, was used for the anointing.[3]

Next came the investiture with the regalia, the symbols of secular government for which the church had created a liturgy. By the eleventh century these were five, the ring, sword, crown, sceptre, and rod, in that order. The ring was 'the seal of holy faith' and with its help the king was to drive back his foes with triumphal power, destroy heresies, unite his subjects and bind them firmly in the catholic faith. The sword was for the protection of the kingdom and the camp of God; with it the king would break and destroy his enemies. The crown was 'the crown of glory and justice', the sceptre 'the rod of the kingdom and of virtue'. With the sceptre went the prayer that God would honour Edward before all kings, establish him on the throne of his realm, visit him with an increase of children, allow justice to spring up in his days, and receive him with joy and gladness to reign in the everlasting kingdom. Finally, the king was given the rod 'of virtue and equity'.

The benediction of the king by the archbishop followed. After calling

[1] Schramm, 'Die Krönung', pp. 234–5; Liebermann, *Gesetze*, i. 214–17.

[2] Richardson, 'The English Coronation Oath', p. 46, 'The coronation', pp. 171–2; M. David, 'Le serment du Sacre', *Revue du Moyen Age latin*, li (1950), 144–51. As Richardson and Sayles have suggested, *The Governance of Medieval England*, p. 137, n. 3, the passage in *VEdR*, pp. 12–13, especially 'leges iniquas evellens, iustas sapienti consilio statuens', may refer to Edward's coronation promises.

[3] Schramm, 'Die Krönung', p. 174.

on the Mother of God, the blessed Peter, the prince of the apostles, St Gregory, the apostle of the English, and all the saints, the archbishop stressed again the main themes. 'May God make you victorious and a conqueror over your enemies, both visible and invisible; may he grant you peace in your days and with the palm of victory lead you to his eternal Kingdom ... May he grant that you be happy in the present world and share the eternal joys of the world to come. May God bless this our chosen king that he may rule like David ... govern with the mildness of Solomon, and enjoy a peaceable kingdom.' Then the anthem: *Vivat rex! Vivat rex! Vivat rex in eternum!* (III Kings (I Kings) i. 34, 39, with Dan. iii. 9).

After which the king's estate was announced: 'Stand and hold fast from henceforth that place ... now delivered to you by hereditary right by the authority of almighty God and by the hands of us, all the bishops and other servants of God ...' If homage was done – and there is no mention of it in the 'Edgar' *ordo* – it would probably have been taken at this point.[1] As there was no queen to crown in 1043 the ecclesiastical ceremonies then concluded with the mass for the ordained king.

From the church there was a procession to the hall for the coronation banquet, at which the king sat in state on the dais, displaying the regalia and flanked by the two archbishops.[2] Here was the king feasting his vassals and we are told that his men drank deep.[3]

Associated with the coronation was the homage or the salutation of other kings and princes. In 973 Edgar had been rowed on the River Dee by six or eight northern kings – the performance of service as a symbol of subjection.[4] In 1043, according to the *Vita Ædwardi Regis,*[5] Henry emperor of the Romans, Henry king of the Franks, the king of the Danes, and many continental nobles, were represented by ambassadors. The first two princes greeted Edward as an equal; the king of the Danes acknowledged him as his lord; and the nobles offered their fealty and

---

[1] Cf. 'Dunstan' *ordo*, 960–73, cap. 7, 'Tunc dicat omnis populus cum episcopis tribus vicibus: *Vivat rex ill. in sempiternum!* Respondeatur: *Amen!* Et confirmabitur cum benedictione omnis populi in solio regni, et osculant principes in sempiternum dicentes: *Amen, Amen, Amen.* (Leofric recension); Schramm, 'Die Krönung', p. 218; L. G. Wickham Legg, pp. 7–8.

[2] *Vita S. Oswaldi*, Schramm, 'Die Krönung', p. 233, *HCY*, i. 438.

[3] 'quo unusquisque iuxta suam aetatem et suum posse bibebat', *ibid.*

[4] *Chron. D*; Florence, i. 142–3; Ælfric, *Life of St Swithun, EHD*, i. 853 (G); Schramm, 'Die Krönung', pp. 176–7.

[5] *VEdR*, pp. 10–11.

service. All made gifts and were given presents in return.[1] Thus Edward was internationally recognized.

The event which completed the ceremonial fashioning of kingship was Edward's marriage to Edith on Wednesday, 23 January 1045.[2] According to one tradition Edith was anointed and crowned;[3] and it is likely that this had indeed been English custom since 856, when King Æthelwulf of Wessex married Judith, daughter of King Charles the Bald of the West Franks, at Verberie (Oise).[4] A service for the consecration of the queen is included in the 'Edgar' *ordo* of 973,[5] and it is unlikely that Emma of Normandy was handed over to Æthelred and then Cnut except on condition that she was crowned. In 1045 Earl Godwin must have coveted this honour for his daughter. The relatively short ceremony consisted in little more than the anointing on the head and the delivery of the ring and the crown, but included an explicit reference to the imposition of hands. The only governmental role ascribed to the queen in the liturgy is that by virtue of the ring she should avoid heresy and through the power of God bring barbarous nations to the knowledge of the truth. After the ecclesiastical ceremonies, the king and queen banqueted separately, the queen dining with the abbots and abbesses.[6]

A very simple view of kingship is expressed by these liturgical texts. The king should behave like a true Christian and be an example to all; he should protect his church and people from all danger; and he should judge with equity and mercy. If he behaved thus he would die in this world but would be joyfully taken up to live with God.[7] The emphasis

[1] For multiple vassalage, which was very common in the eleventh century, see Harmer, *Writs*, pp. 149, 162–3; Jean-François Lemarignier, 'Structures monastiques et structures politiques dans la France de la fin du Xe et des débuts du XIe siècle', *Settimane di studio del Centro italiano di studi sull' alto medioevo* (Spoleto, 8–14 Apr. 1956), iv. 373–82; *Histoire des Relations Internationales*, vol. i, François L. Ganshof, *Le Moyen Age*, p. 139. For the role of gifts in diplomacy, see Ganshof, *ibid.*, pp. 42, 125.

[2] *Chron. CD*.

[3] Osbert of Clare, probably based on the missing portion of *VEdR*, pp. 14–15.

[4] Marriage and Coronation *ordo*, *Monumenta Germaniae Historica, capitularia regum Francorum*, II, ii (Hannover, 1960), no. 296, p. 425.

[5] Schramm, 'Die Krönung', p. 229; L. G. Wickham Legg, pp. 21–2.

[6] *Vita S. Oswaldi*, Schramm, 'Die Krönung', p. 233, *HCY*, i. 438.

[7] Cf. 'ut in bonis operibus perseverans ad aeternum regnum te duce valeat pervenire', 'Edgar' *ordo*, cap. 4; 'et infinitae prosperitatis praemia perpetua angelorumque aeterna commercia consequatur', *ibid.*, cap. 5; 'quatenus et in praesenti saeculo feliciter regnet et ed eorum consortium in caelesti regno perveniat', *ibid.*, cap. 6; 'quatinus . . . eternaliter cum eo regnare merearis', *ibid.*, cap. 8; 'quatenus de temporali regno ad aeternum regnum pervenias', *ibid.*, cap. 16. Cf. 'Ædwardus . . . obiit quidem mundo sed feliciter assumptus est victurus cum deo.', *VEdR*, p. 55;

throughout is on the king as protector and justiciar, and no distinction is made between the classes of people subject to him. Indeed, the sword with which he was girded was a spiritual sword,[1] just as his crown was a *sancta corona*.[2] In the coronation ceremony the church was largely concerned with creating its own lord and master and with attempting to mould him into the shape it desired. It did not explicitly threaten the remiss or recalcitrant ruler; but, because it was a religious ceremony, the implicit threats were understood by all. The bad king, the unjust king, the unchristian king was anathema; and the sanction to many charters proclaimed the fate of such miscreants: 'let him be alienated from the brotherhood of God's holy church and from participation in the holy body and blood of Jesus Christ; . . . and let him be set aside on the left hand with Judas, the betrayer of Christ . . . Nor shall he, apostate, obtain any pardon in this actual life or rest in that to come, but thrust into the eternal flames of hell, be, most wretched creature that he is, everlastingly tormented.'[3]

The torments of hell are excellently described by an abbot whom Edward met in 1054, John of Fécamp:[4]

In that place of living death, called hell, what else can there be but undying flames, everlasting tribulation, endless punishment, and an infinite affliction of total evil, for there is nothing there beyond a river of fire and a foul swamp. Angels of wrath live there, with arms like the heads of dragons, their eyes shooting out fiery arrows, their teeth projecting like the tusks of elephants; and it is as though with the tails of scorpions that they goad men to the tortures. Only to look on them causes trembling, anguish, death. And would that death could come as a release from this prison! But, horror upon horror, the tortured man still lives so that he may be directed to other torments. Gnawed to the bone, he is made whole again so that serpents may never cease from biting him. Dragons feed on the lips of blasphemers; a serpent tears at the breasts of the unfortunate with terrible fangs; and all sorts of monsters in various ways and without rest crucify the souls of the unbelieving. There is always the sound of wailing and lamentation, groans and bellowing, and

'non enim mortuus est sed cum Christo victurus de morte ad vitam migravit.', *ibid.*, p. 80; 'deitas . . . revelat sanctum vivere secum in celo', *ibid.*, p. 81.

[1] 'Edgar' *ordo*, cap. 13.   [2] *VEdR*, p. 27 and *n*.

[3] W. B. Sanders, *Facsimiles of Anglo-Saxon Manuscripts*, Ordnance Survey, 1881, pt. ii, Exeter 11 (Sawyer, no. 971); V. H. Galbraith's translation.

[4] Jean Leclercq and Jean-Paul Bonnes, *Un Maître de la Vie Spirituelle au XIᵉ siècle, Jean de Fécamp* (Paris, 1946), pp. 150–1. For John's meeting with Edward, see below, p. 205.

also everywhere a confused shouting from those oppressed by the engines of torture or burned by the fire . . . There is the coldness of Gehenna, the everlasting ice, the most terrible hunger, immense thirst, perpetual pain and weariness without end, severe plague and unspeakable disease, dense shades and a night of fearsome darkness. There is no rest for the sufferers; all things there are evil; and all kinds of torments are there. In that place is deathless death, unfailing failure, an end without end. Which of the faithful, hearing of these things, and understanding them, shall not quake with fear?

In the eleventh century the coronation ceremonies were not fossilized ritual. They provided a drama which all could understand, and the lessons were meant to teach, to have direct effect. The complementary *imitatio regni* and *imitatio sacerdotii*, whereby the ecclesiastical and secular authorities in turn stole each other's clothes and finery, at least reveal the anxiety of rulers to improve their chances of effectively wielding their pretended powers. They must also have been a part of the process by which government did in reality become more effective. By the coronation ceremony church and king were joining forces to increase royal power – to some extent at the expense of other people, for example, earls and thegns who might aspire to be local tyrants and dominate the churches in their locality.

It is, indeed, not to be doubted that the English kings were among the most effective in Europe because they exercised power over the clergy as well as the laity,[1] because they were, as the coronation texts proclaimed, the judge ruling over the two estates. But we must not accept all this ecclesiastical paraphernalia at its face value. Edward, an anointed king, probably had no more power over his bishops and abbots than had, say, Offa of Mercia, who had not been ecclesiastically ordained. We may think that there was no positive correspondence between piety and power. And it may well be that the bishops invented the coronation liturgy mainly in order to make royal control over the church less offensive to the clergy, and in so doing made rods for their own backs. Medieval history was written by the clergy and we must not be misled by the propaganda. In public kings listened patiently to the clergy, and the laity's ignorance of Latin enabled clergymen to say almost what they liked. But it is probable that in private and in secular society kings were far less respectful. The effective answers to the excessive claims of the church were forgetfulness and evasion.

Although it can fairly be said that English sacramental kingship

[1] Cf. Barlow, *English Church*, pp. 32–5.

reached – to every appearance – twin peaks in Edgar and Edward, this conveys surprisingly little about the actual powers these kings possessed or the way in which they wielded them. What is impossible to tell is whether tenth- and eleventh-century kings were at all interested in political theory and in the claims made for them by the literate church. Was Edward consulted about the royal style used in charters? If he had been offered the choice between *rex Anglorum sive Saxonum, rex Albionis,* and *rex Saxonum, Merciorum Nordanhumbrorumque*[1] would he have had an opinion? Did he approve the form of words in the coronation ceremony which described his claim to the throne? If we were to ask these questions about a twelfth-century king, such as Henry II or John, we should probably answer 'yes'.[2] But a century earlier we are really in the dark. It is easier to believe that kings like Cnut and Edward listened only absent-mindedly to ecclesiastical theories about royal power and acted on quite different assumptions. They had acquired the kingdom as an estate; in the kingdom they had the rights of their predecessors; and these they would exploit because they were theirs. It was as simple as that. No theory was necessary. That every man possessed and should enjoy his rights was taken for granted. There was no need at all to bring God into it.

It is difficult in these matters to steer a sensible course between the fanciful and the unimaginative. Our interest is in the real world of government and politics, not in the abstractions of political theory; but we must allow that in a religious world religious ideas would have exerted some influence. We can start with the common-sense view that the king was two persons, one for the church and one for the laity, and then admit that each role influenced the other. Admittedly the two characters cannot be completely separated in practice. The king was seldom, if ever, exclusively in the company of one of the estates. If he presided over a synod, earls and thegns were there; and if the council was called a *witenagemot,* bishops and abbots were among the *witan.* The king could put a bishop in command of a military campaign and send an earl on a mission to the pope.[3] In his everyday life Edward was surrounded by men both ecclesiastical and lay.

---

[1] 'Edgar' *ordo,* cap. 6, and variant readings: Schramm, 'Die Krönung', pp. 223–4 and *nn.*

[2] Although H. G. Richardson, 'The Coronation in Medieval England', *Traditio,* xvi (1960), suggests that Westminster abbey had a very free hand in revising the ritual. Cf. also his 'The English Coronation Oath', *Speculum,* xxiv (1949), 46.

[3] Bishop Ealdred; Earl Tostig. See below, pp. 208–10.

Moreover, so intrusive was ecclesiastical influence that almost all royal actions had been given a religious significance by the church. In the coronation ceremony the just war was regarded as a Christian duty. The provision of justice was coming so much under the influence of the church that the secular laws were assuming a moral aspect and the king was expected to denounce sin as well as crime. When sacramental kingship was at its height it could assume extravagant and even absurd attributes. With Edgar the royal mistresses were nuns and the offspring of one such union became a popular saint.[1] With Edward it was suggested that – as though he were a priest – 'he preserved the dignity of his consecration with holy chastity and lived his whole life dedicated to God in true innocence.'[2] Indeed, only perhaps when hunting did Edward escape from his religious exercises; and, since he attended mass before the chase,[3] it is possible that the church almost took this activity under its wing.

Thus in return for the heavy hand which secular rulers had laid on the church, the clergy cast a silken net smelling of incense over the laity. It was more than a marriage of convenience: there was a true union. Yet the separateness remained; and it was the church in another mood which emphasized the duality. Only by ruling well in this world would the king progress to live with the saints in the next, passing from death into life (1 John iii. 14). There were Christ's laws and secular laws, the wisdom of God and worldly wisdom, the visible and the invisible, the transitory and the everlasting. The church, although not Manichaean, was an exponent of dualism and partial to antithesis. And it was aware, and taught, that in this world God's sovereignty was disputed by Satan and men were often heedless of Christ's laws. Edward did not always have the eternal kingdom before his eyes,[4] did not always see his political problems in a religious light, did not always take the advice of his bishops and chaplains. Nor can we think that his subjects were greatly impressed by – even possibly aware of – the titles, claims, and aura which the church had created for him.

For the nobility kingship was rich in secular associations. There was the well-known history of the English nation, so that king and nation

[1] Goscelin of St Bertin, *Vita S. Vulfhilde*, ed. Mario Esposito, *Analecta Bollandiana*, xxxii (1913); *Vita S. Edithe*, ed. A. Wilmart, *ibid.*, lvi (1938).
[2] *VEdR*, pp. 60–1.   [3] *Ibid.*, p. 40.
[4] As did William the Conqueror, according to William of Poitiers, p. 116: 'Vir itaque dignus pio parente et piis majoribus neque dum armatus actitabat oculum interiorem a timore sempiternae majestatis dejiciebat.'

went together. There was the heroic poetry, such as *Beowulf* and the Scandinavian sagas, in which kings were associated with great deeds. Above all, kingship went with lordship and would have been emptied of almost all content if divorced from it. As the poem on Edward's death boasted: all men yielded allegiance to King Edward the noble, the ruler of heroes, the distributor of riches.[1] He was the lord king: men owed him reverence and obedience. Among the mass of the farmers and their labourers kingship must have meant less; but in England so wide was the king's demand for allegiance that he was easily called the nation's king.[2] His dead body was washed by his country's tears.[3]

The man crowned in 1043, however, was still twenty-three years away from his death. We would like to know how he looked, whether he was impressive, with what ease he carried the new symbols of power. Various objects carry Edward's image:[4] there are the 'portraits' on the coins and the seal; there is the picture in the St Augustine's copy of the *Encomium Emmae* and those on the Bayeux Tapestry. And there is a literary description in the *Vita Ædwardi Regis*. The effigies on the coinage before the middle of the reign are entirely conventional in design, so that the only possible representation of the young king is in the *Encomium Emmae*.[5] There the man whom we identify as Edward is shown with short hair, cut in front in a fringe, short, curly beard, and possibly a neat moustache. He wears a 'funny' hat and a tunic ornamented with an embroidered band at the neck. He is drawn smaller than his brother and looks rather frail, somewhat startled; but the smallness may be an attempt at perspective and the two men are presumably deliberately portrayed as insignificant young princes, overawed by their mother. Although some of the representations on the later coinage, especially those on types 6 (pointed helmet), 9 (bust facing), and 10 (pyramids), could possibly be attempts at portraiture,[6] it is unlikely that they were. In any case the small and roughly executed images tell us little of interest. The pictures of Edward on the Bayeux Tapestry, executed about a decade after the king's death, are taken from manuscript designs

[1] *Chron. s.a.* 1066.

[2] *Ibid.*

[3] *VEdR*, p. 81.

[4] Only the later iconography is discussed by Laurence E. Tanner, 'Some representations of St Edward the Confessor in Westminster Abbey and elsewhere', *Journal of the British Archaeological Association*, 3rd ser. xv (1952), 1–12.

[5] MS London, Brit. Mus. Add. 33241. See pl. 2.

[6] These are illustrated *VEdR*, facing p. lxiv and see below, pll. 9 and 10.

by an artist who probably never saw the king, and are of no use to us at all.[1]

The description of Edward in the *Vita*,[2] although it appears at the end of the first chapter, immediately after an account of the coronation, is, whether trustworthy or imaginary, a view of Edward in old age. The author, if he ever saw Edward, saw him just before he died; and it was a portrait of the king as he was thought to be at the time of writing that was put most incongruously at the beginning of the book. To this foreign observer Edward was a man of great majesty, still dignified even when in private with his courtiers. He was exceptionally tall, well made, an unblemished royal figure, with milky white hair and beard, round pink face, and thin white hands, the fingers so emaciated as to be translucent. We need not, however, consider if there is anything in this description that we can take back to 1043, for it seems to be completely conventional and was probably adapted from a description of St Audemer, one of the patron saints of St Bertin's monastery.[3] In fact it does not seem that there is a single physical trait which can safely be taken from the iconography. Whether Edward in 1043 was short or tall, muscular or slight, dark or fair, imposing or insignificant, is unknown and unknowable. But perhaps, at least in the eyes of the sycophantic courtiers, 'he was a proper figure of a man, a very royal person.'[4]

Since Edward's character is both obscure and controversial, it can only be discussed satisfactorily in connexion with the interpretation of his actions and policies: it cannot be described and then used to explain his behaviour. A fairly clear picture of his make-up and attitude does emerge by the use of this technique, and one which is rather different from that usually offered. Another advantage in the gradual approach is that the common error of projecting a view of him in extreme old age over the whole of his life is avoided. Naturally his character changed over the years. The eager boy of his father's reign, a tyro among hardened soldiers; the disillusioned exile, living by his wits, hoping for something to turn up; the triumphant king, miraculously restored to

[1] Plates 1, 30, 32. Francis Wormald has pointed out that the royal figure resembles that of David on fo. 30b of a psalter made about 1050 (Brit. Mus. Cotton MS. Tiberius C. VI), *The Bayeux Tapestry* (Phaidon, 1957), p. 31, fig. 11.

[2] *VEdR*, p. 12.

[3] *Ibid., n.* 1. Walcher, when consecrated bishop of Durham at Winchester in March 1071 (an occasion on which the widowed Queen Edith prophesied), is described as, 'cesarie lacteolum, vultu roseum, statura praegrandem', Malmesbury, *GP*, p. 272.

[4] 'hominis persona erat decentissima', *VEdR*, p. 12; cf. 'decentem hominis personam', p. 9.

his patrimony; the choleric man of sixty, full of years and greatly honoured, but still plagued by political and military difficulties: these are in many ways different men. If there is one trait that runs through the whole and can usefully be stressed at the beginning, it is Edward's ability to survive. Despite an inclination to rashness and inflexibility, he was blessed with a saving caution. And there is a general characteristic which must be held in mind. Edward was never a *roi fainéant* or a puppet ruler. Although he was neither a wise statesman nor a convincing soldier, he was both belligerent and worldly-wise. He caused most of his enemies to disappear and outlived almost all who had disputed his authority. He was *rex piissimus*, a fortunate king, blessed by Heaven.

3. Breamore church (St Mary), Hants (tenth or eleventh century). View from S.W. A typical large church of the period. All the fabric is Anglo-Saxon except the twelfth-century porch and the wooden tower. Most of the windows are altered. (*Courtesy National Monuments Record.*)

4(a). Sundial, now placed above the south porch of the church at Kirkdale, N.R. Yorkshire. The inscription records that Orm, son of Gamal, bought St Gregory's church when it was in ruins and had it built anew in honour of Christ and St Gregory in the days of King Edward and Earl Tostig. (*Courtesy National Monuments Record.*)

4(b). Great Paxton Church (Holy Trinity), Hunts. A sophisticated church on royal demesne, probably eleventh century. View of the south aisle. From *Anglo-Saxon Architecture* by H. M. and Joan Taylor. (*Courtesy Cambridge University Press.*)

Chapter 4

THE YEARS OF STRUGGLE
(1043–1048)

Edward began to rule at an age which none among recent English kings, save his father, had even reached. In a society composed largely of young men he must have seemed elderly. Yet he was, for at least the first decade of his reign, a vigorous ruler, spasmodically and somewhat recklessly active, somewhat in the style of his father. He was without much experience of royal government. He probably retained some memories of his father's reign; he had possibly some knowledge of the Capetian court; and he had seen feudal government in action from Brittany to Flanders. This was, however, more than enough. Little technical knowledge beyond the ordinary education of a nobleman was required by a king. The mechanics of administration were the responsibility of clerks. What counted was character. He had to possess the qualities of a lord and king and show them to the people. Edward was not plentifully endowed with lordly virtues. There is no evidence that he was outstandingly brave, loyal, just, and generous, little to suggest that he could inspire great awe or love. But he had not won a crown in order to throw it away; to live comfortably and securely he had to insist on and defend his rights; and in the beginning he had to deal with the established powers in his kingdom. From the moment of his accession, if he was not to remain a nonentity, he had to struggle. And in the first decade of his reign Edward was prepared to take on every challenge to his authority.

Nevertheless he had to advance with circumspection, and he was probably skilled in feeling his way. It was because he could be regarded as the cornerstone uniting the two walls of the English and Danish races that he had escaped civil war in 1042–3. He was his predecessor's half-brother, Cnut's step-son. He had not been put on the throne to inaugurate a revolution but to confirm the possessors in their honours. Such was the influence of the past, and so absent was optimism from men's minds, that, if there was to be an improvement in the state of the

73

kingdom, it could only come from restoration: a rebirth of the nation's fighting spirit, the re-establishment of good laws and true justice, and a renewed respect for Christ and his church.

Although we have no statistics for the wealth or income of the king and the various magnates in 1043, we can get from Domesday Book figures for 1066, which, whatever their significance, can be used comparatively.[1] And, although the relative positions must have altered between 1043 and 1066, figures for the end of the reign at least give us some idea of the possible situation at the beginning. One investigator[2] has valued the king's estates at £5,000, the queen's at £900, the estates of the sons of Godwin (less Tostig's) at £4,000, those of the Mercian family (less Morkere's) at £1,300, and Tostig's as earl of Northumbria (the sum of Tostig's and Morkere's holdings) likewise at £1,300. A useful figure for the earldom of East Anglia is not available. The main change which occurred during the reign was probably the increase in the holding of the Wessex family at the expense of all the others. If so, we see that Edward's position in 1043 was by no means desperate. No earl was as wealthy as he: it is even possible that the combined wealth of the earls was little in excess of his own. But this overall position is misleading. Edward must often have been overshadowed locally. In 1066 in Wessex the lands of the house of Godwin and the king's lands were about equal in value, and in some shires, for example Sussex, Godwin's ancestral home, the earl was a much greater landowner than the king. We have no means of knowing whether Edward's overall superiority compensated for his mediocre position in many of the shires.

A new king had almost always to be a giver of estates. However much he may have wanted to reward some of his own men and dismiss some of the servants he inherited, he was no less anxious to secure the loyal service of the most useful or potentially dangerous of the late king's men. To reward Earl Godwin for his support Edward made his eldest son, Swegn, an earl in 1043 and promoted his second son, Harold, shortly after.[3] In 1044 Edward made a grant of land to 'his familiar bishop', Ælfwine of Winchester, as 'a reward for faithful service'.[4] The very earliest of Edward's surviving charters records a grant to his

[1] See below, p. 153.

[2] Robert H. Davies, *The lands and rights of Harold, son of Godwine, and their distribution by William I* (unpublished M.A. dissertation, University College, Cardiff, 1967).

[3] According to the charter evidence. For this, see Oleson, *Witenagemot*, pp. 117 ff., Harmer, *Writs*, p. 563.

[4] *KCD*, no. 775 (Sawyer, no. 1001).

faithful thegn, Ordgar, one of Cnut's men, and in 1044 he rewarded him again.[1] Edward's next earliest charter is in favour of his thegn, Ælfstan, one of Harthacnut's men.[2] The first grant that Edward is known to have made to one who had not served an earlier king was in 1044 to his faithful thegn, Orc, a man who soon disappears.[3]

The witness lists in the royal charters show massive continuity of personnel between Cnut's and Edward's courts. Edward had perforce to take over the archbishops, bishops, and abbots and could only appoint when a vacancy occurred. He could do little about the existing earls. But where he could have made considerable change, had he wished, among the clerks and thegns at court, he chose, perhaps thought it advisable, to make the minimum disturbance. Of the nine thegns who witness the only charter of Edward's to have survived from 1042 (in favour of Ordgar)[4] at least six were Cnut's men and a further two Harthacnut's. The one new man never witnesses again. In the one charter to survive from 1043 (in favour of Ælfstan)[5] among twenty-three thegns the same six from Cnut's reign reappear together with nine from Harthacnut's. The thegns who commonly witness Edward's charters between 1042 and 1046 are Karl, Osgot, Ordgar, Odda, Ælfweard, Ælfgar, Thored, Ælfstan, Beorhtric, and Ordwulf. The first seven of these were Cnut's thegns and only the last seems to have been introduced by Edward. But only three or four have Scandinavian names. Few can be given historical individuality.[6] Osgot is probably Osgot Clapa, a Danish landholder from the Eastern shires, whom Edward outlawed in 1046. Odda 'of Deerhurst' was a kinsman of Edward who became an earl in 1051. Ordgar and Ælfgar were brothers, West-country thegns, and likewise Edward's kin.[7]

It is possible that most of the men who regularly witnessed royal charters held some sort of office of the king either in the household or in the shires. Some could be called stallers, or placeholders, some may have been reeves or sheriffs. A few were probably the sons of the highest

---

[1] *KCD*, nos. 1332, 770 (Sawyer, nos. 998, 1005).

[2] *Ibid.*, no. 767 (Sawyer, no. 999).

[3] *Ibid.*, no. 772; cf. 778 (Yrc) (Sawyer, nos. 1004, 1010). Oleson omits him from his lists.

[4] *Ibid.*, no. 1332 (Sawyer, no. 998).   [5] *Ibid.*, no. 767 (Sawyer, no. 999).

[6] Oleson, *Witenagemot*, pp. 117 ff., using biographical details collected by Whitelock, *Wills*, Robertson, *Charters*, Harmer, *Writs*, and O. von Feilitzen, *The Pre-Conquest Personal Names of Domesday Book* (Nomina Germanica, 3, Uppsala, 1937) does his best.

[7] *KCD*, no. 1334 (Sawyer, no. 1474). Malmesbury *GP*, p. 203.

nobility being educated at court and hoping for an earldom or at least some important office. A similar mixture is found among the clerks at court.[1] What is disconcerting about these witness lists is the complete absence of the greater men whom Edward is supposed to have brought from Normandy. We can trace the careers of the clerks Leofric and Herman in England from 1041; but we can find no trace of Robert, abbot of Jumièges, and Ralf of Mantes. The former appears neither among the abbots nor until 1046 among the bishops, although he was the successor to Bishop Ælfweard of London who died in 1044. Ralf first appears in a list in 1050. The position can be variously explained. It may be that Robert and Ralf did not in fact accompany Edward in 1041, or at first they may not have held offices at court which qualified them to be regarded as witnesses to the royal acts, or for some reason or other their names were suppressed. Ralf could easily have been a child in 1041, Robert could have acted as a domestic chaplain. At all events Robert, if in England, must have operated at the most 'familiar', domestic level where his influence cannot be gauged.

Edward was not prepared to accept everything that he found. He soon fell foul of his mother.[2] It is possible that she was interfering in the government, continuing to exercise royal rights that she had usurped in Harthacnut's time. After Edward's coronation Stigand, a royal clerk, Emma's confidant, was appointed bishop of East Anglia,[3] and, if we may judge by Edward's later behaviour, appointed by Emma. Edward had so many grievances against her that it only needed a provocative action like this and probably some malicious gossip to spur him into action.[4] Moreover, Emma seems to have been rich; and it was probably believed, rightly or wrongly, that the royal treasury at Winchester had passed into her keeping. On 16 November 1043 Edward rode with Earls Leofric, Godwin, and Siward from Gloucester to Winchester where, after accusing Emma of treason and no doubt obtaining the judgment of his court against her, he deprived her of all her lands and movables, but did not add the extreme penalty, outlawry or exile.[5]

---

[1] Barlow, *English Church*, pp. 129 ff.

[2] The following account is based on *Chron. C, D, E*, and Florence, i. 197. The several versions seem to be biased selections from the common source, and, as there is no contradiction, can safely be conflated. See F. Barlow, 'Two Notes: Cnut's Second Pilgrimage and Queen Emma's Disgrace in 1043', *EHR*, lxxiii (1958), 649 ff.

[3] *Chron. C.E.*   [4] See above, pp. 57–9.

[5] 'And they allowed her to stay there afterwards', *Chron. D*; Florence, i. 197, adds that she was also allowed suitable maintenance. The Miracle of St Mildred (see below, p. 77, *n.* 2) emphasizes, and no doubt exaggerates, her destitution. William of

He then deposed Stigand and confiscated all his possessions.[1] According to the Legend of St Mildred,[2] Emma, when reduced to poverty and despair, had a dream in which the saint promised to help her because she, with Cnut, had patronized the translation of St Mildred from Thanet to St Augustine's, Canterbury. Whereupon Emma borrowed 20s., sent it by means of her thegn, Æthelweard Spearka, to Abbot Ælfstan of St Augustine's, and, miraculously, the king's heart was changed. Edward 'felt shame for the injury he had done her, the son acknowledged his mother, he restored her to her former dignity and he who had proclaimed her guilty begged her pardon.' Everything she had possessed was restored to her; her accusers and despoilers were confounded. Emma's enemies became her son's enemies. And when Æthelweard got back to Winchester he found his mistress entirely reinstated. We know that Edward, while Emma and Stigand were in disgrace, granted to Bury St Edmunds an estate at Mildenhall and the eight-and-a-half hundreds pertaining to Thingoe, all in Suffolk, which Emma had possessed. But he must have returned the hundreds to her because we find him granting them anew to the abbey about the time of her death.[3] In 1044 Edward restored Stigand to Elmham,[4] and the bishop forced Bury to give him the lease of Mildenhall.[5] The incident was closed.

The Legend of St Mildred probably exaggerates both Emma's disgrace and her subsequent return to favour. Styled the king's mother, she witnessed charters regularly until Edward's marriage,[6] which can

---

Malmesbury has the story that while the despoilers were gaping at her treasures, her goldsmith abstracted the shrine containing the head of St Ouen (which she had bought at Rouen, 1013–17) and deposited it at Malmesbury. *GP*, pp. 419–20.

[1] *Chron. C*, 'because he was closest to his mother's counsel, and it was suspected that she did as he advised.'

[2] The first miracle after the Translation, printed in part by Barlow, 'Two Notes', pp. 655–6.

[3] Harmer, *Writs*, nos. 9, 18. The latter, which must be dated October 1051–October 1052 or 1053–7, declares that Bury is to have the hundreds as fully and completely as ever his mother had them, as Ælfric, Wihtgar's son, administered them on her behalf, and as afterwards Edward himself had possessed them. This history of their administration makes it clear that the second grant is not simply a confirmation of the first, like the confirmation at the end of 1065 to the new abbot, Baldwin, *Writs*, no. 24.

[4] *Chron. E*; Florence, i. 199.   [5] Harmer, *Writs*, p. 436.

[6] *KCD*, nos. 767–8, 771, 773–5, 788, 916, 962, 1332 (Sawyer, nos. 998–1002, 1006, 1228, 1391, 1471, 1530) (of varying degrees of authenticity, all to be dated 1042–5) and Robertson, *Charters*, no. 101 (1045 × 47).

only mean that the drafters of these documents did not notice her fall or that it was too brief to leave a trace. Yet her disappearance from court as soon as Edward took a wife shows that she had no influence over her son, and her fate in 1043 proves that she had become even more isolated than she had been in 1035. The northern version of the Anglo-Saxon Chronicle implies that it was the three great earls who advised Edward to disarm his mother,[1] and this league against Emma is one of the most interesting features of the episode. The earls had recognized Edward as king and now they were helping him to establish his rights. They were also, apparently, advising him to take a wife.

But in 1044 Edward had much to do besides choosing a wife. There were some awkward ecclesiastical problems to face and in the summer there was the threat of an invasion. Edward's arbitrary breaking of Bishop Stigand in 1043, even though he pardoned him in 1044, gave notice that he was going to assert his authority over the church. And if he sold the diocese to Grimketel, as some believed,[2] he announced even more sinister intentions. In 1044 two bishoprics became vacant through resignation and both were treated in an irregular way by the king. At Canterbury Archbishop Eadsige withdrew temporarily because of ill health, and with the connivance of Edward and Earl Godwin, he secretly consecrated Siward, abbot of Abingdon, as his replacement, 'because the archbishop suspected that somebody else would ask for it, or purchase it, whom he less trusted and favoured, if more people knew about it.'[3] It would seem that Eadsige secretly approached Edward and Godwin with his plan, and perhaps paid for permission to carry it out.[4] Certainly he believed that bishoprics could be bought and sold. Also occurred the retirement, because of a disease which proved fatal, of Ælfweard, bishop of London and abbot of Evesham. He died at Ramsey abbey on 25 July; and, although we are told that in 'a general council' held at London – presumably to deal with the episcopal vacancy – an Evesham monk, Wulfmaer or Manni, was appointed to the abbacy and consecrated on 10 August,[5] we are told nothing about the bishopric, a quite exceptional silence. Clearly there was some division of opinion.

---

[1] 'the king was advised to ride . . . with Earls Leofric, Godwine, and Siward', *Chron. D*; 'ut illi [comites] consilium ei dederant', Florence, i. 197.

[2] Malmesbury, *GP*, p. 205; Florence, i. 193.

[3] *Chron. CE*.

[4] He may have surrendered the 'third penny' of Kent to Godwin. See below, p. 115, *n.* 2.

[5] *Chron. D*; Florence, i. 198–9, elaborates.

All we know is that from 1046 Robert of Jumièges, Edward's Norman friend, witnesses charters as bishop.[1] It is possible that in 1044 there was a dispute between those who wanted Manni to hold both offices and the king who wished to reward his own servant.

The situation in the church in 1043–4 cannot be fully understood. We are expressly informed that a few years later there was a widespread dispute over patronage;[2] but even then it is not made clear who the rival parties were and what principles were at stake. The most likely explanation is that the will of the king, which may sometimes have meant the wishes of a party of courtiers acting in his name, was being opposed by local interests. This was the situation which the tenth-century reformers had attempted to destroy; and *secularium prioratus*, the domination of the local nobility, operating from outside and also from within the church, may well have returned, especially since Cnut's death. In attempting to recover his patronage Edward could have been supported by reforming prelates and by reformers in his household, by men anxious to prevent the election of unworthy candidates to abbeys and bishoprics through the influence of their kinsmen and friends. But there is nothing to suggest that Edward was interested in anything beyond establishing his rights and, perhaps, in making them profitable.

Equally important for Edward was the military situation. In a royal charter drafted in the Old Minster, Winchester, dated 1044, Edward is made to declare that he is not without anxiety for the peace of his country.[3] Rumours that Magnus of Norway was about to invade England seem to have been in circulation from 1043 until his death in 1047.[4] That Magnus never sailed does not mean that they were without justification and Edward's defence measures may even have had a deterrent effect. In 1044 Edward took command of a fleet of thirty-five ships based on Sandwich,[5] a useful opportunity for the new king to show that he possessed military experience and intended to fight for his kingdom. Indeed, in the next eight years Edward was often in command of an army or navy. Connected, no doubt, with the invasion

---

[1] *KCD*, no. 784 and the St Ouen, Rouen, charter, Donald Matthew, *The Norman Monasteries and their English possessions* (1962), pp. 143 ff. (Sawyer, nos. 1014–15), are the first.

[2] *VEdR*, p. 18.

[3] *KCD*, no. 774 (Sawyer, no. 1006).

[4] Cf. also the story in *Gesta abbatum monasterii S. Albani*, ed. H. T. Riley (Rolls ser. 1867), i. 34–6, that early in Edward's reign the threat of a Danish invasion was taken seriously.   [5] *Chron. CE.*

scare of 1044 was Edward's banishment of Gunnhildr, Cnut's niece, and her children. They returned to Denmark by way of Bruges.[1] Here, too, Edward was making his intentions clear. Those who lost his favour, opposed his will, or aroused his suspicion got short shrift. Edward had no prisons; he was not accused of assassination or poisoning; he banished and outlawed. In 1044 he must have impressed men with his decisiveness and vigour.

Although Edward had not married as soon as he became king, he took a wife at probably the earliest opportunity. The Anglo-Saxon Chronicle mentions the event without comment and no writer before the twelfth century thought it strange.[2] The *Vita Ædwardi Regis* probably devoted at least a paragraph to it in a chapter which has been lost; but all that we can recover from William of Malmesbury's and Osbert of Clare's versions of it is that once peace had been restored to the kingdom marriage plans began to be discussed, and it was decided to look for a wife for Edward among the daughters of the princes. In England one girl alone was found to be suitable, Edith, the eldest daughter of Earl Godwin and Countess Gytha. In her favour were the distinction of her family, her youth and beauty, her good literary education, and her skill in spinning and embroidery.[3] The belief that Edward's choice was limited to the highest English nobility was probably well founded. An insular check on Edward was required.

As Edith's parents married in 1019 she was no more than twenty-five and could have been much younger. Edward was just turned forty. Even if Edith was only half Edward's age, the disparity was not unusual or disadvantageous, and she survived him by only ten years. Edith had been educated in the nunnery at Wilton, a famous seminary for royal and noble ladies,[4] and although her attainments may have been exaggerated, she was more than adequately educated for the highest station. Moreover, she came from a family with long experience of the Anglo-Danish court. We know of nothing which made Edith unfit to be queen. It is quite likely that the match was arranged by the parents. Emma and Godwin would have seen the obvious advantages to both sides in the alliance. For Godwin it set the seal on his wonderful career.

---

[1] *Chron. D*; Florence, i. 199.

[2] There are no observations by the Norman apologists of the Conquest. Malmesbury, *GR*, i. 239, repeats the views of *VEdR* and also gives as an alternative reason for Edward's chastity the king's hatred of his wife's father.

[3] *VEdR*, pp. 14–15. [4] *Ibid.*, pp. 46–7, 95 ff.

For Emma it provided her son with solid support in the kingdom. For both it promised a grandchild to succeed Edward as king.

Edward's feelings cannot be discovered. It is possible that he had always wanted to marry and at last had his chance. He could not have been browbeaten or cajoled into marriage if he had an unshakable antipathy to that state, or into marriage with Edith if he had a strong dislike for her person. If he was merely indifferent, accustomed to a celibate life, not greatly interested in women, there could have been sufficient pressure put on him to overcome his apathy. He usually gave way if resolutely and consistently opposed. The earls were probably tired of the political insecurity. They had given Edward their backing; he was now firmly on the throne; and it was his duty to remove the uncertainty. Edward cannot have failed to see the force of their arguments. It was the custom for men to marry for material or diplomatic advantage. Edward had possibly had some choice of partner. And if such marriages did not always produce happiness, they often produced the children which at least the wife's family desired.

When Edward was invested with the sceptre at his coronation the archbishop prayed that God would visit him with an increase of children;[1] and in the religious ceremonies which accompanied his wedding the archbishop prayed that God would so impart to these his servants the strength of his blessing that according to his will they might be joined together in conjugal fellowship with equal love, like understanding, and identical holiness, and that God would cause them to bear such offspring as would be partakers of his paradise. For Edith he asked that she should be filled 'with the blessings of the breasts and of the womb' (Gen. xlix. 25) and that the blessings of the fathers of old should be strong upon her and upon her seed, just as was promised to Abraham and his seed for ever (Gen. xvii).[2] According to the *Vita Ædwardi Regis* most of these petitions were listened to: the religious pair became, although divided in body, one single person, and the only contention between them was rivalry in good works.[3]

Edith and Edward were not, however, blessed with children. Shortly after the king's death, possibly even in his old age, a rumour was in circulation that the marriage had not been consummated owing

---

[1] 'Visita eum in sobole', Edgar *ordo*, cap. 17, based on the 'Erdmann' *ordo*, *c.* 900, cap. 10, Schramm, 'Die Krönung', pp. 204, 226.

[2] 'Coronatio Iudithae Karoli II filiae', 1 October 856, *Monumenta Germaniae Historica, Capitularia regum Francorum*, II, ii (Hannover, 1960), no. 296, pp. 426–7.

[3] *VEdR*, pp. 3–4, 15, 23, 41–2, 46–9, 79–80.

to Edward's religious scruples; and it was largely on this supposition that the case for his sanctity was to rest.[1] A similar story of virginity and sanctity was attached to Henry II of Germany (1002–24) and his wife, Kunigund, likewise childless and of good religious repute.[2] Such stories cannot be investigated with any hope of arriving at the exact truth. The theoretical possibilities are many. But, although the secrets of the marriage bed can be strange and even when revealed are rarely divulged with full candour, it is hard to believe that a union which lasted for twenty-one years had been a complete nullity. The theory that Edward's childlessness was due to deliberate abstention from sexual relations lacks authority, plausibility, and diagnostic value.

Its lack of authority is obvious. The one source – or at least the sole surviving source – for the story is the *Vita Ædwardi Regis*, and although the author was probably acquainted with the queen, he was not well qualified to judge rumours about the court. Baldwin, the king's doctor, did not apparently carry this story to Bury St Edmunds.[3] Bishops Ealdred and Wulfstan did not tell edifying tales about the royal couple which the Worcester historians could repeat, although Wulfstan seems to have been partial to this kind of discourse.[4] Bishop Leofric, an old and close friend of Edward's, inserted in his pontifical a prayer for a childless king.[5] Archbishop Stigand, it seems, was unimpressed by the king's piety,[6] and no one knew the court better than he. All later references to this subject depend directly or indirectly on the *Vita*.[7]

Moreover, the author's presentation of it is far from convincing. For Edward's miracles he cites 'the joint testimony of good and fitting

[1] *VEdR*, pp. lxx ff., 112 ff., and below, Chapter XII.

[2] *S. Henrici Vita*, auct. anon., Migne, *PL*, cxl, coll. 120, 127. Renate Klauser, *Der Heinrichs- und Kunigundenkult im mittelalterlichen Bistum Bamberg* (Bamberg, 1957), pp. 32–3.

[3] It is not known when Baldwin joined Edward; but he must have served him for some time in order to earn an abbey. He went to Bury on 19 August 1065, Robertson, *Charters*, pp. 196–8, Harmer, *Writs*, nos. 23–5; cf. also Malmesbury, *GP*, p. 156. Baldwin appointed 10s. to supply fish for the monks on the anniversary of Edward, 'the good king', and appointed as much for William I's anniversary, Robertson, *Charters*, pp. 196–8. Edward is most appreciatively noticed in *Miracula S. Eadmundi*, Liebermann, *Ungedruckte*, p. 244, written by Herman, a clerk who had served Bishop Herfast of Elmham and then Baldwin. Herman describes Edward as *piissimus*, but has nothing to say about his chastity or sanctity.

[4] *Vita Wulfstani*, pp. 6–7.

[5] 'Benedictio pro rege . . . Da ei de rore coeli benedictionem et de pinguetudine terrae ubertatem; da ei de inimicis triumphum, de lumbis eius sobolem regnaturum.', *The Leofric Missal*, ed. F. E. Warren (1883), pp. 8b–9a.

[6] *VEdR*, pp. 76–7.   [7] *Ibid.*, pp. xxx ff.

men'.[1] For Edward's chastity we have no separate chapter, not even a paragraph, only scattered hints and random assertions. The author calls no evidence. The one witness who would have inspired respect is Queen Edith. The nearest the author gets to attributing the story to her is when in a poem the Muse asks him, 'Do you forget that often when you talked she called him father and herself his child?'[2] But what does such baby talk mean? Moreover, the writer sometimes forgot his theory. Although, unfortunately, the chapter which dealt with the marriage has been lost, we have the hagiographical version of it which Osbert of Clare produced in the twelfth century, a version from which nothing miraculous would have been omitted:

> This young woman was delivered to the royal bridal apartments with ceremonial rejoicing . . . But merciful God, who preserved his blessed confessor Alexius a virgin, kept, as we believe, St Edward the king all the days of his life in the purity of the flesh. The excellent queen served him as a daughter . . . But she preserved the secret of the king's chastity of which she had learned, and kept those counsels that she knew.[3]

It is most unlikely that the reference to St Alexius appeared in the original text, for it is foreign to the style of the *Vita Ædwardi Regis*. It is just possible that there was a reference to Edith's daughter-like behaviour (although Osbert could have taken this from a later passage), because in the following poem occurs the phrase, 'Edith, a daughter worthy of the great earl, her father, and most worthy of her husband, the king.' But this theme is no more than ambiguous. And the final sentence, which again looks like Osbert's contribution, goes far to destroy his thesis. He is as good as telling us that he obtained here no help from his source; and he provokes the question, if Edith did not tell, who did? So it is unlikely that the author of the *Vita* stated categorically at this point that the marriage was never consummated. And we notice elsewhere, for example in his description of Edward's behaviour towards Edith in 1051-2, of the archbishop of Canterbury's view of the union,[4] and of Edith's despair at Edward's sudden *impotentia* just before his death,[5] that he writes as though he was concerned with an ordinary Christian marriage. Indeed, at the outset, in the prologue,[6] it is their oneness which is emphasized. Edith is Edward's counterpart: they are two in one, one person in two bodies.

[1] *VEdR*, p. 61.
[2] *Ibid.*, pp. 59-60.
[3] *Ibid.*, pp. 14-15.
[4] *Ibid.*, pp. 23, 28.
[5] *Ibid.*, p. 54.
[6] *Ibid.*, pp. 3-4.

No less interesting is William of Malmesbury's gloss on the *Vita*. After a short summary of the lost passage,[1] he adds:

> Edith was suspected of having committed adultery both during her marriage and after Edward's death; but on her deathbed in King William's time she convinced those present of her unbroken chastity (*de perpetua integritate*) by voluntarily taking an oath. The king's treatment of his wife had been neither to remove her from his bed nor to act as a man with her. But whether he did this because of his hatred of her family (which he wisely dissimulated at the time) or because of his love of chastity, I really do not know. It is, however, widely asserted that Edward never marred his purity by intercourse with any woman.[2]

Although William contributes the additional information that Edith, when denying rumours about her unchastity, asserted that she was in fact a virgin, he commits himself to as little as possible. His scepticism cannot be doubted. As for his factual information, it would not have been unusual for a dying woman to protest her honest life; and, if strange stories were already in circulation about Edith and Edward, her words could easily have been misunderstood and misrepresented.

Not only is the story of Edward's virginity without good authority, it is also implausible, and, far from helping us to understand the situation and events, merely obscures. It is a typical example of that irrationality and ignorant credulity with which the eleventh century abounds.[3] There was little knowledge of the physiology of sex. Impotence and infertility lay outside the scope of medical skill: even minor obstructions or abnormalities could probably not be diagnosed and cured. Homosexuality was common and acknowledged,[4] but was discussed only in connexion with sin and allowed no sociological effects, although it may well have had a depressing effect on the birthrate. It is very likely that in vulgar talk there was much coarseness of speech and some shrewdness of understanding gained from animal husbandry; but always there seems to have been the temptation to think in terms of witchcraft, black or white magic, and miraculous powers. We do not know when rumours first began to circulate about Edward and Edith's marriage and whether they were always the same. Such evidence as we have

---

[1] *VEdR*, p. 14.   [2] Malmesbury, *GR*, i. 239.

[3] Cf. Barlow, *English Church*, p. 8. Although the penitential system should have given confessors deep knowledge of human behaviour, it seems in fact to have produced no psychological understanding.

[4] Cf. St Peter Damiani, *Liber Gomorrhianus*, Migne, *PL*, cxlv, coll. 159 ff.

points to the early 1060s as the period when a mysterious holiness began to be ascribed to Edward.[1]

In 1045, however, all men expected, and many hoped, that the marriage would produce the son who would succeed his father on the throne. It was Edward's answer to the several claimants; and, if Edith had conceived at once, that child would have been just nineteen when Edward died. Although in a sense a succession problem existed from the moment that Edward ascended the throne, it did not become acute until men began to suspect that the marriage was going to be unfruitful and to realize that Edward was not going to marry again. Even to the curious and perceptive this diagnosis was not immediately apparent.

Scenes from Edward's domestic life are rare. There is, however, an account of one incident which comes from the earliest years of the marriage.[2] Edward with his wife and mother once visited Abingdon abbey to take refreshment, and, while touring the buildings, came upon the children in the refectory taking their mid-day meal. Edith, because she was a woman of fashion,[3] was surprised that the children were lunching so early (they were, as was the custom, having lunch before the hour appointed for the seniors) and also that they had nothing to eat but bread. And when she was told that they hardly ever had anything else, she called to Edward and asked him if he would assign some revenue so that the children would have an improvement in their diet as a result of this visit to their 'banquet'. Edward received the request with good humour and with a laugh replied that he would be charmed to grant something if only someone would hand him over a bit of property that he could give. And when Edith said that she had just acquired a village and would be delighted if Edward would consent to its gift, he agreed that it was a splendid idea. There is a spontaneity in this episode which inspires some trust in its historical truth, and there is a sidelight on the characters of the newly weds which seems shrewd. A moment of comedy has been well observed.

In the seven years following his marriage Edward to all appearances made himself master in his kingdom. Ecclesiastical business is the most consistently recorded, and we can see that Edward took the traditional royal place in the church, presiding over councils and appointing to

---

[1] *VEdR*, pp. lxxii ff.　　　　　　　　[2] *Chron. Abingdon*, i. 459-61.

[3] 'utpote urbana'. If this means a worldly woman, or a woman of the world, who would not understand monastic customs, the writer shows his ignorance of Edith's education. Edith's unfamiliarity with the monastic *horarium* is a weakness in the story.

bishoprics and probably to the royal abbeys. The secret history of this patronage must have been a complicated story. All that can be discovered now are the principal features. Contemporary, or near-contemporary, observers imagined that in the late 'forties there were two main interests in opposition. According to the *Vita Ædwardi Regis*[1] the kingdom became disturbed and the court divided, 'because, when dignitaries died, one set of men wanted the vacant sees for their own friends while others were seizing them in order to grant them to strangers.' We also gather that the leader of the second party was Edward's Norman favourite, Robert of Jumièges.

It has, therefore, sometimes been imagined that the royal court was divided between those who favoured Normans and those who favoured Englishmen and Lotharingians. But a sort of French versus Teuton feud is most improbable and would not explain the actual appointments which Edward made. A more likely division is between the local interests, who backed the local man, and a court party which advanced strangers – both English and foreign. An earl, supported by some bishops, abbots, and thegns may on occasion have supported a candidate suggested by the vacant church itself, only to find that the king, having taken advice elsewhere, had his own proposal to make.[2] Edward in his promotions usually avoided a local connexion, and such a court policy must indeed have disturbed provincial circles. The identification of these two main interests, although useful, does not, however, entirely elucidate the story. Individual ambitions, particular features, shifting alliances, the kaleidoscope of politics in action, must have enormously complicated the drama. Edward learned to play this game and played to win. He rarely lost.

Most of the plums in the secular church went between 1045 and 1049 to royal clerks.[3] Edward appointed Herman, a Lotharingian, to Wiltshire in 1045, Leofric, an Englishman but educated in Lorraine, to Devon and Cornwall in 1046, Heca, an Englishman, to Sussex in 1047, and Ulf, a Norman, to Dorchester (near Oxford) in 1049. In this same period Robert of Jumièges got possession of London. The appointments in 1046 are particularly interesting. When Lyfing, bishop of Cornwall, Devon, and Worcester, died the obvious successor to the whole collection was Ealdred, who, like Lyfing, had been abbot of Tavistock and who, more recently, had probably been acting as Lyfing's suffragan or

---

[1] *VEdR*, p. 18.   [2] As in the Canterbury election of 1051 (below, pp. 104–5).
[3] Cf. Barlow, *English Church*, pp. 76 ff., 208 ff.

chorepiscopus. But Edward allowed only Worcester to Ealdred and gave the south-western shires to Leofric, thus, apparently deliberately, breaking local connexions.

Edward was also behaving correctly in appointing a clerk to St Germans and Crediton and a monk to Worcester. But in the following year, 1047, he appointed Stigand, bishop of Elmham, to Winchester, although Stigand was a clerk and Winchester was served by monks. This could be regarded as the removal of a local bishop to a diocese where he was a stranger, except that Stigand does not seem to have surrendered Elmham before he became archbishop of Canterbury in 1052[1] and that as a former royal clerk and intimate of Queen Emma he probably knew Winchester well. Moreover, in 1052 Elmham passed to Stigand's brother, Æthelmaer, a local landholder who had once been married.[2] It is probable that both Ealdred and Stigand had support outside the royal household. They were both well-established men with widespread and useful connexions. Yet their promotion should probably not be regarded as victories of an opposition over the king. In these cases the initiative may not have come from within the court, but we cannot doubt that Edward gave his blessing. It is most unlikely that Edward could have been constrained by either an earl or a cathedral chapter in 1046–7, when the tide was running so strongly in his favour. As the author of the *Vita* recognized,[3] the aim of the parties was to get the ear of the king. Whatever the manoeuvres, whatever the counsel taken, the decision rested with Edward.

Even more difficult than elucidating the interplay of interests in the making of these appointments is the investigation of Edward's policy in ecclesiastical affairs. Edward was not regarded by contemporaries as a church reformer and there seems no reason to dispute their view. On the other hand, although his actions could be considered misguided, he was not viewed as an impious tyrant. His appointments to bishoprics and abbeys were respectable enough, and, although there were irregularities, no church was without these. The one charge of simony from this later period seems to have been recklessly preferred and was not sustained.[4] The easiest conclusion is that Edward had prejudices but

---

[1] Æthelmaer does not witness a satisfactory document as bishop before Stigand's promotion to archbishop (cf. *KCD*, no. 956; Sawyer, no. 1478). *KCD*, no. 785 (Sawyer, no. 1055) carries no weight. *Chron.* does not mention Stigand's successor *s.a.* 1047, which seems to be conclusive.

[2] Barlow, *English Church*, pp. 216–17.   [3] *VEdR*, pp. 18–19.

[4] Against Ulf of Dorchester. See Barlow, *English Church*, pp. 215–16.

no policy. He used ecclesiastical benefices to reward his clerical friends and servants. This in itself interfered with local interests and may satisfactorily explain his disregard of the local candidate. It also ensured that a number of foreigners were appointed in the English church.

By exercising his ecclesiastical patronage Edward both increased his influence in the shires, and also strengthened his hand at court. The bishops and abbots were becoming men who owed their promotion to him. And he had shown with Stigand in 1043-4 that loss of royal favour could have serious results. Of the eleven bishops who witness the charters of 1049-50, all but the two archbishops had been appointed by him. The other bishops were, perhaps, becoming infirm or were less welcome at court. As at least four royal clerks had been promoted to the episcopal bench there was considerable change in this group. None of the ten clerks listed in 1049-50 seems to go back to the early years of the reign; and, of these ten, two were to be promoted bishop in 1051-2.[1]

On the secular side the position was rather different. The three great earls whom Edward found in office, Godwin of Wessex, Leofric of Mercia, and Siward of Northumbria, all survived the first decade of his reign; and Edward's only contribution was the favour he showed at first to his wife's family. At a lower level there was change, largely it would seem, as a result of deaths and retirement. A charter dated 1049,[2] commemorating Edward's grant of one-and-a-half perches of land to his faithful thegn, Eadwulf, lists among the secular witnesses below the rank of earl first Earl Godwin's sons, Tostig and Leofwine; then three other nobles, Ordgar, the West-country thegn, Odda of Deerhurst, and Ælfgar, either Earl Leofric's son or Ordgar's brother; and finally twelve thegns, of whom perhaps a third had served Harthacnut or Cnut. But Edward had been eliminating Danes. In 1046 he banished Osgot Clapa,[3] the Danish staller with estates in East Anglia, possibly because he had fallen foul of the new earl, Harold, Godwin's son. And in 1049

---

[1] Barlow, *English Church*, pp. 129 ff., 154-7.

[2] *KCD*, no. 787 (Sawyer, no. 1019). We can also compare an unpublished charter, Nat. Lib. of Wales, Peniarth MS 390, p. 368 (Sawyer, no. 1017), dated 1048, the only charter with this date to survive. It has some obviously unauthentic features. It is a grant of Edward of 2 *territoria* at *Berghe* to his *fideli comiti* [*?ministro*] *Tovig*. But the witness list, except perhaps for the order, is sound. After the two archbishops, four bishops, seven abbots, and five earls, occur the *ministri*, Leofwine, Tostig, Ælfstan, Ælfgar, Odda, Ordgar, Ordulf, Brihtric, and Ælfwine. For this charter, see below, pp. 332-3.

[3] *Chron. CDE*; Florence, i. 200. Edward granted the land which an Osgot had held at Pakenham (Sussex) to the abbey of Bury. Harmer, *Writs*, no. 14.

not one of the witnessing thegns bears a Scandinavian name. On the other hand, we still cannot identify a 'king's party' or a group of foreign favourites among the secular courtiers. Although in 1050 four out of ten royal clerks were foreigners, and three of the four may have been Normans, not one French name appears among the thegns and reeves. The appearance in 1050 of Ralf of Mantes, Edward's nephew, among the earls is the first evidence we have of the king rewarding a foreign nobleman.[1] It is clear that Edward's influence had worked less effectively on secular than on ecclesiastical society. Although he could have claimed that the great position held by the house of Godwin was his creation, it may well be that he would not have boasted of this achievement.

We can form some impression of the ebb and flow of power among the highest nobility. Siward of Northumbria seems to have been the most stable. He had at least two sons, Osbeorn and Waltheof, and was probably uninterested in the politics of southern England. Leofric of Mercia had lost some ground to Godwin of Wessex; but he had a son, Ælfgar, at court[2] and could probably rely on Siward's assistance. Although he may have felt that he was being jostled, he had the deepest roots and could not have been afraid. The most unstable power was the house of Godwin. As it represented the Anglo-Danish interest – Godwin's four eldest boys were given Danish names, the two youngest English – its policies were a cause of suspicion to the king; and its great ambition put it at risk. Godwin himself would not seem to have been sinister. He was a good father and was loved or respected by most of his children. His friends praised his loyalty, gentleness, justice, bravery, and caution, and his eloquence.[3] His enemies created a legend which, apart from allotting him responsibility for the murder of Alfred the aetheling, emphasized the shadier qualities necessary for worldly triumph.[4] Nevertheless, although he was not religious, may not always have been scrupulous, he must have had great talent; and we cannot doubt that his virtues outweighed his vices. His real crime was success.

In 1045, when an earldom was created for Beorn, Estrith's son and Godwin's nephew,[5] Godwin's family held four of the six great earldoms,

---

[1] *KCD*, nos. 791–3, 796, 800 (Sawyer, nos. 1020–3, 1025).

[2] Ælfgar *nobilis* witnesses with Tostig, Leofwine, and Odda in 1049 (*KCD*, no. 787; Sawyer, no. 1019); but this may be the brother of Ordgar.　　　　[3] *VEdR*, pp. 7 ff.

[4] Cf. C. E. Wright, *The Cultivation of Saga in Anglo-Saxon England* (1939), pp. 213–36.

[5] Beorn witnesses from 1045 (*KCD*, no. 781; Sawyer, no. 1008). Freeman conjectured, *NC*, ii. 557 ff., that he succeeded Thuri or Thored as earl of the Middle Angles, that is to say, eastern, or Danish, Mercia.

and there were at least three other sons, Tostig, Gyrth, and Leofwine, waiting their turn. Moreover, the earldoms of Swegn and Beorn included some Mercian shires. Even Harold's earldom of East Anglia, although that province had usually had its own earl, was the natural area for Mercian expansion. There was also Edith at court. The main weakness in the position turned out to be dissensions within the family itself, dissensions which the author of the *Vita Ædwardi Regis* was to lament. The main hazard was the attitude of the king. Edward broke the family in 1051, and it would seem that the causes of his hostility lay in the past. Many violent quarrels are the sudden, unexpected, unwanted eruption of resentments long concealed. Most of these go back ultimately to a physical aversion, and all have a secret history, involving ancient wrongs, almost forgotten grievances. Such quarrels can sometimes be traced through events, but do not usually explain them. The actors are looking always for pretexts to justify emotions which they do not fully understand.

Edward's treatment of his mother in 1043–4 shows that he was capable of this sort of behaviour; and it is easy to suggest episodes which caused, and then nourished, his dislike of Godwin. He may have resented the earl's patronage in 1041–3, his providing him with a wife, his greediness for his sons, his connexions with the Danish interest. There were also men at court, especially Robert of Jumièges, who had their own grievances against Godwin, and did their best to influence the king against him.[1] But there was no public feud between Edward and his father-in-law. The king's unavowed feelings probably showed only in pinpricks, although some of these could have hurt. He was the sort of man who could have taken it out on his wife; he is unlikely to have viewed the family's transgressions with forbearance; and any policy backed by Godwin was bound to be unacceptable. Godwin probably received many affronts, which his men and possibly the rasher members of his family urged him to avenge.[2] But Godwin was a patient man and in the true interests of his family was remarkably long-suffering.[3] He also was embarrassed by the behaviour of his eldest son.

Swegn, who was born about 1023, was the wildest of the family.[4] The church of Worcester disliked him and reported how he claimed that Cnut, not Godwin, was his real father, an assertion which his

[1] *VEdR*, pp. 17 ff.   [2] *Ibid.*, pp. 19, 27.
[3] This is a basic theme of *VEdR*; cf. pp. 19, 25–7, 32.
[4] Cf. Barlow, *English Church*, p. 58; *Hemingi Chartularium ecclesiae Wigorniensis*, ed. T. Hearne (1723), i. 275–6.

mother, Gytha, indignantly denied. The story implies that Swegn was not only reckless but completely Scandinavian in his interests. Swegn's earldom was probably, as in 1050, in the south-west midlands, the shires of Somerset, Hereford, Gloucester, Oxford, and Berkshire.[1] In 1046, in alliance with Gruffydd ap Llewelyn, prince of North Wales, he carried out a punitive expedition in South Wales, and, obviously elated by his success, on his way home through Herefordshire enticed or kidnapped Eadgifu, abbess of Leominster.[2] It is not clear whether this was seduction or rape: it is even possible that Eadgifu was his kinswoman; opinions also differed on Swegn's intentions. But it was a serious crime and a sin, and after a year Swegn fled to Bruges, where he wintered, and then to Denmark, where he caused further scandal.[3] It seems that some of his estates, and possibly his shires, were taken over by his brother, Harold, and his cousin, Beorn, presumably as the next in order of seniority in the family.[4]

The war in Denmark was casting its shadow over England. Magnus of Norway was trying to recreate Cnut's empire; and there can have been few years in which Edward did not take some preventive measures.[5]

[1] Florence, i. 205.

[2] *Chron. C*, 'ordered her to be brought to him and kept her as long as it suited him, and then let her go home.' Florence, i. 201, *s.a.* 1049, names her and claims that Swegn wanted to marry her. Hemming, i. 275–6, has it that Swegn abducted her by force, kept her for a whole year, and surrendered her only because of the threats of Archbishop Eadsige and Bishop Lyfing. As the latter died in March 1046 and the former was in retirement during 1044–8 there are difficulties. In 1051, it seems, Swegn was the father of a son, Hakon (see below, p. 303), but we are not told who was the mother. In 1086 an abbess, who had held in King Edward's day, was still holding part of the manor of Leominster (*DB*, i. 180a ii). This could easily have been Eadgifu, still alive a generation after her lover's death. Also provision was still being made for the maintenance of nuns (*DB*, i. 180a i). It has been conjectured that the convent was suppressed *c.* 1047; but its history is entirely obscure.

[3] *Chron. E, s.a.* 1047; 'and there ruined himself with the Danes', *Chron. D, s.a.* 1049, p. 112. If Swegn kept Eadgifu for a year he spent the winter 1047–8 at Bruges.

[4] See below, p. 99.

[5] T. D. Hardy, *Descriptive catalogue of materials relating to the history of Great Britain and Ireland* (Rolls ser. 1862–71), i. 380, with reference to the 'Translation of St Mildred', London, Brit. Mus. MS, Cotton Vesp. B xx, states that Thanet was once laid waste by order of Edward through fear of the Danes and that Edward placed 700 soldiers in garrison at Canterbury castle. Unfortunately this is a complete mistake. In chapter xxi of the tract, fo. 180, King William I (*prior Willelmus rex*) orders Thanet to be devastated lest it serve as a base for a threatened Danish invasion. In chapter xxiii, fo. 184, William puts 700 mercenary soldiers in the castle at Canterbury as a safeguard against an invasion. These two, possibly separate, actions of the Conqueror have been conflated by Hardy and attributed to Edward.

In the summer of 1045 he again took command of a fleet at Sandwich, perhaps even larger than the thirty-five ships of the previous year.[1] But once more Magnus's threatened invasion did not take place. In the Anglo-Saxon Chronicler's view it was Svein Estrithson's resistance in Denmark which kept Magnus from sailing. But in 1046 Magnus overcame Svein[2] and in 1047 the defeated prince sent to England to ask for fifty ships.[3] Godwin advocated sending these reinforcements and Earl Leofric successfully opposed the plan. Leofric's policy of non-intervention may be said to have been justified by events; but Edward clearly took a risk in refusing to support the weaker party in Denmark; and in 1047, it seems, Magnus became the complete master of the southern kingdom.[4] Svein fled east and was in Lund, preparing to enter Sweden, when messengers arrived from Zealand with the news of Magnus's death on 25 October. This event saved both Svein and Edward. Svein returned to Zealand and was elected king by the men of Fünen and Jutland. He had at last started his long reign over Denmark. To Norway succeeded Harald Sigurdsson (Hardrada), Magnus's uncle, St Olaf's uterine brother, who had shortly before returned from his fabulous adventures in the East in search of a kingdom.[5] According to the Chronicle both Harald and Svein sent ambassadors to England in 1048, the former to negotiate an alliance, the latter to ask again for fifty ships. Once more Svein's request was refused[6] and within a short time hostilities had broken out between the two northern kings.[7]

So far Edward, obviously aided by a great deal of luck, had done extremely well. There can be little doubt that Godwin, through his wife and past history, took an active part in the Scandinavian world and wanted to involve Edward in it. He was a true Anglo-Dane and wished both for Edward's security in England and also for his nephew Svein's success in Denmark. He therefore advocated an alliance with

[1] *Chron. CD*: both entries emphasize the largeness of the force; Florence, i. 199.
[2] 'Magnus conquered Denmark', *Chron. D*; Adam of Bremen, II, lxxviii, lxxix, III, xii, pp. 136–7, 151–2; *Anonymi Roskildensis Chronicon Danicum*, p. 377; *Theodrici monachi Historia de antiquitate Regum Norwagiensium*, pp. 48–50.
[3] *Chron. D*; Florence, i. 200; Plummer, *Two Chronicles*, p. 227.
[4] *Chron. D*; Florence, i. 200; *Anonymi Roskildensis Chronicon Danicum*, pp. 377–8; *Theodrici monachi Historia*, pp. 54–5.
[5] *Chron. D, s.a.* 1048; Florence, i. 200; Adam of Bremen, III, xiii and schol., pp. 153–4; *Theodrici monachi Historia*, pp. 50–7.
[6] *Chron. D*; Florence, i. 200.
[7] Adam of Bremen, III, xiii, p. 154, 'Inter Haroldum et Suein prelium fuit omnibus diebus vitae eorum.'

Svein against Magnus of Norway. Only perversity or secret fears about the intentions of the Danish party could have moved Edward to refuse this apparently sensible policy.

Edward seems indeed to have had cause for suspicion. Svein himself boasted that after Magnus's death he had possessed two kingdoms, that he had immediately fitted out an expedition in order to enforce his claim to England, and that he had allowed himself to be bought off by Edward who offered him tribute and renewed recognition as his heir to England, thus making him the master of three kingdoms.[1] Where the story can be tested it can be shown to be false. Harald took possession of Norway. To an English observer Svein was still a petitioner, not a blackmailer. But it may be that Edward sent him money. Farther than this we cannot go. Edward was showing such hostility to the Scandinavian party that it is impossible to believe he could have promised Svein the succession in good faith. What he could have done, however, is to have made a derisory gesture. He seems to have liked grim jokes and ironical judgments. Simulation and dissimulation were political skills that were highly prized.[2]

At all events Edward's policy of non-intervention had been successful and Godwin had been overruled. A strange coincidence is that Queen Edith is no longer found as a witness to royal charters after 1046[3] until she reappears in 1060. As no charters survive for 1047 this eclipse cannot be put into its exact context. Nor can it be explained. It may be that Edith's childlessness destroyed the little interest that Edward had in her as a woman, and that he chose this method to wound her and through her his father-in-law. It is also possible that the promotion of Ralf of Mantes was intended to irritate her family. Edward made provision for his nephew out of Swegn's earldom, probably when Swegn left England in disgrace late in 1047.[4] It is not surprising that in 1051, after Swegn had returned to England and in the heat of the moment, Ralf was brought into the quarrel; more surprising is how little he was involved in the feud. Godwin and at least some of his sons tolerated, even

[1] Adam of Bremen, III, xii, p. 152.
[2] Cf. *VEdR*, p. 32.
[3] She witnesses regularly in 1045 and two out of four charters dated 1046 (*KCD*, nos. 783 and 1335; Sawyer, nos. 1013, 1016, both Winchester charters and with identical witness lists).
[4] Although Ralf first appears in witness lists as an earl in 1050, French soldiers were already established in Herefordshire by 1051. Admittedly Ralf is missing from two charters dated 1049; but charters for 1047 do not exist, and there is only one for 1048. Oxford also was at some time in his earldom, Harmer, *Writs*, no. 55.

perhaps welcomed, this newcomer among them. Ralf came from the French Vexin, in the marches between the Isle de France and Normandy, a battlefield studded with fortified towns and castles. He was given Herefordshire to hold as an outpost against the Welsh, and, in reorganizing its defences, introduced some French military customs. Castles, presumably of the ring-work (ditch and palisade) type, were constructed; one in the north, Richard's castle, was named after Richard fitzScrob, and another, in the south-west, was called first Pentecost's castle after Osbern Pentecost and then Ewias Harold after Earl Ralf's son.[1] In 1052 a castellan named Hugh was also in this area; and Ralf himself may possibly have had a castle besides the city. The new earl and his captains also began to train their English soldiers to fight as cavalry, like the French.[2]

We should beware of thinking that this French colony in Herefordshire can be linked with other property held by Frenchmen in England to constitute an advance base of the count of Normandy, deliberately created by Edward so as to facilitate the count's succession to the English throne. It is possible that Robert fitzWimarch, who was Norman or Breton, had a castle north of London in 1052;[3] and some Norman and Flemish monasteries had estates on or near the Channel coast. But it was administrative convenience which dictated the location of the monastic estates.[4] A castle at Clavering (Essex) falls into no strategic plan. A castle on the cliff at Dover seems to be a blunder of the twelfth-century annalist 'Florence of Worcester'.[5] And it is impossible to believe that castles were built in the Welsh marches for any but the obvious purpose of defending the frontier.

With his rear thus secured, Edward continued to watch the east. In

---

[1] Cf. J. H. Round, 'Normans under Edward the Confessor', *Feudal England* (1895), pp. 320 ff., Harmer, *Writs*, p. 570. For Richard fitzScrob's spoliation of the church of Worcester, *Hemingi Chartularium*, i. 254–5. Richard is addressed in two Worcester writs, *c.* 1062, and in one Edward calls him 'my housecarl', Harmer, *Writs*, nos. 116–17.

[2] *Chron. C, s.a.* 1055; Florence, i. 213.

[3] 'Robert's castle', *Chron. E, s.a.* 1052, has, since Freeman at least, been generally understood as a castle of Robert fitzWimarch, and a location at Clavering (Essex), one of his *DB* estates, where, we know, a castle once was, was suggested by J. H. Round, *VCH* (*Essex*), i. 345, and has usually been followed.

[4] Donald Matthew, *The Norman Monasteries and their English possessions* (1962), pp. 25–6.

[5] Plummer, *Two Chronicles*, p. 237, *sub* Richard's Castle; R. Allen Brown, *The Normans and the Norman Conquest* (1969), pp. 117, *n.* 48; 177, *n.* 174, for the archaeological evidence.

1048 a Viking fleet of twenty-five ships under Lothen and Yrling, two pirates of whom we know nothing more, sailed from Flanders and raided Sandwich, Thanet, and Essex, after, perhaps, making a first landing on the Isle of Wight.[1] The men of Thanet kept them at bay,[2] and Edward with his earls put to sea against them.[3] But the Vikings managed to withdraw without serious loss to Flanders, where they sold their booty, before sailing east to their homeland.[4]

Edward is not usually regarded as a warrior king; but he may well have been a thwarted hero. It is by no means unlikely that the fleet was mobilized every year for training and defence; and it is certain that Edward with the earls took command whenever there was the possibility of an invasion. Each time the annalist records the mustering of the fleet, and always at Sandwich, Edward is there. And although Edward seems never to have been in action against an enemy, it would have been remarkable if he had been, so rare were battles at sea, so difficult was it to intercept a raider. Edward was providing for the training of his navy, and he gave it leadership when danger threatened. We cannot judge the quality of his generalship; but normally men obeyed his orders and there are no stories of treachery or desertion. By 1049 Edward must have been confident that he could put up a good fight against an enemy, whether from without or within.

[1] *Chron. C* gives Sandwich and the Isle of Wight; *Chron. E* omits Wight but gives a fuller account of the events in the south-east.
[2] *Chron. E.*   [3] *Chron. C.*   [4] *Chron. E.*

Chapter 5

THE VICTORIOUS KING
(1049–1051)

From reading the Anglo-Saxon Chronicle and all accounts based on it the impression is gained that the period 1049–52 was the most remarkable in the whole of Edward's reign. No episode is more dramatic than the fall of the house of Godwin followed so swiftly by its forcible restoration. Moreover there were acts of violence, spectacular embassies, and diplomatic revolutions which were probably exciting in themselves and which certainly disturbed the English aristocracy. But because this is close to the time at which the first version of the annals for this reign was written up, the account of these years is out of proportion. For almost a decade we have a narrative based on near-contemporary recording. It may be that it was because the history of England had become so interesting that the annalist decided that he ought to set it down; but it may be that it is the freshness of the reporting which makes the events seem specially remarkable. Nevertheless, the narrative remains inscrutable. Despite the greater detail and the curiosity which the events have always aroused, a convincing key to the understanding of this period has never been found.

For these years, instead of a random selection of striking events, we have an almost consecutive narrative account, and this encourages the hope that we have only to read intelligently in order to understand. But, although some superficial explanations of the events are provided, such as, 'they had too little support', 'his men went foolishly', or 'he did this with the king's full permission', these rarely, if ever, lay bare the motives of the actors. Moreover, we begin to suspect that even if the events are consecutive they do not always have a strictly causal relationship, that the annalist neither understood all the ramifications nor was able, or wished, to explain fully what little he knew. It is, therefore, impossible from the various versions of the Chronicle, using them either singly or in conflation, to trace with certainty chains of events. Indeed, to make sense of this period we have to reject the annalist's emphasis.

96

The internal crisis, on which he naturally fixed his eye, was probably not Edward's main concern. As usual Edward was looking east, interested in foreign affairs, providing for the safety of his kingdom against external dangers; and it does not seem that the quarrel with Godwin was intimately connected with these matters. The West-Saxon family was forced into rebellion, and then exile, because Edward, largely accidentally, but picking up casual profits as they appeared, provoked Godwin beyond endurance so that both men passed beyond the point of no return. The king and his father-in-law quarrelled within a course of events which was largely outside their control, but which their struggle affected. Passions were aroused, extreme attitudes assumed and tenaciously held, while excitement mounted in the country. These histrionic, Anglo-Saxon attitudes create a drama which masks the basic realism, even cynicism of the players. After the quarrel things were not exactly as they were before, but they were not greatly changed.

Edward's foreign policy was defensive, a simple answer to hostile forces.[1] Since he feared Scandinavian pretenders and raiders, his concern was with their traditional forward bases, the harbours of Flanders and Normandy; and since Count Baldwin V (1035–67) was unfriendly, the containment of Flanders was the fixed point on which England's diplomacy turned. Baldwin was one of the greater powers,[2] far stronger than William of Normandy; and Edward recognized his importance. Lying between Flanders and Normandy were the counties of Boulogne and Ponthieu, and inland, south-east of these, was the Vexin—the county of Mantes, Chaumont, and Pontoise. The rulers of all three counties were closely related, and two of them were directly related to Edward. Eustace II, count of Boulogne, Edward's brother-in-law, may even have had a direct interest in the English throne, for it is possible that he had a marriageable daughter in 1049.[3] If this girl existed she would have been Edward's niece, a descendant of Æthelred and Count Richard I of Normandy. Eustace was also a cousin-once-removed of Hugh II, count of Ponthieu,[4] and step-father of Walter III,

---

[1] Cf. Barlow, 'Edward the Confessor's Early Life, Character and Attitudes', *EHR*, lxxx (1965), 237 ff.; Körner, *Battle of Hastings*, pp. 181 ff.

[2] Cf. the panegyrics in Poitiers, pp. 46–50, and in *VEdR*, pp. 54–5.

[3] See below, Appendix C.

[4] In 'The Carmen de Hastingae proelio', *Studies in International History*, ed. K. Bourne and D. C. Watt (1967), pp. 39, 67, following the chronicler, Hariulf, I made Eustace the half-nephew of Hugh II. It seems, however, that Hugh was not his father's son by Adeliva of Ghent, the widow of Arnulf II of Flanders, but by an

count of Mantes, Edward's nephew. The count of Mantes and probably the other two were friendly towards Edward; the count of Ponthieu and probably the others were hostile to Normandy. It is likely that Edward regarded Normandy as a friendly power. His mother was a reminder to the Norman ruling family that they had an interest in the security of the kingdom; and its harbours do not seem to have been available to Edward's enemies. To put pressure on these maritime counties Edward needed the friendship of the greater powers which lay behind; and this he enjoyed. According to the *Vita Ædwardi Regis* both Henry III, the German emperor, and Henry I, king of France, sent embassies to Edward's coronation; and to the best of our knowledge Edward remained on good terms with both.[1] Moreover Edward welcomed overtures from the reformed papacy which was under German patronage.[2]

Edward could read the international situation in so far as it affected England and made a sensible network of alliances against his enemies. What is more, it is hard to believe that there could have been substantial disagreement in England over the grand strategy. But there was plenty of room for dispute over detail. Earl Godwin could have been among those who advocated coming to terms with Denmark and Flanders. Robert of Jumièges could have been a supporter of a closer alliance with Normandy. The composition of Edward's court gave all interests their chance and should have kept him well informed on foreign affairs.

Between 1047 and 1049 Baldwin V's participation in the Lotharingian rebellion against the emperor created two fairly stable rival leagues, which did not exactly represent Edward's own friends and enemies.[3] On the one side was Baldwin, supported by his brother-in-law, the king of France, who, in turn, relied much on his grateful vassal, William of Normandy. On the other side was the emperor, supported by Pope Leo IX, Geoffrey Martel, count of Anjou (until 1050 married to Agnes, the emperor's mother-in-law), and the kings of Denmark and England. These two leagues were never in general action; but in 1049 the emperor, when making a determined effort to put down the rebellion,

---

earlier wife. Nevertheless a close relationship existed between the two counts, for Arnulf I of Flanders married a daughter of Hugh I of Ponthieu. I owe this correction to Miss Hope Muntz and Miss Catherine Morton.

[1] *VEdR*, p. 10, and *nn.* 4–5.
[2] Barlow, *English Church*, pp. 299 ff.
[3] Barlow, 'Edward the Confessor's Early Life', pp. 245 ff.

asked Svein and Edward to give him naval assistance against Flanders;[1] and the king of France led an army through his northern territories in order to encourage Baldwin and annoy Henry III.[2] Edward summoned a large fleet to Sandwich; and, while he carried out a naval blockade, an event in England entirely unconnected with the Flemish war started a series of incidents which gave the king an opportunity to demonstrate and increase his power.

In the summer Earl Swegn, returning in disgrace from Denmark, slipped through the blockade with seven or eight ships and put into Bosham harbour on one of the family estates.[3] He then travelled overland to the royal fleet at Sandwich in search of Edward's pardon. The accounts of what happened at Sandwich are confused and contradictory. We can, however, see that Swegn pinned his hopes on the intercession of his Danish cousin, Earl Beorn; that Beorn either prevaricated or changed his mind; that Earl Harold was implacably opposed to his elder brother's restoration; and that Edward may have taken malicious pleasure in the discomfiture of those who had profited by Swegn's banishment. Finally, when both Beorn and Harold refused to make room in any way for their kinsman, Edward ordered Swegn out of the country and gave him four days in which to return to his ships. At about the same time news arrived that an Irish Viking fleet, in alliance with Gruffydd ap Rhydderch, king of South Wales, was raiding up the Severn and over the Wye into the Forest of Dean. Either late in July or early in August Bishop Ealdred of Worcester with a small army drawn from Gloucestershire and Herefordshire and some Welsh auxiliaries went against the invaders, but was surprised and defeated.[4] No doubt the main military forces of the region were at Sandwich; and Edward dispatched the Wessex squadron, reinforced by two royal ships, a total of forty-four, under Godwin, Beorn (for some reason replacing Harold), and Tostig to go to meet the enemy and, doubtless, keep an eye on Swegn.[5]

By this time the emperor no longer required English forces in the Channel; but no sooner had Edward dismissed the Mercian squadron, retaining only a few ships of his own, than he heard that Osgot Clapa,

---

[1] *Chron.* For Svein, see Florence, i. 201.

[2] Jean Dhondt, 'Henry Ier, L'Empire et L'Anjou (1043-1056)', *Revue Belge de Philologie et d'Histoire*, xxv (1946), 87-109.

[3] *Chron.* Florence, i. 201-2. Plummer, *Two Chronicles*, pp. 229-31.

[4] *Chron.* E; Florence, i. 203. Cf. J. E. Lloyd, *A History of Wales* (3rd ed. 1939), ii. 362.   [5] *Chron. CDE*; Florence, i. 202.

whom he had exiled in 1046, was at Wulpe, near Sluys, in northern Flanders with twenty-nine ships, having, presumably, followed Swegn from Denmark.[1] Edward urgently recalled the Mercian squadron to meet this new threat, and Osgot, probably alerted to the hazards, disembarked his wife at nearby Bruges, and waited with six ships at Wulpe while the rest of his fleet successfully raided Essex. The raiders were caught in a storm on the way home and the few survivors were captured and massacred somewhere abroad, we are not told where. Osgot possibly returned to Denmark.

Meanwhile the Wessex squadron had made little progress and lay weather bound at Pevensey.[2] Two days after their arrival Swegn joined them and once more appealed to Beorn for help with the king. Possibly because Harold was not there to steady him, Beorn agreed. Whatever assurances Swegn may have offered,[3] Beorn clearly relied on their kinship and took only three men with him for the journey. But, instead of riding east for Sandwich, Swegn got him on some pretext to travel west with him to Bosham.[4] There Beorn was overpowered and carried aboard; Swegn's fleet sailed further west, past Wight and Portland; and at Dartmouth Beorn was murdered and buried on shore.[5] As Swegn could have killed Beorn as easily at Bosham as at Dartmouth, there must have been a further quarrel. It is obvious that Swegn believed that Beorn owed him some service or restitution; but whatever the rights and wrongs in this affair, Swegn's crime was enormous. Harold had his cousin's body recovered and removed to Winchester, where, in the presence of a large concourse of his friends and sailors from London, probably the *lithsmen* whom he may have commanded,[6] he was buried with his uncle Cnut in the Old Minster. Then King Edward and the whole army declared Swegn *nithing*,[7] a scoundrel, a man utterly and irreparably disgraced.

On the evidence, none of Swegn's kin actively supported him in

[1] *Chron. CD*; Florence, i. 202. Twenty-nine ships, *C*, Florence; thirty-nine, *D*. Florence at least makes sense of a not very clear annal.

[2] *Chron. CDE*; Florence, i. 202–3.

[3] *C* states that he offered oaths.

[4] *E*, which tells the story in most detail, has Beorn lured to Bosham by the fable that there was the danger of Swegn's ships deserting.

[5] At Dartmouth, *CD*, Florence; 'they ran west to Axmouth, and kept Beorn with them until they killed him', *E*, which is probably a mistake, although it is not necessarily in contradiction to the others.

[6] *Chron. E*; and see below, p. 102.

[7] *Chron. C*.

1049. It was Swegn, not Beorn, who was the outsider. We can, there-fore, hardly believe the interpretation offered by Adam of Bremen.[1] Adam, who thought that Edward had just named Svein Estrithson of Denmark as his heir, imagined that the sons of Godwin conspired to thwart the plan. They destroyed Svein's prospects in England by, on the one hand, getting rid of his brothers – killing Beorn and exiling Osbeorn – and, on the other, by depriving Edward of everything except his life and the empty title of king. This story contributes little more than the mystery of Osbeorn's career in England. Adam thought that he was an English earl like Beorn; but he cannot be identified as a witness to charters; and his one certain appearance on English soil was in 1069–70, when he invaded William's realm with his brother's navy.[2] Perhaps the main value of Adam's story is in showing that garbled versions of English history were current in the north. But whatever the true explanation of Beorn's death the event cannot have improved relations between the English and Danish royal courts. Moreover, this time Earl Swegn did not go to Denmark. After the murder six of his ships deserted, and of these two were captured by the men of Hastings, who killed the crews and took the ships to Edward still at Sandwich. Swegn with his remaining two vessels sailed for Bruges and was given asylum by Count Baldwin.[3]

In a poem on Godwin's children the anonymous author of the *Vita Ædwardi Regis* describes in obscure imagery the evil part of the family, possibly Swegn.[4] The children are imagined first as the four rivers flowing out of Paradise (Gen. ii. 10), then as trees, family trees. In contrast to the good part, which climbs the skies and, clinging to heaven, fosters its offspring in a nest in a high tree, 'this devouring monster plunges to the depths of the ocean, and, when it suffers damage to its stock, holds the parent trunk hanging from its mouth, while at the appointed time the breath of life creates a living creature from a lifeless mother. Then, once more free, it returns to its plundering.' There is no one but Swegn who can qualify for this part; but it is difficult to identify even his notorious crimes in the passage.

After the excitement of 1049 England settled down to peace. The annal for 1050 has the brevity of a tranquil year; indeed the only royal

---

[1] Adam of Bremen, III, xiv; pp. 154–5. According to schol. 64, 'Harold autem cum esset vir fortissimus, . . . Suein regem Danorum ab Anglia propulit.'

[2] *Chron. DE*, s.a. 1069, *E*, s.a. 1070.

[3] *Chron. CDE*; Florence, i. 203.   [4] *VEdR*, pp. 15–16.

acts described are acts of appeasement. In mid-Lent at a council in London it was decided to pay off nine of the fourteen foreign ships which Edward had been retaining as a standing fleet, and offer only a year's contract to the remainder.[1] In the summer Edward pardoned Earl Swegn.[2] If Beorn had been the captain of the royal fleet,[3] both these events were probably consequences of his death. The London council was an opportunity for Edward's earls and captains to review the military events of the previous year. If Earl Leofric, with his distrust of Danes and dislike of foreign adventure, took the same line as in 1047,[4] he would have argued that, as peace had returned and the English navy was large, Edward should get rid of a burdensome and useless foreign squadron. He and his friends could also have added that England groaned under the burden of *heregeld*, the tax levied to support the royal mercenaries, first imposed by Æthelred some forty years before.[5] Moreover, with Beorn dead, the West-Saxon family had no particular interest in the royal navy; and Godwin, negotiating for Swegn's return, would have wished to avoid awkwardness at any cost. It is most unlikely that Edward was coerced; his personal power was reaching its peak. He was given bad advice and was so ill-advised as to take it. It is likely that he too associated his Viking fleet with the house of Godwin and Scandinavian entanglements. If Beorn had been in command he could have regarded it as a threat to his independence. But by dismissing the mercenary fleet after Beorn's death Edward threw away an opportunity. Although he behaved as though he had gained new freedom and risked some of the most arbitrary and hazardous actions of his reign, it was the lack of a dependable fleet which contributed to their failure. It may well be that the royal ships had not been particularly useful in 1049; but Edward, even if he had forgotten the services which Thorkell Hávi had rendered his family in 1012–16, should have learned from the events of 1049 how desirable it was to have a loyal squadron under his immediate command.

Even more extraordinary was the pardoning of Earl Swegn. Bishop

---

[1] *Chron. C* (1049); *E* (1050).

[2] *Chron. CE*; 'came into England', *E*; 'was reinstated', *C*. Florence, i. 203, 'ibi mansit quoad . . . Aldredus illum reduceret et cum rege pacificaret.'

[3] *Chron. E* specially mentions that Beorn's friends and the *lithsmen* of London went to Winchester for his funeral.

[4] Above, p. 92.

[5] *Chron. D*, *s.a.* 1051; Florence, i. 204; thirty-ninth year, *D*; thirty-eighth, Florence.

Ealdred of Worcester, on his return journey with Bishop Herman of Ramsbury from Leo IX's Easter council at Rome, apparently met the outlaw in Flanders and brought him back to meet the king.[1] Edward may have restored Swegn to some of his honours and in the summer the earl's name appears once more in the witness list to a charter.[2] Presumably Ealdred was convinced that Swegn was penitent and would do penance for his sins. Obviously few in high position regarded the debauching of an abbess or the murder of a cousin as inexpiable crimes. Ealdred could have explained that the temptations had been great. The elimination of Beorn cannot have been regretted by all; and Beorn's death made lands available for Swegn. Edward may still have thought that by pardoning Swegn he was really injuring the family. Godwin may have begged for it, and Harold this time must have acquiesced. The other earls may have thought it a largely private affair; it was no direct concern of theirs. Also in the summer of 1050 Edward made a grant of land to his 'faithful earl', Godwin.[3] The royal family was still holding together, although the concord was possibly bought by concessions made by leading members in turn.

While Edward weakened himself in England by imprudent actions, the situation on the Continent also changed to his disadvantage. In 1049 William of Normandy, possibly with the encouragement of his overlord, the king of France, possibly moving in a direction dictated by his own ambitions, proclaimed his alliance with Baldwin of Flanders by seeking to marry his daughter.[4] This reinforcement of Baldwin's position displeased the emperor; Pope Leo IX at the council of Rheims forbade the marriage; and Edward could only have regarded the alliance between the two maritime powers with anxiety, although he

---

[1] Florence, i. 203; Plummer, *Two Chronicles*, pp. 233-4.

[2] Swegn's position in 1050-1 is most obscure. *Chron. CE* notice Swegn's return, but *C* alone states that he 'was reinstated'. *D*'s silence, followed by Florence, is surprising. Florence, however, *s.a.* 1049 (i. 203), reports that Swegn remained in Flanders until Bishop Ealdred of Worcester brought him back 'et cum rege pacificaret', and, following *D*, has Swegn in the autumn of 1050 raise troops from his earldom, which is described (i. 205). There is also Swegn's attestation of one version of an Exeter charter of 1050, *Ordnance Survey Facsimiles*, ii, Exeter 13 (Sawyer, no. 1021). It is possible that Edward promised Swegn restitution and that Swegn met with local opposition, especially from the French garrisons. *Chron. E*, although *s.a.* 1051 calling Herefordshire Swegn's province, does not refer to Swegn's earldom when describing the distribution of the spoils after the disgrace of Godwin and his sons.

[3] *KCD*, no. 793 (Sawyer, no. 1022); Barlow, *English Church*, p. 154.

[4] See Barlow, 'Edward the Confessor's Early Life', p. 246, *n.* 3.

may have hoped that William would use his influence to reduce Baldwin's ill will.

In 1051 all the affairs in which Edward was most concerned came to a head and severely tested his political skill. He solved each problem in turn, adroitly and economically; and, although each solution may have increased the difficulty of the next problem, for twelve months he could not put a foot wrong. His ability is shown by the fact that, while in almost every crisis there were physical threats and even demonstrations of force, he did not have to fight. The way in which he kept his nerve is impressive. It turned out, however, that he had been mistaken in always aiming at complete success, that by climbing too high he merely increased the distance he had to fall. Indeed, it is apparent that Edward had made a false assessment of his resources; and on this account his political wisdom – as distinct from his cleverness – must be doubted. But, as crisis followed crisis, and Edward came stronger out of each, it must have seemed that nothing could break the run of good luck.

Decisions taken at a council held, as in the previous year, in London in mid-Lent determined most of the political events of the year. Of great importance, and capable of dividing the court, was the ecclesiastical business. On 29 October 1050 Eadsige, archbishop of Canterbury, who had resumed his duties in 1048, died at last, and on 22 January Ælfric Puttoc of York followed him into the grave. The vacancy of both metropolitan sees meant that there would be considerable disturbance in the church, for it was usual to promote diocesan bishops; and it was possibly solely for this reason that the business was not formally concluded until March 1051. The delay, however, allowed factions to emerge. The Canterbury monks wished to elect one of their own number, Ælric, a kinsman of Earl Godwin; and they persuaded the earl to support their candidate.[1] But the king, or the court party, was not prepared to make any concession to the local interest and every promotion went to a royal favourite. Robert of Jumièges, bishop of London, was translated to Canterbury; Spearhavoc, abbot of Abingdon and the king's goldsmith,[2] was given London and paid Stigand for the promotion;[3] and to Abingdon was sent a Scandinavian bishop, Rothulf, a

[1] VEdR, pp. 18–19.

[2] He mislaid a precious ring of Queen Edith before 1046, Goscelin, Historia translationis S. Augustini episcopi, in Migne, PL, clv, col. 46; and, as he was working on a royal commission in 1051, he was certainly persona grata to Edward and most likely the king's personal choice.

[3] Chron. Florence, i. 204; Chron. Abingdon, i. 462–3.

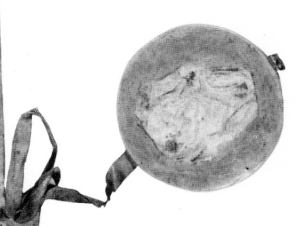

5. A writ of Edward in favour of Westminster abbey (Westminster abbey muniments, XII) to be dated Christmas 1065. See Harmer, *Writs*, no. 96. *(Courtesy Dean and Chapter of Westminster.)*

6. *(overleaf)* A writ of Edward in favour of Saint-Denis, Paris (Archives Nationales, Paris, K. 19, no. 6), to be dated 1053–7, superimposed on the lower part of a charter of Edward, dated 1059, with which it is connected. (See Harmer, *Writs*, no. 55, and pp. 35–6, 243–4, 538–9.) Edward's seal which was originally attached to the writ is now loose. Photographs of its reverse and obverse have here been superimposed. The seal, in brown wax, is one of three known impressions of the only authentic Great Seal of the Confessor, erroneously called the 'second seal'. *(Courtesy Pierre Chaplais, and Manchester University Press for the Seal.)*

Ante domince incarnacionis $\overline{\text{M. L. IX}}$

Anno domince incarnacionis $\overline{\text{M. L. IX}}$ scripta est. hec cartula huic cartis, conscripta

ab. quæ nonnulli inseruntur cartula. signo agie crucis ... condonaui.

+ Ego EDVVARDVS rex eternus br ... ulo concessi

+ Ego EADGYÐ contectalis eiusdem ... cum ...

+ Ego Stigand metropolitan xpi ... quis cum ptophro

+ Ego Kynsinus elmacensis ecclesie archi epc ... fratrum muris consolidaui

+ Ego Wlfsinus Scypealttensis ecclesie epc ... + Ego harold dux

+ Ego Godrico epc conclusi

+ Ego Stigar

+ Ego Gyrð dux + Ego Vlf

Leoðpald cunæ ghter uulpps biscop ... ealle mine þegenas ...

+ Ego Baldum Sci Byonsti monachus. sub regimine abbarð in byʒonis conscripta...
ʒlorum Regis EDVVARDT metlucus. omib; quoð hic adnotata sunt nomina sine cartula ...
scripta huius donacionis confirmaui. de manu eius ... regis ... imperam Sco Dyoni
sio habendi S. V. S. EPI:

kinsman of Edward.[1] Either at this council or shortly afterwards a royal clerk, Cynsige, was appointed to York.[2]

Edward probably disappointed the hopes of not a few candidates and their supporters. The men chosen were respectable if not particularly distinguished; but there was no party devoted to the promotion of the holiest or most deserving men. The views of the monks of Christ Church, Canterbury, had been disregarded. It may be that Stigand, bishop of Elmham and Winchester, already had his eye on Canterbury.[3] Robert of Jumièges, it seems, had wanted William, a royal clerk and another Norman, to succeed him at London.[4] It is possible that Ealdred had hoped to get York, for the tradition that the bishop of Worcester should also hold the northern metropolitan see was strong. We know that Abingdon did not want Rothulf.[5] In these appointments Edward had pleased himself. He had opposed local connexions, refused advice proffered to him, and routed opposition. In all this he was not doing wrong; but those whose advice he disregarded thought that he was ill-advised,[6] and apparently Earl Godwin took the hardest knocks. Godwin may still have been paying for Swegn's pardon, and prepared to pay even more for his son's complete reinstatement; but there was a limit to the demands he would meet; and it seems that he was pressed unconscionably. Moreover, the promotion of Robert of Jumièges probably brought the feud between the bishop and the earl for the first time into the open. Godwin saw the favourite whom he disliked obtain the highest position in the English church, and Robert from this vantage point thought that he could attack the earl.[7] The archbishop accused Godwin of having usurped lands belonging to both the archiepiscopal and the monastic estate, and, as the quarrel sharpened, reported

[1] *Chron. E, Chron. Abingdon,* i. 463–4.

[2] Ælfric's death is mentioned by *Chron. CD,* but only Florence, i. 204, names his successor.

[3] According to *Chron. Abingdon,* i. 462, Stigand was administering Canterbury after the death of Eadsige when he extorted Cerney (Glos) (cf. *DB,* i. 169 a i) from Spearhavoc. This may be a mistake; but the occasion is clearly indicated.

[4] Immediately after Spearhavoc had been expelled, William was given London (*Chron. D*) and consecrated bishop (*Chron. E*).

[5] *Chron. Abingdon,* i. 463–4. Rothulf was old (he was abbot for less than two years) and Abingdon was promised free election on his death.

[6] After Godwin had returned in 1052 all the Frenchmen who had given bad counsel (*unraed raeddon*) were outlawed (*Chron. CD*). Archbishop Robert's banishment 'was God's will, in that he had obtained the dignity when it was not God's will' (*E*). *VEdR,* pp. 17 ff., regards Edward as completely misguided.

[7] *VEdR,* pp. 19 ff. Cf. also D. R. Bates in *Bull. Inst. Hist. Research,* Li (1978), 16.

malicious stories to the king, including, we are told, the incredible, but damaging, slander that just as Godwin had murdered Edward's brother, so now he was plotting to kill Edward himself.

Nor was this the only dissension that Robert's promotion caused. On his return in June from Rome with the pallium he refused to consecrate Spearhavoc as bishop of London on the grounds that the pope had forbidden him to do so.[1] Since it was unprecedented for the pope to interfere with episcopal appointments in England, Robert must himself have secured the prohibition by informing the pope that Spearhavoc was unworthy of consecration, probably by alleging simony. Robert's behaviour may have been justified; but the action further irritated an inflamed situation. Edward had apparently commissioned Spearhavoc to make him a new 'imperial' crown (a commission possibly of significance for Edward's state of mind), and with the king's consent the bishop-elect remained in possession of London during the summer and autumn.[2] Edward was not completely under Robert's thumb, as some of Godwin's friends thought. On St Peter's day 1050 Edward went to Exeter for the enthronement of his clerk, Leofric;[3] but on the same day one year later he was not, apparently, at Canterbury for Robert's installation.[4]

The mid-Lent London council also considered some important secular business. It allowed the last five mercenary ships to leave, it suspended, for a time at least, the collection of *heregeld*,[5] and it probably put the final touches to a treaty with William of Normandy. All these matters were probably connected. An alliance with Normandy could have been used as an argument that a standing fleet was no longer

---

[1] *Chron. E.*   [2] *Chron. Abingdon*, i. 463; *Chron. E.*

[3] Barlow, *English Church*, pp. 116–17, 154.

[4] *Chron. E* makes the point.

[5] The Chronicle states that *heregeld* was abolished, and does not mention it again until after the Conquest. Nevertheless there has not been general acceptance of a long suspension. Cf. Paul Vinogradoff, *English Society in the Eleventh Century*, p. 141, 'Only a temporary respite can have been meant.' Clinching evidence is hard to find. Numismatic evidence (below, p. 184) does not support a long period of freedom; there are references in *DB* which suggest that geld was usually collected, e.g. 'quando geldum dabatur tempore regis Eadwardi communiter per totam Berchesciram', i. 56 b i; and there is the Bury St Edmunds writ, Harmer, no. 15. This includes Earl Ælfgar in the address to the shire courts of Norfolk and Suffolk, and so must be dated October 1051–October 1052 or 1053–7. By the writ Edward frees the 'inland' of the monastery from payment of *heregeld* and all other renders (*gafol*). Such an exemption could have been obtained *ad majorem cautelam*; but it was certainly obtained after the alleged abolition of geld.

necessary. We know of the Norman negotiations only from Norman writers at work after 1071, who used them to justify William's invasion and conquest of England. And although we are probably not dealing with a completely fictitious case, it is an *ex parte* and *ex post facto* statement, rather similar in character to Svein Estrithson's story as reported by Adam of Bremen.

The most elaborate version is given by William of Poitiers, archdeacon of Lisieux, an avowed panegyrist and pleader, who informs us that Edward, with the agreement of his *witan*, appointed William as his heir for three reasons:[1] first, because he was indebted to William and his family for many benefits and honours, especially for help in obtaining the throne; second, because of their kinship; and third, because William was the most fitted of all his relatives to give him aid during his lifetime and succeed him after his death. William of Poitiers names 'Archbishop' Stigand and Earls Godwin, Leofric, and Siward as the principal counsellors who took a corporeal oath that they would accept William as their lord after Edward's death; and he further informs us that Edward sent Robert, archbishop of Canterbury, to make this grant to William and that Edward sent as hostages a son and grandson of Earl Godwin. If the chronicler has made no error in Robert's rank, the embassy was presumably in the spring of 1051, the first stage of Robert's journey to Rome for the pallium.[2] William was twenty-three years old.

Unless we choose either to reject the Norman story out of hand or to swallow it whole, we have to reconstruct it in its historical context. There is every likelihood that Edward was engaged in negotiations with

---

[1] Poitiers, pp. 30–2, 100, 158, 168, 174–6; cf. Jumièges, p. 132. Poitiers states the terms of the treaty in technical language. The consideration for the grant are *dona*, *beneficia*, and *honores* which Edward has received from William (pp. 30, 158, 174). In return Edward appointed William his heir: *haeredem statuere decrevit* (p. 30), *sibi succedere statuit* (p. 168), *me haeredem statuit* (p. 174); and accepted him as a son: *Edwardi regis adoptio, filii loco* (p. 168); cf. *quem loco germani aut prolis adamabat* (p. 100). Such adoptions are discussed, *Histoire des Relations Internationales*, ed. Pierre Renouvin; vol. i: François L. Ganshof, *Le Moyen Age* (Hachette, 1953), pp. 44–5. See also, Raymonde Foreville, 'Aux origines de la renaissance juridique: Concepts juridiques et influences romanisantes chez Guillaume de Poitiers, biographe du Conquérant', *Moyen âge*, lviii (1952), 61 ff.

[2] *Chron. CE*. The obvious error in the story – the description of Stigand as archbishop – is of no consequence; but it does remind us that William of Poitiers could have made a similar mistake with regard to Robert. Hence, although we have a firm *terminus ad quem* (1052) for the mission, we have no secure *terminus a quo*. All the same the transaction fits neatly into the events of 1051.

William in 1051, for Norman friendship was one of the keys to England's security; and Robert of Jumièges might be expected to be an advocate of a treaty and to be appointed the English ambassador if his advice was taken. Beyond this point the discussion becomes much more speculative. The archdeacon, writing long after the event, obviously had no first-class source at his disposal. He made a mistake over Stigand's title, could not name the hostages, and omitted Harold, earl of East Anglia, from the body of magnates who swore to observe the treaty. As it would have strengthened the Norman case considerably to have brought Harold into the story at this point, and in 1073 historical accuracy did not matter, we can only conclude that William of Poitiers did not realize that Harold was one of the greater earls in 1051, and that the list was fabricated by the archdeacon himself in order to provide circumstantial detail.

There is also a major improbability in the structure of the story. Although treaties were normally ratified by the exchange of oaths and hostages,[1] we read only of the English obligations and of Godwin's hostages. We need point to but one event to show how unlikely such conditions were: when Edward banished Godwin's family later in 1051, the duke was left without a security in England. What William needed was hostages from all the great earls. Moreover, although it was in the Norman interest in 1051 to commit Godwin and the rest of his family to the terms, and in 1073 to suggest that he and Harold had given their willing adherence, it is by no means certain that Godwin gave hostages at this time.[2] And, even if he did, it would not have been because he was a supporter of a scheme which insulted his daughter and was advocated by his enemy, Robert of Jumièges, but rather because his opposition to it had been overcome. He may well have favoured the alternative plan of coming to terms with Flanders. In October his third son, Tostig, married Judith, the half-sister of Baldwin,[3] and it was to Flanders that Godwin and Tostig fled shortly afterwards.

The Norman picture of Edward, anxious to repay a debt of gratitude nine years old, also seems out of character. Nor should we take too seriously William of Poitiers' view that Edward was the debtor and solicitor, anxious to confer a benefit on William, for the panegyrist never shows William as a petitioner. When we consider that in 1051

---

[1] *Histoire des Relations Internationales*; vol. i: François L. Ganshof, *Le Moyen Age*, pp. 47, 130–1.

[2] See below, Appendix B.   [3] *VEdR*, pp. 24–5.

William was a youthful count of little note, still in some danger, almost certainly a suitor for the hand of Matilda of Flanders, it is equally probable that William was courting his childless kinsman in England. We need not press this point too hard. In 1051 there may have been a desire on both sides for a treaty of friendship, Edward looking for security, William for prestige. And William, by negotiating with Baldwin, Edward's enemy, could have blackmailed Edward into granting terms specially advantageous to him. But even if Edward did nominate William as his heir in 1051, this clause should not be given the importance that it eventually assumed. Edward could have made the offer merely to annoy his wife's family. Or he could have regarded it as a diplomatic card which could be played repeatedly, now recognizing Svein Estrithson as his heir, now William of Normandy. Nor need he have limited his play so narrowly. Diplomatic promises were cheap. In any case, in 1051 Edward had fifteen more years of active life. No one could have expected that a bequest drawn up in that year would ever be paid.

It is not necessary to explain Godwin's growing despair in 1051 as being caused by Edward's foreign policy. The earl was out of favour, was not listened to, and was being harassed by Robert of Jumièges. By the end of the summer he had obviously taken all that he could stand, and it needed only one more affront to provoke a desperate act. About the beginning of September Eustace of Boulogne came on a visit to his brother-in-law's court, 'told him what he wished', and then went home.[1] The visit was probably connected with Edward's diplomatic relations with the maritime powers; but, although Eustace may have been acting on behalf of Baldwin or William, it is much more likely that he came to promote the interests of his own family. If he had a daughter, there could have been the question of her marriage, for a grandson of Eustace and Godgifu would have stood with Eustace's step-sons, Walter, count of the Vexin, and Earl Ralf, as a possible heir to Edward. All this group may have considered that their claim to the English throne was better than William's or Svein's; they were Edward's, as opposed to his mother's or step-father's, kin; and they may well have wanted at this time to know where they stood.

---

[1] *Chron. E*, cf. *D*; in September, Florence, i. 204. See Plummer, *Two Chronicles*, pp. 235–6. Körner, *Battle of Hastings*, pp. 36–43, when considering the annals for 1051–2, regards *D* as closer to the underlying source because *E* looks as though it has been revised to show Godwin in a better light. This may well be so; but it does not mean that *D* should always be preferred to *E*.

More important, perhaps, than the results of Eustace's mission was the effect of an affray in which he was involved at Dover. The northern (D) version of the Chronicle ascribes it to Eustace's outward journey and has the count then take refuge with the king at Gloucester. The St Augustine's, Canterbury, (E) version maintains that the fracas took place on the return journey, after Eustace had taken refreshments at Canterbury, and that after the disturbance Eustace went back to Gloucester to complain to the king. The authority of E for events which occurred so close to Canterbury cannot be impugned; the D story is probably a simplification. There is, however, no fundamental disagreement over what happened at Dover. Eustace's party required accommodation, and, possibly because of incidents on the outward journey or because it was suspected that Godwin had given orders that they were not to be entertained, they put on their mail outside the town and tried to intimidate the burgesses. According to 'Florence', 'When Eustace's soldiers went ineptly and foolishly in search of lodgings a citizen was killed, and a fellow citizen killed one of the soldiers in revenge. Tempers flared. The count and his men slew a number of men and women with their swords and trampled babies and children to death under their horses' hooves. But when they saw other townsfolk rushing up to join in the fight, they turned tail and fled like cowards, escaping only with difficulty and at the cost of seven dead.'[1] When Eustace reported the incident to the king, Edward accepted the view that Dover was to blame and may have ordered Godwin to punish the town.[2]

It needed little to convince some of Godwin's men that the arrogance of Edward's French friends had become unbearable and little to convince the French favourites that Godwin was seeking their destruction and with theirs the king's. The hothead on Godwin's side was probably Swegn, a man of many grievances, especially resentful of the French colony in Herefordshire, and possibly not yet completely restored to his old earldom. On the other side we gather that Robert of Jumièges, Eustace of Boulogne, and Osbern Pentecost, lord and castellan of Ewias Harold, with his comrade-in-arms, Hugh, were urging Edward to take action against Godwin and his family.[3] Observers favourable to the West-Saxon earl thought that Edward was

---

[1] Florence, i. 204. E puts the casualties as: men of Dover, dead, more than twenty; Eustace's men, dead, nineteen, wounded, unknown. D puts men of Dover, dead, one; Eustace's men, dead, seven.   [2] *Chron.* E only.

[3] For Osbern and Hugh, see J. H. Round, 'Normans under Edward the Confessor', *Feudal England*, pp. 320–6.

not directly involved in the quarrel, that, although he came down heavily on the side of the French, he was simply ill-advised and misled.[1] There is at least a grain of truth here: Edward never completely surrendered to any one group, and in 1051 he behaved much more cautiously than the extremists desired. The other earls, as we can see from their actions, had no great interest in the quarrel. They would protect and support the king; they would, perhaps, welcome a check to Godwin's ambition; but they had no wish to see new men, especially strangers, have it all their own way. In these conditions Edward's success was all the more remarkable.

It was probably when Eustace made his complaint or when Godwin refused to 'carry war into Kent' that Edward summoned his council and army to Gloucester for 7 September.[2] The exact sequence of events is not clear, but the general picture is that each side made accusations against the other while it mobilized, and each exchange stimulated further military preparation. Godwin demanded the surrender of Eustace and perhaps of some of the French garrisons in Herefordshire;[3] Robert of Jumièges accused Godwin of planning the king's death.[4] Godwin and his sons, Swegn and Harold, summoned the armies of their earldoms to Beverstone, fifteen miles south of Gloucester, on the Bristol–Oxford road, where they were well placed to threaten the king.[5] In the other camp, Earl Ralf brought in his troops to protect his uncle and step-father, while Earls Leofric and Siward sent urgently for reinforcements. Edward negotiated with the malcontents while they were strong and he weak; and although, as he grew in strength, he was urged, probably by 'the French',[6] to attack the rebels, there is no suggestion that he was seriously tempted to fight.

[1] *Chron. E* and *VEdR.*

[2] *Chron. E* for the quotation and date; cf. *D*, Florence, i. 205–6, *VEdR*, pp. 20–1.

[3] Eustace and the Frenchmen in the *castelle*, *D*; Florence, i. 205–6, explains this as 'Count Eustace and his companions, as well as the Normans and men of Boulogne who held the *castellum* on the heights of Dover.' *E* does not specify Godwin's demands, but mentions the foreigners (*welisce*) who had built a *castel* in Herefordshire in Earl Swegn's province and were doing injury to the king's men in those parts. To judge by the sequel, the castle in question was at Ewias Harold and the castellan Osbern Pentecost; see Round, *ut supra.*   [4] *VEdR*, pp. 20–1.

[5] According to Malmesbury, *GR*, i. 242, they gave out that they were preparing an expedition against the Welsh, which is a mistranslation of *Chron. E*, Plummer, *Two Chronicles*, p. 237.

[6] Both *Chron. D* and *E* agree that the earls with the king were prepared to go with him against the rebels. According to *E* it was the foreigners, presumably the French garrisons in Herefordshire, who encouraged the king to action.

The two armies were probably well matched; and there was always a middle party, perhaps led by Leofric, which tried to get a peaceful settlement.[1] The only possible compromise was a legal trial; and in the end it was decided that Godwin and his sons should be tried in a council summoned to London for 21 September. There was talk of hostages;[2] but even if some loyalists agreed with Godwin that a treaty was being negotiated and hostages should be given by both sides, Edward, although maintaining a show of impartiality, seems never to have moved from the view that whereas the rebels must give surety that they would stand their trial, he had no obligations to the rebels. And if it was at this time that Godwin and Swegn each surrendered the son who later was held in Normandy, their bitterness and growing despair is understandable. They had been tricked into a dependence on the king's mercy when they knew that Edward and some of his most trusted advisers were actuated solely by *ira et malevolentia*. Nor is it clear what charges Godwin and his sons were to answer, although the chroniclers may have thought the rebellion and treason self-evident.[3] Time was on the king's side. While he remained firm the position of the rebels crumbled. He sapped their strength by summoning the army from the whole of England to be at London for the meeting.[4] As Godwin and his sons followed the southern route to London, some of their thegns deserted to the royal army; Edward outlawed Swegn out of hand,[5] probably because he had

---

[1] *Chron. E* seems to ascribe peace moves to the *witan* as distinct from the loyal earls. *Chron. D* implies that some of the earls became peacemakers because they suspected the secret motives of the foreigners. Florence, i. 206, expands by naming Earl Leofric among those who thought that an attack on Earl Godwin would be *magnum insilium = mycel unraed. Chron. E* views the king as mediating between, or doing justice to, hostile parties.

[2] *Chron. D* and Florence, i. 206, mention negotiations over hostages at this point; *E* transfers these talks to London. It is not unreasonable to think that there was a running debate on the matter. If so, Florence's alteration of *D*'s 'they (royal counsellors) advised the exchange of hostages' to 'hostages were mutually exchanged' is wrong. But it is possible that Godwin gave sureties at Gloucester and considered himself defrauded when the king gave none in return. See below, Appendix B.

[3] The only charge explicitly mentioned in *Chron.* is one attributed to the foreigners at Gloucester, that the rebel earls intended to betray the king (*E*). Even if 'a Frenchman' raised the issue of Alfred's death (*VEdR*, pp. 20–2), it is hardly likely that this would have been a count at the trial. Perhaps we are told only of the wilder accusations.

[4] The *folc* from the earldoms of Siward and Leofric and from elsewhere, *Chron. D*; the best of the *here* from both north and south of the Thames, *E*. Florence, i. 206, cuts 'and from elsewhere' from *D*.

[5] *Chron. E* has the judgment passed at Gloucester when Edward summoned the

forfeited his recent pardon by his behaviour; and by the time that the king and his father-in-law were once more face to face, this time on opposite banks of the Thames, Edward had achieved a decisive military superiority.

Godwin was on his manor of Southwark,[1] apparently deserted by all but his family and a military escort. Edward pressed his advantage home. He summoned Godwin to his trial (perhaps technically the second summons) and, when the earl asked for a safe-conduct and hostages, demanded the transfer to himself of all the thegns still with the rebels. Godwin complied,[2] but got nothing in return. Once again Edward summoned Godwin and his sons to attend the council, ordering them to appear with a suite of twelve men; and once more Godwin requested a safe-conduct and hostages. It is easy to imagine what Godwin feared. According to his panegyrist his one demand was for a lawful trial and the opportunity to purge himself of the crimes with which he was charged. He would offer the satisfaction which the law demanded; he would undergo the ordeal.[3] As we do not know the charges we cannot speculate on the proof-judgment that the court would have awarded. Godwin probably hoped that he would be allowed to meet each charge with his unsupported oath, but feared that he might be assigned multiple oaths or an ordeal beyond his capability. He knew that the court would be hostile to him; he may even have suspected that enemies might have assassins in wait. He would not cross the river and put himself in Edward's power without a safe-conduct and hostages. But the king was probably well within his rights in refusing to give such assurances to men accused of crimes. And so there was no trial and no legal judgments.[4] Edward had not allowed Godwin to stand trial in order to let him escape.

Bishop Stigand of Winchester was the intermediary between Edward and Godwin; and it was probably when he crossed to Southwark to convey the king's final rejection of the earl's request for sureties that he

army and the accused to London. *Chron. D* ascribes it to London after Godwin had transferred all his thegns to the king.

[1] *Chron. D*, Florence, i. 206; cf. *VEdR*, p. 21.

[2] 'Then the king asked for all those thegns that the earls had had, and they were all handed over to him', *Chron. E*. 'And all the thegns of Harold his son were transferred to the king's allegiance', *D*. See Plummer, *Two Chronicles*, p. 237.

[3] *VEdR*, pp. 21–2, cf. p. 26. For the judicial procedure, see M. M. Bigelow, *History of procedure in England from the Norman Conquest* (1880), chs. VI–X.

[4] Edward's 'insoluble judgment' reported by Stigand (*VEdR*, p. 22) can hardly be regarded as the final judgment of a lawful court.

reported Edward's grimly jesting judgment that Godwin could have his peace and pardon if he could restore to him his brother Alfred and all his companions.[1] The bishop was in tears and Godwin knew that he could not win. He pushed away the table at which he had been standing, mounted his horse, and fled. He was refusing to obey the third and final summons to attend the court and plead to the charges; he was, therefore, contumacious and liable to other penalties. The family, either immediately or later on the journey, split into two parties. Godwin, his wife Gytha, and their sons, Swegn and Tostig, with Archbishop Robert in pursuit, rode to their manor at Bosham and embarked at Thorney Island for Flanders. Harold and Leofwine took the road for Bristol, where Swegn had a ship prepared, and sailed for Ireland.[2] Meanwhile, the morning after the flight, Edward with his council and army declared the fugitives outlaws.[3] They had refused to observe the law and were now deprived of its protection. Edward sent Bishop Ealdred in pursuit of those fleeing to the west; but the bishop probably tempered duty with discretion.[4]

This was Edward's day of triumph. He had achieved a spectacular success. The northern chronicler (D) wrote, 'No one in England would have believed that such a remarkable thing could happen, for Godwin had been raised so high that he ruled the king and all England, his sons were earls and royal favourites, and his daughter was married to the king.' It was also, as the *Vita Ædwardi Regis* makes clear,[5] a triumph for Robert of Jumièges; and it was essential for Robert that the revolution should not be undone. He must have known full well that if Godwin returned he could expect no mercy. He must, therefore, have urged on Edward measures designed to block the exiles' restoration. The earldoms of Godwin, Swegn, Harold, and Beorn were in the king's hands. It is possible that Ralf of Mantes was already holding Hereford, Gloucester, Oxford, and Berkshire (Swegn's earldom minus Somerset).[6] Edward granted to Odda of Deerhurst some of Godwin's shires, Corn-

---

[1] *VEdR*, p. 22.

[2] Godwin and Swegn to Bosham, Harold to Ireland, *Chron. E*; Godwin and his wife, Swegn, Tostig and his wife, and Gyrth, well provided with treasure, to Thorney and Bruges, Harold and Leofwine to Bristol and Ireland, *D*, cf. *C*. Florence, i. 206, expands *D* by naming Gytha and Judith. Cf. *VEdR*, pp. 22–5, where the king of Ireland is named.

[3] *Chron. D*, followed by Florence, i. 206. *Chron. E* omits the outlawry and states that Godwin was given five days' safe-conduct to leave the country.

[4] *Chron. D*.   [5] *VEdR*, pp. 17 ff.

[6] Florence, i. 205, ascribes these five shires to Swegn in 1051.

wall, Devon, Dorset, and Somerset, and to Ælfgar, Earl Leofric's son, Harold's earldom of East Anglia.[1] It is possible that Edward kept Wiltshire, Hampshire, Surrey, Sussex, and Kent for himself, although it is not unlikely that, since Archbishop Eadsige had held Kent,[2] Robert claimed the shire as his share of the spoils. Robert also saw to it that Spearhavoc was expelled from London, although Edward probably had no wish for this and must have regretted it when Spearhavoc disappeared not only with all the money he could lay his hands on in his bishopric, but also with the materials provided for making the new imperial crown.[3] In his place was appointed William, a Norman clerk in Edward's household,[4] a man presumably acceptable to both the king and the archbishop.

The queen, Godwin's daughter, was sent to a nunnery. According to the *Vita Ædwardi Regis*, Archbishop Robert, who wanted to destroy her family completely and who feared that she might work for the undoing of the revolution, urged the king to divorce her. Edward, however, temporized. Putting out that she was going into retreat until the disturbances were over, he sent her 'with an imperial escort and royal honour' to Wilton abbey, where she had once been at school. The Anglo-Saxon annalist, in contradiction, has her sent by the king to his sister, the abbess of Wherwell. She was deprived of all her land and movables, according to *E*, and, according to 'Florence', sent without honour and with only one maid.[5] The author of the *Vita* should have

[1] *Chron. E*. Florence, i. 205, describes Godwin's earldom as consisting in the summer of 1051 of Kent, Sussex, and Wessex, and Harold's as Essex, East Anglia, Huntingdon, and Cambridge.

[2] None of Cnut's writs concerning Kent (Harmer, *Writs*, nos. 26, 29, 30) includes an earl in the address, although Edward's (nos. 38, 35, 39) include Godwin and then Harold. In a late-eleventh-century list of estates in which the archbishop of Canterbury had an interest is the item: 'Tertium denarium de comitatu archiepiscopus qui ante Edzinum fuit [Æthelnoth] habuit. Tempore Edzini rex Edwardus dedit Godwino.', David C. Douglas, 'Odo, Lanfranc, and the Domesday Survey', *Historical Essays in Honour of James Tait*, ed. Edwards, Galbraith, Jacob (1933), p. 52. On this evidence the 'Third penny', the earl's fee, went to Archbishops Æthelnoth (1020–38) and Eadsige (1038–50) until it was taken away from the latter and given to Godwin by Edward. This may have occurred in 1044 when Eadsige retired for a time from the archbishopric (see above, p. 78), for while Bishop Siward was coadjutor, Godwin is found acting in Kent. Robertson, *Charters*, no. CII.

[3] According to *Chron. E* Spearhavoc remained in London during the summer and autumn with the king's full permission, but after Godwin's fall was expelled. Florence, i. 204, characteristically attributes his expulsion to Edward. See also *Chron. Abingdon*, i. 463.   [4] *Chron. DE*, Florence, i. 207.

[5] *Chron. D*, expanded by Florence, i. 207; *Chron. E*; *VEdR*, p. 23.

known the truth; and, although he may well have softened the measures so as to minimize Edith's disgrace and Edward's vindictiveness, he is the safer guide. His version also has the merit of keeping Edward and Robert of Jumièges apart. Edward was following policies advocated by Robert only so far as they suited him. He had finally been overborne in the matter of the bishopric of London, but he had not capitulated to his favourite. Indeed, it must be recognized that in all this affair (except on its ecclesiastical side) Edward was the complete master and Robert the servant whom he used. It was the king who profited most by the fall of the house of Godwin; and it was in Edward's interest to keep Edith unharmed in case he was ever forced to make reparations to those whom he had ruined.

The northern chronicler, followed by 'Florence', informs us that 'then Earl William came from overseas with a large force of Frenchmen, and the king received him and as many of his companions as suited him, and let him go again.' This unsupported statement, probably a later insertion into the basic annal and by a chronicler not in the best position to observe the event, has been the subject of much dispute.[1] Cogent arguments can be made both for and against William's visit. But, since there is no reason why the northern chronicler should have invented the journey and it is not easy to see how the entry could be a mistake or the result of confusion, it seems better to allow it to stand. If William entered the kingdom by way of Southampton Water and met Edward at his Christmas court at Gloucester, the northern chronicler is a satisfactory witness. And it is impossible to prove that William could not have found time for a quick trip to England. The Norman apologists tell of Edward's sending a mission to William; but they never show the duke as a petitioner, and may easily have suppressed the return visit. Unless we do not believe that Edward was engaged in negotiations with William at this time, it seems reasonable to think that William probably did make an appearance at the English royal court. In the summer Edward was visited by Eustace and in the late autumn or winter by 'Earl' William. The episodes are described in similar, cryptic words. We are given to understand that both were confidential diplomatic missions.

[1] Körner, *Battle of Hastings*, pp. 158–63, reconsiders the views of those who have debated this problem, especially Stenton, Wilkinson, Douglas, and Oleson. We should notice that it was quite usual at this time for princes to negotiate in person, and the visit of a count to a king would cause no surprise. See *Histoire des Relations Internationales*; vol. i, François L. Ganshof, *Le Moyen Age*, pp. 120–1.

If William came, he probably came as a petitioner, for if he brought great presents they escaped notice. He, like Eustace, wanted to know where he stood. He may even have come to offer Edward help against rebels, to look to the safety of the throne which he aspired to inherit. He may also have come to see his great-aunt, the queen mother, for Emma was close to death. She died in March 1052, probably at Winchester,[1] and was buried in the Old Minster near her second husband, Cnut, her son, Harthacnut, and her nephew, Earl Beorn. Edward seems to have accepted his mother's identification with the Danish royal house, for his own father lay in St Paul's minster in London.

After the banishment of his father-in-law, the repudiation of his wife, and the death of his mother, Edward stood very much alone. In England he was supported by no close relations. This freedom was clearly something that he had desired. In 1052 Edward was about forty-seven, the age at which his father had died; but it must have been clear to all that he was going to last much longer. If William had come over to see for himself what were his chances of succeeding to England, he must have returned discouraged. Edward had fought his way out of tutelage and patronage. He had given proof of his power and authority. It would not be surprising if many men courted even more insistently than before this rich and childless ruler. The *Vita Ædwardi Regis* reports that Earl Godwin sent to Edward to ask for peace and mercy and a lawful trial and that both the count of Flanders and the king of France interceded on the exile's behalf. 'But the malice of evil men had shut up the merciful ears of the king.'[2] For a short time Edward had it all his own way.

---

[1] *Chron. CDE*; Florence, i. 207. She left a messuage in the city to the cathedral church, Harmer, *Writs*, no. 111, and an estate in Norfolk to Bury St Edmunds, *ibid.*, nos. 16–17. It was probably at this time that Edward completed his grant to Bury of her eight-and-a-half hundreds in Suffolk: see above, p. 77.

[2] *VEdR*, p. 26.

Chapter 6

THE REVOLUTION UNDONE
(1052–1053)

No eleventh-century writer described the events of 1051–2 from the point of view of the royal court. The Anglo-Saxon annalist concerned himself almost entirely with the actions of the house of Godwin, and none of the extant revisions has redressed the balance, although *E*, because it was written at Canterbury, gives not only the most detailed account but also the best view of Edward's camp. The Abingdon (*C*) version, which is favourable to the king, simply abbreviates.[1] The author of the *Vita Ædwardi Regis* is here entirely unsympathetic to the king, yet rather surprisingly mentions the charge that Godwin was responsible for the Ætheling Alfred's death and the, for him, far more serious accusation that Godwin had usurped Canterbury lands. Norman apologists for King William ignore the disturbances in England. Although they chose to vituperate Godwin, then twenty years in the grave, and expressed their detestation of his murder of Alfred,[2] they made no use of his disobedience in 1051–2. Their belief that Godwin was in 1051 a supporter of Edward's plan to make William his heir[3] prevented them from describing him as an opponent of the king. And they preferred to use his failure to pass on this policy to Harold rather than his treatment of Edward as a justification of their hatred of the family. William of Malmesbury, faced with the two discordant traditions about Godwin and Robert of Jumièges, did not know what to think.[4]

Although there may have been a few men in England in 1051–2 who regarded Edward's expulsion of Earl Godwin and his family as a victory for righteousness over the ungodly, it is unlikely that anyone thought that the king was behaving like a saint. Indeed, it would seem

[1] Körner, *Battle of Hastings*, pp. 36 ff., discusses the annals and the events of 1051–2. See also above, p. 96.
[2] Jumièges, p. 121; Poitiers, pp. 9–12.
[3] Poitiers, p. 176; cf. Jumièges, p. 132.
[4] Malmesbury, *GR*, i. 236 ff., especially 239–40.

118

that there was more support for the view that the outlaws had been unjustly treated. And when the panegyrist of the house of Godwin came to describe these events, he compared, in one poem, the innocent earl, unjustly punished by his enemies, to Susanna, Joseph, and Jesus Christ,[1] and, in another, to David at the court of Saul.[2] If it was daring to liken Edward to Saul, Saul who, 'fought against all his enemies on every side, against Moab, and against the children of Ammon, and against Edom, and against the kings of Zobah, and against the Philistines, . . . and smote the Amalekites, and delivered Israel out of the hands of them that spoiled them' (1 Sam. xiv. 47–8), Saul who 'secretly practised mischief against David' and 'slew the Lord's priests' after 'the Lord repented that he had made Saul king over Israel' (1 Sam. xv. 35), it was even more daring to liken Godwin to David, the son of Jesse, whom the Lord had provided to rule in Israel after Saul and whom Samuel anointed at the Lord's command. 'The Lord was with David', not with Saul. But we need not take any of these extravagances seriously. None of the protagonists stood for a principle or a cause. In 1051 Edward backed his Norman friends in their vendetta against Godwin, and the earl, 'deserted by fortune',[3] tripped over every stone in his path. In 1052 Godwin and his sons invaded England in order to recover their losses.

Edward's security after the revolution depended on keeping the belligerent support of Earls Leofric and Siward. Even if Godwin had taken great treasure abroad he and his sons would find it difficult to recruit an army which stood any chance against the forces which Edward and the loyal earls could raise. Edward had done well to give Harold's earldom to Ælfgar, Leofric's son; and he probably thought that just as he had kept the exiled Osgot Clapa at bay and dealt easily with Earl Swegn, so he could smother the piratical raids of the new outlaws. Edward was to be undeceived. Godwin was able to rally sympathizers in his earldom and in London and dissuade the other earls from military action. Whereas in 1051 everything ran in Edward's favour, in 1052 the reverse occurred. There was a natural swing of sympathy in favour of the victims, all the stronger because Edward had shown no moderation or mercy. It is possible that some of Edward's

---

[1] *VEdR*, p. 24.

[2] *VEdR*, pp. 28–30. This theme, which may depend immediately on the unction ritual in the coronation ceremony, is also developed by the Norman Anonymous: Karl Pellens, *Die Texte des normannischen Anonymus* (Wiesbaden, 1966), pp. 130–1, cf. 167. [3] *VEdR*, p. 19.

Norman friends were too arrogant after their victory. And if William of Normandy was invited to the English court, this could have caused offence. There was even a destructive raid by Gruffydd ap Llewelyn into Herefordshire.[1] In circumstances such as these the determination of Godwin and his sons to fight for their restoration was decisive. Leofric and Siward had insufficient interest in the new situation to risk their own and their men's lives in its defence. In 1052, as in 1051 and 1065, men shrank from civil war,[2] and this time the house of Godwin was the gainer.

Harold and Leofwine spent the winter of 1051–2 at the court of Diarmaid mac Mael na mbó, king of Leinster and Dublin,[3] Godwin and the rest of the family at Bruges under the protection of Count Baldwin. That the bulk of the family, including the sons, Swegn, Tostig, and Gyrth, should go to Flanders was natural enough. Swegn had fled there in 1047 and 1049; Tostig had just married the count's half-sister; and Gyrth is found in company with Tostig and Judith on a later occasion. The surprising feature is the flight of Harold and Leofwine to Ireland in a ship prepared for Swegn within his earldom at Bristol. Swegn had some acquaintance with the Welsh princes and, from his possession of Bristol, the port for Dublin, at least some knowledge of Irish affairs. But, so far as we know, Harold and Leofwine had no ties with the Celtic West. The likeliest explanation is that Swegn changed his mind at the last minute, decided not to engage in a military adventure but to look to the salvation of his soul; and that Harold, always a bold man, chose to take his place. Harold's move had nothing except its diversionary value to recommend it. He and his brother seem to have had no following at all in the south-west and to have been treated like any other pirates when they returned. Swegn is said to have walked barefoot from Bruges to Jerusalem.[4] If he set out immediately, in winter, his act was the more commendable. And the sooner back, the sooner he could turn to the restoration of his earthly fortune.

[1] *Chron. D.* Florence, i. 207. Lloyd, *History of Wales,* ii. 363–4.

[2] *Chron. CD.*

[3] *VEdR,* p. 25; Plummer, *Two Chronicles,* p. 237; *Annals of the Kingdom of Ireland by the Four Masters,* ed. John O'Donovan (Dublin, 1854; New York, 1966) ii. 861n.; 'The Annals of Tigernach: the fourth fragment A.D. 973–A.D. 1088', ed. Whitley Stokes, *Revue Celtique* (Paris), xvii (1896), 392–3, *s.a.* 1052. Diarmaid does not seem to have succeeded Eachmarcach mac Raghnall in Dublin before 1052, when Eachmarcach sailed to his death in Wales (see below, pp. 200–1). Harold's sojourn in Ireland is mentioned in none of the Celtic sources, which are completely uninterested in English affairs.   [4] *Chron. C*; Florence, i. 209–10.

Communication between the two parties of exiles was possible along the trading routes, and a rendezvous, perhaps in Spithead or Solent, not far from Bosham, was arranged for the summer. An expedition was fitted out which in scope would seem to lie somewhere between Osgot Clapa's raid in 1049 and William of Normandy's invasion in 1066. Godwin and his sons aimed at something much more than annoyance and petty revenge; but it is unlikely that they intended to provoke, and expected to defeat, the best armies that Edward and the loyal earls could deploy. They hoped to recruit sympathizers in England, frighten waverers, and eventually force their way back in the same way as they had been forced out. Chroniclers favourable to Godwin represent him as at all turns restraining his more bellicose followers.[1] This is likely. He had no intention of fighting an unnecessary campaign. But he attained his ends without spilling blood only because he was prepared to fight and because this was known to all.

Godwin's first task, however, was to reanimate loyalty among his thegns and tenants in England, pose as an injured victim, put out propaganda for his cause, and buy support with promises. All sources show him busy with negotiations, some mention that there was an encouraging response. When summer came, Edward, with his usual grasp of the situation, appointed Earls Ralf and Odda to the command of a fleet, estimated at forty small ships, based on Sandwich.[2] He must also have arranged a military command against the western exiles, for the country was prepared for their attack. It was these outlaws who moved first. Harold and Leofwine, with nine ships,[3] no doubt manned by Irish-Norse crews from Dublin, sailed up the Bristol Channel and landed at Porlock in Somerset, near the Devon border, in order to gather provisions. Although Earl Odda was at Sandwich, an army, drawn from the two shires, drove them off, but at the cost of heavy casualties.[4] The two brothers then sailed round Land's End and up the English Channel.

[1] *Chron. E* (p. 125), where *folc* is translated 'men': 'army' or 'soldiers' is to be preferred; *VEdR*, pp. 19, 25-8.

[2] *Chron. E* for the commanders; *Chron. DE*, followed by Florence, i. 208, for the strength of the fleet.

[3] *Chron. E*; 'navibus multis', Florence, i. 208; 'cum magna manu navali', *VEdR*, p. 26.

[4] *Chron. CD*, followed by Florence, i. 208, place the expedition from Ireland first; *Chron. E*, probably followed by *VEdR*, p. 26, introduces it just before the two expeditions meet; but for the St Augustine's writer Harold's invasion is only a side show. According to *CD* and Florence Harold killed more than thirty noble thegns as well

Godwin with a fleet, which one writer thought large, another small,[1] sailed from the River Yser on 22 June, apparently without his sons.[2] He slipped past the royal navy at Sandwich and landed at Dungeness in Kent.[3] All versions of the Chronicle agree that he was warmly welcomed, especially by the sailors from the ports of the region. But Ralf and Odda were determined commanders. They called out a land-army, moved their ships to attack, and forced Godwin to retreat before them to Pevensey[4] in East Sussex. The campaign, however, was halted by a westerly gale which blew both fleets back up the Channel. Godwin returned to Bruges, Ralf and Odda to Sandwich, then London. There was clearly some disarray in the English fleet, and Edward may well have been scornful of its achievements. There was talk, it seems, of finding new crews and appointing new commanders. But nothing was done and the squadron began to disperse.[5] It was like some of the fiascos in Æthelred's reign.[6]

When Godwin had refitted, encouraged by the news he sailed again, this time direct to the Isle of Wight, which he ravaged.[7] From this base he cast about, seeking news of Harold and Leofwine and also reconnoitring the coast. Probably late in August father and sons joined forces at last, possibly down Channel at Portland.[8] The situation was favourable: Godwin knew that they could recruit their supporters unmolested. They stopped ravaging,[9] and sailed up the Channel,

---

as many ordinary soldiers. See also below, p. 172. *VEdR*, p. 26, describes Harold's depredations but does not mention Godwin's.

[1] 'multiplex classis', *VEdR*, p. 26; 'cum paucis navibus', Florence i. 208. Both were probably guessing.

[2] *Chron. E*, possibly followed by *VEdR*, p. 26. No one mentions the presence of Tostig and Gyrth in the fleet although it is implied by all authorities that the whole family was present later in London. Godwin may have chosen not to hazard all his sons in the combat squadrons. [3] *Chron. E*.

[4] *Chron. E*. According to Malmesbury, *GR*, i. 243, the fleets were about to engage when a thick mist enveloped them. After this a gale blew Godwin back to Flanders.

[5] *Chron. E* gives the story in much more detail than *CD*, Florence, and *VEdR*. It is only from *E* that we learn that Godwin returned to Bruges after his first expedition. The others do not contradict: they are merely vague.

[6] Cf. *Chron. s.a.* 1008: an enormous navy was collected at Sandwich 'to protect this country from every invading army. But unfortunately the naval force was no more use to this country than it had been on many previous occasions.'

[7] *Chron. CDE*, Florence, i. 208; the ravaging in *E* and implied in the others.

[8] According to *Chron. E* Godwin ravaged westwards to Portland, where he met Harold; the combined fleets then sailed to Wight where what had been left behind was taken aboard. *CD*, Florence, and *VEdR*, are again vague.

[9] *Chron. CD*, followed by Florence, i. 208.

collecting volunteers or impressing ships and hostages from all the ports from Pevensey to Sandwich, so that by the time they rounded the North Foreland they had assembled forces sufficient for a campaign.[1] As they entered the Thames, part of the fleet went inside Sheppey and burned the royal manor of Milton.[2] It is possible that Ralf and Odda were on the watch, but had to retreat as the invaders advanced.[3]

Edward seems to have received first intelligence of the invasion when the exiles entered Sandwich.[4] He decided to hold London and, as in the previous year, sent urgently for reinforcements.[5] The earls and leading men of the country were in London at the time of Godwin's attack.[6] Clearly, as in 1051, they only had escorts with them, and troops came in slowly to the royal standard.[7] All the same, by the middle of September Edward had a land-army and some fifty ships at his disposal and five earls from whom to choose commanders.[8]

Godwin reached Southwark on Monday, 14 September,[9] and, while waiting for the tide to turn and carry him through London bridge, negotiated with the citizens for a safe passage.[10] This was granted – it is possible that the Londoners were strongly on his side – and, still keeping to the south bank, Godwin moved his fleet within the city defences and came face to face with the royal army and navy. Like Edward, Godwin also had a land-army on the river bank, probably supporters who had come in from his earldom. And reinforcements continued to arrive.[11] With both forces arrayed for battle, but separated by the river, Godwin and Harold demanded the restoration of everything of which they had been deprived. Edward refused.[12] Whereupon Godwin swung his leading ships across the river so as to encircle the royal fleet.[13] Intermediaries were active during a truce and once more Bishop Stigand was

---

[1] *Chron. CDE*, Florence, i. 208–9.

[2] *Chron. E*, which again provides a more detailed narrative.

[3] According to *Chron. E* Godwin sailed up the Thames in pursuit of the earls, although when *E* last mentioned the earls they were in London, about to be dismissed. Only *E* knows anything about the king's camp in London.

[4] *Chron. CD*, Florence, i. 209.

[5] *Chron. CD*, Florence, i. 209; cf. *VEdR*, p. 27.

[6] *Chron. E*.   [7] *Chron. CD*, Florence, i. 209.

[8] *Chron. E*; cf. *VEdR*, p. 27. *Chron. CD* and Florence, i. 209, mention the royal army and navy later.

[9] Date in *Chron. C* and Florence, i. 209.

[10] *Chron. CD*, Florence, i. 209. Cf. also *VEdR*, p. 27.

[11] *Chron. CD*, Florence, i. 209. *VEdR*, p. 27, claims that Godwin was receiving substantial reinforcements.

[12] *Chron. E*.   [13] *Chron. CD*, Florence, i. 209.

prominent.[1] This time Godwin had the advantage. When Edward realized that his men would not fight and that he would have to offer terms, he was mad with anger.[2] Perhaps now at last he was forced to exchange hostages with his father-in-law;[3] and it was presumably at this point that those Frenchmen who feared Godwin's vengeance took to flight.[4] Archbishop Robert, Bishops Ulf of Dorchester and William of London, and some others fought their way out of the East Gate, rode to the Essex coast at the Naze, and escaped abroad. The soldiers rode west to Osbern Pentecost's castle at Ewias Harold or north to Robert's castle, probably a stronghold of Robert fitzWimarch.[5]

On the following day, 15 September, Godwin and Harold went ashore with a suitable escort to attend a large meeting of the king's council, assembled outside London, perhaps at Westminster.[6] Godwin was allowed to declare his and his son's innocence of all the charges which had been brought against them.[7] They were then inlawed, restored to the royal favour, and given back everything of which they had been deprived. To complete the revolution those Frenchmen who had brought the false charges, perverted the law, and been the cause of all the trouble, were outlawed.[8] Thus Godwin recovered Wessex, Harold East Anglia, and the queen her position at court.[9] It is not known whether provision was made for Swegn. But a month or two later news arrived that he had died on 29 September at or near Constantinople on the return journey from the Holy Land.[10] Not only his meritorious end but also his final disappearance from the English scene must have given general satisfaction.

There were, no doubt, checks which prevented Godwin and Harold from pushing their victory too hard: Earls Leofric and Siward would probably not have tolerated the complete humiliation of the king.

---

[1] Stigand mentioned by E.   [2] VEdR, p. 28.

[3] See below, Appendix B, p. 304.

[4] Chron. E; implied by VEdR, p. 28. Chron. CD, Florence, i. 210, mention the flight after full peace had been made on the following day, but are not necessarily in contradiction.

[5] Chron. E. The castle is possibly Clavering (Essex); see above, p. 94.

[6] 'outside London', Chron. E. VEdR, p. 28, mentions the royal palace.

[7] Chron. E; cf. VEdR, pp. 27–8.

[8] Chron. CDE, Florence, i. 209–10, VEdR, p. 28, are in substantial agreement and do not contradict.

[9] Edith's restoration is mentioned by all versions of Chron. and is specially featured in VEdR, p. 28.

[10] Chron. C, at Constantinople; Florence, i. 210, 'in Licia'.

But Godwin hardly needed much external restraint. He wanted to recover his losses and punish his personal enemies, but he wanted also to work again with Edward. The main argument of the poem in the *Vita Ædwardi Regis*, in which Godwin and Edward appear as David and Saul, is that David twice spared the life of the king.[1] Saul is *christus domini*, the Lord's anointed, sanctified by chrism. David, although strong of arm, abhorred the sin of regicide and prevented his men from killing Saul. It is, moreover, unlikely that Godwin was ever tempted to get rid of Edward. He himself cannot have aspired to the crown. His hopes lay in a grandson, as yet unborn. The author of the *Vita* is probably right in thinking that Godwin's main desire was to restore harmony in the royal household. His aim must have been to recreate the conditions under which, even at this late hour, an heir might be produced. Therefore, once those who had poisoned Edward's mind had been removed, everything was done to conciliate the king and soften the blow. Earl Ralf, although he had commanded the fleet against Godwin, was unmolested and Odda seems to have remained an earl until his death in 1056.[2] Edward was allowed to keep those Frenchmen who had been loyal to him and the people – according to the Worcester chronicler, Robert the Deacon, Robert's son-in-law; Richard fitzScrob (of Richard's castle); Alfred, the king's equerry; and Anfrid Cocksfoot.[3] William, bishop of London, was summoned back, because no one had a quarrel with him.[4] Godwin's failing health may also have helped the settlement. He fell ill soon after his return and was dead within seven months.

[1] *VEdR*, pp. 29–30.

[2] Nothing is said in the sources about the fate of Ralf and Odda. In 1055 (*Chron. CD*) Ralf was defending Hereford against the Welsh and so must have retained or recovered some of Swegn's earldom. Odda at his death in 1056 is described as an earl (*Chron. CD*). In a document to be dated 1053 × 5 (*KCD*, no. 956; Sawyer, no. 1478) Ralf witnesses as earl. Robertson, *Charters*, pp. 456–8, suggests that Odda was given the shires of Worcester and perhaps Gloucester. Odda witnesses as earl *ante* 22 December 1053 (*KCD*, no. 804; Sawyer, no. 1409) and 1052 × 6 (*KCD*, no. 805; Sawyer, no. 1408). See also J. H. Round, *VCH, Worcs*, i. 258–60.

[3] *Chron. CD*, Florence, i. 210. Robert, Alfred, and Anfrid are otherwise unknown. R. W. Eyton, *Antiquities of Shropshire* (1854–60), v. 207–9, made 'the hazardous suggestion' (Round) that Robert the Deacon was Robert fitzWimarch. It should at least be noticed that in 1065 Edward gave Robert fitzWimarch a prebend in St Mary's, Bromfield (Salop), which Robert then transferred to his unnamed son-in-law. See *DB*, i. 252 b ii; F. E. Harmer, 'A Bromfield and a Coventry Writ of King Edward the Confessor', *The Anglo-Saxons*, ed. Peter Clemoes (1959), pp. 90–8.

[4] Florence, i. 210.

To judge by later events Edward accepted the return of the house of Godwin at least with resignation. Once he had recovered from the anger and shame caused by his military discomfiture, he may have felt some relief at his release from the dangerous policy to which Robert of Jumièges had committed him and at his escape at so little cost. It had obviously been an exciting time; but Edward may well have preferred to live in a tranquil and secure realm. There is no indication that he ever made any effort to undo the settlement. He probably realized that he had been foolish. He cannot be represented as a prisoner of Godwin and his sons. Leofric and Siward would not have allowed Godwin so much control. Archbishop Robert went to complain at Rome and apparently died at Jumièges soon after his return.[1] He was replaced at Canterbury by Stigand, bishop of Winchester, a prelate probably acceptable to all parties in England. Stigand prudently retained Winchester for the time being and later could not bring himself to surrender it. Ulf of Dorchester was succeeded by Wulfwig, another of Edward's clerks.[2] Ulf, like Spearhavoc, simply drops out of the story. Osbern Pentecost and his comrade, Hugh, surrendered their castles and, with the permission of Earl Leofric, passed through Mercia on their way to Scotland, where they joined King Macbeth, a warrior who could do with brave soldiers.[3]

These expulsions, far from weakening the kingdom, allowed the formation of a new unity of purpose and prepared the way for a firmer attitude towards the Welsh and Scottish princes. While Godwin had been out of the country Gryffydd ap Llewelyn had ravaged Herefordshire. At the Christmas court at Gloucester it was decided to assassinate Rhys, the brother of Gryffydd ap Rhydderch, because of his depredations. Edward gave the order and the head of the victim was brought to him on 5 January 1053.[4] Probably in revenge the Welsh killed a large number of Englishmen on patrol near Westbury.[5] In the

---

[1] Malmesbury, *GP*, p. 35; *GR*, i. 244. His name is included in a list of those present at the 'discovery' of the body of St Dionysius at the abbey of St Denis, Paris, *Recueil des Historiens des Gaules et de la France*, xi (Paris, 1767), 667–74. The event took place after 9 January, not earlier than 1052, because of the witness of Ilenand [Helinand], bishop of Laon, and possibly not later than 1053, because of the presence of Froeland, bishop of Senlis. The *terminus ad quem*, however, does not seem to be very secure. He also functioned at Fécamp for Abbot John before 1055: *ibid.* xi. 363.

[2] For Stigand, *Chron. E*, which is hostile to Robert, and *C, s.a.* 1053; for Wulfwig, *Chron. C, s.a.* 1053.

[3] Florence, i. 210; cf. Plummer, *Two Chronicles*, pp. 243–4.

[4] *Chron. D*, expanded by Florence, i. 211.   [5] *Chron. C.*

following year Earl Siward entered Scotland. There seems to have been in England renewed confidence in the stability of the kingdom.

For Easter 1053 the royal court moved, as was usual, to Winchester. And it was at this family reunion that Godwin, while dining with the king on Monday, 12 April, suffered a stroke. His sons, Harold, Tostig, and Gyrth, carried him into the king's chamber, where he lay speechless until the Thursday, when he died.[1] He was buried in the Old Minster with Cnut and Emma; and his widow, Gytha, Cnut's sister-in-law, made handsome gifts to the church for the redemption of his soul,[2] a tardy atonement for encroachments on ecclesiastical property which some contemporaries thought almost beyond repair.[3] Godwin was, however, extremely popular in Winchester,[4] and, according to the *Vita Ædwardi Regis*, was greatly mourned. All men felt that they had lost a father; and their only consolation was that Edward gave Wessex to Harold.[5] This promotion allowed Edward to restore East Anglia to Ælfgar, Leofric's son.[6] The king may have had little choice in these appointments; but at least he did not attempt the difficult or impossible. In fact the new arrangements probably gave him what he wanted, a fairly even distribution of power between the three great comital families, and so the possibility of getting his own way by playing on their rivalry. In 1053, at the age of forty-eight, with his mother and father-in-law dead, his wife subdued by her recent repudiation, and the new earl of Wessex about twenty-seven years old, Edward had recovered the means to rule as well as to reign. It is, however, by no means easy to get a clear view of his character and policies.

The character of any historical figure is usually best appreciated by way of contemporary opinion, for, although a man's contemporaries may be prejudiced by love or dislike, may misunderstand, may even be incapable of understanding, they have advantages denied to later

---

[1] *Chron. C* and Florence, i. 211, are the most detailed; cf. *Chron. ADE, VEdR*, p. 30.

[2] *VEdR*, p. 30. For Gytha's gifts, including the manors of Bleadon and Crowcombe, see *Annales de Wintonia* in *Annales Monastici*, ed. H. R. Luard (Rolls ser. 1865), ii. 26; *DB, addit.* fos. 266, 510.

[3] *Chron. C, s.a.* 1052, 'Then Godwin fell ill soon after he landed, and recovered again, but he did all too little reparation about the property of God which he had from many holy places.'

[4] In an early-twelfth-century survey of the royal demesne in the borough, which records the tenants 'in the time of King Edward', Godwin is by far the most popular name among the burgesses. The names Edward and Harold are rare. See Barlow, Biddle, Feilitzen, Keene, *Winchester in the early Middle Ages* (1976), 32ff.

[5] *VEdR*, pp. 30–1.   [6] *Chron. CDE*, Florence, i. 211.

observers. Yet some medieval biographers, often because they had a homiletic or hagiographical purpose, not only disregarded but also despised their opportunity to report the naked truth: renounced circumstantiality completely; and many were so incompetent in Latin composition, or so timid, or, possibly again, so little interested in this passing show, that they merely copied appropriate passages from other similar works. The famous description of Edward on his deathbed is derived from a description of St Audemer.[1] The familiar picture of William the Conqueror's appearance and habits is copied from Einhard's *Vita Caroli* and derives ultimately from Suetonius.[2] Asser's *Vita Alfredi* has a similar pedigree and its portrayal of Alfred remains a stumbling block to many historians.[3] Such biographies not only fail to illuminate their subject, they also positively deceive. In the last resort each quality alleged by a biographer has to be tested against indifferently recorded acts.

The Anglo-Saxon Chronicle, based for the bulk of the reign on annals written before Edward's death,[4] makes no observations on Edward's behaviour. But its compilers thought it unnecessary to comment. Edward ruled, commanded the army and navy, punished his enemies and rewarded his friends, got married, like any other king. If he was no hero to the annalist, neither was he a coward, a monster, or a saint. The *Encomium Emmae*, written between 1040 and 1042, and probably hostile to Edward,[5] shows him at one point uninterested in the English crown and leaving the coast clear for Harthacnut.[6] But nothing worse than lack of enterprise is alleged against him. Indeed, the good and generous Harthacnut invites his half-brother to England and associates him with the crown.[7] Edward is to be pitied for his misfortunes, has, perhaps, become unadventurous; but his king-worthiness has not been destroyed.

The one character sketch that has some claim to have been written in the king's lifetime[8] is a sentence substituted by a transcriber for the

[1] *VEdR*, p. 12 and *n*.; cf. pp. 80, 87. See also above, p. 71.

[2] Frank Barlow, *William I and the Norman Conquest* (1965), pp. 177–8.

[3] Marie Schütt, 'The Literary form of Asser's "Vita Alfredi" ', *EHR*, lxxii (1957), 209–20; V. H. Galbraith, 'Who wrote Asser's Life of Alfred', *An Introduction to the Study of History* (1964), pp. 88–128.

[4] Körner, *Battle of Hastings*, pp. 14–20.

[5] Körner, 'The political background of the Encomium Emmae', *Battle of Hastings*, pp. 47–74.

[6] *Encomium Emmae*, p. 48.   [7] *Ibid.*, p. 52.

[8] *Ibid.*, pp. xv–xvi; Körner, p. 74.

original final words of the *Encomium Emmae*.[1] Edward, we are told, was at his accession remarkable for his physical strength and also for corresponding spiritual endowments: courage, determination, and vigour of mind. 'In short, he possessed all the desirable qualities.'

We also have two views of Edward recorded soon after his death, the poem in the Chronicle[2] and the account in the *Vita Ædwardi Regis*. The poem repeats some of the manly qualities stressed by the Continuator of the *Encomium*. Edward ruled over the Welsh, Britons, Scots, Angles, and Saxons. He was a noble king, a dear lord, a ruler of heroes, a dispenser of riches, the protector of his land and people; the English were his eager soldiers. Edward was *craeftig raeda*, strong in counsel (presumably unlike his father, Æthelred, who was *un-raed*); and the words are almost a vernacular rendering of the *virtute . . . consilii . . . praeditus*, the quality of purposefulness, mentioned by the Continuator.

The poem then refers to qualities which have not been mentioned before. Although Edward had been deprived of his throne by the Danes for twenty-eight years, this 'baleless king' had always shown blithe courage.[3] The meaning of *bealuleas* is 'without evil intent': Edward had not returned from exile bent on revenge; he had not been soured or weakened by banishment: he stayed cheerful and resolute. Edward as king was *claene and milde*. The first word almost certainly refers to his sexual behaviour and means that he was not a libertine: he was 'clean-living'. The word *milde* is not quite the modern 'meek and mild' and is better understood as 'merciful', a true royal virtue. According to the poem, therefore, Edward was a good man and king, 'so angels bore his righteous soul to heaven.'

In the poem we have panegyric without reservation and there does not seem to be even unexpressed criticism. The *Vita Ædwardi Regis*, a very strange work, offers us three distinct views of Edward: a formal eulogistic portrait, a critical examination of the king from the point of view of the queen and the house of Godwin, and a hagiographical appreciation. This triptych is probably the result of multiple aims; and, although some of the contradictions and contrasts are highly amusing, it is unlikely that there was a satirical purpose. The author pays full

[1] 'vir virium eminentia conspicuus, virtute animi consiliique atque etiam ingenii vivacitate preditus et, ut omnia breviter concludam, omnium expetendorum summa insignitus', *Encomium Emmae*, p. 52n.   [2] *Chron. CD*, 1065.

[3] Cf. the proverb in *Gnomic Verses*, line 39, 'Blithe sceal bealoleas heorte' (merry shall be the innocent heart), Grein and Wülcker, *Bibliothek der angelsächsischen Poesie*, I, p. 343.

lip-service to Edward's nobility and wisdom. The king was tall and handsome, 'the most fair and noble of English kings', noble in body and mind, majestic in public, dignified in private. He abolished all evil customs, promulgated good laws, and paid special attention to the provision of plentiful and good justice. He defended his realm against all foes, both external and internal. He was like Solomon; he gave peace and plenty to his people, and his reign was a golden age.[1] Here is the ideal king of the coronation service.

Side by side, however, with these grand tributes are some rather irreverent peeps behind the ceremonial curtain. When we meet Edward in his character of military protector of his kingdom, we find him a martial figure, indeed, quick to anger and to threaten war. Yet we cannot but notice that the actual fighting is always done by the king's subordinates, especially the queen's brothers, and that without the co-operation of the earls Edward is powerless, a commander-in-chief without an army.[2] The king's political wisdom receives even harsher treatment. It is not Edward but the queen who is strong in counsel. It was on her advice that the court relied.[3] Edward is emotional, rash, and often misguided; sometimes he imperils the kingdom by listening to favourites, evil men whom the queen's relations have to expel from the court and land.[4] As a justiciar Edward, far from being 'baleless', acts unjustly and shows no mercy. He is unmoved by entreaties from the innocent and their friends. He can give a cynically jesting judgment in a case.[5]

The remarks in the *Vita* on Edward's domestic behaviour are more difficult to interpret, especially as the author wished to present the queen 'as a woman fit to be placed before all noble, royal, or imperial ladies as a model of virtue and integrity in both religious and worldly affairs'.[6] He tells us that Edith was so modest that, unless Edward invited her, she never, except in church or at table, sat on the throne which by custom was provided for her at the king's side, but preferred to sit at his feet.[7] Nevertheless she had great influence in private over her husband. She made sure that Edward, who disliked the pomp of royalty, appeared in public suitably arrayed and with proper ceremony – a solicitude which Edward not only tolerated but even men-

---

[1] *VEdR*, pp. 3, 11–13. See also below, Appendix A.
[2] *VEdR*, pp. 6, 23, 27–8, 32–3, 38, 40, 42–3, 53–4, 57–8.
[3] *Ibid.*, pp. 2–4, 15, 23, 53–4. [4] *Ibid.*, pp. 17–30.
[5] *Ibid.*, pp. 17–30. [6] *Ibid.*, p. 42. [7] *Ibid.*, pp. 41–2; cf. 60, 79.

tioned appreciatively to his intimates.[1] Although it is easy to form the impression that Edward was condescending, even unpleasant to his wife, the passages were probably intended to do honour to both parties. The clerical author, who puts Edward's gracious condescension to women on a par with his mercy to the poor and sick,[2] would hardly have considered uxoriousness a royal virtue.

No less perplexing is the passage on Edward's passion for hunting. In a section devoted to his religious life we are informed that his one secular interest was the chase, to which he devoted most of his time. He loved the sight and company of hawks and hounds.[3] This passage may simply be imitated from Asser's description of Alfred.[4] But, even so, the attribution to Edward of extreme interest in hunting must have had some other significance. Although hunting was the ordinary pastime of kings and nobles, and few bishops and abbots could have been completely innocent of it, the sport was prohibited to the clergy by canon law, and was never regarded by the church as a completely laudable activity. Undue interest in hunting could lead to various abuses; and when the chronicler wrote that William the Conqueror 'loved the stags as much as if he were their father'[5] he was not writing in approval. Nevertheless it may well be that the author of the *Vita* regarded Edward's devotion to hunting as blameless, or as keeping him out of worse mischief, or, most likely, as a venial sin amply redeemed by Edward's prior attendance at mass. Edward's rusticity was an aspect of his simple, 'innocent' behaviour.

Finally, we have Edward presented as a possible candidate for sanctity. Now and then in the narrative passages suggestive epithets and phrases appear. The king is *pius, piissimus, benignissimus, deo devotus* and *deo dilectus*. He is *sanctae memoriae* and *felicissimae mentionis*.[6] These expressions are justified by Edward's religious life. He is a devoted worshipper, enjoys the company of good monks, is generous to clerical visitors to court and builds a monastery.[7] He disapproves of the scandalous state of the English church.[8] He also lived *caste*, chastely, even in

---

[1] *VEdR*, p. 41.   [2] *Ibid.*, pp. 41, 61.   [3] *Ibid.*, pp. 40, 52.
[4] *Asser's Life of King Alfred*, ed. W. H. Stevenson (1904), pp. 58–9.
[5] *Chron. E*, p. 165.
[6] *VEdR*, pp. 3, 17, 19, 34, 40, 44, 52, 54–5. Earl Leofric, too, is *deo devotus*, p. 21; even Earl Godwin is *dei vir*, p. 24, and *deo devotus*, p. 27; Harold and Tostig are *angelici Angli*, p. 38. Cf. Renate Klauser, *Der Heinrichs- und Kunigundenkult im mittelalterlichen Bistum Bamberg* (Bamberg, 1957), p. 29.
[7] *VEdR*, pp. 40–1, 44–6.   [8] *Ibid.*, p. 77.

true innocence, like an angel in the squalor of the world, that is to say, as a monk.[1] Miracles proved that after death he had gone straight to Heaven.[2] And yet even this portrait is not allowed to stand without at least implied criticism. It was the king's brothers-in-law, not he himself, who made the pilgrimage to Rome.[3] The queen was more generous to the church than the king.[4] Tostig was at least his equal in chastity in word and deed and possibly his superior in attacking evil.[5] Archbishop Stigand had no belief in Edward's visionary powers.[6] The author of the *Vita* was writing at a time when various views of Edward were current, and it suited his different purposes to make use of at least three of them.

Although we are offered conflicting views we are not perplexed by the situation. Edward's reign was sufficiently prosperous, and the king sufficiently capable, for writers to pay him the conventional compliments during his lifetime and in the obituary notices. We may not care to take these compliments literally; but they have at least a negative value. Then, once Edward is dead, the contradictory attitudes towards the departed appear. At one extreme Edward could be regarded as a failure, the man responsible for the disasters of 1066, the man who had left his wife and friends in the lurch, a man who could now be criticized. But, if Edward's death had precipitated misfortunes, the greatest disaster was his own absence, for the calamities showed how strong and wise he had been. He was, therefore, sincerely mourned; with him had departed also the golden age. The kingdom was possessed by devils; Edward was with God in Heaven. 'From the fury of the Normans spare us, O Lord.' And why should not men call on Edward too?

The later history of Edward's reputation does not help us much.[7] We merely find that themes which have already appeared are isolated and intensified, such as Edward the warrior (Scandinavian saga), Edward the saint (Westminster legend), and Edward the lawgiver (English tradition); perhaps also Edward the holy simpleton, whose many errors were due to other-worldliness.[8] With these various simplifications we have reached caricature. One of the last to write about Edward before his canonization was the English Cistercian, Ailred of

---

[1] Cf. Jean Leclercq, 'The Fellowship of the Angels', in *The Love of Learning and the desire for God* (Mentor Omega Book, 1962), pp. 62–3.

[2] *VEdR*, pp. 9, 59 ff.   [3] *Ibid.*, pp. 33–7.

[4] *Ibid.*, pp. 41–2, 46–9.   [5] *Ibid.*, p. 32.   [6] *Ibid.*, pp. 76–7.

[7] T. J. Oleson, 'Edward the Confessor in History', *Transactions of the Royal Soc. of Canada*, liii (1959), 28–32, takes a brief look at Edward's posthumous reputation.

[8] 'Simplex', *Vita Wulfstani*, p. 16, Malmesbury *GR*, pp. 317, 353.

Rievaulx, who finished his book *On the Genealogy of the Kings of the English* just before Henry fitzEmpress succeeded to the throne in December 1154. Basing his account of Edward's reign on the chronicles, Ailred wrote, 'gentle and devout,[1] he defended his kingdom more by diplomacy than by war; with a mind raised above anger, averse to greed, and without pride, he walked in the ways of his [grand]father, Edgar.'[2] A decade later, when Ailred revised Osbert of Clare's *Life of Edward* for the translation of the saint after the canonization,[3] he had to tell a different story, the life of a miraculous healer and visionary. Moreover he had to add to the list another deadly sin from which Edward was free, *luxuria*, a tardy acknowledgment of the virtue on which Edward's claim to sanctity had come to rest.

From this sort of evidence it is impossible to display Edward's character in great detail or with intimate understanding. But the main features are clear enough; and it is important that they should not be obscured by the minor uncertainties. A healthy, active man, interested in warfare and with a great love of hunting, Edward spent his life in rural sports which gave pleasure to himself and his companions, and were harmless enough, but which had little bearing on the welfare of his kingdom and its people. He was not unintelligent; it is possible that he had some intellectual curiosity; but his actions were not directed by a serious purpose. It would probably be wrong to imagine that Edward ever had a conscious policy: he lived naturally in his environment and dealt with problems as they arose. All the same, strongly planted in Edward's rustic simplicity was the will to survive and the cunning necessary for survival. On this level he was shrewd and resourceful. By the standards of his age he cannot be considered devoid of statecraft. Even if he showed a tendency to rely on others and have dear friends, this reveals more his understanding of the anatomy of power than his inability to cope. It was the right of a king to have servants and his duty to have hangers-on. Only rarely did Edward surrender himself entirely to a favourite. Normally he ruled his court.

As a person, it does not seem that Edward was more than superficially attractive. Although he was remembered as a gracious prince, no anecdote shows him in a particularly favourable light. More important, there is no evidence from his recorded behaviour that he was

---

[1] 'homo mansuetus et pius', possibly translating 'claene and milde'.
[2] 'De genealogia regum Anglorum', *Historiae Anglicanae Scriptores X* (1652), col. 366.
[3] *VEdR*, pp. xiv, xxxv ff., 130 ff. See below, p. 281.

remarkable for any of the princely virtues: courage, magnanimity, generosity, love of justice, mercy; none that he possessed such humdrum qualities as patience, industry, or good will. There is nothing to suggest that he was outstandingly religious, that he was an enlightened patron of the church, seriously interested in its moral state, artistic activity, or administrative problems. It is, however, clear that, at least in his later years, he lived a respectable life, that he did not run after women. It seems also that in old age there was an aura of goodness about him, perhaps that quietude which sometimes descends on old soldiers when their physical powers are in decay. If it is easier to suggest what Edward was not, this in itself is revealing. He was not a man of great distinction. But neither was he a holy imbecile. He was like many of his rank and time, a mediocrity. Nearly all his characteristics are commonplace.

Nevertheless in comparison with other rulers he seemed a good man. Although severe to enemies and opponents, and even if he ordered the 'execution' of Rhys of South Wales and connived at the assassination of a Northumbrian nobleman at court,[1] he was not so bloodthirsty or cruel in his punishments as Kings Olaf the Saint and Harald Sigurdsson of Norway. According to Snorri Sturluson, Harald himself boasted, after he had contrived the death of Kalf Arnason in battle, by sending him into the attack against the Danes and withholding support:[2]

> Now I have caused the deaths
> of thirteen of my enemies;
> I kill without compunction
> and remember all my killings.
> Treason must be scotched
> by fair means or foul
> before it overwhelms me.
> Oak trees grow from acorns.

Nor had Edward, like William of Normandy, castles full of political prisoners, many of whom never emerged to see the light of day, poisoned, so it was rumoured.[3] By the standard of these princes, Edward was *milde*. Snorri Sturluson summed it up neatly:[4] 'He was nicknamed Edward the Good, which describes him well. . . . By the English he is regarded as a saint.'

[1] Below, p. 235.   [2] *King Harald's [Sigurdsson's] Saga*, caps. 52–3.
[3] Cf. David C. Douglas, 'On poisoning as a method of political action in eleventh-century Normandy', *William the Conqueror* (1964), pp. 408 ff.
[4] *King Harald's Saga*, caps. 75, 77.

Chapter 7

THE ROYAL ESTATE

In the documents with which Edward was most closely connected, the vernacular writ-charters,[1] he is described simply as *cing*. On the seal, which authenticated the writ, he is *Anglorum basileus*,[2] king of the English. On the obverse of the coins he is, in the first half of his reign, EDWERD REX; later, he becomes mostly EADWARD, and his title, REX ANGLORUM, or abbreviations of this.[3] In two royal charters written in the vernacular, and so of doubtful authenticity, the grantor is described as 'ic Eadwerd Englalandes cyncg' (I, Edward, king of England).[4] But in the Latin charters, or land-books, which were drawn up by the beneficiaries (immediate or ultimate), usually important churches,[5] it is quite different. The royal style is given twice, first in the grant and then in the witness list; and the second description is usually different from and simpler than the first. The more elaborate and literary titles, which appear in the grant, are derived from those given to his step-father, Cnut, and his father, Æthelred, but on the whole are somewhat less fanciful. The trend was towards simplicity. Amid the variety it is possible to recognize the 'house style' of the several churches which drafted charters; but there is nothing to suggest that Edward's title was deliberately changed at any particular point or that it evolved significantly during the reign.

As a witness to these charters Edward is almost always *rex*; in the grant he is usually *rex*, sometimes *basileus*,[6] occasionally *monarchus*,[7] in Abingdon

---

[1] For writs, see above, pp. xxv–xxvi.

[2] Harmer, *Writs*, pl. 2. Only the 'second' seal of Edward is genuine: Bishop and Chaplais, *Facsimiles of English Writs to A.D. 1100*, p. xxii. See also above, pl. 6.

[3] For coins, see above, p. xxvi.

[4] Robertson, *Charters*, no. CXX; cf. no. XCV.

[5] For charters, see above, p. xxv.

[6] *KCD*, nos. 767, 783, 801; *769, 770, 813*. Italic type denotes a charter of doubtful authenticity.

[7] *KCD*, nos. *812, 816*; *gubernator et rector*, 793; *monarchiam optinens*, 798; *rex ac defensor*, 814; *regalia sceptra gubernans*, 817.

charters *rex et primicerius*.[1] In the grant, but never in the witness list, Edward is usually 'king by the grace of God'. The phrase *dei gratia* occurs;[2] but there was a preference for elegant variation. The description of his lordship varies within a limited range. *Rex Anglorum* is common;[3] but he is also *Angulsaxonum rex*,[4] *rex Anglorum atque North-unhymbrorum*,[5] *rex (totius) Anglicae nationis / gentis*,[6] *rex totius Albionis*,[7] *rex totius Brittanniae*[8] (the invariable witness style in the Winchester charters), and *industrius rex Anglorum omniumque insularum / cunctarumque gentium / in circuitu persistentium* (Winchester).[9] Two basic traditions intermingle. Edward is king of the English people and he rules over a territory larger than England, the whole of Albion or Britain.[10] And all these titles seem to have been used quite indifferently. A typical example is a Winchester charter, dated 1045, in which Edward appears first as 'king of the English', and then as 'king of the whole of Britain'.[11]

The underlying principle is observed also in the *Vita Ædwardi Regis*. Edward is *rex Anglorum*;[12] he rules over the *anglica gens* and has at his disposal *Anglorum exercitus*, the army of the English.[13] The English kingdom, *anglicum regnum*, contains northern, eastern, and western English.[14] But although the author is happy with the geographical terms *Hibernia, Gallia, Francia, Flandria, Neustria, Normannia, Saxonia*, he avoided *Wallia* and *Scotia*[15] and obviously disliked *Anglia*.[16] In his

---

[1] *KCD*, nos. 792, 796, 800; cf. 797. Cf. *rex et gubernator*, Westminster, 1060 (Sawyer, no. 1031; see below, p. 334).

[2] Cf. Barlow, *English Church*, p. 35. Cf. *largiflua dei gratia*, Westminster, 1060 (see n. 1).

[3] *KCD*, nos. 767, 772, 780, 791, 806, 808, 813; *770, 792, 793, 796, 798, 800, 801, 817*.

[4] Donald Matthew, *The Norman Monasteries and their English possessions* (1962), pp. 143 ff. (Sawyer, no. 1015).

[5] *KCD*, nos. 770, 811; cf. 787, 793.   [6] *KCD*, nos. *774, 775; 787*.

[7] *KCD*, nos. 778, 819; cf. 781, 787, 792, 796, 797.

[8] *KCD*, nos. *774, 775, 776, 780, 781, 783, 797, 1335*; cf. 816. Cf. also 'telluris Brittanice totius rex', Westminster, 1060 (Sawyer, no. 1031).

[9] *KCD*, nos. 776, 783; cf. 1335 (all Winchester); 793, 798. Cf. 'quiescente . . . universali Britannia, cum adiacentium regnorum monarchiarumque angularibus insulis,' *VEdR*, pp. 11–12.

[10] The only styles which make use of England are 'tocius Angliæ basileus' (Evesham), *KCD*, no. 801, and 'Anglicis finibus rex et defensor' (?Exeter), no. 814.

[11] *KCD*, no. 780; cf. 775, 776, 783; cf. also, 'ab ipsis occidentalium Britonum sive Anglorum finibus', *VEdR*, p. 26.   [12] *VEdR*, pp. 3, 11.

[13] *Ibid.*, pp. 22, 54; 30, 42.   [14] *Ibid.*, pp. 25, 52; 50; 26.

[15] Gruffydd was 'rex occidentalium Britonum', *ibid.*, p. 42, cf. 57; Malcolm was 'rex Scottorum', p. 42.

[16] *Anglia* appears three times, always with a qualifying adjective: *tota*, p. 53; *orientalis* (East Anglia), p. 33, and *media* (Middle Anglia), p. 52.

7. A charter of Edward in favour of Leofric, bishop of Devonshire (Exeter, Dean and Chapter, MS. 2072), dated 1050. (*Courtesy Dean and Chapter of Exeter Cathedral.*)

8(a) Seal (the second) of Westminster abbey, early thirteenth century, and engraved before Henry III rebuilt the church, showing (on the reverse shown here) Edward sitting on a throne with his feet resting on the figure of a prostrate king and holding in his left hand a model of the abbey church. On the obverse (not shown) is St Peter, likewise resting his feet on a prostrate king. (*Courtesy Dean and Chapter of Westminster.*)

8(b). Seal of the chapter of Chichester, early thirteenth century, showing either the Saxon church at Selsey (the previous location of the Sussex bishopric) or the Saxon minster at Chichester. (*Courtesy Society of Antiquaries of London.*)

opinion Edward ruled over Britain; it was the British ocean which washed the coast of Kent; and it was to a British port that Alfred in 1036, and Godwin in 1052, crossed from Flanders.[1]

This way of looking at Edward's monarchy is understandable. It continues the tradition that the overlord was both king and *brytenwealda* (broad- or Britain-ruler). The English domination of Wales and Scotland was one of the themes of the *Vita*. According to the obituary poem in the Anglo-Saxon Chronicle Edward ruled over Welsh, Scots, and Britons[2] as well as Angles and Saxons. Certainly Gruffyd ap Llywelyn was constrained to acknowledge that he was an under-king; and after his death in 1063 the subordination of Wales, once again divided into several principalities, was even more obvious. The ruling princes took an oath of fealty to Edward through his vicar, swore that they would be faithful vassals and perform all the customary duties, including military service, and surrendered hostages.[3] But this, it seems, is as far as the dependence went. There is no evidence that Edward normally interfered in Wales, entertained appeals from the courts of the native rulers, or attempted to grant land within the areas under Welsh rule. Over the king of Scots Edward's dominion was probably even less substantial. It can hardly be doubted that Malcolm Canmore, put on the throne by English military power, acknowledged from time to time that he was Edward's vassal.[4] But there is no evidence of regular tribute to be paid, routine services to be rendered, and there is little likelihood that they were. Malcolm was merely within Edward's sphere of influence and anxious for English support against other powers in Scotland. Ireland, however, was completely independent. Neither the native rulers nor 'the foreigners of Dublin' looked to England. They were content to fight among themselves. The Irish annals deal almost solely with insular affairs. The *Annals of Tigernach*, compiled before 1088,

---

[1] *VEdR*, pp. 11, 13; 55; 20, 26.

[2] Plummer, *Two Chronicles*, p. 253, wonders whether these are the Britons of Cornwall or Strathclyde. He favoured the latter. The kingdom of Strathclyde or Cumbria seems to have been at times in the eleventh century an appanage for the heir to the king of Scots. But a writ of Gospatric, lord of Allerdale and Dalston, addressed to his vassals holding land in what was Cumbria, shows at least that English influence there was strong, and probably expanding. Gospatric's act, however, is that of a very independent ruler; and it would not be surprising if he was the Gospatric whose murder was arranged by Queen Edith and Tostig in 1064 (see below, p. 235). For the writ, see H. W. C. Davis, 'Cumberland before the Norman Conquest', *EHR*, xx (1905), 61–5; Harmer, *Writs*, no. 121.

[3] See below, p. 211.   [4] See below, p. 203.

record that in 1051 Laidgnen, son of Maelán Húa Leocháin, king of the Galenga, went to Rome, and died in the East (Britain) on his return journey. But the annal for 1066 omits Edward's death together with all other English events.[1]

Nevertheless the British sea was not the boundary of Edward's lordship. It is likely that a number of French counts accepted fiefs from him,[2] promising service and swearing fealty in return,[3] and that Svein Estrithson, king of Denmark, was, at least in the early years of their reigns, Edward's vassal.[4] Moreover, if Edward occasionally promised the succession to a foreign prince, his adopted heir would surely have entered into some sort of vassal relationship with him. It is one of the major improbabilities in William of Poitiers' story of the dealings between Edward and William of Normandy that he makes the king, not the duke, swear the oaths and give the hostages.[5] Edward was not hawking round a *damnosa haereditas*. The drafter of a royal charter dated 1050 was nearer the mark when he described Edward as, 'king of the whole Anglo-Saxon race and, by the grace of God, governor and ruler of all the other surrounding peoples'.[6]

We have no contemporary account of the rights and duties of an Old-English king. Even Domesday Book, a survey of the kingdom made at the command of William I, in which we are told much about the royal estates and something about the rights that the king had in the various shires and boroughs, provides only an incomplete and incoherent statement of the regalia. The theory, however, although never formulated, seems to have been simple enough: the kingdom was the king's private estate; it was his to manage; and everyone directly under his power or protection owed him tribute. Such a theory was both permissive and restrictive. On the one hand it allowed the king a plenitude of power: the kingdom was his to exploit; and, on the other, it

---

[1] 'The Annals of Tigernach: the fourth fragment, A.D. 973–A.D. 1088', ed. Whitley Stokes, *Revue Celtique* (Paris), xvii (1896), pp. 392, 405–6.

[2] See above, pp. 41–2, 64–5.

[3] Marc Bloch, *La société féodale* (1939–40), i. 267–9; B. D. Lyon, 'The money fief under the English kings, 1066–1485', *EHR*, lxvi (1951), 161; Walher Kienast, *Untertaneneid und Treuvorbehalt in Frankreich und England* (Weimar, 1952), p. 189 and *n.* 2; Jean-François Lemarignier, 'Structures monastiques et structures politiques dans la France de la fin du Xe et des débuts du XIe siècle', *Settimane di studio del Centro italiano di studi sull'alto medioevo* (Spoleto, 8–14 apr. 1956), iv. 373–82.

[4] See above, p. 64.   [5] See above, p. 108.

[6] 'Ego Eadwardus basileus totius gentis Anglo-Saxonum caeterorumque populorum in circuitu habitantium gratia dei gubernator et rector', *KCD*, no. 793.

restrained his arbitrary action by investing him with all the duties of a good lord and, especially, of a good king: his dominions were a trust; he must be a father and protector to his men and, as God's vicar, must exhibit the Christian virtues in the management of his estate. Edward knew – and sometimes was reminded – that after his death he would have to render to God an account of his stewardship.

The economic condition of England in the mid-eleventh century can only be described in the broadest terms, and even these are mostly deductions from what we think was the general situation. The year 1000 should have been awaited less with fear for the end of the world than with joy for the end of a cold spell which had lasted several centuries. It is now accepted by climatologists that the period 1000/ 1100–1300 was one of the warmest and most favourable climatic phases in historical times. The summers were dry and sunny and the winters mild.[1] As Edward's reign lies at the beginning of this era it presumably did not feel the full effect of the change. In the first half of the reign there are a number of references in the Chronicle to extreme weather conditions and attacks of plague. In 1042 (Canterbury) there were storms and disease and great damage to cattle and crops; in 1044 (Canterbury and Abingdon) there was a famine, with the sester of wheat reaching 60d. and more; in 1046 (Abingdon) there was a hard winter, with pestilence and murrain, and in 1047 pestilence occurred again; in 1048 (the north) there was pestilence among men and beasts; in 1052 (Abingdon and the north) there was a strong wind on 21 December; and in 1054 (Canterbury) there was pestilence among cattle. It is possible that in the second half of the reign the weather improved and there was less disease, giving a decade of relative prosperity. At all events, we can assume that there was some amelioration in the climate by 1066, and, as quite small increases in the mean average temperature have great effects on the flora, it can be accepted that farmers were beginning to enjoy sunnier days.

The peacefulness of England since 1016 allowed the improvement in the climate to exert its full effect and was itself a great help towards the well-being of the country. In Æthelred's reign there was frequent fighting and the great drain of silver to Scandinavia. Once these disorders had been corrected the economy was bound to be buoyant; and there is nothing in the history of Edward's reign, except for the Chronicle notices in 1042–54, to suggest that it was otherwise.

[1] Cf. H. H. Lamb, *The Changing Climate* (1966), pp. 208–10.

Accordingly, we can apply to England some of the general views which demographers and economic historians take of this period of European history. A better climate and peaceful conditions led to a rising population, which, in its turn, had important economic effects. Whenever population outstripped supplies there was famine and disease; and it is possible that this is what we find in the first part of Edward's reign. Scandinavian settlement in England may easily have pushed the population up, and these settlers were probably especially fertile. By 1050 the balance may have been restored. Even so, with a rising population there was a steady pressure on existing resources and a land hunger which internal and external colonization could not entirely satisfy. The conditions favoured landlords against tenants and the landless. An abundance of manpower made labour cheap and food dear. Lords, if they chose, could offer less attractive terms, demand higher rents, heavier services. The increased demand for food encouraged improvements in agricultural techniques and inevitably it favoured arable as against pastoral farming. More land went under the plough.

One general result was an accumulation of wealth in the hands of the landlords. Some of this went into capital investment in farm buildings, including mills; some was invested for the good of their souls in church construction; and all these works provided employment and income for landless men. But before 1066 there was little diversion of resources into almost wholly unproductive developments, such as castles. The wealth of the landlords also gave a fillip to the luxury trades, encouraged the growth of towns, and stimulated the import of foreign goods.

Kings normally were less well placed than smaller landlords to exploit such conditions. On royal estates the new profit was probably taken by the reeves and farmers. Nevertheless, it was a time when the king, even if he did comparatively badly, could not have become poorer through the operation of economic forces outside his control. And as the great earls were in the same position as himself, there were no political dangers in the situation. Prosperity among the thegns must have made at least for social and political stability.

The royal revenues were ostensibly very large. There was the yield of the demesne, all those estates which Edward had taken over from his predecessor, the landed possessions of the royal family. There were the profits from the boroughs and the church, which were both in a sense dominical. There were the proceeds of justice, although these, it seems, were usually included in the revenue from the estates. There were those various renders and services owed to the king by all under his direct lordship. There were the many casual rewards, the gifts and offerings. And there was geld, the tax due from almost the whole cultivated area of the kingdom. No other king in Europe had a revenue so broadly based. Edward drew every known type of profit from his kingdom and from its whole area. In England no one had a larger demesne; no one else had the right to tax,[1] even to coin;[2] and no one had a larger clientèle. Nevertheless it does not seem that Edward's net revenue much exceeded his ordinary expenses. His one great capital investment was the rebuilding of Westminster abbey, no doubt a costly undertaking but hardly out of keeping with his position, and he seems to have left no great fortune to his successor. If, of course, Edward did forgo the collection of geld, temporarily or permanently, after 1051,[3] this tightness is explicable. His income would have been reduced very considerably and he would have been deprived of the easiest way of amassing a treasure chest.

A man who enters into his inheritance late, and has no children to succeed him, is not usually a careful and far-sighted manager of his estate, and rarely a reformer. Edward was subject to conflicting economic forces, which, if not producing complete equilibrium, at least allowed only a slow general movement. The pressure on Edward to be generous, to alienate demesne, was immense. Generosity was the royal virtue that all men joined in praising. The magnates and courtiers, both lay and ecclesiastical, had no particular interest in the mainten-ance of the royal demesne. That the king should live of his own was taken for granted – there was nothing else for him to live on – but the scale of his living was not of great concern to others. The clause in the royal charters by which the bishops and magnates consent to the royal alienation of land had disappeared long before Edward's reign;[4] and

[1] Tostig, earl of Northumbria, is said by Florence, i. 223, to have collected an immense tax (*tributum*) c. 1065 from the whole of his earldom. But its collection is described as unjust and as one of the causes of the rebellion against Tostig, and it obviously explains why the rebels broke open his treasury at York.

[2] The profit of a mint sometimes went to a favoured prelate: to Abbot Baldwin of Bury St. Edmunds, Harmer, *Writs*, no. 25; to the bishop of Hereford, *DB*, i. 179 a i.

[3] See above, p. 106.

[4] Maitland, *DB and Beyond*, pp. 294–5.

the few references in Domesday Book to 'the land of the kingdom'[1] seem eccentric. With all the magnates and courtiers wanting grants of land and privilege from the king, mutual jealousy could have had a restraining influence, but could also have led to an almost uncontrollable landslide. It is easy to illustrate royal alienations from Edward's reign: he reduced assessments to geld, perhaps remitted it altogether, and granted land and every type of royal right. Indeed, Maitland thought that he dispersed his jurisdictional rights with complete abandon.[2] Once he even remitted the 'common burdens', the defence duties; but this most unusual concession was in respect of an estate he had granted to his favourite abbey, Westminster.[3] Yet it is hard to believe that Edward was much more generous than his predecessors, for example, Edgar. He had no children and mistresses and few close relations to provide for. The number of foreign favourites he enriched seems to have been small. Since book-land was forfeited for crime, it is even possible that Edward recovered as much land as he granted away.[4] In any case, it must be remembered, many royal gifts were in fact sales and most were 'enfeoffments' in return for service.

There were also restraints on Edward's carelessness and generosity. Even if he had little interest in provident husbandry, the rents and services were fixed by custom, and little effort was required to keep them steady. Nor is it likely that his household advisers and servants would have allowed him to be grossly and continually cheated by the royal agents in the shires. Moreover, Edward seems personally to have been neither avaricious nor extravagant, indeed in some ways he may have been parsimonious. The author of the *Vita* certainly thought Edward frugal, a prince who cared nothing for finery and royal pomp,

[1] 'ad regnum', *DB*, iv. 75; 'de regno', ii. 119; 'ad regionem', ii. 144; 'de regione' ii. 281b, 408b. Maitland, *op. cit.*, pp. 206–7.

[2] Maitland, *op. cit.*, p. 333; cf. Harmer, *Writs*, pp. 126–7. Maitland, however, exaggerates the importance of the jurisdiction surrendered: it was almost all of a petty nature. See below, p. 147.

[3] Sawyer, no. 1031. See below, p. 333.

[4] A case recorded by *KCD*, no. 801 (Sawyer, no. 1026), dated 1055, a charter generally considered spurious, is at least typical. Edward was awarded by the judgment of his thegns and earls an estate at Upper Swell (Glos) because of the crime of Eansige son of Hoc; and this land, rated at 3 hides, he then granted to Abbot Manni of Evesham *in ius ecclesiasticum, ad victum monachorum . . . perpetuo iure*, in return for 6 marks of gold to the king and 1 mark to the queen; the estate still to be liable to the common burdens. Here we have the record of a forfeiture followed by a purchased enfeoffment.

who owed his majesty on state occasions solely to the queen.[1] But here he was pushing too hard the themes of Edward's other-worldliness and Edith's role as Martha. In 1051 Edward commissioned a new crown;[2] and this, together with a reform of the coinage about the same time,[3] suggests that he had some interest in jewelry and the royal image. It is credulous to believe that he lived in unseemly poverty in order to give his savings to good causes. Probably, like most men, he gave generously to some, reluctantly to others, and, although not a big spender, simply spent what he had, and in a variety of ways.

The landed estate (usually called the royal demesne)[4] which Edward inherited from Harthacnut and which he left to Harold was, in its widest sense, the whole kingdom, in its narrowest, the home farms; and there are also some intermediate positions which are worth looking at. If we consider the whole kingdom as demesne, we see it as the land of the king and of his vassals. The conception is not meaningless, for when the king broke an earl he could recover many estates and thegns for himself if he chose. Land and men reverted from 'service' into 'demesne' in a more restricted sense. Even ecclesiastical land, although it was granted in perpetuity out of royal demesne, and dedicated to the service of the heavenly ruler, was still required to perform some earthly services to the king, was under royal control and protection, and provided benefices for the king's ecclesiastical servants. Edward inherited from Cnut and his sons a rather constricted position in England. Owing to the creation of an earldom of Wessex Edward had no great province that he could call his own. But by marrying Godwin's daughter and making use of Godwin's sons he linked their fortunes, although uneasily, together. There was also compensation in the more national character that Edward inevitably acquired. It does not appear that the Northumbrians, Mercians, and East-Anglians regarded him simply as a West-Saxon king, although the more northerly people, who never saw him, cannot have been much interested in his welfare. Moreover, if the great confiscations of 1051 had stood, Edward would have

---

[1] VEdR, pp. 40–2.   [2] See above, p. 106.   [3] See below, pp. 183–4.

[4] I have had some useful discussions on this subject with my colleague, Dr. B. P. Wolffe. Like 'feudalism', the 'royal demesne' is something of a modern invention. Wolffe believes that it is misleading to make a contrast between demesne income (land revenue) and other, more 'public', sources of royal revenue, and that from a very early period receipts from land were only a minor source of the king's income. I agree. But as 'demesne' is a useful term, I would widen its definition rather than avoid it.

considerably increased the royal estate. In any case, endowments were only a loss if the king did not exact the services due. There is nothing to suggest that Edward was a particularly slack master, or that he granted too much land away or bought unnecessary services. His earls and bishops served him energetically, indeed, he may sometimes have thought, even too well.

If we move down a step and subtract the earldoms and the church lands, we are left with the estates which were directly administered by royal agents to yield rents or produce for the king, and the estates of a great number of men of varying wealth and position who by one bond or another were all directly under the king. These range from great nobles, royal thegns with estates in several shires, to small freeholders, subject to the king's jurisdiction or commended to him. All these men in a way owned their land.[1] The more important, certainly the thegns, held book-land. But all owed the king some service, rent, or remunerative custom.

Finally, we can subtract the land of the nobles; and here we come to the scheme adopted by the Domesday commissioners of 1086. In Domesday Book *terra regis*, the land of the king, is contrasted with the lands of the barons, prelates, and great churches. It consists, therefore, of the estates administered for the king by reeves or other speculators, land not granted out for service, together with the estates of, usually, small freeholders who have no other lord than the king. The old boroughs are often put in an ambiguous position: it was not clear whose they were; and if the commissioners had had to make a return which reconstructed the situation in 1066 they would have been faced by other puzzles. But the line they took is easily understandable: using common sense they apportioned to each great man or church what he, or the church's incumbent, regarded as 'his very own'.

If we can trust Domesday Book, Edward's dominical estates were in 1066 very unequally spread within the kingdom. He possessed no manors in Middlesex, Essex, Hertfordshire, Rutland, Lincolnshire,

---

[1] D. A. Bullough, 'Anglo-Saxon Institutions and Early English Society', *Annali della Fondazione italiana per la storia amministrativa* (Milan), 2 (1965), p. 651, *n.* 16, argues, rightly I believe (see my *English Church*, p. 168, *n.* 4), for the use of 'landowner', 'landownership', etc. in preference to 'superiority'. He observes that those who prefer the latter term posit criteria for 'ownership' of land which would seem to deny its existence at almost every period of western European history. It may be added that Maitland, *DB and Beyond*, pp. 278 ff., almost perversely denies the 'reality' of landholding and uses the term 'superiority'.

Cheshire, and Cornwall and few in East Anglia and Yorkshire. Some of these voids were caused by massive alienations to earls, although not necessarily by Edward.[1] Since King William after the Conquest rectified the position, it may have been thought desirable to have a widely scattered estate; but since the change may simply have been due to the forfeiture of the estates of the English earls, the matter must be left in doubt. In any case, for a careful and energetic king the estates of his vassals and servants did not represent a threat to royal power, a diminution of the royal estate. Mintable silver was so scarce that salaried servants were rare. Edward retained a few mercenary troops and doubtless made some cash payments to a number of his domestics. But the usual way in which servants were paid was to grant them an estate which produced a revenue; and one of the purposes of the royal demesne was to enable the king to endow soldiers and the other helpers he needed.[2]

The view that the Anglo-Saxon thegn was granted land as a reward for past services, whereas a feudal vassal was given a benefice to enable him to perform services in the future, has no merit at all.[3] Both propositions are generally true of both types of vassal. In feudal France, as in England, an estate was usually granted as a reward to a faithful servant, to one who had served in the household with this prize in mind; and the grant often marked a partial or final pensioning off. A soldier could not fight for ever. A clerk aspired to retire to a comfortable benefice. Also, it was when the landless man inherited an estate from his father or was granted one by his lord that he was in a position to marry and set up his own household. He acquired cares and responsibilities of his own, and so became less useful to his lord. But, just as neither an English nor a feudal king as a rule granted an estate to a stranger, so the one, no more than the other, did not exempt the endowed servant from all

---

[1] Edward's surviving charters and writs are concerned with lands mostly within the earldom of Wessex, and he made few grants or confirmations north of a line drawn from Lowestoft to Bristol. This pattern is partly determined by the location of the monasteries which preserved charters; but it shows that Edward was not endowing the convents or his thegns with lands in the north, and suggests that the overall distribution of the royal demesne was little affected by his action.

[2] For example, Edward gave land in Berkshire to the wife of sheriff Godric in return for feeding his dogs, *DB*, i. 57 b ii.

[3] On the status of the thegn and the relationship of the thegn to his lord, see Maitland, *DB and Beyond*, pp. 201 ff., 346 ff., 366 ff.; Paul Vinogradoff, *English Society in the Eleventh Century* (1908), pp. 403 ff.; H. R. Loyn, 'Gesiths and thegns in Anglo-Saxon England from the Seventh to the Tenth Century', *EHR*, lxx (1955), 529–49.

future duties. Landed thegns owed the king services;[1] and the liability was hereditary with the land and rank. In this general respect it is impossible to contrast the Old-English thegn and the Anglo-Norman baron. Edward, just as later, say, Henry I, relied on the services of members of families which he or his predecessors had endowed with land; and normally each king rewarded a new set of men who were more responsive to his wishes than the old servants he had taken over.

Two types of document concerned with the grant of land have survived in fair quantity: charters and writs.[2] The Latin charter, normally drawn up by the beneficiary as a dated memorial of the transaction, rehearsed the boundaries of the estate in English and stated what may have been considered the basic conditions. The writ, addressed usually to the shire court, or a group of shires, and written in English, listed the judicial and financial privileges conveyed with the land. The two documents are complementary, but not exhaustive, accounts of the bargain. The surviving charters with a claim to authenticity free the estate from all earthly service except the common burdens, that is to say, military service and the maintenance of bridges and fortifications, and expressly grant an heritable estate: the grantee can bequeath it to whom he chooses. But this is not the whole story. Behind the grant is concealed the contract. All gifts required a counter-gift or counter-performance.[3] We know from other evidence that there could be – perhaps usually was – a purchase price. We may think that often the king expected services from the grantee which were not written into the charter. And it is certain that the land granted was still liable to geld. Moreover, the king was hardly conveying a freehold in the modern sense. Every transaction concerning book-land, as such estates were called, required the king's consent, and royal approval had usually to be bought.[4] At the death of a thegn an appropriate heriot,

---

[1] See below, pp. 147–8.

[2] See above, pp. xxv–xxvi.

[3] H. D. Hazeltine, 'Comments on the Writings known as Anglo-Saxon Wills', *Anglo-Saxon Wills*, ed. Dorothy Whitelock (1930), pp. xviii–xx, xxv–xxvii. Cf. p. xix, 'The gift of land, even the gift of book-land by the king . . . had marked contractual aspects.'

[4] Wills normally state the king's consent and the price paid for it. The bishop of Worcester, when making grants and enfeoffments, mentioned the licence of the king and of the earl; cf. *KCD*, nos. 764, 805, 823. Other examples showing the royal interest are *KCD*, nos. 819, 904, 912, 927, 945, 962–4. There are also examples in *DB*; cf. *DB*, i. 238 b ii *ad fin*. Maitland, *DB and Beyond*, pp. 194, 349–52, discusses restraint on the alienation of book-land.

or succession duty, had to be paid to the king;[1] and often, it seems, the king or the queen expected to get some of the estate back.[2]

The writs inform the local courts of the ancillary rights which the king is granting with the land. These are normally expressed as 'sake and soke, toll, team, and infangenetheof'.[3] *Toll* and *team* give the lord a share in the profits from trade conducted within the estate; *sake* and *soke* grant him petty jurisdiction over the inhabitants of the estate; and *infangenetheof* allowed him to hang and take the chattels of a thief caught on the property. Sometimes the king gave *grithbryce, forstal,* and *hamsocn* as well, jurisdiction over the less serious crimes of violence – minor 'breaches of the peace'. These grants made territorial lords petty royal justices and administrators, and were a necessary devolution of power. Occasionally, and only perhaps for specially favoured churches, the king created greater franchises, sometimes granting a few of the more serious 'reserved' crimes, sometimes putting hundred courts or, less often, the equivalent of shire courts into episcopal and abbatial hands. These large immunities were very few.[4]

Book-land,[5] with which Edward's earls, thegns, and prelates were endowed, had not exactly the same features as the contemporary feudal benefice on the Continent. But it was granted in return for service; there were limitations on its heritability; it formed a petty judicial and administrative franchise; and it served the same purpose as the fief. Moreover, as the Norman Conquest proved, nothing was easier than to treat book-land as fiefs.

The duties of a thegn are listed in a vernacular document known as *Rectitudines Singularum Personarum*, one of a collection of tracts on legal and administrative subjects attributed to Wulfstan, bishop of Worcester 1002–16 and archbishop of York 1002–23.[6] In return for his book-land

---

[1] II Cnut 70–1, laying down the tariff. Cf. Maitland, *DB and Beyond*, pp. 194, 205, 351–2. Since the tenth-century reformation, bishops were not required to pay the king a heriot: Eric John, *Land Tenure in Early England*, pp. 57–8.

[2] Cf. *KCD*, no. 808 (Sawyer, no. 1029), admittedly a charter of doubtful reputation.

[3] Maitland, *op. cit.*, pp. 110 ff.; Vinogradoff, *op. cit.*, pp. 115 ff.; Harmer, *Writs*, pp. 73 ff.

[4] Naomi D. Hurnard, 'The Anglo-Norman Franchises', *EHR*, lxiv (1949), 289–327, 433–60; Maitland, *DB and Beyond*, p. 328; Vinogradoff, *op. cit.*, pp. 111–13; Barlow, *English Church*, pp. 174–5.

[5] Maitland, *op. cit.*, p. 272 ff.; Vinogradoff, *op. cit.*, pp. 253–5; Eric John, *Land Tenure in Early England*, chapter IV; Barlow, *English Church*, pp. 167–9.

[6] Liebermann, *Gesetze*, i. 444; *EHD*, ii. 813. Dorothy Bethurum, *The Homilies of Wulfstan* (1957), p. 46.

the thegn has to perform the three common duties: military service, the repairing of fortresses, and work on bridges, and, in addition, those other services that the king shall require, such as equipping a guard ship and guarding the coast, guarding the lord, military watch, maintaining the deer fence at the king's residence, alms giving, church dues, and so on. This is avowedly an incomplete list of the duties owed, but even so, it is more certain and detailed than any statement we have of the duties of a knight in the early post-Conquest period. Whatever emphasis be put on the more miscellaneous obligations, it cannot be doubted that the thegn's basic duty was military. We may also think that among duties omitted from the list are running his lord's errands, attending his courts, keeping his secrets, and looking after his interests – in short, the performance of a variety of honourable personal services. The thegn was also qualified to hold a royal office: to be appointed earl and govern a province, to have a special place at court, such as steward or chamberlain, or in the shires, as a reeve. Without this class of noble servants, endowed with land and commended to the king, the kingdom could not have been governed.

Contemporaries were not concerned with the problem, which has interested some modern historians, whether the thegn owed these services because of his rank, personal subjection (vassalage), or possession of land (holding a benefice or fief). These are various aspects of noble servitude as it had developed in England over the centuries. We should notice, however, that the author of the *Rectitudines* states categorically that it was because the thegn held book-land that he owed the duties he listed; and, according to a law of Æthelred,[1] anyone who deserted an army which was under the personal command of the king risked losing his property. Even less convincingly can we divide a thegn's duties into those which he owed Edward as king and those he owed Edward as his lord. Edward was the lord king.

The lands of the prelates and great churches likewise served the kingdom and the king.[2] Even in their primary role, the maintenance of the servants of God, they were useful, for they provided for constant intercession with God for the English nation and its rulers, and endowed a *magisterium* whereby the people were instructed in Christian morality and their duties to God and his church. Moreover, although the spiritual head of the church was the pope, and this was fully acknow-

[1] VI Atr. 35; cf. II Cnut 77, 1.
[2] Barlow, *English Church*, chapter II.

ledged by the *ecclesia Anglorum*, the effective head was the king. The history of the *regnum* was also the history of the *ecclesia*; and the tenth-century reformation, carried out by the kings at the behest of the bishops, had renewed the community of interest. The English church was nationalist and royalist, and willingly undertook secular duties not only to secure its authority in local affairs, but also as a contribution to the welfare of the kingdom.

By the middle of the eleventh century, however, many of the services and profits which a lay ruler took from the church were beginning to be regarded by some reformers as unlawful.[1] The main target was simony, the selling of ecclesiastical offices and sacraments. This was denounced as an heretical practice and found no apologists. More radical, and less generally acceptable, was the view that it was wrong for a clerk merely to accept a benefice from the hands of a layman, even though it was given freely, and wrong also to perform any secular services, or services to a layman, on any pretext whatsoever.

So strictly could simony be construed, that it was almost impossible for a king to be completely free from it. If he accepted a gift in return for a benefice, if he merely expected the bargain to be to his advantage, there was scope for the casuist. But it is difficult to be sure that no grosser forms were practised in Edward's reign. On the credit side is that the English bishops survived the scrutiny of the council of Rheims in 1049 and that, although several of Edward's bishops were deposed in 1070, none, it seems, was charged with simony. Also Coleman, St Wulfstan's biographer, wrote expressly, 'No trader in churches, no money-grubber, could ever find anything in Edward's mind which was of profit to his schemes.'[2] Against this is William of Malmesbury's charge that Archbishop Stigand held a public market in bishoprics and abbacies.[3] It is clear beyond doubt that Edward did not habitually sell churches for money. We can hardly believe, for example, that Wulfstan bought Worcester in 1062. But Edward and Edith obviously expected gifts. At least two royal clerks who obtained bishoprics 'lost' an episcopal estate to Edith.[4] And early in the reign there were rumours of simony involving the king.[5] We also know of one case of the buying and selling of a church at Edward's court.[6] St Mary's Huntingdon originally belonged to Thorney abbey. It was pledged by the abbot to

---

[1] *Ibid.*, pp. 99 ff., 301 ff.   [2] *Vita Wulfstani*, p. 18.   [3] *GP*, pp. 35–6.
[4] Herman of Sherborne (*DB*, i. 77 a i.) and Giso of Wells (*DB*, i. 87 a i, 89 b ii).
[5] See above, pp. 78–9.   [6] *DB*, i. 208 a i.

the burgesses, presumably as security for a loan, and then passed into Edward's hands, possibly because he settled the debt. Edward gave it to his clerks, Vitalis and Bernard, who sold it to Hugolin, Edward's chamberlain, who sold it to two priests of the borough.

Edward probably, and some of his courtiers certainly, made a financial profit from royal ecclesiastical patronage; but it was not much and hardly enough to justify a charge of simony. The real profit was in the specialized service he obtained from his bishops, abbots, and clerks. He used ecclesiastical benefices to pay and reward his clerks, and he expected prelates to serve at court and in the shires. Bishops and abbots were the king's counsellors; they were literate and learned, especially in law. They were responsible for royal legislation, both ecclesiastical and secular, and bishops often presided over the shire courts. Prelates conducted royal embassies, commanded armies, and assumed some responsibility for local defence. Royal priests and clerks maintained the religious services at court and on the demesne; in the household they performed secretarial and financial duties; indeed their assistance was required in most aspects and at all levels of royal government. Edward paid well for these services. Some of his clerks, like Osbern and Regenbald,[1] accumulated large estates, indistinguishable from those of royal thegns. Some were given bishoprics and still attracted landed gifts from the king. But although these grants were by charter and in form heritable, Edward seems to have put a restriction on their alienation. In 1060, at the insistence of Queen Edith, he invalidated Archbishop Cynsige's bequest worth £300 to Peterborough abbey,[2] and, urged by Archbishop Stigand and Earl Harold, he stopped Bishop Duduc's bequest to Wells of estates which Cnut had given him.[3] Occasionally a clerk was broken and his estate resumed. About 1065 Edward banished Spirites and took all his estates into his own hands, except an ecclesiastical benefice which he gave to his kinsman and staller, Robert fitzWimarch, a layman.[4]

Besides these personal services performed by ecclesiastical persons to the king, there were also the duties due from church estates. The eighth-century kings of Mercia and later the kings of Wessex had

[1] Barlow, *English Church*, p. 157.

[2] *The Chronicle of Hugh Candidus, a monk of Peterborough*, ed. W. T. Mellows (1949), pp. 70, 73.

[3] *Ecclesiastical Documents: A brief History of the Bishoprick of Somerset*, ed. J. Hunter, Camden Soc. (1840), pp. 15–16; Barlow, *English Church*, p. 75n.

[4] *DB*, i. 252 b ii; *Hemingi Chartularium*, i. 254.

imposed military service and the construction of fortresses and bridges; and these 'common burdens' involved the church deeply in secular affairs.[1] The tenth-century reformation on balance even increased the church's secular duties, for the monasteries not only gained much hidated land but were also granted the administration of hundreds. Thus the bishoprics and abbeys and most of the larger churches owed, because of their estates, military service and the other common burdens, geld, and responsibility for the administration of justice.

The value of the services owed by earls, thegns, bishops, abbots, and other endowed royal servants could not, and cannot be estimated in money. The value, however, of the residuary royal demesne – the home farms and the renders of the smaller royal vassals – could be expressed financially; and in 1086, when the kingdom was surveyed, the 1066 values were entered for each estate. We know from Domesday Book that in Edward's reign the royal demesne was exploited mainly in one of two ways: the individual estates, or manors, were organized into either provisioning or revenue groups. The former supplied a fixed amount of agricultural produce for the king's household on its visits; the latter were leased to a speculator for a fixed money rent. Estates in Old Wessex (Hampshire, Wiltshire, Dorset, and Somerset) were still producing a number of food renders, each in theory enough to support the king and his household for a night.[2] But these were survivals: the movement was towards a money economy.

In Wiltshire Edward held the manor of Amesbury, which had arable estimated at 40 ploughlands, 70 acres of meadow, pasture 4 leagues long and 3 leagues broad, and woodland 6 leagues long and 4 leagues broad. Eight mills paid £4 10s. od. On the demesne were 55 slaves and 2 freedmen with 16 ploughs, and among the 85 villeins and 56 cottagers (*bordarii*) were 23 ploughs. The animal population is not stated. The manor was not assessed in hides and had never paid geld. Nor was it given a money value: together with its appendages it rendered 'the farm of one night' with all customary dues. A supplementary note informs us that Edward in his [? last] sickness granted 2 hides of this manor to the abbess of Wilton.[3] As an example of a

---

[1] Nicholas Brooks, 'The development of military obligations in eighth- and ninth-century England', *England before the Conquest* (Whitelock *Festschrift*, 1971).

[2] A clear account of the arrangement in Dorset is given by Ann Williams, *VCH (Dorset)*, iii (1968), 27–8.

[3] *DB*, i. 64 b ii; *VCH (Wilts)*, ii. 116.

manor providing a money rent we may take Silverton in Devon, a royal manor estimated at 41 ploughlands, 50 acres of meadow, 200 of pasture, and 4 of woodland. Three mills paid 20s. a year. On the demesne were 15 slaves with three ploughs; and there were 45 villeins with 33 ploughs and 31 cottagers (*bordarii*). The animal population included 20 sheep. The manor was not hidated and had never paid geld. It was worth £40 [a year] paid in pennies that had been weighed and assayed.[1]

Besides the agricultural profits of the manors there were also the more urban revenues of the boroughs.[2] These institutions had been created by the kings to serve as fortresses and markets. They were walled towns, sometimes carefully planned, with their streets laid out on a grid plan; and the responsibility for maintaining the fortifications and defending them was laid on the surrounding country. The boroughs were not only defensive redoubts against foreign invaders but also a haven for merchants. Trade was deliberately channelled through them; and all housed one or more mints. Their profit derived mainly from rents, tolls, and the proceeds of the borough court; and this the king had usually to share with the earl, who took 'the third penny', presumably as payment for his duties in connexion with the maintenance of the borough. But few arrangements were as simple as this. For example, at Dover half the profits had been granted to the canons of St Martin, and it was only the other half, worth £18, which was divided between King Edward and Earl Godwin in the proportion 2:1. Permanent inhabitants paid customary dues to the king and were exempted from toll throughout England. The burgesses performed naval service to the king in return for the profits of jurisdiction known as *sake* and *soke*. The town was under the king's peace from the feast of St Michael to St Andrew's day; and if anyone broke it the king's reeve took a fine from all burgesses in common.[3] At Worcester the king had £10 and Earl Eadwine £8. When the shire paid geld, the city was reckoned at 15 hides. The king took no other due there except the tax on the houses collected according to the liability of each. But there was also this customary due: when the coinage was changed each moneyer gave 20s. when he received the dies at London.[4]

[1] *DB.* Addit. fo. 76; i. 100 a ii; *VCH (Devon)*, i. 403–4.
[2] Maitland, *op. cit.*, pp. 213 ff. For tolls and market dues, see Florence E. Harmer, '*Chipping* and *Market*: a lexicographical investigation', *The Early Cultures of North-West Europe* (H. M. Chadwick Memorial Studies), ed. Sir Cyril Fox and Bruce Dickins (1950), pp. 333 ff. Barlow *et al.*, *Winchester in the Early Middle Ages*.
[3] *DB*, i. 1 a i; *VCH (Kent)*, iii. 203.   [4] *DB*, i. 172 a i; *VCH (Worcs)*, i. 282.

As Domesday Book gives the recent history of each estate and its value in 1066 the value of Edward's demesne can in theory be calculated. But the few attempts that have been made to sort out the manors and estates and add up their values have not been altogether fruitful, and for some very good reasons. In the first place, the Domesday information is incomplete. Although the manors which were in direct exploitation in 1066 can be identified fairly easily and their values, which were substantial, added up, the complete reconstruction of Edward's lordship over small freemen and their estates is impossible, for the history of such minor holdings is not fully recorded. Secondly, even if a financial total is produced it has little meaning. It has been calculated that Edward's demesne was worth in 1066 some £5,500 a year.[1] This sum is generally understood as the total rental. But this is not net income. The amounts which twelfth-century sheriffs, who farmed the shires, contracted to pay the king are so much smaller than Domesday statistics would give us to expect that, unless we are prepared to believe that the Norman kings threw away their patrimony with both hands, we must conclude that the difference is largely due to the cost of administration and collection, and that Edward could not have bargained with his reeves for as much as half the amount due to him.[2] And even if we were then to think that Edward may have been owed some £2,500 a year from his agents, what we still cannot discover is how much they paid into the king's chamber and treasury in cash. As we know from later practice, the royal rent collectors disbursed much of the receipts locally, paying for the construction and repair of buildings and the re-stocking of manors, paying salaries, giving customary alms to royal pensioners, buying for the court in local markets, and settling many miscellaneous royal debts. As Edward had no elaborate storage system for money, we may think that the cash receipts were small and that the court lived from hand to mouth.

To be distinguished from the land revenues, but in practice probably often included in them, are what are usually called the perquisites of

[1] W. J. Corbett, *Cambridge Medieval History*, v (1926), 508, estimated William's revenue from land at £11,000, and expressed the belief that this was about twice the amount of the Crown's revenue in King Edward's day. Robert H. Davies, *The lands and rights of Harold, son of Godwine, and their distribution by William I: A study in the Domesday evidence* (unpublished M.A. dissertation, University College, Cardiff, 1967), pp. 3–4, values the royal estates at about £5,000 and Edith's at £900.

[2] R. W. Southern, *The Place of Henry I in English History* (The Raleigh Lecture on History, British Academy, 1962), pp. 158 ff.

government. The most substantial item was the profits of justice; and the extent of the king's judicial rights is often stated under the shire and borough rubrics in Domesday Book. The king took penalties for certain types of offence from certain classes of men; but usually he only received a residual share of the profits. There were special royal forfeitures (not always exactly the same) in all parts of the kingdom, although occasionally the king alienated even some of these. Especially there were those crimes which touched the royal person, such as treason, harbouring an outlaw, breach of the king's peace, giving unjust judgments, desertion from the army, and disobedience to a royal order, and those other heinous, capital crimes, such as murder, arson, attacks on houses, open theft, robbery, and coining.[1] All fines incurred by holders of book-land went to the king.[2] There were royal sokemen – freemen under the king's jurisdiction – in several shires.[3] And on the royal demesne most judicial customs would belong to the king. But, except perhaps in a very few cases, all these jurisdictional profits were shared. Penalties imposed in the public courts at the instigation of the church for breaches of the moral code and other ecclesiastical offences were divided between the lay and ecclesiastical authorities.[4] The profits of the shire courts and of those hundred courts which were not in private hands were shared, in the proportion of two to one, with the earl.[5] And, as these profits were attached to royal manors, the reeves or farmers took their cut as well.

The other main ingredient in the perquisites of government was what the post-Conquest royal secretariat called *oblata*, oblates, offerings or gifts. Presents were an important feature of this society. Probably no bargain was ever struck without the making of token payments in addition; favours were not expected to be gratis; the approach to any great man was through bribed servants; and every gift required something in return. The king, as the grantor of ecclesiastical benefices, landed estates, privileges, protection, favour, and permission for this and that, was promised and accepted many gifts.[6] It is likely that he

[1] II Cnut, 12–15, 58, 61–5; Maitland, *DB and Beyond*, pp. 108–9, 118–19; Naomi D. Hurnard, 'The Anglo-Norman Franchises', *EHR*, lxiv (1949), 289–327, 433–60.

[2] I Atr. 1, 14.   [3] Cf. Kent, *DB*, i. 1 a ii.

[4] Barlow, *English Church*, pp. 137 ff.   [5] Maitland, *op. cit.*, pp. 126–7.

[6] For example, about 1049 Ælfwine, abbot of Ramsey, secured a bequest, despite opposition from a relation of the testator, by buying Edward's favour with 20 marks of gold, Edith's with 5. *Chronicon abbatiae Rameseiensis*, ed. W. Dunn Macray (Rolls ser. 1886), pp. 169–70.

received more in coin and specie than he himself had to pay out. But the claims on his own purse were not insignificant. He was expected to make offerings to churches, to officiating clergy and shrines, give alms to the poor and sick, the widow, the orphan, and the oppressed. Kinsmen, poets, fortune-hunters, flatterers, accredited money-raisers for foreign churches, adventurers of all sorts tried their luck and sought to tap his bounty. We are told that Edward was generous to foreign churches and to the sick and needy.[1] In the obituary poem in the Anglo-Saxon Chronicle he receives the conventional epithet – conventional because also applied there to Cnut and his sons – 'lavish of riches'. Although probably not extravagant, he cannot have been as avaricious and greedy as William the Conqueror.[2]

England was unique in western Europe in being liable to a national tax, *heregeld*, the army tax, which was used to pay the wages of mercenary troops.[3] According to the *D* version of the Chronicle, in the entry for 1051, Æthelred had instituted the tax in 1012 and Edward abolished it thirty-nine years later. It is uncertain, however, whether its collection was suspended for long.[4] Geld was certainly unpopular. Not only was it associated with Viking raids and foreign rule, it also 'was a tax which had to be paid before all other taxes and it oppressed all the English people in many ways.'[5]

Geld was a land-tax; and for its collection use was made of rating valuations, mostly of some antiquity. The north and east of England, except East Anglia, was assessed in terms of carucates, Kent in sulungs, and the rest in hides. The tax was normally collected annually at 2s. the hide, carucate, or sulung. Many small villages, many thegnly estates, were rated at 5 hides; and the abstraction of coin from the farmers in this way must have had important economic effects. By reducing local spending power, the tax must have had a depressing effect on agriculture, industry, and trade. And it caused much social misery, for those who could not pay had their land forcibly sold to those who would.[6] Nor was there merely a redistribution of cash within the kingdom. Much of the wages paid to mercenaries may have gone overseas.

The system of assessment was explored by Round, Maitland, and

[1] *VEdR*, pp. 40–2, 63.   [2] Obituary poem in *Chron. E*.
[3] J. H. Round, *Feudal England* (1895); Maitland, *op. cit.*, pp. 25–30 and *passim*; Vinogradoff, *op. cit.*, pp. 140 ff.; most studies of *DB* are concerned incidentally with geld.
[4] See above, p. 106, n. 5.   [5] *Chron. D*, p. 116.   [6] *Hemingi Chartularium*, i. 278.

Vinogradoff.[1] Except in East Anglia, provincial quotas had been at some time divided between shires, then hundreds, then villages, and finally between the private estates. Investigators have reconstructed from Domesday Book some very neat patterns, for example, Worcestershire with its 1200 hides and twelve hundreds, each mostly containing a hundred hides. But the original system had been much obscured by 1066. What mattered then was the liability of the individual estate to geld. This was carefully recorded in Domesday Book; and whenever a charter was drawn up to record a transfer of land, the estate's assessment was stated: 'Wherefore I, Edward, by the grace of the ruler of Heaven king of the English, freely grant to one of my thegns named Ælfstan ten hides of land at a place called Sevenhampton, to have and to hold, and then leave it to the heir of his choice.' This estate was rated at ten hides to all services, including geld.[2] If the estate were to be divided, so too, unless special arrangements were made, would the assessment. The system in East Anglia was different. Each estate was responsible for so many pence of every pound to be paid by the hundred.

The whole of England was not assessed to geld. In Wiltshire, Dorset, Somerset, and Devon there were large stretches of unhidated royal demesne.[3] The king did not tax 'his very own'. Also unhidated were agricultural settlements made since the assessment had been imposed. It has been calculated (although Maitland declared that counting hides was repulsive work) that in 1086 there were something less than 70,000 rateable units (hides, carucates, sulungs) in England.[4] This figure was considerably smaller than the original assessment, as a result of reductions made by all kings. Because of obvious over-rating, economic disasters, or favouritism, whole shires, hundreds, or individual estates had had their rating reduced. Edward, for example, reduced the hidage of Fareham in Hampshire from 30 to 20 on account of the ravages of the Vikings.[5] Stanford in Berkshire he reduced from 40 to 30; it was subsequently cut to 6.[6] Also there were various franchises.[7] Some favoured churches and nobles held hidated land which did not pay geld. Some monasteries may have collected it for retention from their estates. In Edward's day the gross yield of the tax at 2s. a hide should

---

[1] J. H. Round, *Feudal England* (1895), pp. 3 ff.; Maitland, *op. cit.*, pp. 464 ff.; Vinogradoff, *op. cit.*, pp. 140 ff.

[2] *KCD*, no. 767 (Sawyer, no. 999).   [3] See above, pp. 151–2.

[4] Maitland, *op. cit.*, pp. 464, 586.   [5] *DB*, i. 40 b i.

[6] *DB*, i. 60 b ii.   [7] Vinogradoff, *op. cit.*, pp. 177 ff.

have been £7,000, with something more from East Anglia. If we subtract the immunities and the cost of collection perhaps £5,000–£6,000 would have been left.[1] It probably exceeded the yield of the demesne and produced much more cash. If Edward did not in fact collect geld during the last fifteen years of his reign, he made a deliberate sacrifice of revenue almost unparalleled in history.

This inquiry into Edward's estate reveals two major features: its customary nature and its national extent. Although national taxation rather than income from what may be called the king's private estates was probably the most important source of royal revenue, and jurisdictional profits were an important item in the returns from land, no one made a qualitative distinction between these different kinds of render. Geld, jurisdiction, rents, services, dues were customs which lay on land. All royal customs and rights, whatever their nature, were the king's own; and it was on them, or rather on the fraction of them which ultimately came into his hands, that he had to live. More remarkable than the nature of the royal estate was its extent. Edward had the right to an unusual number of customs, his lands were widespread, and geld lay on almost all the fields of England – and, with very few exceptions – was all paid to the king. Likewise some services, for example *expeditio*, military service, was owed to the king from the whole land, and to nobody else. There were not yet in England duchies or counties from which the king was excluded, in which his only contacts with the inhabitants were through the local ruler. England was about the maximum size that an eleventh-century king could govern through noble and ecclesiastical servants and remain in supreme and direct command. Edward's estate could only just bear the burden of all those who made a living out of it. But, although his customs were pared down at every stage in their journey from the men who rendered them to their final receipt, in the case of money a box under the royal bed, the tributary area was large and, if not uniform, at least all of a piece.

[1] A mid-twelfth-century geld at 2*s*. on the hide should have produced just over £5,000, but with exemptions and pardons was unlikely to yield as much as £3,500. Maitland, *op. cit.*, p. 29.

Chapter 8

THE KING'S GOVERNMENT

Just as the king had rights over his people and their lands, so he owed them duties in return. This responsibility, the royal office, was of interest to contemporaries, as we can see from the literature of the period. The church particularly was concerned with royal power: it had a practical interest in the king's conduct as patron and a theoretical interest in the legitimacy of his authority in spiritual matters. But it had not inherited treatises especially directed to these problems from either the pagan authors or the Fathers. There was material which could be plundered: on the one side, the works of the Roman jurists, and Cicero's *De Officiis*, useful for its vocabulary and some of its concepts; and, on the other, the Old Testament and St Augustine, who popularized the idea of the just king, *rex justus*. But eleventh-century writers made no systematic study of the subject. They were not interested in justifying royal power in its own right, in analysing its various functions. And not only did their treatment lack philosophical or juristic grasp, it also was entirely without political realism. Wulfstan of York's *Institutes of Polity*, an essay in the style of the Carolingian 'Königsspiegel' literature, in which he considers the duties of the English ruling classes, does not come alive. It is a series of sermons.[1]

No one had the confidence or the inclination to write about what he knew at first hand: how the royal court was organized, how the writs and charters were composed and produced, how the mints were run, what were the customs and practices of the law courts, how the various ordeals were prepared and carried out.[2] No one wrote a treatise on the art of war with examples from recent English history. The church had produced a series of practical and useful handbooks for village priests.[3] It seems to have done nothing in that line for the king and his servants.

[1] *Die 'Institutes of Polity, Civil and Ecclesiastical': Ein Werk Erzbischof Wulfstans von York*, ed. Karl Jost (Swiss Studies in English, vol. 47) (Bern, 1959).

[2] The one secular treatise is the *Rectitudines Singularum Personarum*, probably intended for the use of West-country (? Worcester) reeves, attributed to Archbishop Wulfstan.

[3] Barlow, *English Church*, pp. 277 ff.

Nor did anyone consider in writing how the conduct of royal government could be improved, where it should be developed, where restricted. It is, indeed, almost anachronistic to consider royal government as a generally recognizable concept. To most men royal government was a largely unrelated series of royal acts, the exaction of the king's rights. But most men in the end probably made some judgment on the king's behaviour: the king was at least either good or bad, his conduct just or unjust.

The other-worldly bias of some clerks and monks connected with royal government is almost perverse. The proems to charters could be used – and were, for instance, in Germany – for the notification of royal policy. In England the moralizing pomposities usually denied the very utility and purpose of earthly government. In a charter dated 1044 granting an estate to the Old Minster, Winchester, Edward is made to declare:[1]

> Mournful and detestable to all, stuffed with every kind of filth and encompassed by the dire yelpings of obscene and horrid mortality, the sinful offerings (*piacula*) of this troubled world by their very stimulation remind us, who are not without anxiety for the peace of the land we have acquired, that we should, with all the strength of our mind, despise them and cast them away, detest them and flee from them as the disgusting nausea of melancholy, diligently attending to the Gospel mandate, 'Give, and it shall be given unto you';[2] for, as a certain wise man truly says, 'God loves the cheerful giver.'
>
> Wherefore, touched by this salutary warning, I, Edward, by divine mercy king of the whole English nation, counting the perishable things of this world as worth nothing, and, with all creatures of passage, desiring to obtain those things that last for ever, hasten to grant a fugitive and doubtless transitory little estate in order that I may obtain in the kingdom of Christ and of God an everlasting dwelling-place.

Such hysterical expressions of disgust for the theatre of the world are bizarre trappings for an efficient government. Our guides to the secular scene are men who claim to despise and reject it. We have, of course, to take the attitude of the church into account. It is this contempt for the

---

[1] *KCD*, no. 774 (Sawyer, no. 1006). The phrase 'omnique . . . spurcitia saginati' is also used by John of Fécamp in a similar context: Jean Leclercq and Jean-Paul Bonnes, *Un Maître de la Vie spirituelle au XIᵉ siècle, Jean de Fécamp* (1946), p. 150. There is much more in the same vein; cf. pp. 134, 195. John, an active ecclesiastical reformer, was secretly ashamed of his ministry in the world.

[2] Luke vi. 38.

transitory world which discouraged rational thought, political effort, and planning for the generations to come. It is what explains the Middle Ages. But we cannot swallow it whole. Even among the pessimistic extravagances of the Winchester charter the drafter allowed, although somewhat inconsequentially, a sensible phrase to appear: Edward was not without anxiety for the peace of his newly acquired kingdom. It was difficult, even for monks, completely to reject their material setting, their country and its worldly problems. Moreover, although mundane actions were rarely entirely divorced from religion, royal government in northern Europe had a non-Christian origin and retained from its past its own characteristics and independent justification. Kings accepted from the church the *dei gratia* formula, but did not allow it to displace the other supports of their office.

The king of the English was the son and descendant of kings. As Tacitus wrote in his *Germania*, 'They choose kings by ancestry, generals by merit.'[1] Edward's remote ancestors had been priest-kings, and he traced his descent from Woden. He did not rely completely on the Christian church for charisma. In Germanic languages 'king' is derived from the same root as 'kin', and possibly meant originally 'son of the tribe'. Edward was the symbol, the representative, of his people. But the *king* was also *rex*. Isidore of Seville, in his popular *Etymologiae*, stated, correctly, 'Reges a regendo': 'king' is derived from the verb 'to rule';[2] and by showing that the title came from the function, and implying that the title inferred the activity, he contributed an active principle to the office. But Isidore was also aware of the distinction, made earlier by St Augustine, between a king and a tyrant. The difference, wrote Isidore,[3] could be shown by suitable adjectives: a king was 'mild and temperate', a tyrant 'cruel, wicked and harsh'. The two principal royal virtues were justice and *pietas*. Isidore also wrote that, 'He does not rule who does not correct. Therefore, by doing good the name of king is retained, by sinning it is lost.'[4] In the eleventh century the idea of the just king dominated ecclesiastical thinking.

Wulfstan, in his *Institutes of Polity*, urged that the king must be a father and protector of his people, must cherish religion and the church, establish peace and give good justice, support the well-intentioned and

---

[1] *Germania*, 7.

[2] *Etymologiae*, I, xxix. 3. Cf. the Old-English *Gnomic Verses*, line 59, 'A king is eager to rule.'

[3] I, xxxi; II, xxix. 7; IX, iii. 1–5.   [4] IX, iii. 4.

punish the wrong-doers, especially robbers and bandits and the enemies of God. He must be mild to the good and stern to the wicked.[1] Wulfstan returns to the theme in his chapter on the kingdom. Seven things, he wrote, are befitting a righteous king: love of God, love of righteousness, humility before God, sternness towards evil, the comforting and feeding of God's poor, protection of God's church, just judgments in the case of friend and stranger alike.[2] For Wulfstan, a disciplinarian, things were right or wrong. He tried to hammer home a simple code of righteous behaviour.[3]

Something a little more subtle was also available by the mid-eleventh century. When the Norman writer, William of Poitiers, asserted that the king's principal duty was to be just, to uphold equity, he understood from Cicero that the basis of justice was *fides*, that is to say, the constancy and truthfulness of word and covenants.[4] It was the king's duty to uphold the contracts of society, to see that all rights were observed. This theme appears in the *Vita Ædwardi Regis* in the poem on Godwin's children.[5] 'If every river would keep to its own course, fertilizing its own lands, observing the law that the heavenly order has ordained, then everything in the world would be well.' Edith, the queen, was one who helped to preserve this harmony: 'By her advice peace laps the kingdom on every side and warns the nations against breaking the peace treaties.' This golden age, however, was threatened. 'If malignant envy, by calling up the whirlwinds, should break this agreement, alas what ruin there will be. The wretched world will once again be possessed by the Chaos of old.' Justice meant keeping everything in its proper place.

But Cicero's *fides*, on which justice depended, had also other specialized meanings in the eleventh century. For churchmen *ipsa fides* was the true Faith which taught peace and brotherly love;[6] and for all men *fides* meant fealty, the bond between a vassal (*fidelis*) and his lord.[7] The mutual rights and duties of lords and vassals were the concern of justice and should be determined by it.

---

[1] Ed. Jost, pp. 40–51.   [2] *Ibid.*, pp. 52–4.
[3] Barlow, *English Church*, pp. 68 ff., 283 ff.
[4] Poitiers, p. 28; Cicero, *De Officiis*, I, 7; Raymonde Foreville, Poitiers, p. xli, 'Aux origines de la renaissance juridique: Concepts juridiques et influences romanisantes chez Guillaume de Poitiers, biographe du Conquérant', *Moyen âge*, lviii (1952), 53–61, 77–8.
[5] *VEdR*, pp. 15–17.   [6] Cf. *VEdR*, p. 38.
[7] Maitland, *DB and Beyond*, pp. 346–7.

Nevertheless the view that the king was primarily a justiciar and corrector of his people's sins was largely a piece of clerical wishful thinking. It is what the bishops and abbots would have liked him to be, what they had induced Alfred and Edgar to be, what they required the king to promise at his coronation. It was the place they would assign to the king in God's scheme for the world. Doubtless constant repetition of the idea had some effect; but historically the first duty of the king was the leadership and protection of his people, especially in time of war. Justice, no doubt, was often a desirable quality in a king; but a successful leader could not always be just; sometimes he had to dishonour agreements, behave craftily, disregard the law. The preservation of the people came first. Moreover, all observable duties of an eleventh-century king are more easily seen as extensions of this secular function than as aspects of his role as justiciar. In the ordinary course of events he had to maintain diplomatic relations with foreign powers, lead his army and navy against hostile forces, defend his people and country against invasion. He had to maintain law and order within his kingdom, reform the law, provide courts, and punish the evil-doer. He had to see to the economic welfare of his people, encourage trade, and furnish a good currency. He had to protect not only traders but other defenceless classes and institutions, the church, the widowed, the oppressed, the sick, and the poor. And with the church he had to make provision for the spiritual welfare of his people, maintain the shrines, reform the ministers, coerce the ungodly.

These duties were the king's alone. It was often implied that a wise king took good counsel,[1] listened especially to the church; it was always hoped that the king would choose good servants and keep them in order. But no theory of conciliar government was propounded. Indeed, the religious attitudes which made the king answerable to God for his behaviour, not only made him directly responsible to God, but also discouraged other restraints. Edward's was in no constitutional sense a limited monarchy. Wulfstan of York's chapter on 'The *witan* of the nation' gives the counsellors no rights, few duties.[2]

Yet in practice the king was never seen alone. The very fact that he had personal responsibility ensured that he organized a government of some sort. There were duties that he had to perform. Closest to him was his family; in a wider sense his household was also his *familia*; and in its more formal aspects it was his court. Edward was not surrounded

[1] Cf. above, pp. 4–5. [2] Ed. Jost, p. 62.

by a large group of relations. The only persons who are recognized in the royal charters as being in a special blood relationship to him are the royal ladies, his mother, Ælfgifu (Emma), and his wife Eadgyth (Edith).[1] Both, in documents issued in their own names, describe themselves as *seo hlaefdige*, that is to say, *domina* or lady,[2] or expand it with *Eadwardes cyninges modor*,[3] King Edward's mother, or *Eadwardes kinges lefe*,[4] King Edward's widow. Whether either lady appears in the witness list to a royal charter seems to depend on the house style of the drafter. Ælfgifu (Emma), when she occurs, is always described as the king's mother;[5] Edith is given the title of queen (*regina*),[6] except by Winchester and Westminster, which preferred *eiusdem regis conlaterana*.[7] In no royal charter is Edith given any further description.[8]

As Edward and Edith were childless, the royal household did not contain a nursery; but there may always have been plenty of young people being educated at court. We are told in the *Vita Ædwardi Regis* that Earl Godwin and his wife had their children carefully educated in those arts which would make them useful to future rulers,[9] and no place was more suitable for this than the royal court. Godwin's elder children, Edith, Swegn, and Harold, were probably mature at Edward's accession;[10] but Tostig, Gyrth, and Leofwine may have spent some time with their sister in the royal household. At times there were also nephews, like Ralf of Mantes, and Edward's great-nephew and nieces, Edgar the aetheling, Margaret, and Christina.[11] Margaret's future

[1] Except in the unusual Waltham charter (*KCD*, no. 813), where 'Ego Rodbertus regis consanguineus' appears. This is Robert fitzWimarch, described in *VEdR*, p. 76, as 'eiusdem regis propinquus'. In writs Edward refers to his 'dear kinsman', Wigod of Wallingford, and his kinsman, Swegn [? of Essex, son and heir of Robert fitz-Wimarch], Harmer, *Writs*, nos. 104, 92.

[2] *KCD*, nos. 1337; 917 (Harmer, *Writs*, no. 70); cf. *ibid.*, no. 27. This is also the usual style in the vernacular charters: see Robertson, *Charters*, pp. 156, 168, 170, 172, 184, 188, 212, 218.

[3] *KCD*, no. 965 (Robertson, *Charters*, no. XCVI).

[4] *KCD*, no. 918 (Harmer, *Writs*, no. 72).

KCD, nos. 767, 774, 775, 916.

[6] *KCD*, nos. 778, 801, 805, 807, 808, 813, 817, 819, 823.

[7] *KCD*, nos. 776, 780, 781, 783, 1335; Westminster 1060 (Sawyer, no. 1031; see below, p. 335). Cf. 'ipsius huic lateri . . . imperiali quae sociata viget', *VEdR*, p. 3. In *KCD*, no. 916, we get the double formula, 'ego Eadgyth regina eiusdem collateralis regis'.

[8] In a charter of Ealdred, bishop of Worcester, *KCD*, no. 805, she appears as 'regina Anglorum'.

[9] *VEdR*, p. 6.   [10] *Ibid.*, p. 4, *n.* 2.

[11] See above, pp. 50, 76, below, p. 218.

husband, Malcolm of Scots, probably spent some of his boyhood at Edward's court,[1] and there may also have been youthful hostages of noble blood. It is unlikely, however, that the queen's nephews, the bastards of Swegn and Harold, spent much time with their royal aunt and uncle. Beyond this circle it is doubtful whether relationship to Edward counted for much. There was an enormous number of people, English, Danish, and French, who could claim some connexion. His staller, Robert fitzWimarch, who may have been his major-domo, and who was present at the deathbed, was a relation;[2] so was one of his chaplains, Osbern.[3] But there is nothing to suggest that Edward packed his court with kinsmen.

The inner circle of the court was formed by the royal domestic servants. Ælfric wrote in the preface to his third book of homilies, 'Our nation is subject to one king. . . . An earthly king has many servants (thegns) and divers stewards; he cannot be an honoured king unless he has the state which befits him and serving men to offer him their obedience.'[4] A royal charter dated 1062, in favour of Earl Harold and his new minster at Waltham,[5] gives titles to many of the witnesses. The charter is unlikely to be completely authentic in its present form; but the identifications are interesting as an early look at Edward's court. In the witness list, after the two archbishops and eleven bishops, eleven abbots, and five earls, appear Esgar, steward (*procurator*) of the king's hall, Robert, the king's kinsman, Ralf, royal courtier (*aulicus*), Bondi, royal palace official (*palatinus*), Osbern, royal kinsman, Regenbald, royal chancellor, Peter and Baldwin, royal chaplains, Beorhtric and Ælfstan, princes, Herding, the queen's butler, Azur and Lyfing, royal stewards (*dapifer*), Godwin, the queen's steward, and eleven men described as princes.

We are in the world of the *Vita*, with its palace, princes and *palatini*. The description in the charter of a number of thegns as *principes* proves that its forger or editor knew little about Old-English usage, for *minister* was the Latin equivalent of thegn, *princeps* could stand for an earl, instead of *dux*. It would be unsafe, therefore, to put much weight on the other identifications. Most of the men given a court office are called in other sources 'stallers', a Danish title, probably meaning a

---

[1] See below, p. 202.　　　　[2] *VEdR*, p. 76 and *n.* 4.

[3] Barlow, *English Church*, pp. 131–4, 157.

[4] *Lives of Saints*, ed. W. W. Skeat (Early English Text Soc.), 76 (1881), pp. 6–7.

[5] *KCD*, no. 813 (Sawyer, no. 1036).

'place-holder'. Esgar is the man who, according to the *Carmen de Hastingae proelio*, was the leading citizen who surrendered London to the Conqueror.[1] Robert fitzWimarch may also have been sheriff of Essex.[2] Ralf, a Breton, was the father of Ralf de Gael, William's earl of Norfolk.[3] Bondi may have been sheriff of Bedfordshire.[4] Herding was the son of Eadnoth the staller.[5]

If we look at the charter evidence as a whole and consider the customs of other royal courts, we can hardly doubt that Edward and the queen were served by a number of thegns, also called stallers, who had duties in the household, some in the bedchamber, some in the hall, and some in the court yard.[6] Anglo-Saxon equivalents for many of the Carolingian court officials exist, and, although some hardly occur outside vocabularies, some, such as bur-thegn (bower-thegn) for chamberlain, disc-thegn (plate-thegn) for steward, seem to have been in common use,[7] and can be regarded as vernacular titles. Most of these stallers were important men. They were thegns by rank; they were landowners, often in several areas; and it seems that, even if they were not sheriffs, they held leading positions in the shires. Because these men are to us little more than names, and sometimes, like Godwin, cannot be distinguished from other bearers of the name, we must not think them unimportant. One royal servant not mentioned in the Waltham charter, but known from other sources, was Hugolin, one of Edward's chamberlains, presumably French by birth. He was buried in the cloister of Westminster abbey, and when this was rebuilt by Henry III his body, with those of Æthelgotha, wife of King Saeberht of Essex, Abbot Eadwine, and the monk and historian Sulcard, was translated and put in a new tomb situated in the entrance to the chapter house.[8] Westminster remembered him as 'a thegn, the principal

---

[1] *Carmen*, ll. 679 ff. See also R. H. C. Davis, 'The Carmen de Hastingae Proelio', *EHR*, xciii (1978), 250–1.

[2] But see, Harmer, *Writs*, p. 571; Oleson, *Witenagemot*, p. 130.

[3] Oleson, *Witenagemot*, p. 129; and see below, p. 191, *n.* 1.

[4] Oleson, p. 122.   [5] *Ibid.*, p. 126.

[6] L. M. Larson, *The King's Household in England before the Norman Conquest* (1904); Barlow, *English Church*, pp. 115 ff.

[7] The aethelings Æthelstan, *c.* 1013, and Edmund Ironside, 1012, had *discthegns*, Whitelock, *Wills*, p. 61, Robertson, *Charters*, p. 149; *burthein* occurs in Westminster writs of doubtful authenticity, Harmer, *Writs*, nos. 62, 74. The *burgtheines* in *ibid.*, nos. 75, 105, 106 are presumably 'borough-thegns', citizens.

[8] *The History of Westminster Abbey by John Flete*, ed. J. Armitage Robinson (1909), p. 83. See also, Harmer, *Writs*, p. 564.

chamberlain of St Edward the king, always devoted to God, and among all the magnates of this realm Edward's most loyal knight.' The epitaph over his first tomb ran:

> This place holds you, O Hugolin, who fell unjustly;
> You are distinguished by your merits, for in your
> death you equal the martyrs.

And the new common epitaph included, 'the famous Hugolin with the broken crown of his head'. It seems that he lost his life, possibly by execution, in defence of Edward's will or memory.

There is no reason to think that men of this rank and wealth were too grand to perform their duties personally. Queen Edith's *femme de chambre*, Matilda, married a rich English thegn.[1] Edward's doctor, Baldwin, monk of St Denis, was rewarded with an abbey.[2] It is possible that some posts were held by thegns serving in rotation at court. But it is also likely that there was a permanent nucleus of noble household servants.

In addition there were the priests and clerks, whose duty it was to maintain the religious services and perform tasks for which literacy was necessary.[3] Probably all these too came from noble families; and some, like Osbern, were from the highest nobility, at court for their education and while they waited for a suitable bishopric.

The lay and clerical servants of the king and queen formed the most domestic area of the court. But many of the greatest magnates and prelates of the land were almost as much at home there. If we can give any credence to the witness lists to royal charters, there were present, especially perhaps at the great ecclesiastical festivals, when the king held more solemn courts and feasted his vassals, all the great earls, the majority of the bishops, some abbots, and a number of thegns and clerks. Some of these men would be more domestic than others. The queen's family might be expected to be frequently in residence.[4] Archbishop Stigand seems to have been particularly close to the court;[5] and there would be abbots and thegns who were more intimate with the king than the rest. The court was a domestic household to which a great number

---

[1] *Hemingi Chartularium*, i. 253.

[2] Harmer, *Writs*, nos. 23–5. For Baldwin, see David Douglas, *Feudal Documents from the Abbey of Bury St Edmunds* (Br. Acad. 1932), pp. lxi ff.

[3] Barlow, *English Church*, pp. 115 ff.

[4] For Godwin's death at court, see above, p. 127.

[5] Barlow, *English Church*, pp. 77–81.

of men, because of their position or rank, had access; and many men came into the court, paid their respects, did local business, and went out again, as it moved round the country.

Wulfstan of York mentions among the *witan* of the nation bishops, earls, army generals (*heretogan*) – possibly Danish jarls, reeves and judges, scholars and jurists; and the lay categories appear again in his chapter 'On earls'.[1] Obviously he is not giving us a technical inventory of courtiers, nor is he identifying government departments. But his list probably does indicate the main governmental interests of the court: the making of war, the collection of revenue, the administration of justice, and religious education. But how these functions were organized within the court is not known. It is simplest to believe that there was an inner group composed of those whose advice Edward usually asked and normally followed. Among these were (certainly in the later years of the reign) the queen,[2] Archbishop Stigand and probably some other bishops and abbots, and the various 'favourites', like Robert of Jumièges[3] or Earl Tostig.[4] There may also have been some recognized experts in the various subjects. On some issues the king may have desired, may have thought it advisable, to have wider counsel. He would then, as so often happens in the sagas, speak in the hall after dinner and listen to what was said from the mead-benches.[5]

It is when we come to the administrative side that we are almost entirely in the dark.[6] We can imagine the king presiding over an ecclesiastical council in a church or hall; but we cannot show, and can hardly visualize, the court organized as a war council, a bureau of finance, a court of law, or a church patronage office. We must assume that there was a certain number of officials with special responsibilities: someone must have been responsible for the security and policing of the court; someone, possibly a bishop, may have dealt in the first instance with legal matters; someone, probably the principal chamberlain, was the chief financial officer; and someone, possibly an abbot, kept the king's seal and organized the religious services and the secretariat. Some official must have summoned for the king a suitable body

[1] Ed. Jost, pp. 62, 78.
[2] *VEdR*, pp. 15, 23, 42, 53–4.
[3] *Ibid.*, pp. 17–23.
[4] *Ibid.*, p. 50.
[5] Cf. the poem *Andreas*, 'In the desolate gabled hall, the wine-building . . . one warrior often questioned another: "Let him who has gracious counsel, wisdom in his heart, keep it not hidden! Now the time has come, exceeding great trouble; now is great need for us to hearken to the words of wise men" ', 1158–67; cf. also *Beowulf*, ll. 491 ff.
[6] Barlow, *English Church*, pp. 119 ff.

of counsellors to deal with whatever business was before the court. And there was a general office of clerks, hardly specialized, which could keep accounts, write and seal writs, and carry out the other simple duties that were required of them. Even this reconstruction may be too formal. Although we are told in the *Vita* that at mass Edward rarely spoke to anyone unless he was spoken to,[1] it was not unusual to carry out business on such an occasion; and in any case it is likely that much business was transacted while the court was on the move, at times which could be spared from hunting.

When we turn to the royal government at large, the king's administration in the kingdom, the exaction of his rights, the carrying out of his duties, we can see a little more clearly. England was one of the smaller European kingdoms, and, partly because of its size, was more homogeneous, more centralized, and more efficiently governed than the rest. But if we compare it with something much smaller than itself, for example the French county of Normandy, the kingdom appears loosely articulated, decentralized, weakly ruled. The land boundaries were indistinct; there were tracts where men of Scandinavian origin, of doubtful loyalty, were dominant; and into at least half his realm Edward never ventured. Although there were no territorial principalities, as in contemporary France, from which the king's immediate authority was normally excluded, it is quite possible that the earldoms were developing in this way and that England and Germany were set on a similar course.[2] Mercia and Wessex descended hereditarily in Edward's reign. But the point of no return had certainly not been reached. The earldoms still had uncertain boundaries, new earldoms could be created. Edward broke the hereditary succession to Northumbria, and East Anglia was treated as an apprentice's post. The earls remained royal officers governing a province in the king's name; and within their earldoms were bishops and abbots who had no interest in provincial autonomy or princely states, sometimes little interest even in the integrity of their own dioceses. Nor does it seem that the thegns preferred to follow their earl rather than the king. Edward had some trouble with his earls; he may not have been completely successful in his dealings with them; but he did not surrender in any way his claim to be the immediate ruler over the whole of his

[1] *VEdR*, p. 41.

[2] D. A. Bullough, 'Anglo-Saxon Institutions and Early English Society', *Annali della Fondazione italiana per la storia amministrativa* (Milan), 2 (1965), 657-8.

Æthelred: type *First Hand* (Brooke 2) obv. and rev., *c.* 985.
Minted at Stamford by the moneyer Wulfstan.

Cnut: type *Quatrefoil* (Brooke 2) obv., *c.* 1020.
Minted at Leicester by the moneyer Wulfnoth.

Harold Harefoot: type *Fleur de lis* (Brooke 2) obv., *c.* 1039.
Minted at London by the moneyer Brihtmaer.

Harthacnut: type *Arm and Sceptre* (Brooke 2) obv., *c.* 1041.
Minted at Ilchester by the moneyer Godric.

Edward: type *Expanding Cross* (Brooke 5; but Pl. XVII, 8 obv.) obv., (?)1050–3.
Minted at Gloucester by the moneyer Ælfsie.

9. Some English silver pennies of the period (enlarged). (*Courtesy Trustees of the British Museum.*)

Edward: type *Pointed Helmet* (Brooke 6) obv., (?)1053–6.
Minted at Hereford by the moneyer Wulfwine.

Harold II: type *pax* (Brooke 1) obv., 1066.
Minted at Chichester by the moneyer Ælfwine.

Edward: type *Sovereign-Martlets* (Brooke 7), obv. and rev., (?)1056–9.
Minted at Horndon by the moneyer Dudinc.

Edward: type *Facing Head-Small Cross* (Brooke 9) obv., (?)1062–5
Minted at Bedford by the moneyer Sigod.

Edward: type *Pyramids* (Brooke 10) obv., (?)1065–6.
Minted at Steyning by the moneyer Diorman.

10. Some English silver pennies of the period (enlarged). (*Courtesy Trustees of the British Museum.*)

kingdom. And even if he himself never chose, as far as we know, to travel north of Gloucester, this is because he had no need to make such an inconvenient journey. His successor, Harold, visited York twice in the nine months that he reigned. Few medieval kings went beyond the Trent unless impelled by military necessity.

The protection of the land was secured by diplomacy with foreign powers and the provision of military forces. Edward did nothing as spectacular as Cnut's visit to Rome and campaigns in the north. He was, however, clearly involved in continuous diplomatic activity, which at times, for example 1049–52, was intense.[1] The wealth of England, the island's vulnerability to invasion, the question of the succession, the ties which bound the English church to Rome and Edward to other royal and princely courts gave occasion to much coming and going. Edward, as was usual, often sent a group of ambassadors, lay and clerical.[2] Tostig led the great embassy to Rome in 1061 and Harold's visit to Normandy in 1064 or 1065 was probably undertaken on Edward's behalf. But sometimes we hear only of bishops and abbots.[3]

In a sense, too, the English military forces were always on the alert.[4] Edward's reign is called, rightly, an era of peace; but this is relatively speaking. When we remember the insecurity of the early years, the standing threat of a Scandinavian invasion, the incursions of pirates, the constant menace of raids from Wales and Scotland, we realize that Edward and his *witan* must have been always concerned with the efficiency of the army and navy. The composition and size of early

[1] Barlow, 'Edward the Confessor's Early Life', *EHR*, lxxx (1965), 237–8.

[2] *Histoire des Relations Internationales*, ed. Pierre Renouvin; vol. i: François L. Ganshof, *Le Moyen Age* (1953), pp. 39, 122–3.

[3] Edward sent Bishop Duduc of Wells and Abbots Wulfric of St Augustine's and Ælfwine of Ramsey to Rheims in 1049, and Bishops Herman of Wiltshire and Ealdred of Worcester to Rome in 1050. Archbishop Robert was negotiating on his behalf in 1051. In 1054 Ealdred led the mission to Germany. In 1060 Bishop William of London was in Flanders. In the later part of the reign Abbot Ælfwine went to Rome, Saxony, and, perhaps, Denmark. Barlow, *English Church*, pp. 17, 301–2; Harmer, *Writs*, pp. 551–2; *DB*, i. 208 a i. These prelates were, presumably, accompanied by thegns, but, we may assume, not by earls.

[4] Royal laws issued by Æthelred and Cnut ordered the performance of the common burdens (the repair of bridges, the maintenance of fortresses, and army service) and the fitting out of ships, and specified the penalties for desertion from the armed forces. See V Atr. 26–8; VI Atr. 32, 3–35; II Cnut 10; 65; 77; 79. For the army and navy, see Maitland, *DB and Beyond*, pp. 194–202; Vinogradoff, *English Society in the Eleventh Century*, pp. 14 ff.; C. Warren Hollister, *Anglo-Saxon Military Institutions* (1962); Eric John, *Orbis Britanniae* (1966), pp. 128 ff., 292–4. It was Vinogradoff, cf. p. 31, who first got the idea of 'the select fyrd', a distinction elaborated by Hollister.

medieval armies are rarely stated. All kings, and many nobles, maintained some sort of bodyguard; and the easiest way of looking at the armies of the period is to imagine these household troops being reinforced in different ways according to the military requirements. Since the days of Æthelred, English kings and some earls kept housecarls, mercenaries of Scandinavian extraction. How many were in Edward's service is not known. Some were stationed in boroughs on garrison duty.[1] A troop may have accompanied the court; but there would also have been in the household thegns and *cnihtas*, men of higher social rank, to form a retinue for the king.[2] For some purposes no more than an escort was required. Edward also until 1051 kept a small foreign, probably Viking, fleet. In 1050 this consisted of fourteen ships, each with a theoretical complement of 60 'lithsmen' or 'butsecarls'.[3]

These headquarters' troops could be reinforced in a variety of ways. The king was probably rarely without the escorts of some of his companions. When in November 1043 he rode with Earls Leofric, Godwin, and Siward from Gloucester to Winchester in order to despoil his mother, he would have had forces sufficient to overawe Emma's retainers.[4] In 1051, when he was again with his earls at Gloucester, and Godwin's rebellion broke out, both the loyal and the rebel earls set to work to assemble armies.[5] One of their first acts would have been to summon their thegns. And it was by calling the whole army to his own standard and causing thegns to desert the rebel earls that Edward was able to sap Godwin's military power. The armies which the English commanders took into Wales and Scotland were presumably also of this type. Small, mobile, well-trained forces were required.

If larger armies and navies were thought necessary – and these would be needed more for defence than offence – then the king could call up other categories of soldiers and sailors. Most useful, probably, were those who owed the duty because of special arrangements. The Welsh marches had to provide troops for expeditions against Wales.[6] We hear twice of the employment of Welsh auxiliaries,[7] but are not told whether these were mercenaries or contingents owed by Welsh

---

[1] Vinogradoff, pp. 19–22; *VCH* (*Dorset*), iii. 26.

[2] For Robert (of Rhuddlan) serving as a squire at Edward's court, see below p. 191.

[3] Vinogradoff, pp. 17–19; Plummer, *Two Chronicles*, pp. 239–40.

[4] See above, p. 76. [5] See above, p. 111.

[6] Cf. *DB*, i. 179 (Hereford and Archenfield).

[7] See above, p. 99, below, p. 236.

princes. Many of the south-east ports had agreed, in return for a grant of judicial rights, to furnish quotas of ships.[1] Finally there were what can be termed the shire levies. Berkshire and most likely some other areas owed one soldier from each five hides of land.[2] Possibly other customs obtained in the north and east of England; but, assuming that there were no gross inequalities, we can do some interesting sums.[3] England's 70,000 hides should have produced a national army of 14,000 men. Berkshire itself, rated at 2,473 hides, owed roughly 500 soldiers. These figures are not implausible; and they enable us to see that an army raised in this way was far from being a *levée en masse*. The recorded population of Berkshire in Domesday Book is 6,324, mostly family units. Therefore one soldier was sent for every twelve families. If we put any faith in the figure of a million or a million-and-a-half, both based on Domesday, for the population of the whole of England,[4] there was one soldier for every seventy or hundred inhabitants. An army assembled on this basis would not have been a rabble.

Even though a general mobilization of the kingdom is unlikely, on these figures, to have produced in practice more than 10,000 men, such a large army was rarely needed. We know that in 1051, 1052, and 1065 Edward called out the armed forces of the whole kingdom;[5] but each time it was to counter rebellion, and the purpose was as much to deny troops to the rebels as to secure an enormous army for himself. Probably on most occasions a limited mobilization was preferred. Messages would be sent to selected shires and selected magnates ordering them to bring their forces to the assembly point. And these two different 'systems' seem to have worked in harmony: the territorial principle (the assessment of land to military service) and the personal principle (the arrangements made by a lord to acquit the liability lying on his estates). When the king summoned the *fyrd* to Gloucester, he would be able to review, besides the escort troops of himself and his earls, the contingents of the bishoprics of Worcester and Hereford and of some abbeys (each under its own commander) and various other units,

---

[1] *DB*, i. 1 a i; Vinogradoff, *op. cit.*, p. 124.

[2] *DB*, i. 56 b i, cf. 64 b; Vinogradoff, *op. cit.*, pp. 28 ff.; D. A. Bullough, *op. cit.*, p. 655 n. 33.

[3] Statistical tables are conveniently displayed in Maitland, *DB and Beyond*, pp. 463 ff.

[4] Maitland, *op. cit.*, pp. 503–4; J. C. Russell, *British Medieval Population* (Albuquerque, New Mexico, 1948), p. 54.

[5] See above, pp. 111–12, 123, below, pp. 237–8.

possibly representing hundreds not in private hands, led by sheriffs and reeves. Occasionally the composition of an army is stated. When Earl Harold raided the mouth of the Severn in 1052 he was opposed by the armies of Somerset and Devon,[1] theoretically a force of some 800 men. And he killed 'more than 30 good thegns apart from other people', a statement, which, although by no means conclusive, at least suggests that not every man in the army was of thegnly rank.

Beyond this point we can hardly see. It is not unlikely that every freeman had the duty, and right, to bear arms. It is probable that villagers, irrespective of legal obligation, would turn out against pirates and robbers, although here we are passing into police duties, watch and ward and hue and cry. Yet, it seems, in Edward's reign the real cleavage does not occur at this level. The main distinction is between forces which the king or his earls would take on an offensive expedition against an enemy and those which could be called out to defend the coastline and, presumably, to garrison the boroughs.

All English military forces were amphibious and the navy was not completely separate from the army. Edward's mercenaries, the house-carls (soldiers) and the lithsmen (sailors), were distinct. Also the south-east ports had contracted to perform specialized military service. Dover, Sandwich, Romney, and probably some others, each owed 20 ships, each with a crew of 21, once a year for 15 days.[2] There were as well associated customs: for example, whenever the king sent forces to guard the sea, but did not go in person, the burgesses of Lewes had to collect 20s. to give to the men who looked after the arms in the ships.[3] Yet, although the maritime areas may have been accustomed to performing service on sea, possibly all shires had the duty of providing ships for the royal navy,[4] and it is likely that all men liable to military service could be required to fight on sea or on land according to the need. Warships were regarded as platforms for soldiers and the Viking influence on English military tradition encouraged versatility. Edward, therefore, could mobilize a navy in the same way as an army, building upon his standing fleet or, after 1051, possibly on the special duty squadrons. When he called out large forces in 1049 his fleet included,

[1] *Chron. CD*, Florence, i. 208.

[2] *DB*, i. 1 a i, 3 a i, 4 b i, 10 b ii.

[3] *DB*, i. 26 a i.

[4] Vinogradoff, pp. 31–2; Harmer, *Writs*, pp. 266–70; Eric John, *Land Tenure in Early England* (1960), pp. 119 ff., *Orbis Britanniae*, p. 72n.

besides these and the royal ships, the navies of Mercia and Wessex.[1]
And his fleet, just like his army, was commanded by his earls.

The passive defence of the country rested, since Offa, on the
boroughs.[2] These were constructed for the defence of the countryside,
and, especially in Mercia, the shires were created as units for the maintenance and garrisoning of its fortress. Everything suggests that the
duty described in the charters as *arcis constructio regalis*, or some such
phrase, refers to the upkeep of a borough. These, after all, were the
only *arces* throughout the kingdom. As for this task one man was due for
every hide, the earl or sheriff would be able to call out a sizeable labour
force or garrison. But, once again, it is likely that there was some
customary specialization, which enabled the manpower to be divided
between the field army, the defence of the borough walls, and labouring
tasks. A thegn would not dig ditches. And it is in this sphere that the
diocesan bishop may, in practice at least, have had some special
responsibility. Whereas the earl and the sheriffs would normally lead
the troops on campaign, it would often fall to the bishop to see to the
defence of his diocese, particularly at times when it was denuded of its
best fighting men. It is even possible that individual bishops sometimes held large commands. Bishop Ealdred seems at one time to have
been responsible for the defence of the southern stretch of the Welsh
marches, and Archbishop Stigand may possibly have co-ordinated the
coastal defences from the Wash to the Isle of Wight against raids or an
invasion from the Continent.[3]

The history of the private stronghold in England remains controversial.[4] It is by no means certain that the motte and bailey castle,
once regarded as the typical Norman fortress, was in fact common in
Normandy in the mid-eleventh century,[5] or even in England immediately after the Conquest, and it is impossible to believe that England
was without private fortifications before 1066. Apart from the castles

[1] See above, p. 99.

[2] Maitland, *DB and Beyond*, pp. 213 ff. Brooks, as above, p. 151, *n*. 1.

[3] See below, pp. 198–9.

[4] See Brian K. Davison, 'The origins of the castle in England: the institute's
research project', *The Archaeological Journal*, cxxiv (1967), 202–11. The Royal
Archaeological Institute has set on foot an investigation of the problem. For some
early reports, see Davison, 'The Origins of the Castle', *Current Archaeology*, no. 5
(1967), 129–32, 'Sulgrave and Aldingham', *ibid.*, no. 19 (1969), 19–24; Peter Addy-
man, 'Baile Hill, York', *ibid.*, 25–6; G. Beresford, 'Goltho', *ibid.* 56 (1977), 266–9.
See also R. Allen Brown, *Origins of English Feudalism* (1973), pp. 72 ff.

[5] See below, p. 224, *n*. 1.

which Edward's French soldiers built on the Welsh march, and which may indeed have been distinctive in design and a novelty in England, there were the protected residences of the English thegns. The halls themselves were defensible.[1] And, according to a legal treatise of the early eleventh century which possibly refers to the diocese of Worcester,[2] 'if a ceorl [a husbandman] throve, so that he had at least five hides of book-land, a church and a kitchen, a bell-house and a burgh-gate, and a seat and special office in the king's hall, he became entitled to the rights of a thegn.' From this evidence we must accept that a thegn's principal seat was often protected by a stockade, or ditch and rampart, and that this *burh* commonly had a timber gate-house. Whether such a stronghold, a ring-work enclosing a hall, church, and perhaps other buildings and entered through a gate-tower, can properly be called a castle is a matter of definition and usage, and whether such fortifications differed much from contemporary castles in Normandy is a matter for archaeological investigation.

It is unlikely that the whole English army was called out every year for training and manœuvres, or even for a view of arms. But it is quite possible that, as in Edgar's reign,[3] naval units were mustered at least once a year at Sandwich. Without a review of the ships, the royal navy could have disappeared; and it has always been accepted that sailors and marines require a more stringent training than soldiers. The annual assembly of a fleet at a south-east port would also have menaced the pirates in the Channel. Sandwich was a Christ Church, Canterbury, estate, and clearly in this period the main cross-Channel terminal.[4] Edward granted it a mint;[5] and there are several references in Domesday Book to ward duties owed when the king came to Canterbury and Sandwich.[6] Edward would have been specially interested in the custody of the seas and watching the traffic in the Channel during the summer season. In the autumn, it seems, he

---

[1] In the O.E. poetic fragment *Finnesburgh*, a young king and his sixty men 'hold the doors' of the hall without loss for five days in the face of a fierce attack.

[2] *Gethynctho* (On people's ranks), Liebermann, *Die Gesetze*, i. 456; W. Stubbs, *Select Charters*, ed. H. W. C. Davis (1921), p. 88.

[3] Florence, i. 143–4; cf. V. Æthelred 27, VI, 33: the ships shall be equipped soon after Easter.

[4] Hardly any other point of entry from northern Gaul into England is mentioned in *Chron.* in this period, and cf. 'omnium Anglorum portuum famosissimus', *Encomium Emmae*, p. 20; 'portum . . . ad receptionem navium habilem', Osbern, *Vita S. Elphegi* in *Anglia Sacra*, ii (1691), 133.

[5] Michael Dolley, *Anglo-Saxon Pennies*, p. 29.   [6] *DB*, i. 1 a ii.

usually hunted through the forests of Clarendon, Savernake, and Cranborne Chase, through Cheddar up to the Welsh marches and the Forest of Dean, with Christmas often celebrated at Gloucester.[1] It is possible that the Welsh march was kept on a fairly regular war footing with annual manœuvres after the harvest. And it was here that the French garrisons experimented with castles and cavalry.

Old-English and Danish armies were unusual in that they contained few, if any, cavalry units. There can be no doubt that the troops often rode on the march.[2] Even the Vikings seized horses when they could. Thegns would be horsemen from childhood, and no man of that rank walked any distance. Yet, although there has been argument on this point,[3] it does not seem that English troops normally fought from the saddle. The antics of Earl Ralf's cavalry before Hereford in 1055 were regarded as un-English and the cause of the English defeat.[4] It is quite possible that Anglo-Danish forces could make mounted pursuits; but for pitched battles, it seems, they dismounted. There were, however, in the whole of Edward's reign only three military episodes which can be called battles: Siward's victory in Scotland in 1054 and the English defeats at Hereford in 1055 and Glasbury on Wye in 1056.[5] It was difficult for commanders to develop battle tactics when the opportunities for trying them out were so small. And Ralf's discomfiture in 1055 may have discouraged further experiments with cavalry.

Because of the chequered history of English arms in this period – from defeats under Æthelred to the Norman Conquest – the late Old-English military organization has come in for heavy criticism. But, if we cast an eye over the whole of Edward's reign, it does not seem that he neglected the armed forces or that the system, unless there was political hindrance, functioned badly. The military history of the reign really ends with the three great battles of 1066, Gate Fulford, Stamford Bridge, and Hastings. Although two of these were lost, and the pattern of failure is continued, neither defeat was dishonourable

[1] See itinerary in Oleson, *Witenagemot*, pp. 170–1.

[2] Cf. *Gnomic Verses*, 'The earl shall be on the war-horse's back; the host shall ride in a company, the infantry stand fast', Grein and Wülcker, *Bibliothek der Angelsächsischen Poesie*, 1, 344, ll. 63–4. For their love of horses, see Jean I. Young, 'Ungloomy Aspects of Anglo-Saxon Poetry', *The Early Cultures of North-West Europe* (H. M. Chadwick Memorial Studies), ed. Sir Cyril Fox and Bruce Dickins (1950), p. 281.

[3] R. Glover, 'English Warfare in 1066', *EHR*, lxvii (1952), pp. 1–18.

[4] See below, p. 206.

[5] See below, pp. 202, 206–7.

and the one victory was distinguished. It would be perverse to judge from the events of 1066 that Edward had allowed the military strength of his kingdom to decay, or that the English tactics were hopelessly unsuited to the times and conditions. The king was not a helpless prisoner of archaic customs. If he had wanted cavalry troops he could have made arrangements to get them – as in fact at one time he did. And it must not be overlooked that at least one brilliant Norman soldier, Robert of Rhuddlan, received his military training in Edward's household.[1]

The second great duty laid on the king was the maintenance of good internal order and the provision of justice. The drafter of a royal charter, dated 1063 and commemorating Edward's grant of land in Devon to a priest named Scepio, expressed the king's attitude in this way:[2]

> I, Edward, through the contribution of divine providence, by which all things are governed, appointed king and defender of the English bounds, invoke God with unsleeping mind not only that I may be famed for my royal protection,[3] but also that, invested with God's aid, I may prevail in thought and deed against God's enemies and earn the right to advance my kingdom in the quietness of peace. Often, indeed, my mind is troubled, disturbed, and confounded by the vicissitudes of the world; for, lo! everywhere there is the threat that law and justice will be overthrown, everywhere disputes and discord seethe, everywhere wicked presumption rages, money puts off right and justice, and avarice, the nourisher of all evils, kindles them all into flame. But it is our duty courageously to oppose the wicked and take good men as models, by enriching the churches of God, relieving those oppressed by wicked judges, and by judging equitably between the powerful and the humble: all things which are pleasing to God.

It was the church especially which encouraged the king to take an active role in an area which was, to one way of thinking, almost independent of him. The various police and peace schemes were organs of local government; the lawcourts were popular assemblies; the law was immemorial custom, and each shire had its peculiarities; the pleadings, proofs, and judgments were fixed in form.[4] But there was

[1] See below, p. 191.

[2] *KCD*, no. 814 (Sawyer, no. 1037).

[3] 'non solum regiae protectionis nomen ut non habeam', where the second 'non' seems to be a mistake.

[4] Maitland, *DB and Beyond*, pp. 110 ff., 307 ff.; Vinogradoff, *English Society in the Eleventh Century*, pp. 90 ff.; Barlow, *English Church*, pp. 137 ff. See further D. A. Bullough, *op. cit.*, pp. 654–7, *n.* 34, and works cited.

also a strong tradition here, as with so many other Old-English institutions, that popular duties were royal rights, or, equally well, that
popular rights were common duties owed to the king. And in fact
the kings, prompted by prelates who wanted royal protection, had
created most of the courts, devised some of the procedures, and declared and modified the law.[1] Also, royal intervention in the processes
of litigation, far from being resented, was actively courted, at least by
those who hoped to gain from it. The king could interfere effectively
because he was allowed some paramount authority and because the
public courts – shire, borough, hundred, franchisal – and the ecclesiastical tribunals were almost all under presidents who were members
of his own court, bishops, earls, and reeves; and in the shire courts,
and perhaps also in the hundreds, the principal suitors were the king's
thegns. In a sense the king's court broke up in order to hear cases in the
localities; and when it reassembled it could review the judgments that
had been given.[2] For the time it was a remarkably unified judicial
system. And it must have been most profitable to the king, for penalties
were due to him either because of the nature of the crime (usually the
most serious) or because of the status of the person committing it.

How many cases, and what sort, were heard in Edward's ambulatory
court, and how often he heard them in person, are difficult questions
to answer. We know that men, especially the magnates, approached
Edward about legal disputes, devises of land, problems of all kinds;
and Edward's consent to a transaction is often recorded.[3] The part he
could play is well illustrated by the case of the testament of a London
woman, Leofgifu,[4] who, before setting off on a pilgrimage to Jerusalem,
made her will and left the village of Fiskerton, which was her book-
land, to Peterborough abbey. When Abbot Leofric heard of her death
he approached Edward, proved the bequest by witnesses, and asked
for its confirmation. At this point the queen intervened and claimed
that Leofgifu had bequeathed the land to her. A bargain was then
struck. Through the intercession of Edward and Edith's brothers,

---

[1] For regulations concerning the hundred, borough, and shire courts, see II Cnut
16–18; for changes in the rules about vouching to warranty, see II Atr. 9, II Cnut 23.

[2] Cf. Edward's writ, 1053/61, confirming to Christ Church, Canterbury, a grant
of land by a thegn, 'for my will is that the judgment given by my thegns shall be
upheld.' Harmer, *Writs*, no. 35. See also, no. 79.

[3] Cf. *KCD*, nos. 805, 819, 823, 904, 912, 927, 945, 962–4; Harmer, *Writs*, no. 69.

[4] *KCD*, no. 808 (Sawyer, no. 1029), which, admittedly, has not a very good
reputation.

Harold and Tostig, she agreed to abandon her claim in return for 20 marks of gold and church ornaments worth as much. Finally the king confirmed the will, and the king and queen joined in granting the land to the abbey. This was justice of a sort, and exactly the sort which was expected in the eleventh century. Every interested party took his cut. There is no doubt that on most occasions gifts were offered to the king or queen and accepted.[1]

Disputes between the king's vassals must often have been heard in person by the king. Sometimes, no doubt, these matters were settled informally, sometimes, as when in 1065 Tostig accused Harold of inciting rebellion in his earldom, in formal session.[2] The formality of the court when hearing political and treason cases may have varied much; but usually, it seems, the accused was judged in his absence and on occasion, as with Godwin in 1051,[3] was refused permission to answer.

According to the *Vita Ædwardi Regis,* Edward abolished bad laws and with the help of his wise counsellors enacted good ones. He also appointed skilled ecclesiastical and secular judges (princes and palace lawyers) and ordered them to determine cases with equity. He intended always that righteousness should have royal support and evil its due condemnation.[4] We are invited to believe that Edward behaved according to the principles attributed to him by the author of the Scepio charter. But this is a flattering view. Cnut had issued two great codes of English law, one dealing with ecclesiastical, the other with secular jurisdiction, both directed to the proper administration of the local courts, especially the shire court. It does not seem that Edward imitated his stepfather. The *laga Eadwardi,* the laws of King Edward of Henry I's coronation charter,[5] were the laws of England as they had stood before 1066. There is nothing to show that Edward was a law-giver and little evidence that he was particularly interested in justice. His historical reputation as a just judge and a law-reformer probably depends on this passage in the *Vita,* which was taken into the ecclesiastical legend and helped to create the image of sanctity. But, oddly enough, the *Vita* does not show Edward as a just judge. It claims that

---

[1] Cf. the gifts of the abbot of Ramsey about 1049, above, p. 154, n. 6.

[2] See below, p. 237.   [3] See above, p. 113.

[4] *VEdR,* pp. 12–13. As Richardson and Sayles, *The Governance of Medieval England* (1963), p. 137, n. 3, have suggested, this passage may be based on the coronation service: see above, p. 63, n. 2.

[5] Cap. 13; Robertson, *Laws,* p. 282.

in 1051 he denied Godwin justice and behaved in a completely arbitrary way.[1] Nor should we be surprised. In practice impartiality was not expected of a medieval king. It would have been an awkward virtue.

For one royal function, however, superhuman virtue was required. Edward was the patron, in fact the master, of the English church. In return for all the church's services to the kingdom and to him, he was expected to be an enlightened Christian governor. In the Exeter charter of 1050 Edward is made to declare:[2]

> As all things have been founded well by God in his wisdom, heaven and earth, and all things that are therein (Acts xiv. 15), it is clear that, although the incapacity of suffering mankind confuses the acts of men with many mishaps, it will be right and proper for us, Edward, who are said to have been appointed by God as ruler over men, prudently to endeavour, by the inspiration of divine mercy and after the measure of our judgment, to seek for the justice of political science, and, especially, to take in hand, and in kindly measure investigate, the affairs of the church, putting to right those things which in our eyes do not appear to be just, and, when we have established them correctly, directing them to the advancement of innocence and the strengthening of both this and the other life.

As king by the grace of God, *dei vicarius*, Edward had duties and rights in the church. His uncontested right to appoint to bishoprics and royal abbeys enabled him to reward his clerical friends, to establish his own men throughout the kingdom.[3] And nothing demonstrates his power more clearly than his grant to his clerk, Regenbald, of the status at law of a diocesan bishop.[4] His duty to protect and enrich the church, to attack evil, extirpate heathenism, reform morals, was but one aspect of his general responsibility as a Christian king. In all these matters the church expected the king to take clerical advice, but not necessarily in special ecclesiastical synods. Although Edward was canonized, he does not seem to have been an outstandingly enlightened patron of the church or to have paid particular attention to his duties. The great ecclesiastical councils and the royal ecclesiastical legislation, which had characterized the tenth-century reformation and which had persisted into Cnut's reign, were no feature of Edward's. He gave the church, with the rest of the country, peace and protection; but there is no evidence that he particularly favoured the church or encouraged

---

[1] *VEdR*, pp. 20–3.
[2] *KCD*, no. 791 (Sawyer, no. 1021).
[3] Barlow, *English Church*, pp. 46 ff., 76 ff.
[4] Harmer, *Writs*, no. 44.

its ministry. He rebuilt Westminster abbey and made sundry gifts to churches, mostly at a price.[1] His appointments to bishoprics and abbeys, although rarely scandalous, were hardly distinguished. He preferred, certainly in the earlier part of his reign, to promote clerks out of his chapel rather than holy monks; and at his death he left a church which the Normans denounced, although not always with justice, as ignorant and corrupt.

It is doubtful whether Edward ever had an ecclesiastical policy. He was, however, obviously jealous of his rights in the church; and whenever they were opposed by local interests he exerted himself to prevail.[2] Although in a purely devotional sense he may have revered St Peter, he allowed the papal decision to break the combination of York and Worcester to be circumvented and the papal strictures on Archbishop Stigand to be disregarded.[3] The Edwardian church was not by the standards of the time a disgrace, but it was not remarkable for either scholarship or great piety; and although Edward's bishops were probably not inclined to blame his conduct – they were, after all, men he had chosen, men in his confidence, men of his own way of thinking – they could not have been tempted to liken him to Edgar.

Finally we can consider Edward's government in some of its economic aspects. The king had at least a selfish interest in the prosperity of his kingdom; and by providing peace, good internal order, markets, courts, and coinage, he made a great contribution to it. He did nothing to hinder trade and allowed some privileges which encouraged it. His interest in foreign countries and his concern with the south-east ports were also helpful. He granted a group of Sussex ports to the Norman abbey of Fécamp,[4] and he allowed the burgesses of Dover freedom from toll throughout England.[5] It is, however, the coinage which is the most impressive – and enigmatic – memorial to the financial expertise of the Old-English royal government.[6] Coins, although used in trade, were certainly not the only medium of exchange; and there is much to be said for the view that one of the main purposes of issuing coinage, at least in times of peace, was to enable men to pay their rents and taxes,

[1] *KCD*, no. 801 (Sawyer, no. 1026), sale of 3 hides of land to Evesham abbey in 1055 for 7 marks of gold, is a good example, although the charter, in its existing form, is unacceptable.

[2] See above, pp. 78–9, 86.

[3] Barlow, *English Church*, pp. 88, 302 ff.

[4] See above, p. 39, *n.* 3.

[5] *DB*, i. 1 a i.   [6] See above, pll. 9 and 10.

especially the geld.[1] Moreover, it may be thought that one of the most unusual features of the English coinage – the royal monopoly – is also partly to be explained by the existence of royal estates throughout the kingdom and of a national tax.

Intensive study in recent years of the Anglo-Saxon coinage has produced much new information and some interesting theories, but has left many problems unsolved.[2] In Edward's reign a few round half-pennies may have been minted,[3] and some gold coins (probably worth thirty pence, the *mancus*) were struck from the ordinary dies,[4] perhaps for commemorative purposes or for special gifts; but the standard coin, as before and after, was the silver penny. The design was hammered on to thin circular flans, stamped out from sheets of silver at least 900 thousandths fine. On the obverse was a 'portrait' of the king, circled by his name and title, on the reverse was usually a short cross, circled by the name of the moneyer and the place of the mint.

Only one coinage was current in England:[5] there were no seigneurial or episcopal mints as in France and Germany; and foreign coins were banned. The government changed the coinage from time to time (some numismatists believe at regular intervals) and may have required the current issue to be exchanged at the mints for the new type. But no law on this matter has survived and issues could hardly have been demonetized without the sanction of heavy penalties. The dies were all cut in London and distributed to the local mints, in sets of one obverse and two reverse.[6] Minor modifications in the design often occurred while the dies were being produced; and on typological evidence it seems that dies for the most distant mints were produced first.[7] We

[1] R. H. M. Dolley and D. M. Metcalf, 'The reform of the English coinage under Eadgar', *Anglo-Saxon Coins: studies presented to F. M. Stenton*, ed. R. H. M. Dolley (1961), p. 154.

[2] For short bibliography, see above, p. xxvi.

[3] C. S. S. Lyon, 'A round halfpenny of Edward the Confessor', *British Numismatic Journal*, xxxiv (1966), 42–5.

[4] One, struck at Warwick *c.* 1051, is illustrated in the frontispiece to Michael Dolley, *Anglo-Saxon Pennies*.

[5] H. R. Loyn, 'Boroughs and Mints A.D. 900–1066', *Anglo-Saxon Coins*, pp. 122–35; R. H. M. Dolley and D. M. Metcalf, 'The Reform of the English Coinage under Eadgar', *ibid.*, pp. 136–68.

[6] R. H. M. Dolley, 'The Unpublished 1895 Find of coins of Edward the Confessor from Harewood', *Yearbook of the British Association of Numismatic Societies* (1961), pp. 17 ff.

[7] R. H. M. Dolley and F. Elmore Jones, 'Some Remarks on BMC Type VII var. *B* of Edward the Confessor', *Numismatic Chronicle*, 6th ser. xx (1960), 190.

find also that the earliest coins struck were very close to the appointed weight and that the standard could not usually be maintained for long. There was not, however, debasement of the silver. The coinage had been changed since the great reform under Edgar on the average about every six years; but in Edward's reign eleven distinct types, in an order which is now firmly established, were issued;[1] and, although a biennial followed by a triennial change has been suggested, this is by no means certain – perhaps is even unlikely – and the dates now given to the issues must be considered for the most part arbitrary.

Whereas the control of the coinage was highly centralized, minting was so decentralized that in Edward's reign, after he himself had added nine centres,[2] some seventy mints were active; and in the more populated areas of England few men lived more than fifteen miles from an exchange. The mints were in boroughs, and there were few boroughs which did not possess at least one mint. The efficiency of the system is proved by Harold's coinage. New dies were cut after Edward's death, to a novel and most distinguished design; and coins from forty-two mints have survived, although they could have been struck for less than twelve months.[3]

It is difficult to explain the monetary system satisfactorily without attributing to the government a grasp of economics which seems unlikely in the eleventh century.[4] The simplest explanation of the frequent change of issue is that it increased the royal revenue, for the moneyers had to pay for the new dies.[5] But this cannot be the whole

[1] Peter Seaby, 'The sequence of Anglo-Saxon coin types, 1030–50', *British Numismatic Journal*, 1955–7, xxviii (1958), 111–46; R. H. M. Dolley, 'New light on the order of the early issues of Edward the Confessor', *ibid.*, xxix (1960), 289–92; Dolley and Metcalf, 'The Reform of the English Coinage under Eadgar', pp. 152 ff. J. J. North, *English Hammered Coinage* (Spink and Son, 1963), i. 128–30. Not all numismatists, however, accept that coin-types were changed on every sixth Michaelmas day after Edgar's reform: cf. John D. Brand, 'Meretricious Metrology', Spink and Son Ltd., *The Numismatic Circular*, lxxv (1967), 63–5. It may in any case be doubted whether it was ever decreed that from henceforth the coinage would be changed at regular determined intervals. To legislate for six years ahead would often be legislating for a successor.

[2] Bedwyn, Berkeley, Bury St Edmunds, Horndon, Hythe, Newport (unidentified), Pershore, Petherton, Reading, Sandwich, and an unidentified Dyr/Dernt' near Ipswich, *Anglo-Saxon Pennies*, pp. 28–9.

[3] Michael Dolley, *Anglo-Saxon Pennies*, pp. 29–30.

[4] See Dolley and Metcalf, 'The Reform of the English Coinage under Eadgar', pp. 154–5.

[5] Loyn, 'Boroughs and Mints', p. 125.

story. When the coinage was changed it was always possible, and in Edward's reign the opportunity was increasingly taken, to alter the weight of the coins.[1] Edward's early issues were mostly at 18 grains, once falling to 17. But in the middle of the reign, possibly in 1051, the weight was increased spectacularly to 27 grains. In 1053 (if we accept one scheme of dating) it was reduced to 21·5, and then it see-sawed: 20·5 in 1056,[2] 21·5 in 1059, 17 (the lowest point) in 1062, and back again to 21·5 for Edward's last issue in 1065. It was at this weight that William held the coinage until 1080, when it was advanced to 22·5. The government was carrying out a monetary policy which alternated between inflation and deflation.

What considerations influenced the government, and to what extent it understood the effect of its actions are difficult questions to answer. It is unlikely that there was any intention to influence foreign trade or foreign exchange. But even if we confine our attention to the home scene, there is so much that we do not know that an economic analysis is hardly worth while. We can, however, make a few observations. The silver penny had a purchasing power somewhat similar to that of a gold half sovereign before World War I, and because of its high value easily acquired a token significance. But even so we can only explain the readiness with which the population exchanged coins weighing 27 grains for a new issue at 21·5 by assuming that the penny was substantially over-valued, that it never contained a pennyworth of silver and was not worth melting down.[3] Most of the royal revenue had to be paid either by weight or in assayed currency: in neither case did alterations in the coinage affect the true value of the receipts.[4] Perhaps, therefore, the weight was changed simply in order to control the number of coins in circulation. But it is hard to see for what reasons this was done. It is possible that the general deflation that occurred in the second half of the reign can be associated with greater prosperity, for it seems that after 1054 there was less disease among cattle and better harvests.[5] Once we can suggest an historical context. The greatest jump of all, from 18 to 27 grains, may have occurred in 1051 as a result of Edward's dismissal of the lithsmen and his supposed

[1] Table in P. Grierson, 'Sterling', *Anglo-Saxon Coins*, p. 273.
[2] A round halfpenny was also minted from this die: see above, p. 181.
[3] Dolley and Metcalf, 'The Reform of the English Coinage under Eadgar', p. 158.
[4] Sally Harvey, 'Royal Revenue and Domesday Terminology', *Ec. Hist. Rev.*, 2nd ser., xx (1967), 221–8. See also below, pp. 186–7.
[5] See above, p. 139.

abolition of geld:[1] the government calculated that fewer coins would be needed and decided that the opportunity should be taken to produce a heavier coin which would give enhanced prestige. If this theory is correct, the numismatic evidence suggests that geld was soon reimposed. The other changes in weight cannot be associated with any political or economic event. The Anglo-Saxon annalist took no interest in the coinage; and we may, therefore, assume that whatever the reason for the manipulations neither the general public nor the monasteries felt the effect.

Edward's coinage is also interesting for its design. In the first half of the reign the portrait of the king on the obverse was the traditional bust, clean-shaven, wearing a crown or diadem, facing left, normal in England since the late tenth century and deriving ultimately from Roman models. In the last five issues, after the change in weight, there was much more variety. The revolution started possibly in 1053, when the designer, although he used features which he took from older English coins, produced a new and lively image.[2] He turned the bust to face right, introduced a beard, and substituted a helmet for a crown. We have, in place of a debased classical theme, a more naturalistic, barbaric, vigorous effigy. On the coins of the next issue (? 1056), when the weight was reduced a little, the king is shown facing, enthroned in majesty, a design imitated from a Roman coin:[3] and on the reverse, between the arms of the cross, are the mysterious 'martlets' (possibly doves rather than eagles).[4] It was this reverse which provided medieval heralds with Edward's coat of arms. After a return in (?) 1059 to a greater weight and the bust facing right, this time crowned, in (?) 1062 the lightest issue since the very beginning of the reign was given the most unusual design, a facing bust, bearded and crowned, possibly inspired by an Ottonian model.[5] Finally, in (?) 1065, with the restora-

[1] Michael Dolley, *Anglo-Saxon Pennies*, p. 29. For the suspension of geld, see above, p. 106.

[2] F. Barlow, 'Two Notes: Cnut's Second Pilgrimage and Queen Emma's Disgrace in 1043', *EHR*, lxxiii (1958), 655; *VEdR*, p. lxxvii; R. H. M. Dolley and F. Elmore Jones, 'Some Remarks on BMC Type VII var. *B* of Edward the Confessor', *Numismatic Chronicle*, 6th ser., xx (1960), 183–90.

[3] P. D. Whitting, 'The Byzantine Empire and the Coinage of the Anglo-Saxons', *Anglo-Saxon Coins*, p. 35, pl. III, 13–15.

[4] R. H. M. Dolley and F. Elmore Jones, 'A new suggestion concerning the so-called "Martlets" in the "Arms of St Edward" ', *Anglo-Saxon Coins*, pp. 215–26, argue for eagles. For doves (symbolizing perhaps the Holy Ghost), see Percy Ernst Schramm, *Sphaira, Globus, Reichsapfel* (Stuttgart, 1958), pp. 117–18 and pl. 32.

[5] P. D. Whitting, *op. cit.*, p. 35; Michael Dolley, *Anglo-Saxon Pennies*, p. 29.

tion of the 21·5 grain standard, was restored also the bust turned to the right. Harold promptly turned the bust to face left. Artistic considerations apart, it seems that whenever Edward's government found it necessary to reduce the weight of the penny it also provided a new and intriguing design, presumably to encourage men to make the exchange.

We must also take some account of the iconography. The persistence with the old style during the first half of the reign is a sign that the government was traditional in policy and that Edward had no wish to dissociate himself from his Danish predecessors. When the design was dramatically changed Edward must have been making a proclamation. A more naturalistic picture of a bearded warrior-king, inspired mainly by a coin of Cnut, suggests that Edward was assuring the people that although his mother and father-in-law were dead, the Anglo-Scandinavian monarchy would continue, and that the king was strong and resolute. The design balanced neatly continuity and revolution. The other unusual patterns can all be interpreted as intended to draw attention to the king or the monarchy. They indicate a confident government. Where the inspiration for this improved coinage came from is uncertain. On the technical side German artificers, whom we know to have been in the country,[1] may have made their contribution. In the government many prelates, including both archbishops, were interested in metal work.[2]

Although there are inequalities and unusual features in Edward's coinage, it seems unwarranted to view this as a sign of administrative incoherence. The abandonment of the 'sexennial issues' is not evidence of confusion, nor should the experiments be seen as a breakdown in the system.[3] The ability to increase the weight of the coins on three separate occasions proves that the direction, even if restless, was entirely competent.

The coinage was not unconnected with the collection of the king's revenue. We do not know a great deal directly about the financial machinery of Edward's government;[4] but we can be fairly confident

---

[1] Poitiers, p. 258. For the goldsmith Theodoric, see Barlow, *English Church*, p. 123, n. 4.

[2] *Ibid.*, pp. 79–80, 89–90.

[3] R. H. M. Dolley and D. M. Metcalf, 'The Reform of the English Coinage under Eadgar', p. 158: 'The pronounced tendency for hoards of the period 1042–66 to be "multiple-type" is perhaps a sign that a breakdown was threatening the system of regular renewal of the coinage, and may also reflect a decline in public morality of which there is evidence in other aspects of English life.' But see below, p. 287, n. 1.

[4] Vinogradoff, *op. cit.*, pp. 199–200, and Ann Williams, *VCH (Dorset)*, iii. 116–17, discuss the collection of the geld.

that the Norman-Angevin system at least developed out of Old-English procedures and carry the basic post-Conquest customs back to Edward's day.[1] The king's reeves, probably for the most part shire-reeves (sheriffs), 'farmed' the king's revenues, that is to say, they agreed to pay a fixed rent which was much below the value of what they had the right to collect.[2] Wulfstan of York, in his *Institutes of Polity*,[3] wrote that it was proper for reeves to work zealously for their lords; but, he claimed, since Edgar's reign they had become robbers, especially of the defenceless, the poor and the widowed. They cannot have been popular officials.[4]

The reeves paid their farms, less allowances and deductions, plus items outside the farm (certainly geld), in two instalments, one at Easter, the balance at Michaelmas, at one of the royal treasuries. There is not much evidence for a centralized royal treasury at this time; but Winchester and London seem to have been the main depositories.[5] Nothing very elaborate was required, but something rather more sophisticated than was usual in eleventh-century Europe, for the receipts were relatively large and Edward's treasuries, or some of them, could assay, or blanch, the coins proffered, reducing them to their bullion value.[6] From these treasuries, or from the reeves direct, the court took in the money necessary for current expenses; and this treasure, in boxes or barrels, was apparently kept in the king's bedchamber by the chief chamberlain. We cannot describe in detail the accounting system; but it would have been simple, for it was mostly concerned with deductions from fixed renders. Edward would have been personally interested in the state of his affairs; and it is most likely that the tradition that the king celebrated Easter at Winchester[7] developed out of his concern with the treasury accounts. There is one scrap of

[1] Domesday Book assumes the continuity of the whole financial system.

[2] For a discussion of this, see R. W. Southern, *The Place of Henry I in English History* (The Raleigh Lecture on History, British Academy, 1962), pp. 164 ff.

[3] Ed. Jost, pp. 81–2.

[4] They were often admonished in Cnut's reign to avoid unjust and oppressive behaviour: cf. Cnut 1020, cap. 11; Cnut 1027, cap. 12; II Cnut, 69; Harmer, *Writs*, no. 29.

[5] V. H. Galbraith, *Studies in the Public Records* (1948), pp. 41–6; Barlow, *English Church*, pp. 121–4.

[6] J. H. Round, 'The Origin of the Exchequer', *The Commune of London* (1899), pp. 65–9. However, Miss Harvey has shown (below, p. 187) that blanching could mean no more than counting 20*d.* to the ora instead of 16.

[7] *Chron. E, s.a.* 1086; *Vita Wulfstani*, p. 34.

evidence which points to the extreme efficiency of the royal financial administration towards the end of the reign. According to Domesday Book, the most usual monetary unit in which royal renders were paid was the 'ora' containing 20 pennies. As there were only 16 pence in the ordinary ora, the heavy unit represents a surcharge of 25%, and may have been introduced in (?) 1062 when the penny was reduced from 21·5 grains to 17.[1] A government which could protect the royal revenue against the effects of its own devaluation of the currency and keep the surcharge in force after it had returned to the old standard was outstandingly powerful and resourceful.

The economic state of a country which relied almost entirely on agriculture – and, moreover, on mixed farming – depended basically on the climate and weather. In the eleventh century the climate was improving; but England with its changeable weather did not reap the full advantage, and could only become really prosperous under the most favourable political conditions. Although Edward's government cannot be considered enlightened, and it is easy to believe that there could have been much injustice and oppression at lower levels which remained unpunished, the government possibly kept a near optimum course between harshness and laxity. Greater slackness would have led to more disorder and more widespread extortion from the agricultural classes; greater severity and rapacity would likewise have caused poverty and famine. The system when pushed hard, as by William I, struck men as stark and fierce.[2] In comparison Edward was a wise ruler.[3]

[1] Sally Harvey, *op. cit.*
[2] Obituary poem on William in *Chron. E.*
[3] Obituary poem on Edward in *Chron. CD.*

Chapter 9

THE RULE OF SOLOMON
(1054–1064)

The second decade of Edward's reign is more obscure than the first. The narrative sources almost dry up and the charter evidence nearly fails. It does not seem that there are identical reasons for this double decline, although the Norman Conquest may have contributed to both. The dearth of chronicle information appears to have been caused less by the absence of memorable events than by the carelessness of the annalist or of the monastic house where the annals were kept. These were brought up to date about 1053, then continued currently, but with dwindling zeal. The annals from 1059 to 1061 are brief, and for two years, 1062 and 1064, no entry was made. In 1065, however, the Chronicle suddenly expands again. Either, therefore, there was a re-birth of interest towards the end of Edward's reign or, more likely, it was Edward's death which caused the monastery to write up the period from 1059; and by that time fading memory or diminished interest worked to prevent the reinforcement and elaboration of the available jottings.[1] There can be no doubt that the revolutions of 1066 temporarily diminished interest in recent history. The author of the *Vita Ædwardi Regis* cut short his accounts of Harold's campaigns in Wales and Tostig's in Scotland 'until a surer investigation and a suitable time gives us the opportunity to unfold' them.[2] And, of course, the opportunity never came. The triumphs of the house of Godwin were turned into sad, or sour, memories by the battle of Hastings. Harder to understand is the sparsity of reliable and useful charter evidence in the second half of Edward's reign. It is possible that the writ was becoming a more popular title deed and that fewer charters were drawn up. It may be that charters written close to the Conquest were more often superseded and replaced.

[1] The Abingdon (*C*) version omits the years 1057 to 1064 (inclusive); St Augustine's (*E*) for that period is very brief; only the northern version (*D*) has some substance.
[2] *VEdR*, pp. 42–3.

Whatever the cause, the scarcity of information left a space which later historians felt bound to fill. As Edward himself almost disappears from the scene, the earliest interpreter, the author of the *Vita*, set the pattern by turning his attention to Edward's sporting and religious activities, which withdrew the king from the public stage, and to the exploits of the sons of Godwin, which allowed Edward to go into semi-retirement. The thesis is that in the children of Godwin Edward found trusted helpers whom he allowed to take much of the burden off his shoulders.[1] Although we must remember the author's purpose in writing the *Vita* and be prepared for exaggerations,[2] this interpretation is probably not entirely devoid of truth. And it seems better substantiated than the view that Edward's mode of life was the result of premature senility. There is ample evidence in the *Vita*, confirmed by the Chronicle, of the king's continuing physical and mental vigour. Where the *Vita* most seriously misleads is in making so strong a contrast between the earlier and later part of Edward's reign. To claim that before 1052 Edward was often misguided to the great harm of the kingdom and that after 1052, when he was in good hands, everything went well, is patently untrue. Even the author of the *Vita* had to recognize that the rule of Edith, Harold, and Tostig brought the country to ruin.[3] The truth may be that after 1052 Edward's life was much as before, only the lieutenants were changed. In this connexion we should note the attitude of the Worcester chronicler. 'Florence' always stresses that Edward took the initiative, and, when he translated an Anglo-Saxon annal which described the actions of an earl, often inserted *jussu regis*, by the king's command.[4] It is doubtful whether he had any authority for this view beyond his belief that it was kings who gave orders and earls who carried them out; but he was probably right in correcting the impression of anarchy given by the annals.

The directions in which Edward's most intimate advisers pushed him are difficult to see: perhaps they, no more than the king, had not steadfast policies. But if Edith's interests are unknown, her character shows clearly through evidence which is mostly equivocal. In the *Vita*, although she is always placed modestly behind the throne, the author does not minimize her power or completely conceal her will. Whenever

---

[1] Cf. *VEdR*, p. 40. [2] See below, Appendix A.
[3] Because of the rivalry between the brothers.
[4] E.g. the execution of Rhys in 1053 (i. 211), Siward's invasion of Scotland in 1054 (i. 212), Ælfgar's outlawry in 1058 (i. 217), and the Welsh wars of 1063 (i. 222). Cf. also *VEdR*, p. 57.

we catch sight of her elsewhere, we see a determined woman, interfering, hard, probably bad-tempered. For example, we are told in the chronicle of St Riquier,[1] a monastery in Ponthieu, that Abbot Gervin was a friend of Edward and Edith and often visited their court; but when, on one occasion, Edith offered him a kiss of greeting and peace, he drew back in horror. This made her wild – a queen snubbed by a monk – and she took away the gifts she had made him. But after Edward had reproved her and courtiers had intervened, she understood, relented, and gave the abbot an amice ornamented with gold and precious stones, which was later coveted and eventually acquired by Guy, bishop of Amiens (1058–75), the probable author of the *Carmen de Hastingae proelio*. And Edith, we are told, was converted to Gervin's way of thinking and henceforth complained to her own bishops and abbots of their habit of receiving salutations from women. Edith was a woman of importance.

Changes in this period among the royal servants were of some moment. The revolutions of 1051–2 caused upsets at court; but more important than political upheavals were the deaths of the men who had dominated the earlier years of the reign. With the death of Godwin the era which had its roots in the reign of Cnut began to dissolve. In 1055 Siward of Northumbria died, in 1056 Odda, and in 1057 Leofric of Mercia and Ralf of Mantes. Although all the replacements had been born well before Edward's accession, probably none had sentimental attachments to the Danish monarchy. Moreover, the years 1051–3 appear to have been a barrier that few of the greater thegns at court passed through; and the only known exception, Ralf 'the Staller', does not witness before 1050.[2] In the episcopate, however, despite the shake-up in 1051–2, when both provinces and two dioceses received new incumbents, there was, because of the permanence of the office, much greater continuity. Seven bishops and one archbishop died between 1053 and 1062; but, even so, in 1064 both archbishops were men who had begun their careers under Cnut, and two bishops, Leofric and Herman, had accompanied Edward to England. What is more these four men ruled two dioceses apiece.[3] In 1064 more than half the fourteen bishops had been royal clerks.

A strange feature of the royal court after 1052 is the apparent increase

---

[1] Hariulf, *Chronique de l'abbaye de Saint-Riquier*, ed. F. Lot (Paris, 1894), pp. 237–8.
[2] *KCD*, no. 791 (Sawyer, no. 1021).
[3] Stigand: Canterbury and Winchester; Ealdred: York and (effectively) Worcester; Leofric: Devon and Cornwall; Herman: Ramsbury and Sherborne.

in the number of foreigners. By 1057 most of the earls had Scandinavian names and so had some of the royal thegns, such as Bondi and Esgar, while one, Maerleswegen, had an Anglo-Danish compound. Also among the courtiers were two of Edward's French friends, Ralf 'the Staller' and Robert fitzWimarch, both Bretons, at least in part;[1] and the king had a godson named Baldwin, who, apparently, became a monk at Westminster.[2] Another Frenchman at court was Robert, later to be known as Robert of Rhuddlan. According to Orderic Vital,[3] Robert, a member of the important Giroie and Grandmesnil families through his mother, and the son of Humphrey of Tilleuil, was brought to England as a boy by his father and served Edward as a squire. When his apprenticeship was over and he had received knighthood and rich gifts from the king, he obtained permission to return to his parents. But after the Conquest he came back again, this time with his cousin, Hugh, *vicomte* of Avranches; and after Hugh had been appointed earl of Chester, Robert started his own brilliant career of conquest against the Welsh. He was slain in 1093. In ecclesiastical society the position was rather different. The only bishop with a Scandinavian name was Stigand (whose brother had the English name Æthelmaer); and in 1061 the foreigners on the bench were four Germans and a Norman.[4] The abbots, however, seem to have been solidly English by name and by birth.[5]

This racial variety at court is a symptom of a relaxed atmosphere in the kingdom. Even if some of those with Scandinavian names were of mixed descent, or Englishmen in disguise, this reinforces the diagnosis. It is characteristic of the period after 1052 that Ralf of Mantes was

[1] Ralf, who was probably made earl of Norfolk by the Conqueror, died before April 1070 and was succeeded by his son, Ralf, lord of Gael in Brittany, broken for conspiracy in 1075. For the father's grants to the abbey of St Riquier during Edward's reign, see Hariulf, *Chronique de l'abbaye de Saint-Riquier*, ed. F. Lot, pp. 240–5. Opinion has been divided on Robert fitzWimarch's nationality: see Round, *Feudal England*, p. 331, and Professor Foreville, Poitiers, p. 170, *n.* 1; but at least one of his contemporaries, William of Poitiers, claimed him as a Norman (*ibid.*). It is possible that he was Norman-Breton rather than Anglo-Breton.

[2] *DB*, i. 154 b 1: 'Has dedit rex E. S. Petro de Westmon. et Balduino suo filiolo.'

[3] Ordericus Vitalis, ii. 111, 219 (ed. Chibnall, ii. 128, 220, 260, and genealogical table, p. 370), iii. 280–1, 283; iv, pp. xxxiv–xxxviii, 136, 138.

[4] Leofric of Exeter, Giso of Wells, Walter of Hereford, and Herman of Ramsbury and Sherborne; William of London.

[5] In 1044 Manni, who also had the alternative English name of Wulfmaer, became abbot of Evesham, and in 1046 Sihtric became abbot of Tavistock. Baldwin, abbot of Bury St Edmunds in 1065, had been prior of Leberau in German Alsace.

living with his wife, Gytha, and their son, Harold (both Danish names), on their estates in Herefordshire,[1] while Earl Harold's mistress, Edith, bore sons whom they called Godwin, Edmund, and Magnus. The Anglo-Danish queen, Edith, had a French serving woman named Matilda, who married the rich English thegn, Ælfweard.[2] Such a tolerance of strangers, the absence of prejudice in the choice of personal names, the adaptability which the linguistic difficulties alone must have required, reveal among the aristocracy a sophistication which, although seldom completely absent from the English royal court, had, perhaps, been on the decline since the reigns of Athelstan and Edgar. It was again an elegant society. We can see on the Bayeux Tapestry Earl Harold and his company dressed in the height of fashion; impeccably noble; graceful, if a little affected, in manners; the distinguished embassy of a great and wealthy king. The long blond hair and the moustaches of the men were, it is true, outlandish, a Viking habit denounced by moralists;[3] but even this fashion had its admirers in Latin countries. All men knew that the *Angli* were akin to the angels, and all could see that the younger men were as beautiful as girls.[4] Yet English society was not effeminate or decadent. It was a military community. Earl Harold was renowned for his strength of body and will; and his love of women was notorious.[5] Edward gained prestige from such a court. It is not surprising that men began to liken him to Solomon,[6] which, as the learned knew, signifies 'peace'.[7] In the eleventh century, the name was not particularly associated with wisdom.[8]

Edward's main domestic problem after 1053 was to satisfy the ambition of the queen and her brothers without antagonizing the other leading families. It was awkward that Godwin had fathered so many sons, all of whom expected to be promoted earl; although, given

[1] For Gytha, see *DB*, i. 148 a ii; for Harold, Freeman, *NC*, ii, Appendix KK.

[2] *Hemingi Chartularium*, i. 253.

[3] Cf. *Chron. D'EF*, s.a. 959, written or inspired by Wulfstan of York, and Wulfstan of Worcester, *Vita Wulfstani*, p. 23.

[4] Cf. Poitiers, p. 260.

[5] 'luxuria foedum', Poitiers, p. 166. Cf. also Freeman, *NC*, iii, Appendix NN.

[6] *VEdR*, p. 3; 'Heremanni archidiaconi miracula sancti Eadmundi', F. Liebermann, *Ungedruckte Anglo-Normannische Geschichtsquellen* (Strassburg, 1879), pp. 238-9.

[7] Cf. Ælfric, *Treatise on the Old and New Testament* (Early Eng. Text Soc., 160, 1922), p. 37; Jerome, *Liber de nominibus Hebraicis*, Migne, *PL*, xxiii, col. 887, 'Salomon, pacificus, sive pacatus erit.'

[8] *Carmen*, l. 735; 'sapientia Salomonis', *Die Texte des normannischen Anonymus*, ed. Karl Pellens (Wiesbaden, 1966), p. 167.

moderation and goodwill on the part of the older brothers, it was possible to reallocate the existing family holding of shires so as to make provision for their juniors as they came of age. But the first major change spectacularly increased the influence of the house of Godwin. Early in 1055 Earl Siward of Northumbria died – according to the saga,[1] on his feet harnessed for war, unlike the outlawed Osgot Clapa, whom death had just surprised in bed.[2] And Siward was buried in the church he had built at York and dedicated to the Viking saint, Olaf Haraldsson, Æthelred's sometime naval captain. Siward's elder son, Osbeorn 'Bulax', and his sister's son, Siward, had been killed on the Scottish expedition in the previous year; and his one surviving son, Waltheof, was young.[3] Edward summoned his council to meet at London a week before mid-Lent to deal with this problem.

Through the influence of Edith and Harold,[4] their brother, Tostig, was appointed to succeed Siward,[5] and, at the same council, Earl Ælfgar of East Anglia was outlawed. According to the Abingdon (*C*) version of the Chronicle, which is hostile to the house of Godwin, Ælfgar was innocent of crime;[6] according to the northern (*D*) version, he had committed hardly any wrong; according to the St Augustine's (*E*) version, Ælfgar was charged with being a traitor to the king and all the people in the country, a charge which he involuntarily admitted in the council. Obviously he had advanced his own claim to Northumbria, perhaps intrigued both locally and nationally to achieve his aim. His punishment proves that his father, Leofric, now an old man, was without much power and that the queen's party was ruthless. Part of Ælfgar's earldom was taken away and entrusted to Gyrth, the next son of Godwin to be approaching manhood.[7] It would help us to understand the internal politics of the years 1057 to 1062 if we knew why Edward and his advisers were so hostile to Ælfgar. Although the author of the *Vita Ædwardi Regis* believed,[8] probably rightly, that there was a feud between Tostig and the sons of Ælfgar, this is not evidence for open

---

[1] As reported by Henry of Huntingdon, *Historia Anglorum*, ed. Thomas Arnold (Rolls ser. 1879), pp. 195–6.

[2] *Chron. CD, s.a.* 1054, 'died suddenly as he was lying in bed'.

[3] 'adhuc parvulus', Henry of Huntingdon, p. 196. He was executed in 1076. For Siward's death and the council, *Chron. CDE*; Florence i. 212; *VEdR*, p. 31.

[4] *VEdR*, p. 31.

[5] He also succeeded Siward in, or obtained later, the earldom of Northampton (including Huntingdon) and Nottinghamshire, Harmer, *Writs*, p. 575.

[6] Florence, i. 212, with its 'sine culpa', here follows *C* instead of *D*.

[7] Norfolk, *VEdR*, p. 33. [8] *Ibid.*, pp. 50–1.

enmity between the Wessex and Mercian families. Ælfgar's sons had every reason to hate Tostig. The evidence suggests that Ælfgar was a wild man, rather like Swegn Godwinsson, and that it was his imprudent behaviour which aroused the hostility of men inclined to be critical of Mercian policies. However that may be, Ælfgar was expelled and went to Ireland and Wales.[1] As the rights and wrongs of the case are beyond our understanding, all that can profitably be discussed is Edward's political wisdom.

The lawlessness of the north and the Scottish war made the succession of Waltheof impossible. He was not in disgrace. An agreement between him and Abbot Leofric of Peterborough concerning two vills which should have fallen to the abbey on Siward's death was ratified by the king.[2] Nor was he neglected: by 1065 he was holding a subordinate earldom in the north;[3] and he was earl of Northumberland under the Conqueror from 1072 until his forfeiture three years later. Although there were probably several adult nobles in Northumbria descended from Earl Waltheof I, who flourished towards the end of the tenth century,[4] Edward wisely took the opportunity to go outside the native candidates and try to bring the province under closer royal control. This was his steadfast policy with regard to the archbishopric of York. In the circumstances, once these basic decisions had been taken, the earldom was Tostig's. It must have been obvious that Leofric of Mercia had not long to live and that Ælfgar's claim to succeed him could not be denied. It would, therefore, have been most imprudent of Edward

[1] To Wales, *Chron. E*; to Ireland and then Wales, *Chron. CD*; Florence, i. 212–13, with additional detail.

[2] *KCD*, no. 927 (Sawyer, no. 1481), a post-Conquest Peterborough memorandum of land transactions done before Edward. Waltheof was allowed to keep one of the vills for life and only returned the other in return for 5 marks of gold. The vills, in Rutland, had belonged to the widow, Godgifu, whom Siward had married perhaps after Ælfleda, Waltheof's mother.

[3] He must have been an earl under Harold, for, described as earl, he was one of the hostages taken by William to Normandy in February 1067, *Chron. D*, Poitiers, p. 244. Since there is evidence that later he held the counties of Huntingdon and Northampton, which we know were held by Tostig and possibly Siward as detached members of Northumbria, and it is likely that William was restoring him to his old office, Freeman's suggestion, *NC*, ii. 560, that Waltheof obtained these two shires when Tostig was exiled, is persuasive. For Waltheof's later earldom, see Ordericus Vitalis, ii. 221 (ed. Chibnall, ii. 262), interpolation of Robert of Torigni, in Jumièges, p. 327. Waltheof also signs as earl *KCD*, no. 810 (Sawyer, no. 1033), a royal charter in favour of Rouen with a witness list dated and congruent with 1061. But we cannot identify his earldom at this time.

[4] See chart in Barlow, *English Church*, p. 172.

to let Ælfgar transfer from East Anglia to Northumbria. It offered no immediate advantages and would for certain cause trouble later. A man of rare qualities, who would settle down to the task, was required to rule Northumbria; and in Tostig Edward thought he had the man.

As Tostig had secured the hand of Judith, half-sister of the count of Flanders, in 1051,[1] it must have been understood that he would receive an important earldom at the first opportunity.[2] His distinguished Danish ancestry through his mother, Gytha, and his even more distinguished marriage made him particularly suited to rule Northumbria. He also had qualities which fitted him for the office. The author of the *Vita Ædwardi Regis* naturally praised Edward for this wise appointment.[3] With Harold defending the south and Tostig the north the tranquillity of the kingdom and the carefreeness of the king were assured. It is on this occasion that the family's encomiast makes an interesting comparison between the brothers. They had in common good looks, physical strength, and courage. Both were serious and responsible, never foolhardy or inept, and both could disguise their intentions. In all other respects they were different. Harold was the taller and had the greater physical stamina;[4] he also had the more open character and the sunnier temperament. He could stand being contradicted; he liked to discuss his plans with friends; he was honourable and easy-going. Occasionally he was too slow to act. Although, like Tostig, he was persevering, he liked to enjoy himself on the way; Tostig always pressed on to the goal. Harold was more intelligent than Tostig, more wily; but the writer infers that he did not always make the fullest use of his talents. Tostig was the more secretive; he kept his own counsel, which gave him the advantage of surprise. He was the more inflexible and was slightly at fault in his ruthless pursuit of evil-doers. He always kept his word and never changed his purpose. Unlike Harold he was a good and religious man, generous to the church, faithful to his wife, clean-mouthed.

Edward's choice of Tostig for Northumbria was in the short run

---

[1] *VEdR*, pp. 24–5. She was Edward's cousin once removed.

[2] He is called dux in *VEdR*, p. 24, on the occasion of his marriage. He does not, however, witness as earl any document which can be dated earlier than 1055. *KCD*, no. 806 (Sawyer, no. 1060), which can be dated 1055 × 60, would seem to be the earliest.　　　　　　　　　　　　　　　　　　　　[3] *VEdR*, p. 31.

[4] According to *King Harald's Saga*, cap. 91, Harald Sigurdsson said of his namesake before the battle of Stamford Bridge, 'What a little man that was; but he stood proudly in his stirrups.' The Norwegian Harald was, however, exceptionally tall.

justified. Tostig ruled Northumbria firmly, or harshly (according to the point of view), for ten years. He was often out of his earldom, but had a capable deputy, Copsig.[1] He enforced severe justice and seems to have introduced some West-Saxon laws,[2] presumably those less favourable to blood feuds and other lawlessness. He kept peace in the north. He and his wife, Judith, patronized the church of Durham.[3] Although his rule was unpopular, and in the end he was expelled, it was only as a result of discreditable intrigues at court.[4] Thus Tostig probably did even better than expected. Nor does it seem that Edward could have appointed Ælfgar. But in the long run this choice marked a decisive change in royal policy. Hitherto Edward had always relied on the earls of Mercia and Northumbria to counterbalance the influence of the earl of Wessex. In 1055 that position was abandoned. Ælfgar was put to shame and became a discontented, awkward man. Edward could only recover freedom of action through dissension between the children of Godwin. To what extent rivalry already existed in the family, and how far Edward was tempted to exploit it, is difficult to see. After the events of 1065–6 it was only natural to imagine that Harold and Tostig were rivals of long standing;[5] and it is, indeed, possible that the younger brother both envied Harold's advantages and disapproved of his way of life. It was this rivalry, according to the author of the *Vita*, which in the end destroyed the kingdom.[6] Yet Harold and Tostig co-operated in 1063 and there is no good evidence for disagreement between them before 1065. Nor can it be thought that Edward gave Northumbria to Tostig in 1055 in order to play off the one brother against the other. The house of Godwin was in power and determined to extend it, although stopping short of enormities.

[1] Symeon, *HDE*, p. 97.

[2] Edward, when he allowed the Northumbrians to expel Tostig in 1065, renewed for them the law of King Cnut, *Chron. DE*.

[3] *VEdR*, p. 32, and *n.*; Symeon, *HDE*, i. 94–5; 'Godwini' and 'Tosti' are written in letters of gold in Durham's *Liber Vitae*, fo. 12ᵛ, Surtees Soc., xiii (1841), p. 2. But Tostig and his men seem to have cared little for Durham's right of sanctuary: see the story in *Historia translationum S. Cuthberti*, ed. Hodgson Hinde, Surtees Soc., li (1868), 168–70; Symeon (Rolls ser.), i. 244–5; Bertram Colgrave, 'The post-Bedan miracles and translations of St Cuthbert', *The Early Cultures of North-West Europe*, ed. Cyril Fox and Bruce Dickins, p. 312; Barlow, *English Church*, pp. 257–8.

[4] See below, p. 237.

[5] *VEdR*, pp. 15–17, 37–40, 53–4, 56–7. The story of how Harold and Tostig fought each other as boys at court, and Edward prophesied the events of 1065–6, first appears in Ailred of Rievaulx's *Vita Sancti Edwardi*, written in 1163, Migne, *PL*, cxcv, col. 763.

[6] Below, Appendix A, pp. 295 ff.

In the autumn of 1057 Earl Leofric and in December Earl Ralf died.
Ælfgar, who had been reinstated in East Anglia, was allowed to succeed
his father in Mercia. The house of Godwin divided up the rest. Gyrth
took over the whole of East Anglia. The next younger brother, Leofwine,
was given a new earldom created out of the south-eastern shires, and
Harold took Ralf's earldom in compensation.[1] Since Gyrth sometimes
paired with Tostig and Leofwine with Harold,[2] the whole rearrange-
ment may have been acceptable to all concerned. There is no reason to
think that Edward opposed this further extension of the power of his
brothers-in-law; there was probably in practice no alternative available
to him. Ralf had left only a young boy as heir to a marcher earldom;[3]
Ælfgar had no adult sons. Unless Edward was to raise up entirely new
men – like Ralf 'the Staller', Robert fitzWimarch, Esgar, or Ulf of
Lincoln – he had to accept the queen's brothers. The fact that in this
period he appointed to an earldom no man from outside the great ducal
families he had inherited from Cnut shows that he was either without
the power or without the will to follow an autocratic course. A realist,
Edward probably accepted here a situation which he could not greatly
change.

Although England was not without internal tensions between 1053
and 1065 these must be kept in perspective. In that same period
William of Normandy campaigned almost every year against one or
more of his neighbours and sometimes against his overlord, the king of
France. In Germany the Emperor Henry III was still troubled by the
Lotharingian rebellion. In England, although the concentration of
earldoms in the hands of the queen's brothers was in the end bound to
lead to some sort of revolution, while the brothers worked together
under the king the monarchy could mobilize all its potential strength.
The author of the *Vita*, in a poem,[4] described Harold and Tostig as,

---

[1] Freeman, *NC*, ii, Appendix G, 'The great earldoms during the reign of Eadward.'
Gyrth had, as well as Norfolk and Suffolk, probably Cambridgeshire, possibly Bed-
fordshire, and, certainly later, Oxfordshire. Leofwine had Kent, Surrey, Middlesex,
Essex, Hertford, and probably Buckinghamshire. For Harold and Hereford, see
Harmer, *Writs*, no. 49; for Leofwine, *ibid.*, p. 567. See also below, p. 359.

[2] Leofwine went with Harold to Ireland in 1051, Gyrth accompanied Tostig to
Rome in 1061. But Gyrth may have marched with Harold against Tostig in 1066
(*The Foundation of Waltham Abbey*, ed. W. Stubbs, 1861, p. 25), and both he and
Leofwine were in Harold's army at Hastings after Tostig's death.

[3] He was under age in 1066, when, according to *DB*, i. 129 b i, 'Hoc manerium
tenuit Heraldus filius Radulfi comitis, quem custodiebat regina Eddid cum manerio
ea die qua rex Edwardus fuit vivus et mortuus.'   [4] *VEdR*, pp. 37–40.

'two brightly shining offspring of a cloud-born land, as strong as Hercules; when united in peace they seem to the English the kingdom's hearts of oak. And just as in the ancient world it was Atlas and Hermes who jointly supported the weight of the skies and thus kept heaven and earth in their place, so now these two angelic Angles, combining their strength, keep the English frontiers safe. . . . O holy mother Concord, grant us peace, lest from the royal kin and faithful stock the hostile fire should laugh to have procured an endless stubble, fuel for its sparks.' The only danger to the king and kingdom was discord between the brothers.

Especially interesting in this period are the ecclesiastical empires which some favoured bishops assembled. Ealdred, a monk, administered from 1055 to 1058 the three dioceses of Worcester, Hereford, and Wilt-shire and the abbey of Winchcombe. Once he also held Gloucester abbey. Later he had to be satisfied with York and *de facto* control over Worcester. Stigand did even better. When in 1058 he consecrated Siward, abbot of Chertsey, to Rochester and Æthelric, monk of Christ Church, Canterbury, to Selsey, he linked his dioceses of Winchester and Canterbury by putting his own men into the bishoprics which separated them.[1] To the north, after the interruption of the diocese of London, his brother, Æthelmaer, ruled East Anglia. And we must not forget that Spearhavoc, abbot of Abingdon, who may have been another of this group, almost obtained London in 1051. Stigand also administered several abbeys.[2] There were obviously various reasons for this pluralism. Occasionally it was almost accidental, at the time administratively convenient. There may have been an unavowed, perhaps even uncon-scious, desire among the leading bishops to recover parity with the great earls, their secular counterparts. Some of these accumulations may also have had military significance. Ealdred's responsibility for the defence of the southern marches against the Welsh has, because of his implication in Anglo-Welsh diplomacy and warfare, always been obvious. Stigand was ecclesiastically responsible for the arc which faced the Continent. The coastline from the Wash to the Isle of Wight, save only Essex, was under his eye. Sandwich, the main Channel port, was one of his (Christ Church) manors. We never hear of the archbishop

---

[1] Rochester, which was subject to Canterbury, seems to have had no bishop of its own between 1046 and 1058. In those 12 years it was, presumably, ruled directly by the archbishop.

[2] For all this, see Barlow, *English Church*.

being engaged in military affairs. It is indeed unlikely that he had any taste for warfare. But, as a landowner and prelate, he was responsible for large contingents of troops, for the maintenance of many fortresses and bridges, and he may well have had some administrative responsibility for the defence of this most vulnerable coastal sector. Attention has often been directed to a few littoral estates in the hands of French monasteries. Much more important were the earls and bishops who ruled the provinces in which they lay.

There may also have been in this pluralism occasionally a reformative purpose, such as had been present in England in the tenth century and in Normandy in the eleventh.[1] Although with Stigand, Ealdred, and Leofric of Peterborough as the greatest pluralists,[2] the motive was hardly the spiritual regeneration of the communities, it could easily have been to secure more efficient government and prevent the haphazard wastage of monastic estates. However that may be, there was in the latter part of Edward's reign if not a reform movement in the English church at least much local improvement. Bishops Leofric of Exeter (1050-72), William of London (1051-75), and Giso of Wells (1060-88) reorganized their cathedral chapters, and in the diocese of York Archbishops Cynsige (1051-60) and Ealdred (1060-9) remodelled, enriched, and adorned their four great minsters. Earl Harold founded a collegiate church at Waltham. Because these were not monastic reforms they did not meet with the entire approval of the monastic chroniclers, and so have often been undervalued. But at the lowest estimation they were leaven in the mass; and even in the Benedictine houses the movement was not entirely from bad to worse. At Sherborne under Herman (1058-78) and Worcester under Wulfstan (1062-95) the tone of the monastic chapters was much improved. All these bishops were appointed by Edward (all but the monks Ealdred and Wulfstan out of his household), and all must have been his friends. It is unlikely that Edward rewarded them with dioceses because they were reformers.

[1] John of Ravenna, abbot of Fécamp, ruled other monasteries outside Normandy. All the same, he attacked pluralism, 'Enim vero nullus inter abbates invenitur tam infimus qui uno iuxta decreta canonum velit esse contentus monasterio. Ille fortunatus, ille baro laudatus qui multas habens abbatias cum equis et equitibus [Ezech. xxvi. 7] discurrit per regiones et regna.' Letter 'tuae quidem', Jean Leclercq and Jean-Paul Bonnes: *Un Maître de la Vie spirituelle au XIᵉ siècle, Jean de Fécamp* (Paris, 1946), p. 202. Cf. also L. Musset, 'La contribution de Fécamp à la reconquête monastique de la Basse-Normandie (990-1066)', *L'Abbaye Bénédictine de Fécamp, Ouvrage Scientifique du XIIIᵉ Centenaire, 658-1958*, i (1959), 57-66.

[2] Barlow, *English Church*, pp. 78-9, 87-8, 57, and (2nd edn., 1979) Appendix 2.

They had earned their promotion through efficient service at court, and they had at least some of the qualities that go to make a good bishop.

Whatever Edward's foreign policy may have been in the crisis years, there are no signs of a diplomatic revolution either when Godwin returned or when he died. Perhaps Edward's policy was nothing more than keeping on good terms with all his neighbours, in order to discourage Viking aggression. If so, Godwin's return was a help. There is no evidence that the Wessex family was actively opposed to an alliance with Normandy; Tostig's marriage to Judith of Flanders helped to appease a hostile power; and Svein of Denmark was a first cousin of the queen and her brothers. The only possible enemy outside English influence was Norway, where Harald Sigurdsson (Hardrada) ruled. Even if English diplomacy made little contribution to the pacification of the North Sea after 1052, Godwin's was the last hostile invasion across the Channel before 1066. Svein Estrithson was under Norwegian pressure until 1064, when he made a treaty with Harald. But he was, as Earl Tostig, according to Snorri Sturluson,[1] pointed out to Harald Sigurdsson in 1065, a popular king, supported by all the chieftains. He was able to harness aristocratic energy to the defence of his kingdom: he would neither allow his nobles to go a-viking nor tolerate internal disorder, as the well-known story of how impatient he became with his unruly nephew and foster-son, Asmund, shows.[2]

Norway, on the other hand, was very turbulent under Harald. Chieftains whom he exiled and those out of his control raided the west coast of Britain by way of the Orkneys, where Thorfinn Sigurdsson, Thorfinn the Mighty, was earl from 1014 to 1065, and Dublin, where Margad Rognvaldsson (in Irish: Eachmarcach mac Ragnall) ruled from 1046 to 1052.[3] In the late 'forties Kalf Arnason, exiled from Norway, was raiding from winter quarters in Orkney;[4] and at the same time, or a little later, Guthorm Gunnhildarson, a nephew of King

[1] *King Harald's Saga*, cap. 79.

[2] *Ibid.*, cap. 49. Asmund was so unruly that in the end, when he became a Viking and even ravaged Denmark, Svein encouraged the commander of his defence forces, Hakon Ivarsson, to bring Asmund to book. Hakon sought him out, killed him, cut off his head, and took it to Svein. The king made no comment at the time, but later dismissed Hakon from his service on the grounds that, although he himself wished him no harm, he could not answer for his kinsmen.

[3] *Annals of the kingdom of Ireland by the Four Masters*, ii. 851, 861; *The Annals of Tigernach* in *Revue Celtique*, xvii (1896), 392–3.

[4] *King Harald's Saga*, cap. 51.

11–12. Scenes from the Bayeux Tapestry (embroidered possibly in Kent about 1075). (Courtesy Phaidon Press Ltd.)

11. Edward's death. The inscription (in translation) is 'Here King Edward in bed addresses his vassals. And here he is dead.' The figures in the upper picture are (following *VEdR*) Queen Edith at Edward's feet, Robert fitzWimarch at his head, Archbishop Stigand and Earl Harold. Edward and Harold are about to clasp hands.

12(a). The funeral procession to the church. The inscription (in translation) is, 'Here the body of King Edward is carried to the church of St Peter the Apostle'.

12(b). Westminster abbey church. A man is about to fix the weather-cock.

Harald, raided from his winter quarters at Dublin.[1] In 1052, when Guthorm and Margad were looting Wales, the jarl commanding five warships, the king sixteen, there was a quarrel in the Menai Straits over the division of the booty, and Guthorm slew Margad. This victory against the odds on 28 July was won with the help of St Olaf, Guthorm's uncle, and in thanksgiving Guthorm had a tenth of the silver coin they had collected from Wales made into a crucifix ten feet tall to put in the church at Trondheim in which St Olaf was buried. Although we do not hear of further raids on Britain before 1058, when Magnus Haraldsson led a substantial Norwegian expedition into the Irish Sea,[2] conditions were probably so unsettled in this area as seldom to inspire special mention.

Freedom from continental entanglements, from invasion and civil war, made it almost inevitable, as in the reigns of Athelstan and Edgar, that Edward and his earls should pay some attention to the other powers in the British Isles. Edward had, it seems, no ambition to widen his empire: his policy towards Scotland and Wales, like his Scandinavian policy, was purely defensive. His desire was to have respectful neighbours who observed the bounds. But his actions passed into folk-history. A century later Walter Map told stories of Gruffydd and Edward, and Gerald of Barry stories of Harold. The reign of Macbeth became even more famous. The kingdom of Scotland[3] had taken shape in the tenth century after Edmund's lease of Cumbria to Malcolm I in 945[4] and Edgar's grant of Lothian to Kenneth II about 973.[5] As a result one of the most famous Anglo-Saxon monuments, the eighth-century Ruthwell Cross in Dumfriesshire, eighteen feet high, covered with scenes in relief and inscriptions in the Northumbrian dialect (including some lines from the poem *The Dream of the Rood*), is now in Scotland. Although England's loss of its northern territories was confirmed by Malcolm II's defeat of Uchtred, earl of Northumbria, at Carham on the Tweed in 1016,[6] the boundary remained not only ill-defined but capable of violent fluctuation. In the north, vast areas of the mainland as well as the islands were held by Scandinavians. Nevertheless, under Duncan I (1034–40), unsuccessful as he was, there was a recognizable kingdom

---

[1] *King Harald's Saga*, caps. 54–5; cf. 45.   [2] See below, p. 209.

[3] William Croft Dickinson, *Scotland from the Earliest Times to 1603* (1961); R. L. Graeme Ritchie, *The Normans in Scotland* (1954); Plummer, *Two Chronicles*, pp. 243–4.

[4] *Chron.*: 'On condition that he should be his ally both on sea and on land.'

[5] Roger of Wendover (xiii cent.), *Flores Historiarum*, ed. H. O. Coxe, i (1841), 416.

[6] Symeon, *HDE*, i. 84, *HR*, ii. 155–6.

comparable to the kingdom of England. Succession to the crown was disputed among the descendants of the ninth-century Kenneth Mac-Alpin, king of Alba: representatives of the several collateral branches dethroning each other whenever the opportunity occurred. On 14 August 1040 Macbeth killed Duncan and, aided by his wife, Gruoch, became an effective ruler. In 1050 he made a pilgrimage to Rome and was generous with alms.[1]

Duncan, like Cnut's earl, Siward, had married a woman descended from Earl Waltheof of Northumbria – perhaps Duncan and Siward were brothers-in-law – and so, after his death, his elder son, Malcolm Canmore (Big Head), about nine years old but already king-designate of Cumbria, was taken for safety to his uncle. Although Malcolm's presence at Edward's court is not attested, it was later believed in Scotland that the exile was educated there;[2] and it is more than likely that he spent some time at both courts. Edward probably had a special interest in exiled princes, and in the summer of 1054, when Malcolm was about twenty-three, ordered Siward to invade Scotland and place Malcolm on the throne.[3] Edward supplied at least some of his own housecarls to the army and navy[4] which advanced by the eastern route into Scotland; and on 27 July Siward brought Macbeth to battle north of the Tay in Perthshire. In this fierce engagement both sides suffered serious casualties. On the Scottish side were killed all those Frenchmen from Herefordshire who had joined Macbeth two years before;[5] on the English, Siward's elder son, Osbern, his sister's son, and many English and Danes, including housecarls.[6] It was, however, a victory for the invaders. Macbeth was put to flight and, while Siward returned to England with great plunder, Malcolm took possession of Lothian as well as Cumbria. On 15 August 1057 Malcolm killed Macbeth in battle and in 1058 Lulach, Gruoch's son.[7] He had obtained complete control of the kingdom.

---

[1] Florence, i. 204.

[2] Johannes de Fordun, *Chronica Gentis Scotorum*, ed. William F. Skene (1871), i. 188–9, 190–91.

[3] *Chron. CD*; Florence, i. 212; *VEdR*, p. 43; Fordun, i. 203–4.

[4] Their death is mentioned in *Chron. D*. The expeditionary force is called *here*, a Danish army, in both *C* and *D*; but *D* then distinguishes between the *scyp here* and the *land fyrd*.   [5] Florence, i. 212.

[6] *Chron. C*, followed by Florence, *ibid.*; full detail only in *D*. The battle with its heavy casualties is mentioned in *The Annals of Tigernach* in *Revue Celtique*, xvii. 395.

[7] Fordun, pp. 205–6. *The Annals of Tigernach*, pp. 398–9, where it is stated that Lulach, 'king of Scotland', was treacherously slain by Mael-Coluimb, son of Donchad.

In 1059 Malcolm, escorted by Earl Tostig, Cynsige, archbishop of York, and Æthelwine, bishop of Durham, came to Edward's court at Gloucester,[1] no doubt to return thanks and probably to acknowledge Edward as his lord. On this occasion he could have met his future wife, Margaret, the daughter of Edward 'the Exile', then about thirteen years old and since 1057 resident in England.[2] According to Scottish tradition Edward offered this match;[3] but Malcolm chose to ally with the Scandinavian north. He married Ingibjorg, daughter of Thorfinn, earl of the Orkneys and Caithness, who bore him a son, Duncan.[4] Indeed, Malcolm's gratitude to Edward seems to have been short-lived; and it may have been because of his fourteen years' stay in England that he acquired the ambition to annex Northumbria. Tostig is said to have defeated Scottish pressure more by cunning diplomacy than by war;[5] and one of his schemes was, no doubt, to become Malcolm's 'sworn brother'.[6] But in 1061, while Tostig was absent on his pilgrimage to Rome,[7] Malcolm could invade without violating the compact; and he ravaged deep into Northumbria.[8] After this, Tostig seems to have restored the understanding with Malcolm, perhaps taking hostages for Edward;[9] and it was to Malcolm that the exiled earl sailed in 1066 before joining forces with Harald Hardrada.

If Edward's achievements in Anglo-Scottish affairs were modest they were at least not outclassed by those of his Norman successors. It is, indeed, likely that in 1066 the boundary was further north than it was

---

[1] Symeon, *HR*, ii. 174, probably followed by Gaimar, *Lestorie des engles*, ed. T. D. Hardy and C. T. Martin (Rolls ser. 1888–9), ll. 5087–98, and *Annales Dunelmenses*, in *Monumenta Germaniae historica*, ed. G. H. Pertz, Scriptores, xix (Hannover, 1866), p. 508.   [2] See below, p. 218.

[3] Orderic (ed. Chibnall), iv. 270, states that Malcolm, when he invaded Northumbria in 1091, asserted, 'Fateor quod rex Edvardus, dum mihi Margaritam proneptem suam in conjugium tradidit, Lodonensem [Lothian] comitatum mihi donavit. Deinde Guillelmus rex quod antecessor ejus mihi dederat concessit . . .' now at Alençon, printed Le Prevost, *ibid.*, v, p. liv. William of Malmesbury, *Historia Novella*, ed. K. R. Potter (Nelson's Medieval Texts, 1955), p. 4, was another who believed that Edward had arranged the marriage. 'Porro Edwardus . . . proneptem suam Margaritam ex fratre Edmundo Ireneside Malcolmi regis Scottorum nuptiis copulavit.' All these writers are probably in error, confusing here Edward (her father) or Edgar (her brother) with King Edward.

[4] Ritchie, pp. 16–17.   [5] *VEdR*, p. 43.

[6] Symeon, *HR*, ii. 174–5. For artificial brotherhood, see Plummer, *Two Chronicles*, pp. 25–6.   [7] See below, p. 210.

[8] Symeon, *HR*, ii. 174–5, 221, presumably followed by Gaimar, ll. 5101–4. It is strange that even *Chron. D* omits this episode.   [9] *VEdR*, p. 43.

at any time in the Conqueror's reign. In his tardy but thorough defeat of a resurgent Wales Edward was even more successful.[1] He inherited a frontier which had been pushed west of Offa's dyke by English colonization, but had to cope with an enemy unusually united and exceptionally well led. As a result the English encroachments were turned into a belt of devastated and depopulated land.[2] It was probably in this period that the familiar English view of the Welsh, most noticeable in twelfth-century writers, was being sharpened. The Welsh only kept peace until they felt able to do mischief;[3] as Walter Map said to Archbishop Thomas Becket of Canterbury, 'While you hold the sword they will beseech you; when they hold it they will command.'[4] The glory of the Welsh was in plunder and theft; their anger was foolish and unreasonable; they were swift to shed blood.[5] Gruffydd ap Llywelyn, from 1039 ruler of north and central Wales (Gwynedd and Powys) and from 1055 master also of the south (Deheubarth), exemplified the typical Welsh qualities. In legend he was, like Alexander and all great conquerors, generous, vigilant, quick, bold, courteous, affable, bountiful, audacious, and cruel.[6] When charged with the murder of all those whom he feared as future rivals, he said, 'I kill no one; I only blunt the horns of Wales lest they wound their mother.'[7] For a time, 1044–55, Gruffydd was resisted in the south by a namesake, the son of Rhydderch, a leader almost as great as he. These two princes were also the scourge of the English.

Gruffydd ap Llywelyn heavily defeated the forces of Mercia in 1039 in an ambush at Rhydd y Groes, on the upper Severn near Welshpool, when Earl Leofric's brother, Eadwine, was killed;[8] and in 1052, thirteen years later to the day, during an invasion of Herefordshire, he defeated near Leominster the French castellans commanding both French and English troops.[9] In the south Gruffydd ap Rhydderch, in alliance with Danish pirates, had invaded in 1049 across the Wye and defeated Bishop Ealdred commanding the local defence[10] forces, and in

---

[1] See J. E. Lloyd, *A History of Wales* (3rd ed., 1939), ii. 357 ff.; 'Wales and the coming of the Normans', *Cymmrodorion*, 1899–1900 (1901), 122–79.

[2] As we see in *DB* from Chester to Gloucester.

[3] Walter Mapes, *De Nugis Curialium*, ed. Thomas Wright (Camden Soc., vol. 50, 1850), p. 99.

[4] *Ibid.*, p. 100.   [5] *Ibid.*, p. 103.   [6] *Ibid.*, p. 98.   [7] *Ibid.*, p. 104.

[8] *Chron. C*; Florence, i. 193; cf. *Annales Cambriae*, ed. John Williams ab Ithel (Rolls ser. 1860), pp. 23–4; *Hemingi Chartularium*, i. 278. J. E. Lloyd, 'Wales and the coming of the Normans', pp. 129–31.

[9] *Chron. D*; Florence, i. 207.   [10] See above, p. 99.

1053 had raided Westbury on Severn.[1] There are no signs that Edward was as yet alarmed. It is even possible that he did not spend Christmas 1054 at Gloucester, for on 4 December the saintly Abbot John of Fécamp left his abbey to visit its English possessions, Winchelsea and Rye on the Sussex coast, and afterwards, presumably at a place closer to the Channel than the Welsh march, had an audience with the king at which he asked for the church at Eastbourne.[2] In 1055, however, the northern prince instigated the death of the southerner and began to rule over the whole of Wales. This was a situation which no English king could welcome.

The defences against the Welsh were considerable and were greatly strengthened by Edward. The ditch and embankment known as Offa's dyke was a formidable obstacle;[3] it is hardly likely that any cities were unprotected by earthworks or walls;[4] and Ralf of Mantes was encouraged to defend Herefordshire in the French fashion, with castles and cavalry garrisons.[5] All the estates had the duty of producing troops for a field army and there were some special arrangements for watch and ward.[6] In military command were the earls, supported by the bishops. As Æthelstan, bishop of Hereford, was old and from 1043 until his death in 1056 blind,[7] the bishop of Worcester had the main responsibility. Above all, Edward himself took a lively interest in Welsh affairs. He often held his court at Gloucester;[8] and if the chief attraction was hunting in the Forest of Dean, the main business to be transacted there was the co-ordination of the defences.

---

[1] See above, p. 126.

[2] *Neustria Pia* (Rouen, 1663), p. 223; J. Mabillon, *Annales Ordinis Sancti Benedicti Occidentalium Monachorum Patriarchae* (Paris, 1703–39), iv. 547. Donald Matthew, *The Norman Monasteries and their English Possessions* (1962), pp. 19–21. Cf. J. Mabillon, *Vetera Analecta* (Paris 1723), p. 451a.

[3] Cyril Fox, *Offa's Dyke* (Brit. Acad., 1955).

[4] The English Chronicle would have us believe (see below, p. 206) that Hereford was unprotected by a perimeter defence until 1055, when Harold built fortifications. But the *Brut y Tywysogion*, ed. John Williams ab Ithel (Rolls ser. 1860), pp. 42–3, in the annal for 1054, distinguishes between the *gaer* (fortress), which Gruffydd depopulated and demolished, and the *tref* (town), which he burned. It is, indeed, almost inconceivable that Hereford was ever a completely open city. Philip Rahtz, 'Hereford', *Current Archaeology*, no. 9 (July 1968), pp. 242–6, reports on excavations in the city which reveal a series of ramparts. He identifies one with tenth-century defences against the Vikings and another with Harold's works.

[5] See above, p. 94.

[6] Cf. the entries under Hereford and Archenfield, *DB*, i. 179.

[7] Florence, i. 214.

[8] Cf. Oleson, *Witenagemot*, Appendix O.

The Welsh princes had never been completely isolated from English influence; and the more ambitious the prince, the more likely he was to become involved. In 1046 Earl Swegn had helped the northern Gruffydd against his southern rival.[1] After 1055, when Gruffydd became ruler of all Wales, the Welsh prince began to play for even higher stakes. In that same year Earl Ælfgar, when banished from England for treason,[2] returned from Ireland to Wales with eighteen ships, made an alliance with Gruffydd, and led their combined forces against the city of Hereford.[3] On 24 October Earl Ralf offered battle two miles before the city; the Anglo-French cavalry fled before a spear was thrown;[4] and, after the Welsh had killed about four or five hundred of the defenders, they were able to put Hereford to the sack. Cathedral clergy defending the doors of the church were killed; the new cathedral, St Æthelberht's minster, was looted and then burned; captives were led into slavery; the whole city and part of the county[5] was ravaged. Probably as a result, Bishop Æthelstan's coadjutor, the Welsh bishop, Tramerin, died shortly afterwards and Æthelstan himself only lasted until 10 February. Edward put Harold in command of an army which was summoned from almost the whole of England (perhaps Northumbria was excused) to report at Gloucester.[6] Harold advanced a short distance into Wales, but found no enemy to fight. Leaving part of his forces to protect his flank, he went to Hereford where he had additional defence works constructed, a ditch to surround the city and fortified gates.[7] It is unlikely that Harold had any quarrel with Ælfgar; and it was decided to split the coalition. At Billingsley in Archenfield, south of Hereford, it was agreed that Ælfgar should make his peace with the king and recover his earldom of East Anglia,[8] and we must assume that

---

[1] Above, p. 91.　　　　　　　　　　　[2] Above, p. 193.

[3] *Chron. CDE*; Florence, i. 212–14. All the accounts, of which *C* and Florence are the longest, appear to be complementary; there is no disagreement. The Welsh account, *Brut y Tywysogion*, p. 43, is also in harmony.

[4] *Chron. C* alleges that the English army fled because they were on horseback; Florence describes Ralf as *timidus*, claims that he forced the English to fight on horseback and alleges that it was Ralf and the Normans who first took to flight. It is, indeed, possible that Welsh and Viking war cries frightened the horses and some of the riders and started an uncontrollable flight.

[5] 'Rex Grifin et Blein vastaverunt hanc terram T.R.E. et ideo nescitur qualis eo tempore fuerit', under Archenfield, *DB*, i. 181 a i.

[6] 'from nearly all over England', *Chron. C*; 'de tota mox [? *recte* vix] Anglia', Florence, i. 213.　　　　　　　　　　　[7] *Chron. C*, Florence, i. 213–14.

[8] Florence, i. 214, states explicitly that after the peace made at Billingsley by Harold, Ælfgar went to the king for reinvestiture with his earldom. Cf. *Chron. C*.

Gruffydd was left in possession of at least some of his conquests.[1] The Viking fleet sailed to Chester to await the pay which Ælfgar had promised. None of Edward's men came out of this affair with an enhanced reputation; but Harold was still without much military experience, and it was probably this intervention in Wales which made him ambitious for fame.[2] He was to prove a ready learner.

The year 1055 was clearly a turning point in Anglo-Welsh relations. The English court decided to destroy the presumptuous Gruffydd; and the steadfastness with which this policy was pursued, using different expedients until success was achieved, shows that Edward, when the safety of his kingdom was threatened, was at his shrewdest and most tenacious. Until 1058, however, the English failed in all their undertakings, and from 1058 until 1063 there is a gap in our knowledge. At first the English position even worsened. Earl Leofric of Mercia, although he had never been the hammer of the Welsh, indeed had no military reputation, was at least entirely loyal. His son, Ælfgar, who succeeded him in October 1057, seems never to have abandoned the alliance he made with Gruffydd in 1055, and gave him, presumably after 1057, his daughter in marriage.[3] It is one of the earliest examples of a situation which was usual enough later: a marcher lord, when threatened by the English king or a court party, making common cause with Celtic princes.

Edward's first scheme was to appoint a warrior bishop. When Æthelstan of Hereford died in February 1056, Earl Harold's clerk, Leofgar, was appointed to the see, a man of whom the annalist disapproved because he wore moustaches until promoted bishop and because his first concern as bishop was to go to war.[4] Eleven weeks after his consecration he led an army against Gruffydd, only to be overwhelmed on 16 June, probably at Glasbury on Wye. There were slain with the bishop some of his priests, the sheriff, and many thegns. After

---

[1] Freeman, *NC*, ii. 399, on the strength of *DB*, i. 263 a i, suggests, perhaps rightly, that Gruffydd was mulcted of land to the west of the Dee.

[2] According to Florence, i. 213, the Welsh would not fight Harold because they knew him to be 'virum fortem et bellicosum'. Poitiers wrote, p. 104, that William of Normandy took Harold on the Breton campaign because he knew him to be 'ferocem et novi nominis cupidum'.

[3] Ordericus Vitalis, ii. 119, 183 (ed. Chibnall, ii. 138, 216); Orderic's interpolation in Jumièges, p. 192; Lloyd, p. 369.

[4] *Chron. CD*; Florence, i. 214–15; Lloyd, pp. 367–8; Lloyd, 'Wales and the coming of the Normans', p. 135.

this disaster there was more campaigning, apparently with little success on the English side, until peace was negotiated by the aged Earl Leofric, accompanied by Harold and Bishop Ealdred. Gruffydd swore that he would be a loyal and faithful under-king to Edward[1] and must again have been confirmed in his possessions as a counter-gift. It is possible that Walter Map's popular story of the meeting of the two kings on the Severn between Beachley and Aust refers to this occasion:[2] the place is the traditional ferry crossing, not far from Gloucester. According to the story, there was a dispute over which king should cross the river to meet the other. Gruffydd claimed that he was the senior king, Edward that they were equals. Gruffydd argued that his people had conquered the whole of England with Cornwall, Scotland (or Ireland), and Wales from the giants, and that he was their direct descendant; Edward retorted that his predecessors had obtained England from its conquerors. In the end Edward embarked and set off to meet Gruffydd; and the Welsh prince, overcome by this humility, threw off his ceremonial mantle and plunged into the water to greet him and apologize. He carried Edward to land on his shoulders, set him on his mantle, and with joined hands did him homage.

The arguments attributed to the kings by Walter Map do not ring very true. The historical pleas are possible: the Welsh claiming once to have been in possession of the whole of Britain; Edward maintaining that he represented the Germanic conquerors. But the argument on dignity would seem to be an illustration of Map's view of their characters: Gruffydd boastfully claiming precedence, Edward modestly accepting equality. But since we know so little about diplomatic exchanges in this period it is impossible to be sure. As boasting was socially acceptable, it may have been an ordinary part of diplomacy. However that may be, the peace, wrote Map, this peace so admirably begun, did not last long.

It was probably because of the Welsh threat that after Bishop Leofgar's death in 1056 it was decided that Ealdred of Worcester should administer also the diocese of Hereford;[3] and as a defender of the marches the monk was at least more prudent than the clerk. In the following year there seems to have been no attempt at court to prevent Ælfgar succeeding to Mercia; but he was almost immediately expelled

---

[1] *Chron. C*; Florence, i. 215.
[2] *De Nugis Curialium*, p. 99, where Gruffydd is again called *Luelinus*.
[3] *Chron. CD*; Florence, i. 215.

and outlawed on a charge of treason.[1] The substance of the charge must have been treasonable correspondence with Gruffydd and perhaps the marriage alliance. But we are given no details. We are told only that in 1058 Ælfgar returned by force with the help of Gruffydd and with the fortuitous support of a Norwegian invasion. 'It is tedious', wrote the chronicler, 'to relate fully how things went.' The Viking fleet, drawn from Norway, Orkney, Hebrides, and Dublin, was under the command of Magnus, King Harald's son,[2] but the invasion was, presumably, more a raid for booty than a serious attempt to conquer England, such as Harald himself attempted in 1066. Edward seems to have held his Easter court at Gloucester this year, 1058,[3] an unusual deviation which shows how concerned he was with Welsh affairs. The unexpected combination of dangers, however, forced Edward and his advisers once again to temporize, and, if we may judge from the chronicler's shame, to buy the enemy off. If there had been fighting we should have heard of it.

It is at this point that we lose track for a time of Anglo-Welsh affairs. With Earl Harold on the watch from Hereford, Earl Ælfgar behaving more responsibly, and Gruffydd content with his good fortune, there may have been an interlude of peace. It is evidence for a *détente* that in 1058 Bishop Ealdred set off for Jerusalem by way of Hungary,[4] leaving the sees of Worcester and Hereford untenanted for at least six months,

---

[1] *Chron. D*; Florence, i. 217, says that Ælfgar was outlawed 'a rege Eadwardo'. Reference to the Norwegian invasion makes it certain that we are not concerned with an erroneous duplication of the earlier outlawry. *Chron. C* has no entry for the years 1057-1064, inclusive.

[2] *The Annals of Tigernach* in *Revue Celtique*, xvii (1896), 399; *Annales Cambriae* (Rolls ser.), p. 25; *Brut y Tywysogion* (Rolls ser.), p. 45. Körner, *Battle of Hastings*, pp. 151-4.

[3] According to *Chronicon Abbatiae de Evesham*, ed. W. D. Macray (Rolls ser. 1863), pp. 87-8, when Abbot Manni became paralysed, he chose the prior, Æthelwig, to govern in his place and sent him to Edward, who was holding his court at Gloucester. The king approved the arrangement and had 'Archbishop' Ealdred consecrate Æthelwig 'in paschali solemnitate' on the festival of St George the Martyr. Æthelwig then ruled the abbey for seven years in Edward's reign. Macray, followed hesitatingly by Freeman, *NC*, ii. 669-70, identified the year as 1059. This is impossible if Ealdred was the consecrator, for, not yet archbishop, he left for Jerusalem in 1058 and could hardly have been back by April 1059. But we need not dismiss Ealdred, even if wrongly described, for 1058 suits the indications better. St George's day is 23 April. If the year is 1059, Æthelwig ruled for seven years less three months before Edward's death; if 1058, seven years plus nine months. More decisively, in 1059 Easter day was 4 April, so that St George's day was hardly in Easter; but in 1058 Easter day was 19 April, the saint's festival thus falling on the Thursday of Easter week. [4] *Chron. D*; Florence, i. 217.

that Harold may have travelled through France to Rome,[1] and that in 1061 Tostig, Countess Judith, Gyrth, Ealdred, and other English nobles and clerks went on a great embassy to the holy city.[2] It is also evidence that the Welsh threat was not taken too seriously at Edward's court. But it was not forgotten. Earl Ælfgar is not heard of again after the summer of 1062 – possibly it is because there is no annal for this year that we are ignorant of his fate[3] – and Ælfgar's disappearance upset the established position.

It is probable that, as in 1055, Edward assembled a council to advise him on the succession to the vacant earldom. Rather surprisingly in view of Ælfgar's shortcomings, it was decided to appoint to the office his elder son, Eadwine, a boy probably in his teens.[4] A number of factors may have contributed to this decision: a general feeling that it would be unjust to bring to an end the Mercian dynasty; the possession of an earldom by all the queen's brothers; a position within Godwin's family so nicely balanced that no one cared to disturb it; and Harold's realization that, with a boy as earl of Mercia, Gruffydd would be without an effective ally and could be attacked at will. Moreover it is possible that at first Eadwine ruled in name only. He took no recorded part in the Welsh wars of 1063 and is not mentioned in the Chronicle before the autumn of 1065.[5] Ælfgar left also a younger son who had been given the Scandinavian name Morkere. One day an earldom would have to be found for him.

Gruffydd misread the times. Undeterred by the fact that the new earl was his wife's brother, he regarded the death of his ally as bringing the peace to an end. Mercia could once more be raided, and, he may mistakenly have thought, with impunity. But the English nobles regarded the renewed Welsh hostilities as an insult not to be borne. There may also have been trading disputes on the Usk.[6] At Edward's Christmas court, held in 1062 as usual at Gloucester,[7] it was decided to put an end

---

[1] VEdR, p. 33 and n.

[2] Chron. D; Florence, i. 218; VEdR, pp. 34–7; Vita Wulfstani, pp. 16–17; Malmesbury, GP, pp. 251–2.

[3] Alternatively, if there was something shameful about Ælfgar's death, the annalist may not have wished to record it.

[4] As his younger brother became an earl by rebellion in 1065, Eadwine must have been at least fourteen in 1062.

[5] As earl he is the recipient of a writ, Harmer, Writs, no. 96.

[6] Plummer, Two Chronicles, pp. 250–1, quoting from the Life of St Gundleius. But the actual incident described in this source seems to belong to 1065.

[7] Chron. D; Florence, i. 221; both s.a. 1063.

to Gruffydd's lawlessness in the same way as Rhys ap Rhydderch had been stopped nine years before.[1] Harold was dispatched with a cavalry force to surprise Gruffydd at Rhuddlan, his 'palace' in North Wales on the River Clwyd, and kill him. But the Welsh prince was warned just in time to escape by ship. And Harold, without sailors, could do no more than burn the hall and the remaining ships before returning to report his failure.[2] During the spring a more elaborate campaign was planned. In the last week of May Harold sailed with a fleet from Bristol to ravage the Welsh coastline and prevent Gruffydd escaping by sea, while Tostig invaded North Wales, presumably from Chester. The brothers had a spectacular success. Although Gruffydd had already slipped through the net before they joined forces, probably in North Wales, they had received the submission of most of the Welsh nobles; and when they continued to ravage, there was a general surrender and renunciation of Gruffydd. Harold and Tostig did not pursue the fugitive into the wilderness of Snowdonia. They left the kill to the Welsh. On 5 August Gruffydd was slain by his own men, and his head and the ornaments of his ship were brought to Harold. The earl delivered them in person to Edward.[3] It was decided that North Wales should be divided between Gruffydd's two half-brothers, Bleddynn and Rhiwallon. Harold put them in possession of their shares and took from them oaths, confirmed by hostages, that they would be faithful vassals of King Edward, perform military service for him on land and sea, and pay all the customs that had ever been due from Wales. They seem to have taken oaths to Harold as well.[4] In Deheubarth two new men emerged as leaders, Maredudd and Rhys ab Owain, and in Morgannwg, Cadwgan ap Meurig, the son of the former ruler, rose to power.[5] Wales had once again fallen to pieces. And the opportunity seems to have been taken of pushing the boundary west almost all along the line.[6]

Not since Agricola, and never again for many a year, was Wales so insolently invaded, so easily cowed by force of arms. Even if Gruffydd had been losing his countrymen's support, even if Welsh disunity facilitated the entry of a determined enemy, the English success in 1063 was in striking contrast to the earlier failures. It marks the rebirth of

[1] See above, p. 233.   [2] *Chron. D*, developed by Florence, i. 221.
[3] *Chron. D*; Florence, i. 221-2; cf. *Chron. E*; *VEdR*, pp. 42-3, 57-8.
[4] *Chron. E* completely ignores Edward's part; *Chron D*, and more so Florence, bring Edward into the story.
[5] Lloyd, 'Wales and the coming of the Normans', pp. 146-7.
[6] Freeman, *NC*, ii. 683-6.

England as a military power. According to the Welsh Chronicle,[1] 'Gruffydd ap Llewelyn, the head and shield and defender of the Britons, fell through the treachery of his own men. The man who hitherto had been invincible, who had taken immense spoils, countless treasures of gold and silver, jewels and purple vestments, was left in the glens of desolation.' The 'most noble king of the Britons' was dead. But these are the reflexions of a later age. There is little sign of Welsh patriotism in 1063. There is, however, much evidence of English pride and rejoicing. We see Edward as he is described in his obituary poem, 'a ruler of heroes, the governor of the Welsh, Britons, and Scots.' We can hardly believe that when Harold came into his presence to hand over Gruffydd's head, he addressed him as, 'O thou more saint than king'.[2] The author of the *Vita Ædwardi Regis* described the war in thirty-two lines of verse.[3] He took the view that Gruffydd – presumably because he had broken his word – had done a shameful injury to Edward; and, like the northern English chronicler, he regarded Edward as the one who planned and ordered the criminal's punishment. For him, too, the great day was when the earls returned in triumph, parading the hostages surrendered by the Welsh nobles and the spoils of war before their king, Edward 'the glorious, deservedly renowned'.[4]

The magnitude of the English achievement is proved by the anecdotes remembered in the twelfth century about Edward's wars. Harold's ruthlessness had made a great impression. Gerald of Barry believed that Harold had almost exterminated the people,[5] and erected inscribed pillars as monuments to his victory. John of Salisbury, in his *Policraticus*, cited Harold's campaigns as a good example of that training in warfare required by all nations in order to keep them healthy and free from the emollient vices of peace. He thought that Harold enacted a law that any Welshman found east of Offa's dyke carrying a spear should lose his right hand and that he had slain so many men that Edward, to prevent the disappearance of the Welsh race, gave the women permission to marry Englishmen.[6]

[1] *Brut y Tywysogion* (Rolls ser.), p. 45.

[2] Alfred Tennyson, *Harold, a drama* (1877), Act I, sc. ii, Gruffydd's widow, 'Aldwyth', reporting the style used by Tostig and other sycophants at court.

[3] *VEdR*, pp. 57–8.   [4] 'preclari meritis [et] nomine regis', p. 57.

[5] 'tam valide totam Kambriam et circuivit et transpenetravit, ut in eadem fere mingentem ad parietem non reliquerit', *Descriptio Kambriae*, in *Opera Omnia*, ed. J. F. Dimock (Rolls ser. 1868), vi. 217.

[6] *Johannis Saresberiensis episcopi Carnotensis Policraticus*, ed. Clement C. J. Webb (1909), Bk. VI, cap. vi, ii. 19–20.

Not only had the English kingdom recovered its military confidence, there are also signs of prosperity and fulfilment. In the introductory poem to the *Vita* the Muse tells the Poet to describe,

> How [with Edward's accession] . . .
> A golden age shone for his English race,
> As after David's wars came Solomon and peace,
> Which drowned the grievous moans in Lethe's stream,
> And Plenty poured profusely for her king
> Abundant riches from a bounteous horn;
> How, when this leader, patron, king was there,
> The dreadful anger of the foe withdraws;
> And how with locks of snowy white he blooms,
> The glass of virtue, the beloved of God.[1]

It is in the context of the English victories over the Welsh and Scots that the author of the *Vita* paints a picture of a rustic king, enjoying both the earthly and the heavenly paradise, a figure drawn at once from the mythology of some religion of nature and from the ranks of those soldiers who were converted to the ascetic life, a picture which may well have caught some of the features of this ruler in his declining years.[2] After early mass, the chase; and after the labour of the day, the company and discourse of holy abbots and clerks. With his mind no longer turned to war or royal pomp, Edward lived like an angel in the squalor of the world,[3] feeding and clothing the poor and sick, and vying with his religious consort in the performance of good works. The most spectacular products of their rivalry were the monastic churches at Wilton and Westminster, both dedicated in 1065 and so, presumably, at least started in 1063. This mellow, autumnal hue is the product of idealization; but to one looking back from Christmas 1066 over Edward's reign, the years 1063–4 may with some justice have appeared as the brightest spot in a golden age. All the inherited difficulties had been overcome. Edward had struggled through to shine like another Solomon. And in 1063 he was still outside the shadow cast retrospectively by his death.

---

[1] *VEdR*, p. 3. [2] *Ibid.*, pp. 40 ff.
[3] That is to say, like a monk: Jean Leclercq, *The Love of Learning and the desire for God* (Mentor Omega Book, 1962), pp. 62–3.

Chapter 10

THE KINGDOM BEQUEATHED

The standing problem in Edward's reign was the succession to the throne. But during the first decade it was more a lure to attract kinsmen and a means of keeping them in order, a diplomatic gambit, a matter of interest in high society, than a problem which had to be solved. After Edward's marriage in 1045 there was always the possibility of the birth of an heir (Edith cannot have been more than forty-six when widowed): and even if at different times Edward promised the succession to Svein of Denmark and William of Normandy,[1] these promises, whatever their recipients may have claimed later, must have been conditional on the absence of a nearer claimant, especially a child of the marriage. Such a speculative bargain, unlikely even in 1054, when Edward was approaching fifty, to be honoured within a decade, cannot have been taken very seriously by any of those concerned. It is impossible to believe that if Edward had died between 1051 and 1053 the English magnates would have sent for either Svein or William; and it does not seem that either prince would have been in a position to invade. More likely, a regency council would have been set up, as on Cnut's death in 1035, to rule while search was made for a suitable descendant of Æthelred. The Norwegian chieftains behaved in this way in 1035, sending to Russia to invite Magnus, the illegitimate son of St Olaf, to return from the court of King Jaroslav and drive out the Danes.

The death of Godwin in 1053 ended the first phase. Unlike the queen mother, who died the year before, the earl had only one string to his bow; and it is clear that he never lost hope that he would be the grandfather of an heir to the throne. It is, however, likely that Edward by this time had come to realize that he could not have a son, at least from Edith; and it would seem, too, that, whatever may have been the significance of his repudiation of the queen in 1051, he had decided that the marriage should continue. In these circumstances a more serious, more realistic search for an heir was set on foot. In 1054, as in 1041, it

[1] Above, pp. 93, 107-9.

was planned to bring to England out of exile an aetheling whom most of the nobles and bishops would accept on the king's death. As Bishop Ealdred of Worcester led the search, the impetus probably came from those counsellors whose loyalty was attached primarily to the Old-English royal dynasty, and who feared the intervention of foreigners.[1] But Edward cannot have disagreed. With Godwin dead and Siward and Leofric reaching the end of their lives, he must have had a fairly free hand. Certainly Ealdred travelled to Germany 'on the king's business', as Edward's ambassador to the German emperor, bearing royal gifts.[2] He may have been accompanied by Abbot Ælfwine of Ramsey,[3] another in whom the king trusted.

According to Worcester tradition,[4] which should here be sound, Ealdred left England after 17 July and was received with great honour at Cologne by Archbishop Herman and the Emperor Henry III. These were just back from Aachen, where the emperor had had his young son, the future Henry IV, crowned king; and Edward's problem no doubt aroused their sympathetic interest. To the emperor Ealdred conveyed Edward's request that messengers should be sent into Hungary to bring back Edward's half-nephew and namesake, the son of Edmund Ironside, and have him conducted to England. The church of Worcester also knew that in 1016, when Cnut had been advised to kill Edmund's sons, he decided instead to send them to the king of Sweden with a request that they should be murdered; but the king of Sweden sent them for their safety to King 'Solomon' of Hungary. The younger son, Edmund, died there; the elder, Edward, married Agatha, a daughter of the Emperor Henry II's brother, and had three children, Margaret, the future queen of Scots, Christina, later a nun, and Edgar the aetheling.[5]

Ealdred remained for a whole year at Cologne, obviously waiting either for the aetheling or at least for news about him, and then returned to England, although not empty-handed,[6] without the prince. It was believed in England that Edward had a distinguished position

---

[1] Cf. 'they did not wish the country to be laid the more open to foreigners through their destroying each other', *Chron. CD*, s.a. 1052.

[2] *Chron. D.* [3] *DB*, i. 208 a i. Freeman, *NC*, ii. 649.

[4] *Chron. D*, Florence, i. 212; *Vita Wulfstani*, pp. 5, 15–16. Körner, *Battle of Hastings*, pp. 196 ff.

[5] Florence, i. 181. Cf. also Ordericus Vitalis, i. 178, and (ed. Chibnall), iv. 272.

[6] Among the gifts he received in Germany were the Peterborough sacramentary and psalter which Cnut had sent to Germany, *Vita Wulfstani*, pp. 5, 15–16.

at the Magyar court,[1] but naturally the details were a little hazy, and they cannot be made much clearer now. The ruler of Hungary from 997 to 1038 was Stephen I, St Stephen, who in 1008 married Gisla, the sister of the Emperor Henry II. The Agatha whom Edward married has never been identified with complete certainty. If the Worcester story is correct, she was probably the daughter of Henry II's only brother, Bruno, who lived for a time at Stephen's court before becoming bishop of Augsburg, and the niece of Stephen's queen. Alternatively, she was the daughter of Stephen and Gisla.[2] Ealdred was an adventurous man and a bold traveller; at Cologne he was on the main road for Hungary; the dukes of Swabia and Bavaria, the intermediate countries, were close relatives of the archbishop; and all three were in the confidence of the emperor;[3] so the only reason for the bishop's failure to complete the journey must have been either that he had other business to transact in Germany or that he was advised to stay where he was because of the political situation. The Magyar kingdom had been in revolt against Germany since 1046, when Peter, Stephen's nephew, was dethroned by Andrew, a representative of the nationalist party. In 1054 the Hungarians, in alliance with Kuno, the deposed duke of Bavaria, invaded Carinthia. When Ealdred arrived at Cologne communications between Germany and Hungary were probably broken.[4]

[1] *Chron. D*, *s.a.* 1057. It has been pointed out by P. E. Schramm, *Herrschaftszeichen und Staatssymbolik*, Schriften der Monumenta Germaniae historica (1954–6), pp. 774 and *n.*, 944, that an Anglo-Saxon *ordo* was used for the coronation of Solomon, Andrew's son, in 1059.

[2] The problem of Agatha's identity has been considered at length by Freeman, *NC*, ii. 650–1, Sándor Fest, 'The Sons of Eadmund Ironside, Anglo-Saxon king at the Court of St Stephen', *Archivum Europae Centro-Orientalis* (Budapest), iv (1938), 115–46, and, more profitably, by R. L. Graeme Ritchie, *The Normans in Scotland* (1954), pp. 389–92. Basically there is a choice between Worcester tradition, presumably deriving from Ealdred, which stresses Agatha's relationship to the emperor, and the view of Orderic Vitalis, i. 178, and Ailred of Rievaulx, *De Genealogia Regum Anglorum*, Migne, *PL*, cxcv, col. 715, in which the Hungarian connexion is emphasized. Ailred, although writing in 1153, had been steward at the court of David king of Scots, Agatha's grandson, so that his opinion cannot be rejected out of hand. At the same time it could be a simple mistaken assumption from the exiles' residence in Hungary. Worcester tradition, with its 'unlikely' detail, seems to be the sounder.

[3] Moreover, Herman should have been sympathetic to the English mission. He had been greatly concerned over Henry III's lack of an heir.

[4] Körner, *Battle of Hastings*, p. 204, argues that Ealdred's mission failed for political reasons: (a) as the bishop arrived after Henry's victorious campaign against Flanders, he could not offer Edward's services, and (b) 'it was not in the emperor's interest to encourage co-operation between England and Hungary.' All this seems rather far-fetched.

Moreover, it is impossible to believe that the aetheling was anxious to return to the land from which he had been separated in infancy. Edmund Ironside had married Sigeferth's widow in the late summer of 1015 and if Edward and Edmund were the children of that marriage, the elder cannot have been more than six months old when his father died.[1] In 1054 Edward was about thirty-six, a married man with three children. He, like his family, probably spoke no English. Although it was believed at Worcester that King Edward had decreed that his nephew should be appointed his heir,[2] this may be too simple a story. Neither Edward nor his counsellors could have bound themselves in advance, before they had even seen the exile. And if Ealdred had to make conditional offers and half-promises through a chain of messengers and interpreters it is no wonder that nothing was achieved at first. In the end the worsening situation in Hungary may have persuaded the aetheling to leave. Anti-German feeling was strong during the reign of Andrew, and the death of the Emperor Henry III on 5 October 1056 reduced German influence in Hungary to its lowest level. In November Earl Harold was at St Omer,[3] possibly on a journey to or from Germany and Rome, possibly also under instructions to escort the aetheling to England. In 1057 the exile arrived in England; and shortly afterwards he died in London and was buried in St Paul's, before he had seen the king.[4]

The northern chronicler, who could draw on the church of Worcester for information, and who quotes here from a poem written probably after 1066, claims that for some reason the aetheling was kept away from his uncle; but, although he laments the death and pictures it as a great misfortune for the kingdom, he does not hint at foul play.[5] The death of the aetheling was a misfortune for those who wished to see an English prince recognized as heir because his only son was a child. We

---

[1] For the marriage, *Chron. s.a.* 1015; Plummer, *Two Chronicles*, p. 194. The two boys could have been born posthumously. We may assume that they were taken abroad by their mother; but we have no information.

[2] 'Decreverat enim rex illum post se regni haeredem constituere', Florence, i. 215, *s.a.* 1057.

[3] P. Grierson, 'A visit of Earl Harold to Flanders in 1056', *EHR*, li (1936), 90–7. Körner, *Battle of Hastings*, pp. 205–6, throws doubt on the visit.

[4] *Chron. DE*; Florence, i. 215.

[5] There seems to be no good reason why we should regard his death as 'one of the unsolved mysteries of the period' (*The Anglo-Saxon Chronicle*, ed. Dorothy Whitelock, D. C. Douglas, and Susie I. Tucker, p. 133 n.). See also Körner, *Battle of Hastings*, pp. 207–9.

are not told that Edward was accompanied to England by Agatha, Margaret, Christina, and Edgar;[1] but as Edgar was in England in 1066 and all four fled to Scotland in 1067,[2] it is likely that the family had travelled together. Edgar was the same age as Robert Curthose, the Conqueror's eldest son, and so would be no more than five, and perhaps less, in 1057.[3] The two daughters were probably older. Later writers believed that the family arrived with great treasure, with many holy relics, including the Black Rood.[4] Unless they had difficulty in getting their possessions out of Hungary, this must have been the case. Edward is said to have brought the children up as though they were his own.[5] This, too, is what we would expect. In 1058 Ealdred travelled to Jerusalem by way of Hungary;[6] but we do not know whether this had any connexion with the aetheling's death.

It is possible that with his great-nephew as his ward, Edward considered that the problem of the succession was solved. He had only to live another decade for the boy to be old enough to be taken seriously as a candidate, old enough, indeed, to press his claim. We should not assume that Edward was greatly interested in what would happen when he died. Even if he turned his thoughts increasingly to the life hereafter, the problem of who would reign after him in England may not have been one of his favourite subjects for meditation. It may be that the closer he came to death, the more distasteful the topic became. In the vision[7] which Bishop Beorhtweald of Wiltshire had at Glastonbury during Cnut's reign of Edward's coronation by St Peter and of the saint's indication that Edward would remain a bachelor[8] and reign for

[1] Except in the fourteenth-century Johannes de Fordun, *Chronica Gentis Scotorum,* ed. William F. Skene (1871), i. 206, 208.

[2] *Chron. DE, s.a.* 1066; *Chron. D, s.a.* 1067, cf. *E*; Florence, i. 228. Symeon *HR,* p. 190; Poitiers, pp. 214, 236–8, 244.

[3] Orderic (ed. Chibnall), v. 272, 'ducemque sibi coaevum et quasi collactaneum fratrem diligebat.' We do not know when Robert was born; but it is usually assumed that he was born a year after his parents' marriage, which took place between 1049 and the end of 1053, possibly in 1052.

[4] Ailred of Rievaulx, *De Genealogia Regum Anglorum,* Migne, *PL,* cxcv, coll. 715, 734. Fordun (quoting Turgot of Durham), i. 213.

[5] Ordericus Vitalis, i. 178.   [6] *Chron. D;* Florence, i. 217.

[7] *VEdR,* pp. 8–9, 85–6. See also below, Appendix A, pp. 293–4. The original vision may well have been revised in the light of later information before it was recorded by the Anonymous. William of Malmesbury, for example, changed the secret length of Edward's reign into twenty-four years.

[8] 'celibem ei vitam designare'. As Edward remained a bachelor until 1045 this may have been the original meaning of the words. Later, however, and especially in view of Edward's marriage, they were understood as 'a chaste life'.

so many years, Peter answered Edward's natural question about who then would reign after him, with, 'The kingdom of the English is the kingdom of God; and he has already made provision for your successor according to his will.' One important feature of this story is its resigned attitude towards the problem: God will provide. And this may well have been Edward's reply to those who importuned him to take more decisive action.

From the death of Edward 'the Exile' until the eve of Edward's death we have no news about the succession problem. The Anglo-Saxon Chronicle is at its scantiest and there are no other sure sources of information. But there may have been no public developments to report. Nor does it seem that in this period the number of claimants with a possible chance was much reduced. Some fell out. The deaths of Earl Ralf (1057) and Walter III, count of Mantes (*c.* 1064),[1] removed Edward's closest kin, the sons of his sister, Godgifu. Walter died childless. Ralf left a young son, Harold, who was in Queen Edith's wardship in 1066.[2] Some were eclipsed. The few cousins on Edward's mother's side who were still alive[3] could not assert a claim in rivalry with their overlord, the duke of Normandy. But as the number of blood relations with a chance was reduced, so the hopes of relations by marriage were raised. Although the claim of Eustace II, count of Boulogne, Godgifu's second husband, but since about 1049 married to Ida of Bouillon, was another blighted by William's interest, the ambitions of two of the queen's brothers, Harold and Tostig, were probably at this time taking form.[4] However that may be, it was also in this period that the three foreign claimants who actively intervened after Edward's death, Harald Sigurdsson (Hardrada) of Norway, Svein of Denmark, and William of Normandy, established the position which made their expeditions possible. Although Svein was utterly defeated and almost killed by Harald at the battle of the Nissa in 1062, two years later on the River Gota the rivals made a firm and lasting peace, guaranteed by oaths and hostages.[5] In north-west France William was freeing himself

[1] Walter intervened as a claimant to Maine (he was married to Biota, the sister of Hugh IV of Maine), was captured by Duke William in 1063 and with his wife imprisoned at Falaise. They did not survive the captivity. See Poitiers, pp. 88–92, Ordericus Vitalis, ii. 102–3, 259 (ed. Chibnall, ii. 116–18, 312).

[2] *DB*, i. 129 b i.

[3] The most important of these were probably Richard, count of Evreux, Robert, count of Eu, and William, count of Corbeil.

[4] See also below, Appendix A, pp. 297 ff.

[5] *King Harald's Saga*, caps. 61–5, 71.

from all obstacles. His marriage to Matilda of Flanders secured his northern flank, his conquest of Maine in 1063 improved his security in the south, and the minority of the king of France freed him from worry about an attack from the rear.

Edward must have been aware of the shifting situation; and as his expectation of life diminished, interest in his intentions must have grown; but nothing of the diplomacy between 1057 and 1064 or 1065 has survived. If we may judge from what seems to be the set pattern of Edward's behaviour, he would have balanced the various interests as best he could. At home he could balance Tostig against Harold and use Edgar Ætheling and possibly Harold, Earl Ralf's son, against both. Abroad he could play off the Scandinavians against the Normans, and keep the foreign claimants reminded of the men in England who aspired to the throne. Those who play this game most astutely often have a favourite on whose side they intend to come down in the end. And sometimes this secret bias can be discovered. But in Edward's case the evidence is quite inadequate. To choose William as the candidate whom Edward intended to win is to accept the Norman thesis which is at least exaggerated. To pick on Tostig is, perhaps, to pervert the general view of the anonymous author of the *Vita Ædwardi Regis*.[1] It is by no means impossible that Edward regarded his great-nephew, Edgar, as the heir presumptive and tried to manage the other candidates so that the boy would at least have his chance. Edward knew from experience that in this kind of contest the winner was unpredictable, that God 'removeth kings and setteth up kings', that with the Lord 'all things are possible', texts used by his biographer.[2]

However inconclusive the result, an inquiry at this point into Edward's attitude towards the succession is essential, for in 1064 or 1065 Harold visited Normandy; and the event is brought to our notice, and explained, by post-Conquest continental, especially Norman, writers. The journey was known to Guy of Amiens, William of Jumièges, William of Poitiers, and the writer of the *scenario* for the Bayeux Tapestry.[3] Although it is ignored by the Anglo-Saxon Chronicle, there is an allusion to it in the *Vita Ædwardi Regis*.[4] The ultimate literary

---

[1] See below, Appendix A, p. 298.
[2] Dan. ii. 21; iv. 25; Matt. xix. 26. *VEdR*, pp. 7, 76; 78.
[3] *Carmen*, ll. 291 ff. Jumièges, p. 132. Poitiers, pp. 100 ff., 176. Tapestry, pl. 1 ff.
[4] *VEdR*, p. 53.

source of the story may be the legal case which the duke's advisers drew up in 1066 in order to win the support of the pope and other princes,[1] and which later served to justify the Conquest. And there can be little doubt that we have to face the almost impossible task of taking the event out of a piece of special pleading and putting it into its historical context. We also have to consider whether we can put any trust in the more developed versions offered by William of Poitiers and the tapestry.[2] Unfortunately Harold's embassy cannot even be dated exactly. William of Poitiers places it after events which occurred in 1063 and on the eve of Edward's death. The Anglo-Saxon Chronicle records nothing between Edward and Harold's completion of the Welsh business in the autumn or winter of 1063 and the earl's invasion of South Wales before August 1065. It is most unlikely that Harold went to Normandy during the Welsh war of 1063 or after the summer of 1065. If we can trust William of Poitiers' observation that the corn was green in Brittany and there was a dearth of food,[3] Harold's visit would have been in the early summer of 1064 or of 1065. The author by his treatment of the episode implies that it took place in 1065; but this may well be artistic foreshortening.

William of Jumièges gives the story in its simplest form. Edward sent his richest and most powerful earl, Harold, to William to swear fealty concerning the crown and to confirm the succession by oaths. Harold, captured en route by Guy, count of Ponthieu, was freed by William's threat of war,[4] and successfully completed his mission. Guy of Amiens refers to Harold's delivering a ring and a sword to William as earnest of the bargain.[5] But it is the archdeacon of Lisieux who provides the circumstantial detail. He describes the event twice. The second (shorter)

---

[1] F. Barlow, 'The Carmen de Hastingae Proelio', *Studies in International History*, ed. K. Bourne and D. C. Watt (1967), p. 36; Raymonde Foreville, 'Aux origines de la renaissance juridique', *Moyen âge*, lviii (1952), 61 ff.

[2] Barlow, 'Edward the Confessor's Early Life', pp. 240 ff. Körner, *Battle of Hastings*, pp. 107–21. Barlow, 'The Carmen de Hastingae Proelio'.

[3] Poitiers, pp. 110–12.

[4] 'violenter illum extorsit', p. 133. Poitiers alters to 'nec violentia compulsus', p. 102; cf. 'eum prudentia ac fortitudine eripui', p. 176.

[5] 'Hoc quia perplures testantur (et asserit idem)
    Assensu populi, consilio procerum
Etguardus quod rex ut ei succederet heres,
    Annuit et fecit; teque favente sibi
Anulus est illi testis concessus et ensis,
    Quae per te nosti missa fuisse sibi.'
Carmen, ll. 291–6, William addressing Harold.

version occurs in a speech which he attributes to William on the eve of the battle of Hastings:[1]

> Finally Edward sent Harold himself to Normandy so that he could swear to me there in my presence what his father and Earls Leofric and Siward and Archbishop Stigand had sworn to me here in my absence. On the journey Harold incurred the danger of being taken prisoner, from which, using diplomacy and force, I rescued him. Through his own hands he made himself my vassal and with his own hand he gave me a firm pledge concerning the kingdom of England.

Here we may have the basic text from which he developed his longer version. But the oddity about this rendering is that it disagrees with all the others over the danger which threatened Harold on the journey. Harold 'in periculum captionis incidit', 'he experienced the hazard of being captured'; which is not the same as being captured.[2] And we are reminded of the words of the author of the *Vita*, 'he came home, passing with watchful mockery through all ambushes, as was his way.'[3] If here we have caught William of Poitiers unawares, we have no difficulty in accepting that the other descriptions, especially his own second version, of the terrible danger in Ponthieu from which William rescued Harold are simply exaggerations. Moreover, if the archdeacon could draw on his imagination in one place he could do it in others. He contributes to the story the English hostages,[4] the detailed analysis of Harold's oath, and the Breton campaign. None of these contributions can be taken simply on trust.

Harold's embassy and the Breton war are also shown on the Bayeux Tapestry; and, although it would seem that the man who planned the tapestry had read William of Poitiers' account – and probably William of Jumièges too – he refashioned the story a little, partly no doubt so as to suit the different purpose, partly, perhaps, because he did not accept all the chronicler's detail. There is even enough idiosyncrasy in the tapestry's presentation of the embassy to suggest that at some points it differed widely from the literary sources.[5] One of the most remarkable

---

[1] Poitiers, p. 176.

[2] Professor Foreville, p. 177, translates, 'il tomba en péril de captivité'; but D. C. Douglas and G. W. Greenaway, *EHD*, ii. 224, give, 'Harold fell into a perilous captivity.'

[3] *VEdR*, p. 33.   [4] See below, Appendix B.

[5] It is surely wrong to dismiss the Ælfgifu episode (pl. 18) as a trivial erotic ornament. We cannot understand it, but the enclosing towers and also the 'ubi' of the legend show that the event took place in William's palace, or at least at Rouen; and

features is that in the brief Latin chronicle beneath the border, which
professes to explain the pictures, we are told neither why Edward
dispatched Harold nor what the earl swore to the duke on the relics,[1]
omissions probably to be explained by the wish to evade commitment
on these issues and the desire to avoid deliberate untruth. The episode
is also mentioned after 1066 by English and Anglo-Norman writers,
who usually explain Harold's mission quite differently.[2] Although some
of the explanations spring from a fanciful interpretation of the tapestry,
it is possible that the Norman version never won universal acceptance
in England.

In William of Poitiers the anecdote is the second part of an elaborate
and quite sophisticated legal case in support of William's claim to the
English throne. On the two basic points, the nomination in 1051 and
the mission of Harold to swear fealty, or take an oath, to William in the
matter of the crown, the two Norman writers and, by implication, the
tapestry are in agreement. When William of Poitiers furnishes more
detail he may be going beyond his brief, but with what justification it is
difficult to determine. Indeed, his longer version of the story of Harold's
embassy raises so many difficulties that it is advisable to scrutinize it in
his own words. The essential parts of his statement, which occurs as a
narrative account in its appropriate chronological place, are as follows:[3]

> About the same time (1063) Edward, king of the English, gave William,
> whom he loved like a brother or son[4] and whom he had already appointed
> his heir, a pledge even weightier than he had given before. For this man
> of saintly life, striving towards heaven, believed that the hour of his death
> was approaching and wished to make his dispositions before that inexor-
> able fate. He, therefore, sent Harold to William to confirm his promise by
> oath, Harold, the most distinguished, richest, most honourable and

---

it would seem to be the copula between the meeting of William and Harold and the
Breton campaign, which otherwise would follow without explanation. No satisfactory interpretation has been offered; but, as Freeman pointed out, *NC*, iii. 699,
Harold had a sister named Ælfgifu (*DB*, i. 144 b i: 'homo Alveve soror[is] Heraldi
[com. *interlined*]). Unfortunately, this is the end of the trail.

[1] '. . . Bagias ubi Harold sacramentum fecit Willelmo duci.' It would have been
easy to give 'sacramentum de corona' or 'de successione'.

[2] For the explanations furnished by Eadmer and William of Malmesbury, versions
designed to free Harold from blame, see Körner, *Battle of Hastings*, pp. 114–21.

[3] Poitiers, pp. 100 ff.

[4] 'quem loco germani aut prolis adamabat', p. 100. This is a *cliché* which the
archdeacon uses, rather inappropriately, to describe William's love for Lanfranc, an
older man and his father in Christ: 'diligens ut germanum aut prolem', p. 126.

powerful of his subjects, whose brother and nephew (*fratruelis*) had already been taken as hostages in connexion with the succession to the throne. . . .

After William had rescued Harold from Guy, count of Ponthieu, into whose hands he had fallen while on his way to Normandy, the embassy was entertained at Rouen.

. . . In a council assembled at Bonneville-sur-Touques Harold took an oath of fealty to William in a religious ceremony; and, according to the testimony of truthful and distinguished men of high repute who were present, Harold, in the final stage of his oath, of his own free will made these distinct promises: that he would be William's proxy in the court of his lord, King Edward, for as long as the king lived; that after Edward's death he would use all his influence and resources to secure the English kingdom for William; and that in the meantime he would deliver the town[1] of Dover to the custody of William's soldiers and fortify it at his own pains and cost – likewise other towns which the duke would require to be fortified in various parts of the kingdom – and that he would furnish the garrisons with abundant supplies. William, for his part, after he had accepted Harold as his vassal by the ceremony of taking hands, and before Harold had taken the oath, confirmed to Harold at his request all his lands and privileges. For it was believed that Edward, already sick, would not last long. . . .

William then honoured Harold by taking him on a campaign against Brittany.

. . . When William had returned home he kept his dear guest, Harold, with him for some time, and then let him depart, laden with gifts worthy of them both and worthy of Edward, who, in order to increase his honour, had ordered Harold to come. With Harold there also returned his nephew, one of the hostages, released for his sake.

---

[1] *Castrum*, William of Poitiers' usual term for Dover (pp. 240, 264), although once he uses *castellum* (p. 210), means not a castle, but a fortified town, one defended by walls and often containing *firmamenta*, *munimenta*, *munitiones*, and, occasionally, an *arx*. In 1066 *firmamenta* were made in London (p. 236), while in 1067 a *munitio* was built within Winchester (p. 238). Individual, isolated castles, especially counter-fortifications, are called *castella* (cf. pp. 18, 36, 58), and, significantly, only one is named, the *castellum sancti Jacobi*, built by the Normans on the frontier with Brittany. These are, probably, ring-works or motte and bailey castles. Brionne, Vernon, Arques, Alençon, Ambrières, Mayenne, and Dol are *castra*. J. H. Round, in his 'amusing' attack on Freeman, 'The attack on Dover, 1067', *The Antiquary*, xii (1885), 49–53, sheds little light on this matter. For the present state of our archaeological knowledge of the castle at Dover, see *Medieval Archaeology*, iii (1964), 254–5. For recent thinking about eleventh-century castles, see above, pp, 173–4.

With this account we have a problem within a problem. There is the basic case and there is William of Poitiers' embroidery of it. We can put little trust in the chronicler's unsupported statements. He was writing a panegyric of the duke and a justification of the conquest of England and the killing of Harold, making use of everything that came to hand in a completely biased way. His theme was that William never fought an unjust war.[1] He was not, apparently, very well-informed about events, and, since he was not writing history, was probably not interested in historical truth. Where his detail can be checked it is often found to be incorrect, and usually, it seems, he was not an eye-witness of the events he describes. He makes it clear that he was not present when Harold took his oath. It must be recognized that if the oath had taken place at Bonneville, William of Poitiers was in a position to gather information, for Bonneville is near Lisieux, of which see William was archdeacon. But the tapestry locates the oath at Bayeux,[2] and Orderic Vitalis expressly corrected William of Poitiers' text to put the oath at Rouen.[3]

There are also some obvious exaggerations, difficulties, and improbabilities in the archdeacon's version. He claims that the purpose of the embassy was to increase Edward's honour – presumably by the acquisition of such a distinguished heir; but it is inconceivable that the appointment of a bastard count should have been regarded in this way by the English aristocracy. He does not hold a completely consistent view of the efficacy of the oaths taken in 1051, and it is not clear how Harold's oath was a weightier pledge than the oaths taken previously by the *witan*. We have also seen that he is not sure whether Harold was in danger of capture by Guy or was actually captured.[4] The greatest difficulty, however, is the flimsiness of the guarantee that William of Poitiers describes. Harold did homage to William, asked for and was granted William's confirmation of all his English lands and privileges, and swore on relics (although little is made of this)[5] an elaborate oath

---

[1] Poitiers, p. 118.

[2] But, surprisingly, does not indicate a church or show the presence of Odo of Bayeux.

[3] Ordericus Vitalis, ii. 117 (ed. Chibnall, ii. 134–6).　　　　　[4] Above, p. 222.

[5] Harold swore 'sancto ritu christianorum' (p. 104), 'sacrosancto jurejurando' (p. 114). It is not until the morning of the battle that we have an explicit reference to the relics: William took the eucharist; 'appendit etiam humili collo suo reliquias, quarum favorem Heraldus abalienaverat sibi, violata fide quam super eas jurando sanxerat' (pp. 180–2). In the first passage the archdeacon is probably following William of Jumièges' 'christiano more sacramentis firmaret' (p. 132). The theme of the relics seems to be an ornament which the tapestry develops further.

of fealty, in which the precise services which he was to perform were listed. But this was a gentleman's agreement unlikely to satisfy any serious negotiators of the period. Treaties were usually warranted by the swearing of many oaths and the exchange of several hostages.[1] If Edward really was conscious of his approaching death and wanted to make certain that William could succeed, he would surely have sent more and better hostages. The duke, one would have thought, would have wanted to have Edgar the aetheling and a son of each of the earls in his power. But, according to William of Poitiers, the duke, far from improving his hold, actually allowed Harold to take one of the two existing hostages back to England. The only mention of an investiture or delivery of seizin is in the equally unreliable *Carmen de Hastingae proelio*, where it is related that Harold brought a ring and a sword from Edward.[2] But these symbols play no part in the archdeacon's case; nor are they shown on the tapestry.[3] Ideally, William should have been conducted to England, and, if not crowned in Edward's lifetime, at least put into possession of some key places. Edward, from his experiences in 1041–3, knew all about this. Moreover, since, in English eyes at least, Edward was doing William a favour, it would be expected that the duke would have given something substantial in return: possibly a great reward or, if he was promising aid, oaths and hostages as a guarantee that he would honour his side of the bargain.

William of Poitiers paints the picture of a politically naive duke wronged by a criminally ambitious earl from perfidious Albion.[4] It is quite impossible to believe that Duke William was simple and in-experienced. It is, however, likely that Harold could deceive. There are it seems, in the *Vita Ædwardi Regis* some covert references to Harold's dealings with William, or, at least, some general observations which can be applied to this business. We are told that Harold, like Tostig, could cleverly disguise his intentions; but he often discussed his plans with friends whose loyalty he trusted, and sometimes delayed action far too long. Although ambitious and persevering, he was cautious and thoughtful in his approach, moving circumspectly toward his goal and

[1] Cf. above, p. 219.

[2] See above, p. 221, *n*. 5.

[3] Only in the scenes showing Harold at the court of Guy of Ponthieu is a sword featured. An anecdote about Harold's sword at Beaurain may have suggested this story to Guy of Amiens.

[4] Cf. Poitiers, p. 100, 'ut ipsius [Heraldi] opes et auctoritas totius Anglicae gentis dissensum coercerent, si rem novare mallent perfida mobilitate, quanta sese agunt.'

enjoying life on the way.[1] He studied, both through servants and also in person, the princes of Gaul, their characters, policies, and resources, 'and adroitly and with natural cunning – and at great length – noted down most carefully what he could get from them if he ever needed their services in any of his projects. And in this way he acquired such an exhaustive knowledge of them that he could not be deceived by any of their proposals.'[2] He was, alas, too free with oaths.[3] He passed with watchful mockery through all ambushes, as was his way.[4] It is possible that by putting together these sentences, some widely separated in the book, we give them a meaning which was not intended. But, at the least, we learn that Harold could dissemble, that he studied personally the situation in Gaul, and that he was skilled in avoiding traps. We should also ponder the passage which contrasts the different ways in which Harold and Tostig worked towards their objectives.[5] Tostig was secretive and schemed alone: sometimes he was so cautiously active that his action seemed to come before his planning. This was to his advantage. On the other hand Harold's openness and procrastination were to his disadvantage. Both may have been scheming how to succeed Edward.

Harold's behaviour is one of the major improbabilities in William of Poitiers' story. It follows from the archdeacon's thesis that Harold decided at some point in the short time between the oath and Edward's death to become a traitor to his lord, the Norman duke, and worse, to his heavenly Lord; that his succession to the throne was entirely unpremeditated, completely unplanned. Admittedly the *Vita Ædwardi Regis*, perhaps commissioned by Queen Edith at about the same time as the embassy, was not intended to justify Harold's succession, although clearly it was propaganda in the interest of Edith and her four brothers.[6] And more decisive actions are the result of unexpected opportunities, thankfully accepted, than is commonly allowed. It could be that it was this very embassy which implanted the ambition in Harold. It is possible that it was not until Edward was on his deathbed that Harold realized that the crown was his for the taking. And we should not expect from Harold great foresight or long-concealed ambitions. The Normans

---

[1] *VEdR*, pp. 31–2. For some of these passages, see also Körner, *Battle of Hastings*, pp. 213–17.

[2] *Ibid.*, p. 33.

[3] *Ibid.*, p. 53, 'citius ad sacramenta nimis, proh dolor, prodigus'.

[4] *Ibid.*, p. 33. [5] *Ibid.*, p. 32.

[6] See below, Appendix A.

regarded him as a violent usurper rather than a cunning deceiver.[1] Nevertheless it is difficult to believe that twenty months, at the outside, before Edward's death Harold was completely innocent of designs on the throne.

The truth about Harold's embassy to Normandy in 1064 or 1065 cannot be established: the evidence is too unreliable. All we can do is to list the main possibilities. It may be that the archdeacon's story is basically true. In which case we can explain the episode either by Edward's return in old age to the concerns of his youth or by his policy of playing off the claimants against each other: Harold was becoming the strongest of the English candidates, so, with cruel humour, he was sent to confirm the bequest to William.[2] But it may be that the archdeacon was mistaken, or deceitful, about Harold's business in Normandy, and that the oath was extorted from Harold, probably in reluctant gratitude for the duke's rescue of him from Guy of Ponthieu. The oath, moreover, may not have been as comprehensive as William of Poitiers describes it; Harold could merely have taken an oath of fealty and promised to be a true vassal, maintaining William's interests in England. Or we can follow what seems to be a lead in the *Vita Ædwardi Regis* and think that Harold was touring the Continent in order to get support for some scheme of his own, or at least for some scheme favoured by his family, and that when he tried to enlist William as an ally he ran into trouble from which he extricated himself with difficulty.[3] Finally, we can reinterpret the whole episode in a way which does no real violence to the essential facts but which completely contradicts the archdeacon's thesis. It is possible that Harold's visit was entirely unconnected with the succession, that no one had any suspicion that Edward's life was almost at its end, and that Harold simply swore to observe the long-standing treaty of amity between the king and the duke and in return was granted the release of his nephew. This refashioning, although it

[1] The duke acknowledges his *sapientia* (Poitiers, p. 156) and Harold is described as sending out spies (*ibid.*, pp. 154–6). But the essential charge against Harold is his 'invasion' of William's rights, not his premeditated deceit. Cf. *ibid.*, pp. 114, 206–8, 230.

[2] Cf. F. Barlow, *Edward the Confessor and the Norman Conquest* (Hastings and Bexhill Branch of The Historical Association, 1966), pp. 14–15.

[3] If so, Harold went on to Rome (*VEdR*, p. 33), where he could have obtained absolution from engagements extorted from him. We should also notice Poitiers' account of the Norman nobles' view of Harold's power in 1066 (p. 156): 'Thesauris illum abundare, quibus partis [? *recte* parti] suae duces et reges praepotentes conducantur.'

goes most against the Norman version, accords best with the 'insular' view of Edward and his reign.

Whatever may be the truth about Harold's embassy, it is doubtful whether the episode had any direct effect on later events. It is unlikely that William's decision to invade England in 1066 was immediately dependent on a promise or an oath; and Harold's own behaviour does not seem to have been affected by this incident. So much happened in the three months before Edward's death that all deep-laid plans were probably upset; as the political scene changed dramatically the various pretenders must have improvised at every turn. There is even evidence of intrigue in the royal household. Late in the reign, probably in 1065, Edward banished Spirites, a clerk whom he had inherited from his Danish predecessors and who had become rich in the royal service. Part of the confiscated estate Edward gave to Robert fitzWimarch.[1] Although we are not told why Spirites was exiled, 'treason' would be the likeliest crime. But no less remarkable is the apparent tranquillity of the English political scene between Harold's return from the embassy and the upheaval in the autumn of 1065. We get the impression that hunting was the main interest of all the English leaders and that no one expected the hunting season to be disturbed by vexatious events. No one behaved as though Edward had not long to live; and the king himself seems to have been completely unaware of his approaching end.

Such plans as Edward had made for his death had been laid down a long time ago. According to the *Vita Ædwardi Regis*[2] Edward chose Westminster as his burial place and rebuilt that obscure and poverty-stricken monastery as a worthy mausoleum. We do not know when the work was begun;[3] we only know that it was barely finished in time. Nor is it perfectly clear why he chose Westminster. As the Danish royal family and his mother and father-in-law were entombed at Winchester

---

[1] *DB*, i. 252 b ii; Barlow, *English Church*, pp. 131–2, 135, 156, 174–5.

[2] *VEdR*, pp. 44–6.

[3] The time taken to build a church obviously depended on the wealth and attitude of the builder; but it is difficult to give eleventh-century examples, because the only date commonly available, that of the dedication, tells us nothing except that some progress with the building had been made. Holy Trinity and St. Stephen's, Caen, were started after 1059. Lanfranc was appointed abbot of the latter in 1063 and the church was dedicated in 1077. Holy Trinity was dedicated ten years earlier. Cnut's church at *Assandun*, begun after November 1016, was dedicated in 1020. William I's monastery at Battle was dedicated in February 1094, twenty-eight years after the slaughter. Edward granted an estate to Westminster in 1060 (Sawyer, no. 1031, and below, p. 333) and it is likely that the rebuilding had started before then.

and his father was buried at St Paul's, London, we may assume that he was asserting his independence and pleasing himself. Harold Harefoot had been buried in Westminster until Harthacnut threw the body out; but this was probably of no account. The author of the *Vita* maintains that Edward loved the place and held St Peter in special honour. This may be the simple reason. At about the same time Edith, in devout rivalry, began to rebuild the nunnery at Wilton where she had received her education.[1]

We know something about Edward's church, which stood until it was rebuilt by King Henry III, for it is described in the *Vita* and illustrated on the Bayeux Tapestry.[2] It was designed in a romanesque style which had spread from Burgundy into Normandy, probably through the agency of William of Volpiano and his pupils. William and his nephew, John of Ravenna, went from the abbey of Fruttuaria to Dijon, where William founded St Bénigne; in 1001 William began to reform the Norman monasteries and in 1017 sent John to St Trinity, Fécamp, to replace Thierry, another from St Bénigne, whom he had appointed abbot of Jumièges. Fécamp became the head of a congregation, which included the monastery of Bernay in the diocese of Lisieux; and in 1052 John became abbot of St Bénigne as well.[3] Thus Burgundian influence was strong in the Norman monastic church; and it has been usual to assume that the model for Westminster was Jumièges and the link Robert II, abbot of Jumièges (1037-?), bishop of London (? 1044-51), and archbishop of Canterbury (1051-2), who was buried in the sanctuary of his old home shortly after his expulsion from England.[4] The eleventh-century church at Jumièges, it is thought, was started by Abbot Thierry (1017-28); and he is credited with the great western works and the definition of the whole plan on the ground. Robert is believed to have begun in the usual way from the east, and built the presbytery and transepts. The nave and the lantern were finished by Abbot Robert III (1048-78), the main altar being dedicated in 1067. Jumièges is, therefore, later than Bernay and Avranches, and contemporary with Mont

---

[1] *VEdR*, pp. 46-9. [2] Pl. 30-1, and see above, pl. 13.

[3] Jean Leclercq and Jean-Paul Bonnes, *Un Maître de la Vie spirituelle au XIe siècle: Jean de Fécamp* (Etudes de Théologie et d'Histoire de la spiritualité, Paris, 1946), pp. 13-14.

[4] For Jumièges, see Georges Lanfry, 'Fouilles et découvertes à Jumièges: le déambulatoire de l'église romaine', *Bulletin Monumental*, lxxxvii (1928), 107-37, and *L'abbaye de Jumièges, Plans et documents* (Rouen, 1954); Jean Taralon, *Jumièges* (Nefs et Clochers: les éditions du Cerf, 1955), which has a useful bibliography, p. 40.

St Michel, started in 1023. It is quite likely that Westminster was indeed inspired by Jumièges; but John of Fécamp visited Edward in 1054[1] and any architect familiar with recent building in the duchy – and by 1050 several major churches were going up – could have designed Westminster for Edward. In fact of the master-masons for whom we have a name, two, Leofsi Duddesson and Godwin Gretsith, were English and the third, Teinfrith, was probably a German.[2]

It seems, however, fairly safe to interpret the literary description in the *Vita*, which was acceptable to the Westminster monk Sulcard in the late eleventh century,[3] the picture on the tapestry, and the few archaeological discoveries,[4] with reference to the existing remains at Jumièges and other Norman evidence. Westminster, built in dressed Reigate stone, had a long nave of six double bays (two longer than Jumièges), a lantern tower over the crossing, and a presbytery of two bays. There may also have been a western porch which connected the new church to the old. According to a thirteenth-century poem,[5] there were two western towers. The nave had aisles, communicating with the main area by rows of arches. This ground arcade consisted of six bays, defined by great compound piers, each divided by a pair of round arches resting on a plain cylindrical column. The alternation of massive and simple piers, found also at St Vigor, Bayeux, and Le Pré at Le Mans, may have been derived ultimately from St Bénigne. Above this high arcade was the triforium stage, with a gallery surmounting the vaulted aisles; and finally there was the clerestory. The nave was probably timber roofed. The transepts, each with an eastern apsidal chapel, were covered at the triforium level by a large gallery, which carried the nave galleries into the presbytery, and also provided ample space for chapels. The tower was borne over the crossing by lofty arches which sprang at the clerestory level and hardly obstructed the view. The presbytery of two bays continued the line of the nave arcading. It was surrounded at Jumièges,

---

[1] See above, p. 205.

[2] Harmer, *Writs*, no. 87, 'Three Westminster Writs of King Edward the Confessor', *EHR*, li (1936), 98, *n*. 1.

[3] Sulcard, when describing his own church, simply adapted the Anonymous's description: Bernhard W. Scholz, 'Sulcard of Westminster: "Prologus de Construccione Westmonasterii" ', *Traditio*, xx (1964), 91.

[4] W. R. Lethaby, *Westminster Abbey Re-examined* (1925), pp. 3–19; Laurence E. Tanner and A. W. Clapham, 'Recent discoveries in the Nave of Westminster Abbey', *Archaeologia*, lxxxiii (1933), 227–36; Barlow, *VEdR*, pp. 45–6. See also above, pl. 13.

[5] 'En miliu dresce une tur,/ E deus en fiunt del occident.': Univ. Lib., Cambridge, Ee iii. 59, ll. 2295–6.

as at Mont St Michel, the eleventh-century cathedral at Rouen, and at Fécamp, by an ambulatory, innocent, it seems, of side chapels. This may also have been the arrangement at Westminster.[1]

The nave at Jumièges was 25 metres high; and the diminishing height of the stages, the alternating piers, and the semi-circular shafts which run centrally up the face of the great piers, across the triforium stage to the clerestory, thus dividing the nave into segments, all emphasize its vertical lines. But also at Jumièges there is a great sense of length, of unbroken space, of continuity from one end to the other. Contemporaries were certainly impressed by Westminster. It was probably not only a large, but also a very beautiful church, its clean lines uncluttered by ornamentation. With greater length than Jumièges, there may have been near perfect proportions; and the lantern was bound to be sublime. It was, indeed, the central tower which especially struck the imagination of the author of the *Vita*: 'a tower reaching up with spiralling stairs in artistic profusion, and then with plain walls climbing to a wooden roof which is carefully covered with lead.' Outside, according to the tapestry, there was a cluster of turrets round the main tower.

Little is known about the queen's undertaking at Wilton except that wooden structures were replaced by stone and that it was a less ambitious project than her husband's.[2] Once, when it was almost finished, it was devastated by fire; but even so it was ready before Westminster. It may have been in connexion with these enterprises that one year, before Christmas, which the court was to spend at Gloucester, Edward and Edith ordered several of the neighbouring monasteries to send their reliquaries there so that (as it was feared at Evesham) the queen could choose the best relics for herself.[3] Evesham safeguarded itself against the greatest loss by sending the relics of St Odulf instead of those of St Egwin, its principal patron. And Odulf defended his church stoutly. On the day after Christmas Edith ordered a goldsmith to open the shrines for her inspection; and when he came to the Evesham chest and put his hand inside, Edith was suddenly blinded. Overcome with grief at this affliction, she ordered the smith to stop, promised God she would never

[1] This has not usually been accepted by English writers about Westminster. But the language of the *Vita*, p. 45, 'ambitus autem ipsius edis . . .', suggests an ambulatory: and it was not known before Lanfry's excavations in 1927 that Jumièges had this arrangement. [2] *VEdR*, pp. 46–8.

[3] 'Translation and Miracles of S. Odulph', *Chronicon abbatiae de Evesham*, ed. W. D. Macray (Rolls. ser. 1863), pp. 317–18.

13. Westminster Abbey: excavated remains of Edward's church. (above) South arcade. Base of first compound pier from west; (below) Bases of south arcade looking east from pier of south-west tower. (*Courtesy Society of Antiquaries of London.*)

14–16. Edward's miracles: six thirteenth-century coloured miniatures on two leaves inserted into an abbreviation of Domesday Book. (*Courtesy Public Record Office, London, E 36/284.*)

14(a). Edward accuses Earl Godwin of the murder of the aetheling Alfred.
  (b). Godwin (extreme right) prepares to undergo the ordeal.

again offer violence to saints if through the merits of St Odulf he would restore her sight, and, moreover, offered a precious pall on the shrine she had violated. Whereupon she recovered the use of her eyes, and the king and his warriors rejoiced. Thus the Evesham admonitory story.

Wilton was dedicated in 1065, apparently before the autumn.[1] Westminster was dedicated on 28 December while Edward lay dying. Present at both ceremonies was a possible author of the *Vita Ædwardi Regis*, Goscelin of St Bertin, a Flemish monk in the household of Bishop Herman of Wiltshire and Sherborne.[2] Goscelin was closely associated with Wilton, and between 1077 and 1082 wrote a life of St Wulfsige of Sherborne, a life of St Edith of Wilton, and 'A book of comfort' for Eve, a girl whom he had known and loved while she had been receiving her education in the nunnery, the daughter of a Danish father and a Lotharingian mother. And Goscelin recalled both ceremonies in his *Liber confortatorius*, written about 1081, because he associated them with Eve.[3] The girl was with her mother, Olive, at the banquet after the dedication of Wilton. Goscelin sent her a fish, and it may have been a symbolical offering. The author of the *Vita* composed 'a metaphorical epithalamium on the dedication ceremony of this new bride of God [the nunnery]',[4] full of erotic imagery, employed, as was usual, to convey a spiritual meaning. Goscelin then took Eve, dressed in black, to the celebrations at Westminster: she was 'a Mary by the grace of the Lord for three days'. But there is no poem on this subject in the *Vita*.

Between the two dedications there was a rebellion in Northumbria. In the spring of 1065 Harold invaded South Wales, possibly because of the 'ill-treatment' of some English traders at Newport; and after he had ravaged as far as the Usk and subdued the territory, he had some buildings put up at Portskewet, south-west of Chepstow.[5] These may have

---

[1] *VEdR*, p. 50.   [2] For Goscelin, see *VEdR*, Appendix C.
[3] C. H. Talbot, 'The Liber confortatorius of Goscelin of Saint Bertin', *Studia Anselmiana*, fasc. xxxvii = *Analecta Monastica*, 3rd ser. (Rome, 1955), pp. 28–9; Barlow, *VEdR*, pp. 92, 94, 97–9.   [4] *VEdR*, pp. 48–9.
[5] *Chron. CD*; *Vita Sancti Gundleii* (St Gwynllyw), cap. 13, in *Lives of the Cambro-British Saints*, ed. W. J. Rees (Welsh MSS Soc. 1853), pp. 153–4, and A. W. Wade-Evans, *Vitae Sanctorum Britanniae et Genealogiae* (1944), pp. 184–6. According to this twelfth-century source, in King Edward's reign some English merchants, trading to the mouth of the Usk [Newport], refused to pay the customary toll, whereupon Rhiryd, son of Ifor and *nepos* of King Gruffydd, cut their anchor away and offered it at the shrine of St Gwynllyw [in Newport]. The merchants reported their shameful loss to Earl Harold, who assembled an army and invaded and ravaged Glamorgan. Some of his troops violated the church of the saint. But they failed to see the anchor while collecting the booty they found in the church, and when they started to cut

been intended to serve as a safer haven for English merchants; and in the summer Harold invited Edward to join him there for a hunting party. But on 24 August Caradog ap Gruffydd, the son of Gruffydd ap Rhydderch, attacked the site, slew most of the workmen, and carried off the stores and equipment.[1] The remark of the northern (*D*) chronicler, 'We do not know who first suggested this conspiracy', is possibly just another of his dark sayings,[2] or a hint that someone was plotting against Harold. In the autumn Edward was hunting in Wiltshire in company with Earl Tostig, both obviously without any suspicion of danger,[3] when news arrived of an even more destructive plot, this time aimed at Tostig. The Northumbrian rebellion had a decisive effect on future events. And it is this tragedy, rather than the Norman Conquest, which throws its shadow far back over the *Vita Ædwardi Regis*. It was caused by, or led to, the fatal discord between Harold and Tostig. It was the reason why Edward's reign collapsed in ruin. The author of the *Vita* devoted a whole poem to the theme and alluded to it in other verses.

> Why then, Ill Fortune, menace these two men
> With thickened gall, with more than double spite,
> And, set for Theban pyres, intent on dreadful war,
> From both sides furnish torches for the dead?[4]

He regarded the queen as the peace-maker:

> By her advice peace wraps the kingdom round
> And keeps mankind from breaking pacts of peace.[5]

But when the family harmony was broken,

> O what ruin comes!
> The wretched world again old chaos keeps.[6]

It was the quarrel between Harold and Tostig which destroyed the purpose of his book, turned his song of praise into a *Thebaidis*:

> Alas, those brothers' hearts too hard![7]

---

up the cheeses these began to bleed. At this terrible sign the soldiers abandoned their loot and Harold made an offering at the altar. 'Immediately afterwards, in the next month, because of this wickedness and his other sins, Harold was defeated and killed by King William at the battle of Hastings.'

[1] *Chron. CD*, Florence, i. 222–3. Cf. *DB*, i. 162 a i.
[2] Cf. his remark on the death of Edward 'the Exile', above, p. 217.
[3] *VEdR*, pp. 50, 52.　　　　[4] *Ibid.*, p. 38.　　　　[5] *Ibid.*, p. 15.
[6] *Ibid.*, p. 16.　　　　[7] *Ibid.*, p. 56.

The Northumbrian rebellion was against Tostig, not the king; but this was no help to Edward. It was a conspiracy among the nobility which aroused a great deal of aristocratic support, even outside the earldom. Although the grievances of the rebels are reported differently in the several sources,[1] they come to much the same thing: the severity and partiality of Tostig's rule. He had used the law to deprive his enemies of life and land; he had despoiled churches of their property; he had taxed the whole of Northumbria heavily and unjustly. Three of his murders are noted by the Worcester chronicler and one of these involves the royal court. Tostig had had Gamel son of Orm and Ulf son of Dolfin killed by treachery in his chamber at York when they were there under a safe-conduct, and Queen Edith, for love of her brother, had had Gospatric killed by treachery in the royal court on 28 December.[2] All these men were probably members of the highest Northumbrian aristocracy, descendants of Earl Waltheof I.[3] There can be no doubt that Tostig because of his repressive government was unpopular in his earldom. There can be no doubt also that the leaders in the conspiracy had intrigued with Eadwine and Morkere of Mercia and possibly with Harold. The Mercian brothers had clearly promised their support, and it was on the strength of this that the rebels came into the open. Harold's position is more doubtful. Tostig, apparently, accused him of instigating the insurrection, a charge which Harold denied.[4] If Tostig had incited Caradog to attack Portskewet, Harold could have retaliated by encouraging his brother's enemies. At some point Harold acquired large estates in Mercia.[5] But once again the evidence is insufficient for a firm conclusion.

[1] *Chron. C*; *VEdR*, pp. 50 ff.; Florence, i. 222. *Chron. DE* give no reasons.

[2] Florence, i. 222.

[3] See genealogical table in Barlow, *English Church*, p. 172. H. W. C. Davis, 'Cumbria before the Norman Conquest', *EHR*, xx (1905), 61–5, followed by Harmer, *Writs*, p. 562, identifies Gospatric as the third son of Earl Uchtred of Northumbria (murdered in 1016) and also as the lord of Allerdale and Dalston who issued writ no. 121. Less can be objected to the second identification than to the first. According to Symeon, *HR*, pp. 197–8, cf. 383, Uchtred was succeeded as earl first by his brother, Eadwulf Cudel, then by his two sons in turn, Ealdred and Eadwulf. The third son, Gospatric, who was never earl, had a son, Uchtred, and a grandson, Eadwulf Rus, one of the killers of Bishop Walcher of Durham in 1080. It seems unlikely that a man would be assassinated as a political nuisance fifty years after the death of his father. Gospatrics were common among the Northumbrian nobility. A youngish Gospatric was in Tostig's suite on his embassy to Rome in 1061, *VEdR*, pp. 35–6.

[4] *VEdR*, p. 53; see below, p. 237.

[5] See below, p. 243.

On 3 October 1065 a large number of Northumbrian thegns, led by three men who are otherwise unknown, marched on York, killed as many of the earl's housecarls and servants as they could find, and plundered his armoury and treasury.[1] They then outlawed Tostig – perhaps the first of several such renunciations intended to legalize their behaviour[2] – sent for Morkere, recognized him as their earl, and under his leadership marched south, by way of Lincoln and Nottingham or Derby to Northampton, collecting reinforcements and killing Tostig's men and plundering his lands as they went.[3] When the rebel army came into Mercia it was joined by Eadwine with the forces of his earldom and some Welsh auxiliaries.[4] From Northampton, where much damage was done, at least part of the insurgent force pushed on to Oxford.[5] The rebellion had in effect split England at the Thames, just as had happened in 1035 and 1051.[6] Northumbrian 'separatism' may have played a part, but only, it seems, within the more general distrust of Wessex. The revolt was not inspired simply by Northumbrian patriotism; the rebels did not choose Waltheof, Earl Siward's son, as their new earl and leader, but Morkere of Mercia, a man who had no obvious connexion with the Anglo-Scandinavian society of the north. It appears that the insurgents were protesting to a West-Saxon king against the misrule of a West-Saxon earl and had the political skill to propose an alternative which was not out of the question.

When Edward learned of the rebellion he made his headquarters at

---

[1] *Chron. DE* (identical), expanded by Florence, i. 223, who supplies the date and names; *Chron. C* is short. Freeman, *NC*, ii. 479, identifies the leaders in *DB*. Florence claims that 200 Northumbrian thegns killed 200 of Tostig's men. *VEdR*, pp. 50–1, also stresses the killing and destruction.

[2] *Chron. DE* place the outlawry after the attack on York and before the invitation to Morkere. *VEdR*, p. 50, agrees that it was immediately after the events at York that the rebels negotiated with 'the sons of Earl Ælfgar'. But *C* places the outlawry of Tostig 'and all those with him who had committed lawless deeds', followed by the adoption of Morkere as earl, after the council of Oxford on 28 October, and Florence, i. 223–4, agrees on the date of the sentence, but omits all reference to Morkere. In this matter *DE* seem to have the most acceptable order of events, although it is possible that Tostig was renounced on several occasions and that no one source gives the whole story.

[3] *Chron. DE* mention the collection of troops from Nottinghamshire, Derbyshire, and Lincolnshire; *VEdR*, p. 51, refers to the slaughter at Lincoln.

[4] *Chron. DE*; cf. Florence, i. 224, *VEdR*, p. 50.

[5] *Chron. C*, Florence, i. 223, and *VEdR*, p. 52, mention a meeting with the rebels at Oxford. *Chron. DE*, probably mistakenly, locate both parleys at Northampton.

[6] Above, pp. 43, 111.

Britford,[1] near Wilton, and summoned his counsellors to him. Only in the *Vita Ædwardi Regis* is there an account of what took place at court,[2] and as the author in this section is sympathetic to Tostig, he may do less than justice to Harold. The anonymous author relates that there were angry scenes at court, charges and counter-charges. Some men accused Tostig of being himself responsible for the disaster: his misgovernment was the cause. Tostig countered by accusing Harold of having artfully instigated the rebellion. He made a formal charge in Edward's presence; and Harold cleared himself by swearing that he was innocent of the crime. It was decided in the first place to negotiate with the rebels. We are reminded of the crisis in 1051, how Edward, by negotiation, procrastination, and the threat of war, defeated his opponents. But in 1065 he was unable to repeat his success.

Harold had talks with the rebels at Northampton and then on 28 October at Oxford.[3] All versions of the Chronicle agree that the insurgents utterly refused to take Tostig back and asked that Edward should recognize Morkere as their earl. According to the northern and Canterbury versions Harold conveyed Edward's acceptance of the demands to the second meeting (which they, probably mistakenly, locate at Northampton) and renewed for the rebels the laws of Cnut – the good old laws that Tostig had disregarded. It is clear from the Chronicle that this capitulation was followed by the departure of Tostig and his family from England; and the one must be regarded as a direct consequence of the other: Edward must have agreed to expel the fallen earl. The *Vita* tells us much more about what went on at court and seems to explain the events which the Chronicle records. Edward sent an ultimatum to the rebels: lay down your arms, and then I will hear your complaints against Tostig and do you justice. But the rebels replied with another ultimatum: either dismiss Tostig from the court and country or we will make war also on you. Exchanges of this kind would explain the advance of the insurgents from Northampton to Oxford. When the negotiations failed, according to the *Vita*, Edward summoned the army from the whole of the land, with the intention of crushing the rebellion by force. We are again reminded of Edward's

[1] *Chron. C*; *VEdR*, p. 52. The latter holds that Edward only moved from the forest to Britford when the negotiations failed.

[2] *VEdR*, pp. 52–4.

[3] *Chron. C*, followed by Florence, i. 223, gives the two meeting places and supplies the date. *Chron. DE* agree with *C* on the date, but place both meetings at Northampton. *VEdR*, p. 52, refers to negotiations with the rebels only at Oxford.

measures in 1051. By calling out the army he probably hoped, as on the previous occasion, to cause desertions from the rebel standard. But no troops appeared. Some of the counsellors blamed the lateness of the season and the unsuitable weather; all shrank from civil war. They tried to calm the king, and in the end they simply refused to obey him. Edward called down God's vengeance on those who neglected their duty and withheld their service. Edith wept. Tostig went into exile.

In its broadest outlines the story is clear enough. Edward was powerless in the face of a Northumbrian and Mercian conspiracy against Tostig and had to accept the rebels' terms. But as the conspiracy was against Tostig and his household alone, all that Edward was required to do was dismiss Tostig and appoint Morkere.[1] In 1052 Edward had allowed Archbishop Robert, Bishop Ulf, and some others of his friends to be driven from the country. We are on familiar ground. What we must investigate, however, is why Edward with, so far as we know, all the earls of Godwin's family at his side, could do nothing for Tostig, and why Tostig could do nothing for himself. The latter question is the easier to answer. Tostig obviously had only a small escort with him while he hunted with Edward in Wiltshire; his housecarls had been slain at York and Lincoln by the rebels; and the northern thegns were in arms against him. But there were the armies of his brothers, Harold, Gyrth, and Leofwine, and all the troops that could be raised from Wessex. The explanation in the *Vita* is simple: Harold deserted Edward and Tostig. In one sense this explanation must be true. Harold obviously refused to fight; and in the next year, after Edward's death, he is found in close alliance with Eadwine and Morkere against Tostig. By 1066 the quarrel between Harold and Tostig had become deadly. But this does not necessarily mean that the brothers were enemies in the summer of 1065.

The *Vita* may be in error when it suggests and hints (largely by omissions) that Harold was playing an underhand game throughout the autumn and made no real effort to help Tostig. The Anglo-Saxon

[1] According to an early-twelfth-century tract, 'De Northymbrorum Comitibus', *Symeonis monachi Opera Omnia*, ed. T. Arnold (Rolls ser. 1885), ii. 383, Edward granted the earldom jointly to Eadwine and Morkere, who in their turn committed the land between Tyne and Tweed to Oswulf, the son of the Earl Eadwulf whom Siward had killed and replaced. This Oswulf after the Conquest killed Copsig, William's appointment to the earldom, and was then himself killed by a robber. Their replacement was Gospatric, Oswulf's cousin. It is also possible that in 1065 Edward detached the shires of Huntingdon and Northampton and gave them as an earldom to Waltheof, Siward's son. See above, p. 194 *n.* 3. Cf. also Symeon *HR*, pp. 198–9.

Chronicle gives no support to this view. The northern and Canterbury versions simply relate that Harold was engaged in negotiations, carrying messages between the sides. The Abingdon version and the Worcester chronicle maintain that Harold tried to calm the rebels, get an agreement, and make peace between them and Tostig. The *Vita* does not hide from us the total lack of sympathy for Tostig among Edward's counsellors: they thought that he had brought the trouble on himself. It may well be that Harold did all he could for his brother short of war, that in the end he refused to champion a lost cause, declined to fall with Tostig, shrank from a suicidal civil conflict. At the worst he was calculating and selfish, aware that the elimination of Tostig would remove one obstacle which lay between him and the throne; but most men probably thought him wise. Tostig, however, never forgave this 'treachery'. And the quarrel caused the death of both.

> A wind
> Most wanton, parts in twain the flames above
> The pyre for brothers killed by mutual blows.[1]

[1] *VEdR*, p. 39, cf. Lucan, I, 550-2; Statius, *Thebaid*, XII, 431.

Chapter 11

THE END OF THE REIGN

The Northumbrian rebellion was followed three months later by Edward's death. Although the one need not have been the cause of the other, the events which took place in October must have been a great shock to the king. The author of the *Vita Ædwardi Regis*, who describes how Edward was shaken by paroxysms of rage in 1052, when Earl Godwin forced his way back into England,[1] relates that he was even more shattered by the refusal of his counsellors to obey his order to restore Tostig to Northumbria by force of arms. He became ill from grief; and from then until his death his mind was affected.[2] Tostig went into exile after 1 November;[3] Edward died eight weeks later. It is possible that the king suffered at Britford the first of a series of strokes.

The author of the *Vita*, however, because of his purpose, pays more attention to the condition of the queen.[4] In his opinion Edith had for some time been the real power behind the throne. Edward relied much on her advice and cheerful courage; the court regarded her as a stabilizing influence. But now, with the quarrel of her brothers and the illness of her husband, she lost courage and broke down. Her tears, her inconsolable grief, were a sign to all that the end was at hand, disaster imminent. The author of the *Vita* implies that Edith foresaw the death of her husband, the death of Tostig at Stamford Bridge, and the deaths of Harold, Gyrth, and Leofwine at Hastings. 'All men deduced future calamities from the signs of the present.' But if Edward was seriously ill, sometimes out of his mind, for most of November and December, if it was reasonably clear that he was not going to survive, there must have been great activity at court. We cannot believe with the *Vita* that the whole palace joined Edith in her mourning. Most men would have been looking to the future, and would not necessarily have been oppressed by the problems or dismayed by the prospects. The *Vita* was probably

[1] 'paulatim defervente animi motu sedatus', *VEdR*, p. 28.

[2] 'egrum trahebat animum', *ibid.*, p. 53.

[3] Florence, i. 223–4. In the *Vita*, however, Tostig arrives in Flanders a few days before Christmas, p. 55.   [4] *VEdR*, pp. 53–4.

being written at this very time, and the changing circumstances seem to have affected its attitude and progress, and to have blurred its purpose. It is likely that Edith commissioned the work so as to prepare the English magnates for the implementation of a 'Godwinist' plan on Edward's death. But we are not told clearly what the scheme was.[1]

If, however, we can trust the *Vita* on Edith's mental state, we must conclude that in November her own dearest hopes, whatever these may have been, were, or were about to be, disappointed. It is possible that she mourned her husband's passing. We can believe with the Anonymous that for such an ambitious woman her husband's unexpected incapacity was a terrible blow. She was going to lose her position as queen when she was still in her forties. She would not have been ignorant of what had happened to her mother-in-law in 1035 and 1043. And, as it turned out, she was reduced after 1066 to complete obscurity. Some of Edward's last words, as reported in the *Vita*,[2] show that he too feared for her state in widowhood.

What we would most like to know is how the quarrel between Harold and Tostig affected Edith. Was she sad simply because two of her brothers, equally beloved, had fallen out? Or did she regard a house divided as a family inviting its own ruin? Had she set her hopes on Tostig and seen him as the most suitable successor to Edward? Or, with the balance between Harold and Tostig lost, did she regard the chance of some other candidate, on whom Edward and she had agreed, as seriously reduced? And in this last case we need not go beyond the aetheling Edgar, Svein of Denmark, and William of Normandy. There is nothing to suggest that Edith was a supporter of Edgar. Apparently she was not in London after the battle of Hastings when Edgar was chosen king by some of the remaining English leaders;[3] and although Margaret (Edgar's sister) and Malcolm III of Scots called five of their children Edward, Edmund, Æthelred, Edgar, and Edith, we cannot be sure which royal Edith was being remembered. As for Svein of Denmark, although the queen was herself half Danish by blood and Svein was her first cousin, after her brothers her closest kinsman, again there is no known connexion between the two and little sign that Edith was interested in Scandinavia.[4]

---

[1] See below, Appendix A.   [2] *VEdR*, p. 79.

[3] The accounts in *Chron.* and Florence, i. 228, omit her. The *Carmen de Hastingae proelio*, ll. 626–35, implies that she was on her dower estate at Winchester.

[4] Her Danish mother, Gytha, is not mentioned by name in *VEdR*.

Edith's relations with William of Normandy are more open to investigation but no more certain. The widowed queen was unmolested after the Conquest and, so far as we know, linked with none of the conspiracies against the Conqueror. But there is no reputable evidence that she was an active or even positive supporter of the Norman. From 1066 until her death in 1075 she seems to have lived in complete retirement from court and public affairs. If she did nothing to harm William, equally she did nothing to help him in any way. It is only from William of Poitiers that we learn that she hated Harold and supported his victor.[1] The duke's panegyrist tells us that Edith, whom he does not identify by name, like Tostig fought against their wicked brother, although she, being a woman, could fight him only with prayers and stratagems. 'This woman, as intelligent as a man, who could distinguish good from evil and always honoured goodness, wanted William, her husband's adopted son and appointed heir, to rule in England, because she knew that he was wise, just, and strong.' Only if we accept William of Poitiers' thesis can we also accept that Edith tried to carry out her husband's wishes after his death.

Something a little more persuasive can be adduced to support the view that Edith hoped that Tostig would succeed. The *Vita Ædwardi Regis* can be interpreted in this way. If Edith had preferred Harold, she would not have been so desperate when Tostig was sent into exile. The author presumably follows Tostig's fortunes at this point in his story not only because the earl went to Flanders, but also because his fate was of special interest to his patron, the queen. And Edith's love for Tostig is the only one of her preferences to be corroborated. As we have already seen,[2] the Worcester chronicler believed that Edith had contrived the murder of one of Tostig's Northumbrian enemies. But Tostig's own attitudes and ambitions are hopelessly obscure. He was related by marriage to the duke of Normandy. He was welcomed in Flanders,[3] by William's father-in-law. He sailed to Scandinavia, imploring in turn Svein of Denmark and Harald Hardrada to join with him in an invasion of England,[4] although both were rival claimants. In 1066 he harboured in Scotland, although Malcolm might have disputed Northumbria with him. The evidence suggests that Tostig was an opportunist who would accept anything that was going; and it is not

[1] Poitiers, pp. 166–8. [2] Above, p. 235.
[3] *VEdR*, p. 55. Cf. *Chron. CDE*, Florence, i. 224.
[4] *King Harald's Saga*, caps. 78–9.

impossible that he and his sister had taken their hopes seriously. Although one chronicler believed that Tostig was in touch with William,[1] and it could be suggested that Tostig and Edith were both in favour of William's succession, even William of Poitiers did not claim Tostig for an ally, and Tostig's own behaviour in 1066 rules this out completely. If he supported William he had only to sail to Normandy and join the invading forces. Instead he played for his own hand.

Even if Tostig's banishment from England was not part of a plot hatched by Harold to remove a rival – and from what we know of Harold this would be too harsh a judgment on his hesitations in October 1065 – it was after Tostig had left for Flanders that Harold must have brought his ambition into the open and counted his friends. From subsequent events we know that no one of importance actively supported any of the foreign claimants. When Tostig led Harald Hardrada into Yorkshire every man's hand was against them.[2] There were no defections to William's camp before the battle of Hastings and only reluctant submissions afterwards. Even as late as 1073 William of Poitiers addressed an impassioned plea to the English to acknowledge William as their king. 'And you, England, you also would love him and regard him as one of the truly great, and joyfully throw yourself at his feet, if, casting aside your foolishness and wickedness, you could judge more wisely what sort of a man he is who now has power over you.'[3] For William 'removed from your neck the proud and cruel despotism of Harold, killed the hateful tyrant who had reduced you to ruinous and shameful slavery.'[4] But, as William of Poitiers acknowledged, that is not the way in which the English saw it.

At some point Harold came to an understanding with the Mercian family. He had never been on bad terms with Ælfgar or his sons; and by allowing Morkere to remain in Northumbria he put the brothers in his debt. Before Edward died it must have been agreed that Eadwine and Morkere would support Harold's claim to the throne and that Harold would marry their sister, Ealdgyth, Gruffydd ap Llywelyn's widow,[5] and protect them against Tostig. It may also have been at this time that Harold obtained substantial tenements in Mercia, valued in Domesday Book at over £250.[6] Harold was getting the best of the

[1] Ordericus Vitalis, ii. 120–1 (ed. Chibnall, ii. 138–40).

[2] However, according to *King Harald's Saga*, cap. 86, Tostig's friends and kinsmen joined the invaders. [3] Poitiers, p. 228. [4] *Ibid.*, p. 230.

[5] Ordericus Vitalis, ii. 119 (ed. Chibnall, ii. 138).

[6] Robert H. Davies, *The lands and rights of Harold, son of Godwine, and their distribution*

bargain; but the brothers were in a weaker position than is often allowed, and there was no alternative alliance open to them. Even if they had preferred Edgar the aetheling as king, it would have been suicidal for them to champion Edgar against Harold. At Christmas 1065 Edgar was not more than fourteen years old. He had been given no earldom; he is not known to have held large estates.[1] Although he was a boy of promise,[2] obviously he had no following in the country. But, equally obviously, if the earls had decided to have him as their king, the bishops would have accepted the choice and there would have been no opposition. He was regarded as throne-worthy, for after Hastings the bishops and the surviving earls recognized him as king. It is, therefore, good evidence for a true understanding between the West-Saxon and the Mercian earls that Edgar was passed over. He would have been the obvious compromise candidate.

Because it was decided to consecrate Edward's new church at Westminster and also, perhaps, because the sick king could not hunt, the Christmas celebrations in 1065 were not held at Gloucester. A great concourse 'from the whole of Britain' assembled at Westminster for the double ceremony.[3] News of the king's illness may also have encouraged a large attendance. Two twelfth-century Westminster forgeries,[4] charters of Edward in favour of the abbey dated 28 December, the day on which the church was dedicated, have almost impeccable witness lists[5] which may have been taken from a genuine instrument or from

---

by William I: A study in the Domesday evidence (unpublished M.A. dissertation, University College, Cardiff, 1967), pp. 51–2.

[1] According to Poitiers, p. 238, King William granted him large estates, because he was a kinsman of Edward and to console him for having been deprived of the crown to which he had been elected. There is little sign of this in Domesday Book (1086).

[2] Orderic (ed. Chibnall), v. 270–2, describes him in 1098–9, when he was with Duke Robert on the First Crusade, as, 'Hic corpore speciosus, lingua disertus, liberalis et generosus, utpote Eduardi regis Hunorum filius, sed dextera segnis erat.'

[3] Sulcard and Osbert of Clare, based on *VEdR*, pp. 71–2.

[4] KCD, nos. 824, 825 (Sawyer, nos. 1043, 1041). See Pierre Chaplais, 'The original charters of Herbert and Gervase abbots of Westminster', *A Medieval Miscellany for Doris Mary Stenton* (Pipe Roll Soc. 1962), pp. 91 ff. A spurious Westminster charter dated 1065, printed Richard Widmore, *Enquiry into the time of the first foundation of Westminster Abbey* (1751), Appendix II, pp. 14–18 (Sawyer, no. 1040), with 16 witnesses, provides no other names.

[5] The one obvious error is that in no. 825 Bishop Godwin, presumably of Rochester, is added to the eight bishops, including Siweard of Rochester, common to both schedules.

a contemporary memorandum. Together they list, besides the king and queen, the two archbishops, eight of the twelve bishops, eight abbots, three royal clerks, the king's 'chancellor', five earls, seven thegns, and five 'knights'. The bishops omitted from the list, Æthelric of Selsey, Æthelmaer of Elmham (Stigand's brother), Leofwine of Lichfield, and Æthelwine of Durham, were all removed from the bench after the Conquest and may have been considered by the fabricator of the list unworthy of inclusion. The abbots listed as present – Westminster, St Augustine's, Ramsey, Peterborough, Bury, Bath or Chertsey, Evesham, and Pershore – are a typical selection from the heads of the larger houses. The three 'chaplains' are among the most famous of Edward's clerks, for they were all promoted to bishoprics;[1] and Regenbald was the clerk whom William probably employed for a time as his chancellor. On the lay side the Mercian and West-Saxon earls all appear, but Waltheof, whose witness appears on no authentic document, is omitted. The nobles and court officials inspire confidence: Ralf, Robert fitzWimarch, Esgar, Eadnoth, Bondi, Wigod, and Æthelnoth, all well-known men, large landholders, stallers, and in several cases sheriffs. We notice that Edgar the aetheling is not included among them, but his name appears on no extant charter. Most of the five men described as *milites* are also thegns known from other sources.

Although the witness lists may be synthetic, the persons listed are all men whom we might expect to find at this Christmas celebration, and, although these thirty-nine courtiers were hardly 'from the whole of Britain' – a line drawn from the Wash to the middle Severn would be the northern limit of the territorial interests of most of them – they will be found to be the usual heterogeneous assembly. Monks (one archbishop, three bishops, and eight abbots) outnumber the secular clergy, and one of the monk-bishops, Wulfstan of Worcester, is a saint. There are Scandinavian, French, and German names. All the foreign bishops, the one Norman, William of London, and the four 'Lotharingians', Walter of Hereford, Leofric of Exeter, Herman of Ramsbury and Sherborne, and Giso of Wells, are there. Among the abbots is Edward's Alsacian doctor, Baldwin of Bury St Edmunds. The three chaplains were all of Norman origin. Of the twelve leading nobles listed, three earls (Harold, Gyrth, Morkere) and three stallers have Scandinavian names, and two of the stallers were French. If these thirty-nine men were

---

[1] Osbern of Exeter (1072–1103), Peter of Lichfield (1072–?84), and Robert, possibly the future bishop of Hereford (1079–95).

indeed present at the Christmas court, it was not packed and could not have been overawed. It was thoroughly representative of the various interests in the land, and any decision it took can be considered the voice of the kingdom. William of Poitiers' claim that Harold got the crown by a *coup d'état* instead of by 'a public election',[1] is not good evidence for thinking that at Christmas 1065 Edward was surrounded only by conspirators in Harold's pay. Moreover, the archdeacon does not tell us why Duke William was not at Westminster, although, if the duke was really heir-designate, his absence needs explaining.

The other important absentee was, of course, Tostig, in exile at St Omer in Flanders. Although Tostig's absence must have cast a cloud over the festivities, it is difficult to see whether it would also have inspired fear. There is certainly a tradition that the earl was an experienced military commander, and we know from later events that his sole interest in exile was to raise an army, or enlist allies, so as to return by force. The author of the *Vita*, himself probably a monk of St Bertin's at St Omer, tells us that Count Baldwin, the earl's brother-in-law, made him military governor of that town, in command of the garrison and in receipt of its revenues.[2] Snorri Sturluson, in the very confused account of Tostig's exile which he included in *King Harald's (Sigurdsson's) Saga*,[3] made Tostig the eldest son of Godwin, and commander-in-chief of the English army, with authority over all the other earls and in complete charge of the nation's defences towards the end of the reign.[4] This is to attribute to Tostig Harold's position; and although Tostig fought bravely at Gate Fulford and Stamford Bridge and in the latter battle flew his own flag beside Harald Sigurdsson's banner, 'The Landwaster', Harald had told Tostig that the Norwegians would not serve under the earl's command, for 'people say that the English are not entirely to be trusted.'[5] Moreover, in a passage in the *Vita* where Harold and Tostig are compared, the elder brother is considered the hardier soldier.[6] Even if Edith was filled with forebodings and wept incessantly, Harold, Gyrth, Leofwine, Eadwine, and Morkere were probably confident that they could deal with Tostig. And it should not be overlooked that a few months later, when Harald Sigurdsson sailed from the Solund Isles for Shetland and Orkney, men had the most horrid dreams of ogresses and ravens, and almost all the portents were ominous.[7]

[1] Poitiers, p. 146.   [2] *VEdR*, p. 55.   [3] Caps. 75–93.
[4] Cap. 77.   [5] Cap. 79.   [6] *VEdR*, p. 31.
[7] *King Harald's Saga*, caps. 80–2.

Our detailed knowledge of what happened at Edward's Christmas court is derived exclusively from the *Vita*.[1] The author used the occasion not only to mount a brilliant set-piece but also to expound his view of the situation. The characters play the parts which he has assigned to them, and the set purpose conspires with artistry to produce something more impressive than life. At the same time there is nothing unlikely. We are not in either a strictly conventional or a fancifully idealized world. The actors behave in a way in which we can believe; and at the lowest historical valuation we are given a typical scene. In the eleventh century men died and made their last wills in public. Death was a familiar visitor. Many men saw Edward die and many more saw him dead.

Edward became ill – possibly he suffered another stroke – on Christmas Eve, which was a Saturday. He recovered sufficiently to go through the Christmas Day festivities, the service in the abbey and the banquet, but on Boxing Day had to retire to his chamber. On Wednesday, 28 December, the festival of the Holy Innocents, the new abbey church at Westminster was consecrated in his absence;[2] and a week later he died. Towards the end he sank into a coma in which there were some intervals of delirium; and shortly before he died he became so restless that the watchers tried to rouse him, and succeeded in doing so. There were at that time in the bedchamber the queen, who was sitting on the floor warming his feet in her lap, Earl Harold, Robert fitzWimarch, and the archbishop of Canterbury. This scene is shown on the Bayeux Tapestry, where the designer has put Robert at the king's head, supporting him so that he could sit up, and Stigand[3] and Harold on either side of the bed.

When Edward recovered consciousness, he ordered his household to be assembled; and, as soon as the company was present, speaking with a strong voice, he recounted a vision he had just had.[4] He had seen two monks whom he had known very well when he had been in exile in Normandy and who were long since dead. They had told him that

[1] *VEdR*, pp. 74–81.

[2] The date is also in *Chron. CDE* and Florence, i. 224.

[3] It has sometimes been suggested that the priest at the deathbed cannot be Stigand because his appearance is quite different from the figure later identified as Stigand by name. But the likeliest explanation is that different models were followed in the different scenes. See above, pl. 11.

[4] *VEdR*, pp. 75–6, 88–90; and for some general observations on Edward's visions, see F. Barlow, 'The Vita Ædwardi (Book II); The Seven Sleepers: some further evidence and reflections', *Speculum*, xl (1965), 391 ff.

because all the magnates in England, the earls, bishops, abbots, and other clergy, were servants not of God, but of the Devil,[1] God had cursed the kingdom, and a year and a day after the king's death would deliver it into the hands of the Enemy, so that devils would 'come through all this land with fire and sword and the havoc of war.' To this Edward had replied that he would bring his people to repentance and ask for God's mercy, which surely would not be withheld. But the monks had answered that the people would not repent and God would not pardon. Edward had then asked when God's punishment would come to an end, and had been told that God would cease to punish England for her sins when a green tree, a tree in full leaf, which had been felled halfway up its trunk and the part cut off carried three furlongs away, should by its own efforts, without the aid of man or any kind of stake, join up again, and through its rising sap break into leaf and bear fruit. When that marvel happened, God's anger would be stilled.

Although we cannot doubt that the vision, even in this primitive state,[2] bears the marks of the events of the year 1066, we can easily believe that Edward related a dream and prophesied woe, and that it struck terror into the hearts of some of those present. According to the *Vita* the queen was one of those who was convinced that her husband had spoken the truth; she was aware of the scandalous state of the English church and believed that dire punishment was about to descend on the people of England. But at least one man was not carried away. Archbishop Stigand, who had had such a dazzling career in Edward's reign, who was the chief of those whom the author of the *Vita* regarded as servants recruited by the Devil through the lure of riches and worldly glory, 'who would repent either far too late or not at all'; this man, who knew all the secrets of the court, whispered to Harold that the king

---

[1] A contemporary 'Norman' moralist, John of Ravenna, abbot of Fécamp (1027–1078), made similar generals trictures in a letter 'Tuae quidem': 'Quid ergo melius mundus dici potest quam reges et duces, marchiones et comites, carnales episcopi et omnes personae quae sunt terrenis desideriis deditae . . . Et cum sint pessimae vitae homines, fornicatores, adulteri, rapaces, homicidae, avari, ebriosi, et cunctis flagitiis implicati, non timent servi Dei veste mutati eorum praedia quaerere, pecunias recipere et velut omni laude dignos praedicare.' Jean Leclercq and Jean-Paul Bonnes, *Un Maître de la Vie spirituelle au XIᵉ siècle, Jean de Fécamp* (1946), p. 203.

[2] It was several times revised to suit the changing circumstances; see the references above, p. 247, *n.* 4. Essentially we have a rustic metaphor about the impossibility of a felled tree joining up again; and this has been given a scriptural polish from Luke xxiii. 31 and Dan. iv. 14, 15, 23.

because of senility and sickness was simply out of his mind: the prophecy was no more than delirious raving. Stigand was obviously one of those who were committed to making Harold king; he did not want their champion upset by death-bed hysteria.

While his vassals wept and the queen cried unceasingly Edward spoke his last words and made his final will and testament.[1] To his men he said, 'Do not weep, but pray to God for my soul and give me leave to go to him. He who allowed himself to die will not permit me not to die.' Edward kept on trying to comfort the queen by saying that she was not to fear, for by God's mercy he would not die then, but would become well again.[2] And he did his best to safeguard her future. He exclaimed, 'May God repay my wife for her dutiful and loving service. For she has certainly been a devoted servant to me and has always been at my side like a beloved daughter. May God's mercy reward her with eternal joy in heaven.' Then, offering his hand to Harold, he said, 'I commend this woman and all the kingdom to your protection. Remember that she is your lady and sister, and serve her faithfully and honour her as such for all the days of her life. Do not take away from her any honour that I have granted her.' Edward then commended to Harold all his foreign vassals and servants, and asked that Harold should offer them service under him and give those who declined a safe-conduct to return home with all that they had acquired in the royal service. The dying man also gave instructions about his burial. 'Have my grave prepared in the minster in the place which will be shown to you. I beg you not to conceal my death, but send out the news promptly to all parts, so that all the faithful can beseech the mercy of Almighty God on me, a sinner.'

The last rites were administered to Edward, and he died, probably

[1] The *verba novissima*, the will declared on the deathbed, was the basic, usual, and completely valid method of disposing of goods and property. Writings were merely evidential. See H. D. Hazeltine, 'Comments on the writings known as Anglo-Saxon wills', Whitelock, *Wills*, pp. vii ff. Hazeltine regards Anglo-Saxon 'wills' as *donationes irrevocabiles post obitum* – irrevocable contracts. And so the question could be raised – though perhaps to no great profit – whether, if Edward had in fact made an 'irrevocable' grant to Svein of Denmark or William of Normandy (if he had made such a grant to both the question would hardly arise), he could properly abrogate it without the legatee's consent. It would have to be considered whether a bequest of the throne pertained to private or public law, and whether such a distinction had meaning at the time. Raymonde Foreville, 'Aux origines de la renaissance juridique', *Moyen âge*, lviii (1952), 63 ff., considers some of these matters.

[2] The author of the *Vita* says that Edward meant, and Edith understood him to mean, that he was passing from death to eternal life.

from a cerebral haemorrhage, on 4 or 5 January 1066, possibly on the Wednesday night between the two.[1] 'The beloved of God, languishing from the sickness of mind with which he had been stricken, died indeed to this world, but was joyfully taken up to live with God.'[2] The glory of his soul ascending to God was reflected in the beauty of his corpse; for his face blushed like a rose, his beard gleamed lily-white, and his hands grew pale. He looked more like one in blessed sleep.[3]

Thus the *Vita*. It is not a simple story that the author tells. He is pained, perplexed, and sometimes, perhaps, uncertain. His patron is the queen, and she must be served; but it was impossible for him suddenly to vilify Harold, one of the heroes of the earlier pages of the book. While he attributes to holy monks in heaven the view that all the English earls were in the Devil's service, he describes in neutral terms Harold's part in this last drama. Indeed, the man to whom all eyes must have turned, the man who must have been racked by hopes and fears, because of the author's tact is almost left out of the picture. The one great sinner named is Stigand, presumably a convenient and at the time of writing a harmless scapegoat. But he may have been unwisely chosen, for he seems to have been one of Edith's friends. She visited him in his disgrace after 1070 and urged him not to give way to despair and to take better care of himself.[4] The anonymous author was probably on safest ground when he attributed all mishaps generally to the sins of the church and the people and to God's vengeance. None of his contemporaries would have disagreed with that.

The author's greatest difficulty, however, was caused by his knowledge of future events. We can see that his whole presentation of the death-bed scene is controlled by his awareness of what came after. The

---

[1] 'pridie nonas Januarii' (4 January), *VEdR*, p. 80; 'on the eve of the Epiphany' (5 January), *Chron. CDE*, followed by Florence, i. 224, who identifies it, correctly, as 'feria 5', Thursday. See also below, p. 253, *n.* 1. Although Edward's translation on 13 October [1163 and 1269] was by the fifteenth century fairly generally commemorated in English Benedictine monasteries, the January festival, despite the little competition, was never popular. Westminster itself observed it on 5 January (with the octave on the 12th), and this is the date in the calendars of Abingdon, Christ Church Canterbury, Chertsey, Malmesbury, and Winchester (?Hyde). The Winchester festival was of the *depositio* (burial). The *VEdR* date for the death, 4 January, is supported only by Crowland. At Ely the festival was on 8 January. See Francis Wormald, *English Kalendars before A.D. 1100, English Benedictine Kalendars after A.D. 1100* (Henry Bradshaw Soc. lxxii, lxxvii, lxxxi, 1933, 1938, 1943-4); and for Westminster, see also below p. 265.

[2] *VEdR*, p. 55.   [3] *Ibid.*, p. 80.

[4] Malmesbury, *GP*, p. 252.

stage is wrapped in a gloom which the quarrel between Tostig and Harold and Edward's own death cannot justify. The king's death, he claims, was a funereal and mournful head to the body of a year which they would have to watch, month by month, becoming weaker because of calamities and all sorts of disasters.[1] This foreknowledge probably completely distorts the picture. To some of the actors Edward's death may have come as a great relief from tension, for many it would have offered the interest of change and novelty, to a few it was the opportunity which had long been awaited.

Among the more obscure sentences attributed in the *Vita* to Edward is that referring to the succession. 'I commend this woman with all the kingdom to your protection',[2] preceded and followed by passages almost exclusively concerned with the queen, is hardly an unambiguous statement that Edward bequeathed the kingdom to Harold. Indeed, it looks rather like a studied evasion. But since Edward next commended all his foreign servants to Harold and wished him to take an oath of fealty from them and to protect and retain them, otherwise allow them to return to the Continent, we can hardly believe that the author is describing Edward's appointment of Harold as an executor of his will in favour of someone else (unnamed), to whom he would eventually transfer these vassals.[3] The author of the *Vita* is at once being discreet and protecting the artistic presentation. Since he is writing the last Act after Harold's death, the earl can hardly be shown plainly as the king's favourite, receiving an unjust award.

There are ambiguities also in some of the other sources. On the Bayeux Tapestry Edward is pointing to a figure which we understand to be Harold; but there is no explanation. The caption reads, 'Here King Edward in bed addresses (or consoles) his vassals.'[4] And in this context the picture could mean that Edward was reminding his brother-in-law of the oath he had taken to William. The poem in the Abingdon and northern versions of the Anglo-Saxon Chronicle has 'Yet the wise ruler entrusted the realm to a man of high rank, to Harold himself', which in expression is not greatly different from the statement of the *Vita* and may even be its source. But the verses were almost certainly

---

[1] *VEdR*, p. 80.   [2] *Ibid.*, p. 79.

[3] Raymonde Foreville, 'Aux origines de la renaissance juridique', *Moyen âge*, lviii (1952), 69–72, seems to believe that the author of the *Vita* regarded Harold as an executor, and, more hesitatingly, that William of Poitiers also had this possibility in mind. But even if this were so (and it seems not), they were obviously in error.

[4] 'Hic Eadwardus rex in lecto alloquitur fideles.' See above, pl. 11.

intended to mean that Edward bequeathed the kingdom to Harold, for the St Augustine's, Canterbury, version is, 'And Earl Harold succeeded to the realm of England, just as the king had granted it to him, and as he had been chosen to the position.'[1]

This story could, of course, have been concocted by Harold's friends in order to justify his seizure of the throne. But the bedchamber does not seem to have been packed. After 1066 Edith and Robert fitz-Wimarch, whom William made sheriff of Essex, could have told the Normans that the story was a lie, that Edward *in articulo mortis* had either been speechless or had reaffirmed his nomination of William as his heir. But if there was a conspiracy, it was a conspiracy in which all who witnessed Edward's death were involved. The proof of this is the attitude of William of Poitiers, the advocate of the case that William was the lawful heir and Harold the usurper. The Norman writer twice admits that Edward on his deathbed bequeathed the throne to Harold. He allows Harold's messenger to say to William just before the battle of Hastings, 'Harold knows also that the kingdom is his by right, for it was granted to him by the gift of that same king, his lord, in his last moments. And it has been the general custom among this people, ever since St Augustine came into the land, that a gift made *in articulo mortis* is a valid act.'[2] In William's reply to Harold this point is not directly met. Then, in the ironical words addressed by William of Poitiers to the slain Harold, we find, 'Your end proves how justly you were raised to the throne by Edward's grant on his deathbed.'[3] William of Poitiers accepted the English evidence that Edward had bequeathed Harold the throne, although it was inconvenient for his case. He made the point that Harold could not accept the bequest: acceptance made him a perjurer; the act was a nullity. This was a serious argument; but, as it was unlikely to cut much ice in the faithless society of the time, it was only the best he could do in the circumstances.

One argument which was open to William of Poitiers, but one which, for obvious reasons, he chose not to use, is that Edward was out of his

---

[1] The tradition culminates in Florence, i. 224: 'subregulus Haroldus . . ., quem rex ante suam decessionem regni successorem elegerat, a totius Angliae primatibus ad regale culmen electus, die eodem ab Aldredo Eboracensi archiepiscopo in regem est honorifice consecratus.' This is almost too good to be true. Cf. also Eadmer, *Historia Novorum*, p. 8, 'et juxta quod ipse [Edwardus] ante mortem statuerat in regnum ei successit Haroldus.'

[2] Poitiers, pp. 172–3. This is not found in the archdeacon's known sources.

[3] *Ibid.*, pp. 266–8. This, too, is not based on the *Carmen*.

mind when he bequeathed the throne to Harold. And it is the failure of any contemporary to consider this point which makes our own treatment of it hazardous. The author of the *Vita* was certainly of the opinion that Edward suffered from a mental illness; he expressly mentions coma and delirium, and lets us know that Stigand thought Edward's vision the ravings of a sick man. It is extremely doubtful, even if Edward did recover consciousness just before the end, speak with a loud voice, and make some sensible remarks, whether, by modern standards, he was of sound testamentary capacity. Moreover, we must admit that pressure could have been put on the dying man to say what was required, or words uttered indistinctly could have been interpreted by the archbishop in the sense that he wanted. But these caveats were not open to contemporaries. Both English and Normans, even if for different reasons, were inclined to believe that Edward had a claim to sanctity; delirium and visions were clear signs that Edward was inspired, was swinging between life and death, was vouchsafed foretastes of eternal truth; and words spoken *in articulo mortis* were the most solemn that medieval man could imagine. But although if we could solve this problem, we should be helped in our understanding of Edward's sympathies and policy, it is profitless to investigate it further. And we must probably accept that Harold had decided to take the throne, bequest or no bequest. Indeed, it was presumably because Harold and his friends had made this decision that the bequest was made or the story of it put about.

Edward was buried in Westminster abbey on Thursday, 6 January,[1] perhaps one whole day after his death. The funeral procession is shown on the Bayeux Tapestry. Although the scenes are unlikely to be based scrupulously on first-hand accounts, they probably represent contemporary custom. We see Edward's body, almost completely prepared for the ceremony, wrapped in a woollen binding, but with the face still uncovered, while a prelate, apparently the one who appears in the death-bed scene, watches and gives his blessing. We are also shown the simple procession from Westminster Hall to the minster. The corpse, now completely shrouded, is carried head foremost on an open bier laid with a richly embroidered pall. Four men in front and four behind shoulder the poles; and there is an acolyte with bells on either side. The

---

[1] 'On the feast of the Epiphany', *Chron. CDE*, and Florence, i. 224, agrees. According to *VEdR*, p. 81, the corpse was taken to the minster where prayers were said all that day and the following night; and on the morrow Edward was buried. If, therefore, Edward died in the night of 4/5 January all accounts would be in substantial harmony.

bier is followed by a group of clergy, four choristers singing the anthem. In the church a stone sarcophagus would have been prepared, which we know was sunk in the pavement before the main altar, that dedicated to St Peter. But it does not seem that the gravestone was inscribed, for within a relatively short time it could not be identified with certainty.[1]

Osbert of Clare's description of the opening of Edward's tomb in 1102[2] gives us a little more information about the burial. When the top slab was removed, a wonderful fragrance filled the church – which suggests that the body, if not embalmed, had at least been packed with aromatics. Edward's body was seen to be wrapped in a precious pall, and there was a sceptre by his side and a crown on his head. His limbs were, apparently, free, for we are told that the hands were soft and the joints flexible, a ring was on one finger, and the sandals were not stained by any corruption. The pall covered the king's head, and, to see the face, it had to be cut beneath the chin and the long beard extracted. There was sufficient interference with the tomb on this occasion to make the translations in 1163 and 1269 untrustworthy sources of evidence for the original conditions.

According to the *Vita Ædwardi Regis* Edward was buried with full honour and ceremony.[3] A month of prayers for the dead was ordered and large sums of money were given to the poor. Edward's body 'was washed by his country's tears'. His tomb was also from the start the scene of religious manifestations. The anonymous author, echoing the 146th psalm, which was in the Office for the Dead, claimed that at the tomb, 'the blind receive their sight, the lame are made to walk, the sick are healed, and the sorrowing are refreshed by the comfort of God.'

Meanwhile, on 6 January,[4] on the day of the funeral itself and in the same church, Harold was crowned king. It is most unlikely that anyone thought it unseemly for the funeral baked meats to furnish coldly the coronation banquet. Eleventh-century man was a realist: when he required delay it was for a practical reason.[5] There could have been no

---

[1] See below, pp. 263–4.

[2] 'La vie de S. Edouard le Confesseur par Osbert de Clare', ed. Marc Bloch, *Analecta Bollandiana*, xli (1923), 121. For commentary, see Barlow, *VEdR*, pp. 113 ff. and below, pp. 268–9.

[3] *VEdR*, pp. 80–1.

[4] Date only in *Chron. E*, followed by Florence, i. 224. Poitiers, p. 146, agrees that the coronation was on the same day as the funeral.

[5] Widows were not to remarry within a year, to avoid doubt over the parentage of any child born after the first husband's death.

question of indecent haste about a coronation. William of Poitiers did not reproach Harold with ascending a throne which was still warm from Edward's occupation but with anticipating 'a popular election'.[1] To many it must have appeared that a house so quickly united was one which could withstand the storms. The omens were good.

[1] Poitiers, p. 146.

Chapter 12

THE ETERNAL KINGDOM

'King Edward, the beloved of God, weakened by the mental disease from which he was suffering, died indeed to this world, but was joyfully taken up to live with God.' 'This gem of God stripped off the corruption of his earthly body and obtained a place of eternal splendour in the diadem of the heavenly king.' 'For he has not died, but has passed from death unto life, to live with Christ.'[1] The poem in the Anglo-Saxon Chronicle expresses the same belief:

> till on a sudden came
> Death in his bitterness, bearing so dear
> A lord from the earth. And angels led
> His righteous soul to heaven's radiance.

Both Christian and pagan belief were at one in expecting a good lord to get immediate recognition in the other world. For Christians it was a hope, based on the New Testament[2] and enshrined in the Office for the Dead,[3] which was rather more optimistic than the church would allow in some other contexts, for example in its teaching on purgatory. In some degree it must be considered a popular error, part of that sub-Christian theology, that underworld of superstition, which the church largely tolerated, sometimes made use of. Few men could resist the idea that the heavenly kingdom reproduced in perfect form the pattern of the earthly kingdom;[4] that a king in this life must remain a sort of king, under 'the king of kings',[5] in the next; that a good and powerful man, such as Edward, 'lives with God as a saint in heaven.'[6]

The tradition was exceptionally strong in England. Edward's grand-

---

[1] *VEdR*, pp. 55, 79, 80.

[2] Cf. especially, John xi. 25–26; 1 John iii. 14; 1 Cor. xv. 20 ff.

[3] John xi. 25–6 and 1 Cor. xv. 20 ff. are incorporated; and cf. 'Oratio: pro uno defuncto, . . . sanctorum tuorum iubeas esse consortem' and 'Oratio: in die depositionis defuncti, Absolve, quaesumus domine, animam famuli tui N. ut defunctus saeculo, tibi vivat . . .'

[4] Cf. 'Angels in thousands stood outside around the Princely One, thegns about their king', *Andreas*, ll. 871–2. [5] 1 Tim. vi. 15. [6] *VEdR*, p. 81.

256

father, King Edgar, had a cult at Glastonbury; his aunt, St Edith, was revered at Wilton; his uncle, St Edward the Martyr, at Shaftesbury; while his brother, Alfred, was not without honour at Ely.[1] In two writs for Bury St Edmunds, issued in the mid 1040s, Edward referred to St Edmund (king of the East Angles) as his kinsman.[2] And the foreigners at court would not lag behind when it came to the apotheosis of an anointed ruler. King Henry II of Germany (1002–24) and Queen Kunigund, a healthy, apparently devoted, but childless couple, were reputed virgins, saints and confessors.[3] In *Francia* the church had done everything possible to increase the people's reverence for the weak Capetian monarchy,[4] and Robert the Pious (996–1031) had cured a blind beggar with the water provided for rinsing his hands and lepers by touching their faces and making the sign of the Cross.[5] There are indications in the *Vita Ædwardi Regis* that the French, probably Normans, led the way in attributing thaumaturgical powers to Edward.[6] But the first expressions of belief in his sanctity, that he had gone direct to Heaven and could intercede with God for earthly petitioners, were probably almost automatic. There was grief at his death, there could have been uneasiness about the future, and there may already have been in circulation rumours about his exceptional goodness and, perhaps, his chastity.

The first writer to investigate the religious aspects of Edward's life was the monk from St Bertin's monastery at St Omer in Flanders, possibly either Goscelin or Folcard, who wrote the *Vita Ædwardi Regis*.[7] This work, because of its multiple and changing purpose, is difficult enough to interpret without the further complications of the survival of only a revised edition, probably made about 1100 at Christ Church, Canterbury, in a manuscript which is now defective. The loss of folios at two different points has deprived us of the author's account of Edward's

[1] See the chart in *VEdR*, p. xii, and Barlow, *English Church*, pp. 31–3.

[2] Harmer, *Writs*, nos. 13, 14.

[3] Cf. *S. Henrici Vita*, auct. anon., Migne, *PL*, cxl, coll. 120, 127. Henry was canonized in 1146: see Renate Klauser, *Der Heinrichs- und Kunigundenkult im mittelalterlichen Bistum Bamberg* (Bamberg, 1957).

[4] Helgaud, *Epitoma vitae regis Roberti pii*, Migne, *PL*, cxli; Jean-François Lemarignier, *Autour de la royauté française du IXe au XIIIe siècle*, Bibl. de l'Ecole des Chartes, cxiii (1955), 9–13.

[5] Helgaud, *op. cit.*, coll. 915, 931.

[6] *VEdR*, pp. 62, lxxiii.

[7] *Ibid.*, pp. xiii ff.; F. Barlow, 'The Vita Ædwardi (Book II); the Seven Sleepers: Some further evidence and reflections', *Speculum*, xl (1965), 385 ff.; above, pp. xxii–xxiii.

marriage to Edith and destroyed an early version of some of the miracles. And the revision which the work has suffered was directed towards increasing the miraculous content. Nevertheless, this edition is still uncontaminated by Westminster influence, and is all the more credible for that. The original work was produced either in the royal court or within the curial circle. It was not intended to glorify the abbey in which Edward was buried.

The *Vita*, which had been started, possibly in 1065, in honour of Queen Edith's family and was originally intended to show how the king and kingdom flourished when the advice of Edith's father and brothers was taken, and possibly to demonstrate that one of the brothers was a suitable heir to the throne, could hardly after the events of 1066 be ended on any preconceived plan.[1] Edith's husband and brothers were dead; the house of Godwin was in ruins. It needed skill to turn this disaster into a triumph. But, as all men knew, 'O death, where is thy sting? O grave, where is thy victory?'[2] There was a possible outlet in Edward's victorious translation to Heaven. England was being punished for its sins; Edward because of his virtues was being rewarded; and the pious Edith would eventually be reunited with her spouse, whose virtues she had encouraged, whose weaknesses she had masked. Edward had gone before to prepare a place for her.[3] The anonymous author, by giving his work this twist, could both achieve an artistic conclusion and also hope to retain the queen's patronage and favour.

It is possible that the author lightly revised the earlier part of the work when he came to salvage his undertaking; but the essential feature of the new scheme was the addition of a second book, in which, starting again, he reinterpreted Edward's life. A second prologue gives a straightforward explanation of the change of plan.[4] The Poet complains to his Muse that she has deceived and misled him. All his labour has been lost, for the kings and earls, his lords whom he set out to praise, are dead; and the story of this disaster cannot possibly please the queen. But the Muse rebukes him for his unreasonable despair and shows him how to overcome the difficulty. An even nobler theme awaits his pen. He is to write about Edward's virtues and depict him in Heaven. He is to make known the signs with which God revealed that Edward, while still in the flesh, was pleasing to him and, when resting in the tomb, lived in Heaven. In other words, the Poet was to describe the miracles

---

[1] See below, Appendix A.
[2] 1 Cor. xv. 55.
[3] Cf. *VEdR*, p. 79; John xiv. 2–3.
[4] *VEdR*, pp. 56 ff.

which Edward worked both during his life and after his death. This new task the Poet accepted, but sadly, because of his mourning.[1]

Although the author was, perhaps, over-optimistic in his prologue, he honoured some of his promises. He reminds us of the way in which Edward was chosen king by God even before he was born,[2] and of the circumstances in which he was consecrated king more by divine providence than by man.[3] He then asserts, 'He preserved with holy chastity the dignity of his consecration, and lived his whole life dedicated to God in true innocence.' This sacrifice, he tells us, was acceptable to God, and God glorified him by certain signs, some miraculous cures which occurred while he was still 'in this life of corruption'.[4] The author's bold stroke in applying to the consecration of a king the new sacramental theology, which demanded absolute chastity from a priest as a consequence of his holy orders and prevented him from marrying, produces an elegant pattern. Edward had been marked out by God to rule over the English, had been supernaturally consecrated king, and consequently had lived a celibate life dedicated to the service of God. It is no matter that such an interpretation of Edward's life was completely fanciful, indeed rather absurd. The author is no longer in any way concerned with history.

The anonymous writer claimed to have learned of the miracles from the joint testimony of good and fitting men, that is to say, from oral tradition.[5] Owing to the lacuna in the manuscript, only two miracles can be read in the form in which they appeared about 1100, and this seems already a little removed from the primitive state.[6] Nevertheless it can hardly be doubted that shortly after Edward's death a written record was made of four or five cures with which the king was thought to have been associated, and an attempt was also made to push these signs much further back. The author of the *Vita* states immediately after his account of the first miracle,[7] 'Although this seems strange to us, the

---

[1] There is deliberate contrast here with the conclusion to the first preface, *VEdR*, p. 5, where the Poet gladly accepts the commission.

[2] *Ibid.*, pp. 60, 7–8.

[3] *Ibid.*, pp. 60, 8–9.

[4] *Ibid.*, pp. 60–1, lxxv–lxxvii; 1 Cor. xv. 42 ff.

[5] 'bonis et idoneis viris contestificantibus', *VEdR*, p. 61. The phrase almost suggests an inquest with jury.

[6] Barlow, 'The Vita Ædwardi (Book II)', pp. 394–5.

[7] *VEdR*, p. 62. This observation is rather awkwardly placed after the first of four or five miracles. It could indicate a state when only one miracle was in the text or it could be an interpolation.

Franks aver that Edward had done this often as a youth, when he was in Neustria, now known as Normandy.'

The miracles are unremarkable and could have appeared in any saint's life of the period. All the cures are performed by anointing with the water in which Edward had washed his hands; but only in the first miracle does the king himself administer the water; in the others it is done by courtiers, in the last case unbeknown to the king. In the first three cases the postulant had been instructed in a dream to approach Edward and ask for this favour. There is no suggestion that Edward ever took the initiative; indeed the impression is given that his reluctance and incredulity had to be overcome, apparently by courtiers and servants who encouraged, or at least tolerated, this business.[1] In his later years Edward maintained many poor and sick men at court,[2] and it was probably in this miserable and sycophantic society that belief in Edward's thaumaturgical power took root. But the recorded miracles are few in number. The author of the *Vita* may have been encouraged by much vague talk about Edward's miraculous powers only to find on closer investigation that there was little substance beneath it.

He probably described four or five cures.[3] The first was of an unidentified scrofulous and barren woman at a place and time unknown. When cured she conceived and bore twins.[4] The second was of a blind man on the eve of All Saints day. This man, after being cured, lived a long time at court. The other miracles we have only in twelfth-century versions. The third was of a blind man from Lincoln (and there was still a witness alive who remembered him before and after the cure). The fourth is the only one for which we have individual detail. Wulfwi 'Spillecorn', the son of Wulfmaer of Ludgarshall in Buckinghamshire, a workman helping to build a royal hunting lodge at nearby Brill, suddenly went blind, and at Windsor was informed by a woman that nineteen years later, after he had visited eighty, or eighty-seven, churches, he would be cured by the king's washing water. After the cure, which was indeed performed at Windsor, Edward appointed him keeper of the royal palace at Windsor (William of Malmesbury) or at Westminster (Osbert of Clare), where he still was in 1066. Westminster

---

[1] Cf. *VEdR*, p. 62. William of Malmesbury exaggerates this feature; Osbert of Clare erases it, by showing the servants as obstructive; cf. *ibid.*, p. 65.

[2] *Ibid.*, p. 41. The first cure at the tomb was of a poor cripple who had been maintained by the king: below, p. 262.

[3] *VEdR*, pp. 61 ff. Barlow, 'The Vita Ædwardi (Book II)', pp. 385 ff.

[4] According to Malmesbury, *GR*, i. 273, who gives a somewhat different version.

abbey claimed that Windsor was one of the estates that Edward granted it in 1066;[1] and we probably owe the uncharacteristic detail of this story to its having been worked up in the monastery. In the final miracle a courtier, who had witnessed the previous one, took what remained of the water and with it cured four beggars, three totally blind, the leader monocular.

This is a poor collection of miracle stories. Contemporaries would have noticed the general lack of circumstantial detail (all the more noticeable because of the one exception) and the failure to name the witnesses. They would have been as unimpressed as are we. Even more disconcerting is the failure of the author to give us that account of the posthumous signs which he promised in the prologue. It is possible, of course, that in our unique manuscript we have an incomplete edition of the work, that the final section had been lost between 1067 and 1100. But neither was it present in the manuscript used by William of Malmesbury before 1125. And the only miracles that we have for 1066 and the next few years are provided by Osbert of Clare, prior of Westminster, in the new book on St Edward that he wrote in 1138. At least the first two of these could have been based on the concluding pages of the *Vita Ædwardi Regis*; but as the next three are in content and style quite unlike the earlier work, and all five are Westminster abbey stories, it would seem that the whole group was first brought into the legend by Osbert, presumably in order to remedy the defect he found in the plan of the *Vita*.[2] If this is so, it is unlikely that the author of the *Vita* ever completed his revised scheme. As with the earlier signs, so with those at the tomb, rumour may have promised much and furnished little. And as those months became 'weak from tribulation and manifold disaster',[3] the author may have realized that the whole project had indeed been labour in vain. In 1066–7 there was no honour or profit to be had from publishing an account of the queen's family, even one showing Edward as a saint.

The five miracles provided by Osbert of Clare for the period immediately after Edward's death are, just as before, a scraping of the barrel. Osbert several times remarks on the vast number of miracles that he has

---

[1] *KCD*, no. 824, p. 178 (Sawyer, no. 1043): one of Osbert of Clare's forgeries.

[2] Marc Bloch, 'La vie de S. Edouard le Confesseur par Osbert de Clare', *Analecta Bollandiana*, xli (1923), pp. 112 ff. They are not unlike the five miraculous stories which Osbert inserts earlier into the life, *ibid.*, pp. 75, 80, 82, 83, 91. See below, pp. 273–4.

[3] *VEdR*, p. 80.

left untold, so as not to weary the reader;[1] but one feels that in fact he had to make use of everything capable of exploitation. Within eight days of Edward's death a Norman cripple named Ralf, who had been maintained by royal alms, was cured at the tomb; and within thirty days six blind men, led by one who was monocular,[2] likewise were miraculously cured. These two events occurred during the *tricenarium*, the month of prayers for the deceased, and should have been known to the author of the *Vita*. Next comes a vision which Abbot Ælfwine of Ramsey had in his sleep when King Harold was marching north against Harald Hardrada of Norway and Tostig. Edward told Ælfwine to encourage his lord with the news that he would be victorious (at Stamford Bridge). Although this patriotic story also could have been in circulation while the anonymous author was writing, it is not in its present form of that period. Since Harald (Sigurdsson) is called Harold 'Fairhair', the story is based on the Anglo-Saxon Chronicle,[3] and so is a literary composition. The fourth miracle is the cure of a blind bell-ringer in Westminster abbey, who, when resting before nones one summer afternoon, saw in a dream Edward leave his tomb and tell him to summon the monks for the noon office. When he awoke he could see.

With the fifth miracle we enter that world of fabricated history which Osbert of Clare was to make so much his own.[4] The story of Ælfwine of Ramsey may be an essay in this vein; but in the account of how Archbishop Lanfranc tried to depose Bishop Wulfstan of Worcester in a council held at Westminster we see Osbert up to all his tricks. According to the story Wulfstan insisted on giving his crozier back to Edward, who had invested him with it, and Edward refused to let it go again. The metal spike went into the stone of the tomb as though into wax. The quality of Osbert's historical reconstructions is shown by the fact that, although the only time when Wulfstan could have been in danger was

---

[1] 'La vie de S. Edouard', p. 123; cf. *The Letters of Osbert of Clare*, ed. E. W. Williamson (1929), p. 84.

[2] It is perhaps mere coincidence that Osbert's six blind men with a monocular leader balance the three and the four (including a one-eyed leader) cured in Edward's lifetime.

[3] 'agnomine vocabatur lingua danica rex eorum predictus Haroldus pulcre crinus'. *Chron. D, s.a.* 1066, has 'Harold Harfagera', and is followed by all the English chroniclers. Cf. Körner, *Battle of Hastings*, p. 27.

[4] It was Osbert who first identified the original founder of the monastery as Saeberht, the early seventh-century king of Essex, J. Armitage Robinson, *Flete's History of Westminster Abbey* (1909), p. 9. And it was possibly he who named Saeberht's wife, Æthelgotha: see above, p. 165.

in 1070, when papal legates deposed Stigand and some other English bishops, not only is Lanfranc made president of the council, but Bishop Gundulf of Rochester (1077–1108) is given a part in the drama. It is possible that the story first came into being to explain a decoration over the tomb which in the twelfth century was attributed to William the Conqueror's amazement at this miracle.[1]

As the next series of miracles at Edward's tomb does not start until about 1134,[2] we can hold with assurance that a popular cult of the king had hardly begun to show at Westminster when it virtually came to an end. This, after all, was the usual pattern. Grief created an interest which soon waned. Each new cult had to compete with those already in existence. Only exceptional momentum in extraordinarily favourable circumstances could carry a new shrine through the slump which followed the cessation of intensive prayers for the dead. Although Abbot Eadwine (1049–70) may well have encouraged respect for Edward's memory,[3] it is unlikely that his Norman successors, Geoffrey, Vitalis (c. 1076–? 1085), and Gilbert Crispin (? 1085–1117),[4] would have taken much interest in it. We can get some idea of the attitude under Vitalis from Sulcard's history of the abbey. Sulcard was possibly a newcomer to the house and relied mostly on written sources. Certainly he read the *Vita Ædwardi Regis* and used it to describe the church and its dedication in 1066.[5] But the only saint he was interested in was St Peter, who had personally dedicated the earlier church. He completely ignored all the hagiographical elements in the *Vita*, and concluded his rather cool account of their latest royal benefactor with the words, based on the *Vita*,[6] 'He survived, alas, only a few more days. After he had been fortified by the last rites, he died and was buried, it seems, before the very altar of the prince of the apostles amid the groans of England and

---

[1] 'Qua de causa triumphator Anglorum Willelmus super sanctum regem Eadwardum ex auro et argento capsę fabricam condidit, quę utique in odiernum diem [1138] in ecclesia beati Petri apostoli gloriosum corpus obumbrat et tegit.', Osbert, cap. xxix, ed. Bloch, p. 116. William of Malmesbury, who has little to say about Westminster, regarded the Conqueror as a greater benefactor of the abbey than Edward. *GP*, p. 141.

[2] *VEdR*, pp. 124 ff.   [3] *Flete's History of Westminster Abbey*, pp. 82–3.

[4] Geoffrey, formerly abbot of Jumièges, was sent back there by William and Lanfranc. Vitalis had been abbot of Bernay, a cell of Fécamp. Gilbert was a monk of Bec, a pupil of Lanfranc and Anselm. For these men, see *ibid.*, pp. 84–7, 141–2, and J. Armitage Robinson, *Gilbert Crispin, abbot of Westminster* (1911), pp. 1 ff.

[5] *VEdR*, pp. xxxiv–xxxv, 71–2; Bernhard W. Scholz, 'Sulcard of Westminster: "Prologus de construccione Westmonasterii" ', *Traditio*, xx (1964), 91.

[6] *VEdR*, p. 72, *n.* 3; ed. Scholz, p. 91.

the neighbouring lands.' The cautious way in which he locates the grave
is most revealing. About fifteen years after Edward's death the monks
were not absolutely sure which was Edward's tomb. There could hardly
have been a constant stream of pilgrims to the grave.

If there was no strong popular cult at Westminster in the early
Norman period we could hardly expect to find one elsewhere. The
hagiographer, Goscelin of St Bertin, who between 1080 and 1107 wrote
saints' lives in the monasteries of Peterborough, Barking, Ely, Ramsey,
and St Augustine's, Canterbury, did not refer to Edward as a candidate
for sanctity in any of his identified writings, although he was steeped in
England's religious history and at first was hostile to the Normans.[1]
Between 1077 and 1079 Goscelin wrote the life of St Wulfsige for his
patron, Bishop Herman of Sherborne. Wulfsige, a Londoner, was oblate,
monk, and abbot of Westminster before holding the bishopric of Sherborne in plurality. Goscelin brings St Edward, king and martyr, and
St Edith into his story, but not the even more obvious Edward, the son
of Æthelred.[2] Coleman, writing at Worcester,[3] Herman at Bury St
Edmunds,[4] Turgot at Durham,[5] Eadmer at Christ Church, Canterbury,[6] Dominic at Evesham,[7] and Orderic Vital at St Evroul[8] treated
Edward with a varying degree of respect, but did not consider him a
saint. William of Malmesbury knew the *Vita* and made use of it in his
histories.[9] He reported the marvels, but refused to commit himself. He
did not know what to make of Edward and his reign.

We get the impression from Ailred's *Vita sancti Edwardi*, in a section
probably based on a collection of miracles provided by Osbert of Clare,[10]
that by the time of Henry I's death miracles were no longer taking place
at Edward's tomb. On one anniversary Osbert, when suffering from

---

[1] *VEdR*, pp. l–li, 91 ff.

[2] C. H. Talbot, 'The Life of Saint Wulsin of Sherborne by Goscelin', *Revue Bénédictine*, lxix (1959), pp. 68–85.

[3] *Vita Wulfstani*. Moreover Wulfstan was partial to stories about women as tempters
and how they could be withstood: see pp. 6–7, 12; cf. 31.

[4] 'Heremanni archidiaconi miracula sancti Eadmundi', *Ungedruckte Anglo-Normannische Geschichtsquellen*, ed. F. Liebermann (Strassburg, 1879), pp. 238–9, 244.

[5] *Vita S. Margaretae Scotorum reginae*, in *Symeonis Dunelmensis opera*, ed. J. Hodgson
Hinde, Surtees Soc., li (1868), p. 237.

[6] Cf. *Historia Novorum*, pp. 5–8.

[7] 'Liber de miraculis S. Ecgwini', *Chronicon Abbatiae de Evesham*, ed. W. D. Macray
(Rolls ser. 1863), p. 44.

[8] Orderic, *passim*; cf. ii. 118 (ed. Chibnall, ii. 136), 'piae memoriae rex Eduardus'.

[9] Malmesbury, *GR*, i. 271–8. See also his *Hist. Nov.* ed. K. R. Potter, p.4.

[10] Migne, *PL*, cxcv, coll. 783–9; *VEdR*, pp. xxxvi f., 124–8.

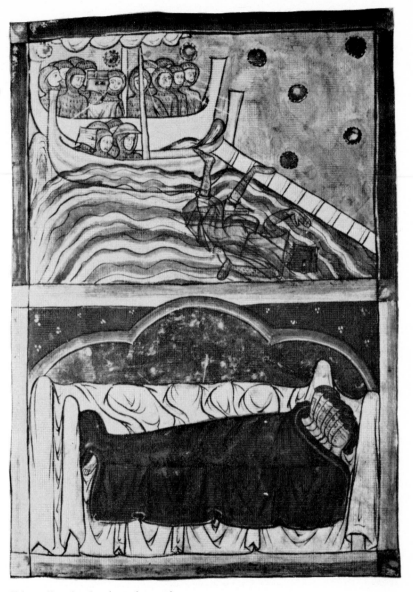

Edward's miracles (see plate 14)

15(a). Edward's vision of the drowning of King Svein of Denmark.
  (b). Edward's vision of the Seven Sleepers of Ephesus.

Edward's miracles (see plate 14)

16(a). Edward and Earl Leofric at mass in Westminster abbey see Jesus in the flesh.
  (b). Edward recovers from a pilgrim the ring which he had given to a beggar who
        was St John the Evangelist in disguise.

fever, prayed at the tomb and asked, 'Where are the marvels that our forefathers have told about you? Where are the miracles you worked in their days?' It was, indeed, probably the liturgy which kept Edward's memory alive at Westminster and provided a basis on which either popular fervour or monastic interest could build.[1] Although for the pre-canonization period we have no details of a special mass, with its own proper, for Edward's anniversary, it is most unlikely that the day was not continuously commemorated or that special prayers were not devised. About 1137, when the abbacy was vacant, the prior, Osbert of Clare, celebrated the anniversary mass on 5 January,[2] and, after the Lesson, preached to the large congregation, which, we are told, had, as usual, flocked to the abbey from the city to be present both at the vigil (the nocturnal office) and the mass. Among the worshippers was the keeper of the royal palace at Westminster, a knight named Gerin,[3] who was so inspired by the sermon that he kept vigil at the tomb the following night and was cured of a fever. 'Edward heard Gerin and Christ Edward.' Osbert had preached about Edward's humility, patience, and chastity, and had proved his special standing with God from his miracles, including the one which he himself had experienced. It is unlikely that Osbert had introduced, or reintroduced, the commemorative mass; but clearly he was transforming it into a feast for a saint.

The liturgy always made possible a local renewal of popular interest in Westminster's royal benefactor, and in the twelfth century Edward's reputation began to improve. In the reign of Henry I (1100–35) things English began to come back into fashion. Henry, who had been born in England, married Edith, the daughter of Margaret and Malcolm of Scots. At the Scottish court the view was already developing that the children of Margaret were in the true line of descent from the Old-English kings.[4] Within two years of the marriage Edward's tomb was opened and the body inspected.[5] Henry's coronation charter gave back

---

[1] See Renate Klauser, *Der Heinrichs- und Kunigundenkult im mittelalterlichen Bistum Bamberg* (Bamberg, 1957), pp. 36 ff.

[2] The eve of the Epiphany, coll. 786–7. Cf. also Osbert's cure the year before, col. 785.

[3] Abbot Gervase made a grant to Gerin, described as 'ministro regis et homini meo', Pierre Chaplais, 'The original charters of Herbert and Gervase abbots of Westminster (1121–1157)', *A Medieval Miscellany for Doris Mary Stenton*, ed. Patricia M. Barnes and C. F. Slade (Pipe Roll Soc. 1962), pp. 101–2.

[4] Cf. F. M. Powicke, *The Life of Ailred of Rievaulx by Walter Daniel* (Nelson's Medieval Classics, 1950), pp. xli–xlii.

[5] Below, pp. 267 ff.

to his people the *laga Eadwardi*, the laws of King Edward; and it was not long before these laws were collected together.[1] The rebuilding of so many churches had aroused an interest in the bodies which were disturbed, and new Latin Lives of English saints were produced in many monasteries. William of Malmesbury thought it disgraceful that so little was known about England's ecclesiastical history, and in 1124-5 wrote his *Gesta pontificum Anglorum* to remedy the ignorance.[2] And not only were Normans becoming more tolerant of the English past and English culture, but also the English were beginning to assert themselves again. About the year 1112, through the faith of Englishmen, miracles began to occur in Crowland abbey at the tomb of Waltheof, the earl whom the Conqueror had had executed in 1075 as a traitor. And although at least one of the monks derided this cult, the abbot decided not to interfere.[3] In the late twelfth century there was an attempt to rehabilitate Harold Godwinesson, and marvellous tales were told about him.[4] At some point in this swing of fashion a reappraisal of Edward was almost inevitable.

When we remember that Westminster abbey did not possess a fashionable shrine, that it was outshone by the East minster, St Paul's, with its cult of St Erkenwald,[5] and that it owned a copy of the *Vita*, it is the monastery's slowness in exploiting Edward which is remarkable. All the more so, because it seems that there was always some popular interest in Edward.[6] It must be that Abbot Vitalis and then Gilbert Crispin actively discouraged it. Both may have considered it subversive; Gilbert may have had an aristocratic contempt for the more vulgar

---

[1] William Rufus may have made similar promises in 1088 after his accession: *Chron. E*, p. 167; Florence, ii. 23; *Ann. Winchcombe*, ed. R. R. Darlington, *A Medieval Miscellany for Doris Mary Stenton*, p. 119. Henry I's charter, caps. 13, 9, *Select Charters of Eng. Const. Hist.*, ed. W. Stubbs and H. W. C. Davis (9th ed. 1911), p. 119. *Leges Edwardi Confessoris, c.* 1130-5, Liebermann, *Die Gesetze*, pp. 627 ff.

[2] *GP*, p. 4.

[3] Ordericus Vitalis, ii. 288-90 (ed. Chibnall, ii. 348-50); 'Vita et passio Waldevi comitis', *Chroniques Anglo-Normandes*, ed. F. Michel (Rouen, 1836), ii. 111-23; 'Miracula S. Waldevi gloriosi martyris', *ibid.*, pp. 131-42. Most of those cured have English names. See also Malmesbury *GP*, p. 322.

[4] *Vita Haroldi*, ed. W. De Gray Birch (1885).

[5] In the early-eleventh-century guide to the shrines of England, which was translated into Latin and lightly revised before 1085, Bishop Erconwald's tomb 'on Lundenbirig' is listed, but Westminster is omitted. *Die Heiligen Englands*, ed. F. Liebermann (Hannover, 1889), pp. 13-14.

[6] In 1086 the jurors in Babergh Hundred, on the Sussex–Essex border, south of Bury St Edmunds, described Edward thrice as *rex gloriosus*, *DB*, ii. 415b, 416b, 425.

types of popular religion. We know from Gilbert's life of Herlwin, the founder of Bec, that he was a highly intelligent man, deeply religious, spiritual, the flower of reformed Benedictine culture. But we also see that however tempted he may have been to portray Herlwin as a saint, he stopped just short. After describing Herlwin's victories of faith, he wrote, 'These are miracles that we relate, and much to be preferred to the kind which the mob regards as such, although even those were not lacking.'[1] So fastidious a man would not have allowed his abbey to be turned into a sensational hospital.

Nevertheless, it is possible that the pressure had begun to build up. Edward's widow died at Winchester a week before Christmas 1075, and William had her body brought to Westminster, where he was keeping the festival, and buried with great honour near her husband.[2] He then wrote to John, abbot of Fécamp, about appointing Vitalis, one of his monks, to Westminster, a place he held in great veneration, for entombed there were 'his lord, King Edward' and Edward's 'illustrious wife'.[3] In 1102 it was decided to open Edward's grave.[4] Our only authority for this event is Osbert of Clare, writing in 1138, a man whom we know to have been deeply involved in fraud. What is more, the condition of the corpse was an important point in the case he was making for Edward's sanctity. But there is reason to think that the grave was opened in this period,[5] and Osbert's account contains no improbabilities. Osbert does not give us the exact reason for the inspection, which, although there seems to have been no removal of the body, he calls the first translation.[6] Perhaps Abbot Gilbert Crispin wanted to settle once and for all the exact location of Edward's tomb; perhaps the abbey was about to erect that ornament to which Osbert ascribes an earlier origin;[7] but it may well be that some persons, perhaps Westminster monks, who had read the *Vita Ædwardi Regis*, were claiming

[1] J. Armitage Robinson, *Gilbert Crispin, abbot of Westminster*, p. 92.

[2] *Chron. DE*; Florence, ii. 11. Malmesbury *GR*, p.332.

[3] J. Mabillon, *Vetera Analecta* (1723), p. 450.

[4] Osbert, ed. Bloch, p. 121, where it is stated that Edward had been in the tomb for thirty-six years. In 1160 (see below, pp. 314–15, 321, 323) the abbey claimed that Edward had been buried [? more than] thirty-five years, seven *lustra*, when the inspection took place.

[5] Osbert clearly had confidence in the tradition; and a rifling of the tomb is the easiest explanation of how Edward's crown and sceptre came into the abbey's possesssion: see below, p. 269.

[6] Ailred of Rievaulx, *Vita sancti Edwardi regis*, Migne, *PL*, cxcv, col. 781 follows Osbert in this obvious exaggeration.   [7] See above, p. 263.

that Edward was a saint. In the autumn of 1102 Archbishop Anselm held a council in the abbey at which it was decreed, *inter alia*, that no one, innovating rashly, should, as had been known to happen, pay reverence to the bodies of the dead, springs of water, or other objects as something sacred, without the authority of the diocesan bishop.[1] This prohibition may have brought the matter to a head. The simplest way to answer all the questions that were being asked was to open the tomb.[2]

According to Osbert, Abbot Gilbert invited many honest persons, including Bishop Gundulf of Rochester, to the ceremony. It is probable that Westminster claimed to be exempt from the jurisdiction of the bishop of London; but in any case, Gundulf seems to have been regarded as the prelate most suitable to take part in this sort of rite.[3] As Edward had been dead for thirty-six years, not a few of the company thought that he would be reduced to ashes. Some, with religious longing, were expecting a sign of divinity in him because the virginity of his body had never been harmed. And there were some saintly monks, who had had the good fortune to see him when he was alive, who were moved by their great love for him to want to gaze again on his dear countenance. This is Osbert of Clare in an unusually restrained mood: only a few of those attending the ceremony predicted marvels. But Osbert had no reason to exaggerate here; it was before he had opened men's eyes to the truth. When the top slab of the sarcophagus was removed a sweet fragrance filled the church and the body was found to be whole and in no way decomposed. After Gundulf had released the head and beard from the covering pall, he tried to pull out a hair from

---

[1] Eadmer, *Historia Novorum*, p. 143.

[2] A similar investigation of St Cuthbert's tomb at Durham was carried out on 24 August 1104: 'Capitula de Miraculis et Translationibus sancti Cuthberti', *Symeonis monachi Opera Omnia*, ed. T. Arnold (Rolls ser. 1882), i. 247 ff. There were doubters who attacked the official view that the church possessed the incorrupt body of the saint. Some alleged that the body had been removed elsewhere and explained the miracles at the tomb as due only to its persisting influence; some argued that, although the tomb doubtless contained sacred relics, to believe that the body was incorrupt was to go against the law of nature, to accept something which was entirely unproved, and to expect a marvel which was denied to the majority of saints. The controversy was harmful to the brethren's faith and a cause for shame. But completion of the new church and the need to translate the relics allowed the matter to be put to the test. St Cuthbert was found to be present and incorrupt.

[3] H. Wharton, *Anglia Sacra* (1691), ii. 285; R. A. L. Smith, 'The place of Gundulf in the Anglo-Norman church', *EHR*, lviii (1943), 257–72. In inviting outsiders they were wiser than the Durham monks in 1104, who had to allow a second, impartial inspection after not only another abbot but also their own bishop had doubted their findings, *loc. cit.*, pp. 254–9.

the beard, but desisted when rebuked by the abbot. Finally 'they shut up in the sepulchre the holy body that they had found completely intact', apparently replacing the same slab that they had removed.[1]

But if the abbot strained at a hair, he may have swallowed more serious depredations. According to Osbert the king had a crown on his head, a sceptre at his side, and a ring on his finger. Only the ring, or a ring, seems to have been there when next the grave was opened;[2] and it is quite likely that it was by abstracting the other regalia from the coffin that Westminster started that collection of coronation ornaments of which it became so proud. Osbert was fond of associating Edward with a crown and sceptre; and in the forged charters, for which he seems to have been responsible, it was claimed that Edward had bequeathed his crown and other regalia to the abbey.[3] We may be sure that the Conqueror would not have allowed crowns, sceptres, and other symbols of royal power to exist outside his own treasuries. Edward's 'bequest' was probably executed surreptitiously thirty-six years after his death.

Just as we do not know the exact reason for the inspection of 1102, so also we are ignorant of the effect it had on Edward's posthumous reputation. Osbert subjoined the statement that many marvels took place at the tomb, which, however, he would not describe for fear of wearying the reader.[4] We must assume, therefore, that nothing of much importance occurred, or, at least, nothing which the monastery thought worthy of record. The discovery that Edward's body was incorrupt was not a decisive turning point. Nevertheless we know from writs of Abbot Gilbert that Edward's tomb had become a recognized place of sanctuary for criminals.[5] It may merely have been a convenient spot before the high altar, but at least it kept the king in the public mind. We also see in Henry I's reign the first signs of royal interest in Westminster and Edward. There was no national mausoleum for the Norman and Angevin kings of England. William I was buried in his monastery of St Stephen's at Caen, William II at Winchester, Henry I

---

[1] At the translation of 1163 Archbishop Thomas obviously believed that he was removing the stone into which Wulfstan had stuck his staff: see below, p. 284.

[2] See below, p. 282.

[3] *Inspeximus* in 1335 of a diploma dated 1067, *Calendar of the Charter Rolls Preserved in the Public Record Office* (1912), iv. 330.

[4] *Vita beati Eadwardi*, ed. Bloch, p. 123.

[5] J. Armitage Robinson, *Gilbert Crispin, abbot of Westminster*, p. 37; W. Dugdale, *Monasticon Anglicanum* (1817), i. 310, where similar letters testimonial of Abbots Herbert, Gervase, and Laurence are printed.

in his foundation at Reading, and Stephen in his foundation at Faversham. Henry III was the first of the foreign kings to be buried in Westminster abbey. But Henry I's wife, Edith or Matilda, the daughter of Margaret of Scots, Æthelred's great-great-granddaughter, died in 1118 at Westminster and was buried there. She had been educated at Wilton and may have taken some interest in her namesake, Edward's queen, who had been a great benefactor of that nunnery. It was presumably by her own wish that she was buried on the other side of Edward to form a balancing family group. The St Albans chronicler believed that she proved she dwelt in Heaven by working some miracles at her tomb.[1]

It is sometimes claimed that Henry I touched for the king's evil, that is to say, scrofula or tubercular infection of the lymphatic glands. If he did, there could be some connexion with the cult of Edward. The evidence is very obscure.[2] By the late thirteenth century touching had become an established royal activity in both France and England. In the Capetian line Louis VI (1108–37) and Robert the Pious (996–1031) can be claimed as isolated forerunners. For England the prehistory is even less substantial. After the claims made for Edward, William of Malmesbury provides in 1118–25 some ambiguous material. He was interested in medicine and popularized the term *morbus regius* (the royal disease, or King's Evil), which for him meant leprosy. His study of Anglo-Saxon history had familiarized him with royal saints and miracles; and he included in his *Gesta Regum* the cures attributed to Edward which he found in an extended version of *Vita Ædwardi Regis*. He repeated the anonymous author's remark after the first miracle (the cure of the woman with diseased glands), 'whereas this cure may seem a novelty to us, the French [i.e. the Normans] say that Edward did this often when he was a young man in Normandy.' But he then added, 'And so today some men set out to deceive by asserting that the power

[1] *Chron. E*, Florence, ii. 71; Orderic (ed. Chibnall), vi. 188. She was buried while the abbey was vacant after the death of Abbot Gilbert (6 December 1117). Osbert was probably elected prior and, perhaps, abbot during the vacancy: see below, p. 272. For the miracles, see *Rogeri de Wendover Chronica*, ed. H. O. Coxe (Eng. Hist. Soc. 1841), ii. 194–5; Matthew Paris, *Historia Anglorum*, ed. Sir F. Madden (Rolls ser. 1866), i. 222; Matthew Paris, *Historia Majora*, ed. H. R. Luard (Rolls ser. 1874), ii. 144.

[2] Marc Bloch, *Les rois thaumaturges* (Strasbourg, 1924); J. F. Lemarignier, *Autour de la royauté française du IXe au XIIIe siècle*, Bibl. de l'Ecole des Chartes, cxiii (1955), 10–11; R. W. Southern, 'The First Life of Edward the Confessor', *EHR*, lviii (1943), 389–91; P. E. Schramm, *A History of the English Coronation* (trans. L. G. Wickham Legg, 1937), pp. 122 ff.

to cure this sort of disease is not the product of holiness, but an hereditary royal prerogative.'[1]

This dictum is probably an answer to an anecdote in Guibert of Nogent's *De pignoribus sanctorum*. The abbot, when illustrating how God works through unlikely agents, claimed that he had once seen Louis VI touch the scrofulous and that even his father, Philip I (1060–1108), had touched before he lost the power because of his sins. No English king, he added, to the best of his knowledge had ever attempted such a cure.[2] William answered that it was holiness not royalty which allowed some kings to cure the sick. It may also be inferred that, except for Edward, he did not dispute Guibert's observation on the English kings. Indeed, it seems most unlikely that anyone thought that William I or his sons had curative powers. The subject is neglected by the unidentified theologian known as the Norman Anonymous. If anyone of ecclesiastical importance in Normandy and England in the late eleventh century believed that the Anglo-Norman kings had this power, he would have known and the matter would have been grist to his mill. He was one of the greatest apologists for Anglo-Norman sacramental kingship; it has even been suggested that his collection of essays are a course of lectures intended to be delivered to important clergy at the royal court;[3] and his disregard of this topic cannot be brushed aside.

After the flurry of interest in the 1120s there is no further evidence for France until the 1250s and nothing in England, apart from an inconclusive remark of Peter of Blois in the 1180s, before the fourteenth century. The archdeacon of Bath, in a rhetorical exercise in defence of clerks entering royal service, wrote that there was something holy about serving the lord king for by virtue of the sacrament of unction at his coronation he was *christus* and could banish the disease which attacks the groin and cure scrofulas.[4] This remark shows that thaumaturgical powers had been, or were still being, made on behalf of royalty, Capetian, Angevin, or both. But it is cautionary to notice that there is no reference to royal cures in the extensive polemical writings concerned with the Becket affair, although they would have served as a useful royalist debating point.

[1] Karl Pellens, *Die Texte des normannischen Anonymus* (Wiesbaden, 1966), pp. xv, xxix ff., 45 *n.*, 51 *n.*, 95 *n.*
[2] Migne *PL*, clvi. 616.
[3] *GR*, i. 273.
[4] Epp. 14, 150, Migne *PL*, ccvii. 42, 439. For the date, J. A. Robinson, 'Early Somerset archdeacons', *Somerset Historical Essays* (1921), pp. 113–14.

On the evidence it is unlikely that Henry I touched or that it was ever claimed that he did. But William of Malmesbury created a splendid background for his 'new monarchy', provided him with an *antecessor* who worked miracles, and set in motion a new type of rivalry with the French dynasty. In these circumstances a champion of Edward's sanctity was almost bound to emerge. In 1121, after a four years' vacancy at Westminster, Herbert, the almoner, was appointed abbot; and we can form an idea of Westminster's attitude towards Edward in 1122 from the monastery's *titulus* in the mortuary roll of Abbot Vitalis of Savigny.[1] Westminster first asked for reciprocal services for the souls of King Edward (written in majuscules), Abbots Vitalis and Gilbert Crispin, and six monks. But the list was then corrected. Before Edward's name were inserted Kings Offa and Edgar, and after it was added Queen Matilda (i.e. Edith). Some monks had thought that only one lay patron was worthy of honour; others had disagreed and had imposed their will.

It is from this same period that we can trace the career of Osbert, whose campaign on Edward's behalf, although itself a failure, enabled others to obtain the canonization. Osbert, who came from Clare in Suffolk, was a monk, and perhaps prior and probably a candidate for the abbacy, when the king appointed Herbert.[2] He was a man who espoused causes; and although we do not know when he first became interested in Edward, he had in the vacancy of 1117–21 at least the opportunity to develop schemes of his own. He soon quarrelled with Herbert and suffered the first of several banishments to other monasteries. Exile probably hardened his resolve. The movement to get Edward recognized as a saint was part of a general restatement of Westminster's rights and claims in which Osbert, or a group of monks led by him, became engaged. It is likely that Osbert believed that he was acting in defence of the true privileges of the abbey against all oppressive authorities, including worldly abbots appointed by the king. Certainly he posed as a reformer in his quarrel with Herbert;[3] but,

---

[1] *Rouleau Mortuaire du B. Vital, abbé de Savigni*, ed. Léopold Delisle (Paris, 1909), pl. xxvii, tit. 100.

[2] See J. Armitage Robinson, 'Westminster in the twelfth century: Osbert of Clare', *Church Quarterly Review*, lxviii (1909), 337–47; reprinted in *The Letters of Osbert of Clare*, ed. E. W. Williamson (1929), 1–20; Williamson, *ibid.*, pp. 21–37; Pierre Chaplais, 'The original charters of Herbert and Gervase abbots of Westminster (1121–1157)', *A Medieval Miscellany for Doris Mary Stenton*, pp. 89 ff.

[3] H. G. Richardson and G. O. Sayles, *The Governance of Medieval England* (1963), pp. 413 ff., regard Herbert as a dilapidator and his successor, Gervase of Blois, as a respectable abbot.

although he had every reason to criticize, his attitude was not devoid of self-interest, for his several reminders from exile of his desire for a healthy and free church[1] were not without reference to his own disappointed ambitions. It was possibly when he began to attack Herbert's dilapidations that he discovered that the abbey's muniments were defective and entirely unsuitable for an age which paid increasing attention to *ius scriptum*. Apparently there was little documentary proof of the grants of lands and privileges which the monastery attributed to Edward. No doubt some writs had been preserved, but, possibly because of Edward's untimely death, no charters, or at least none answering to the needs of the twelfth century, had been drawn up. Osbert and his friends remedied this deficiency by 'reconstructing' a series of charters granting the rights to which they thought the monastery was entitled. They produced, however, very clumsy forgeries, which are no credit to Osbert's historical scholarship.

This activity had a crucial effect on Edward's reputation. As he was being proclaimed the abbey's greatest patron, he was deserving of every honour; and the creation of memorials to his generosity, piety, and far-sightedness helped in the campaign to get him recognized as a saint. Moreover, if he was a saint, his charters would have unassailable authority; and if his sanctity was recognized, pilgrims to his tomb would increase not only the monastery's fame but also its revenue. Hence Edward, like the muniments, had to be refurbished. Some work was done on revising the *Vita Ædwardi Regis*.[2] It is likely that between 1100 and 1124 the account of the miracles was expanded, the vision of the Seven Sleepers was added,[3] and Edward's death-bed prophesy was brought up to date. It was in this form that William of Malmesbury knew the *Vita*. Also material concerning Edward was either collected or fabricated. Edward's vision of the Seven Sleepers of Ephesus and its interpretation were not Westminster creations; but once the fable was known to the abbey it probably served as a model for some similar stories. There were produced Edward's vision of the death of Svein junior, king of Denmark, drowned when embarking to invade and

[1] *The Letters of Osbert*, nos. 2 (p. 51), 3 (pp. 54, 56), 4 (pp. 60–1).

[2] F. Barlow, 'The *Vita Ædwardi* (Book II); the Seven Sleepers: some further evidence and reflections', *Speculum*, xl (1965), pp. 391–5.

[3] The story of how Edward one Easter Sunday, when dining in his palace at Westminster after mass in the abbey, broke into indecorous laughter because he had seen the seven saints at Ephesus, sleeping in their cave on Mt Celius, turn over from their right sides to their left – a sinister event presaging disaster. *Ibid.*, pp. 385 ff.

conquer England;[1] the story of how Edward at the dedication of a church to St John the Evangelist gave a ring to a beggar who was St John in disguise and who returned it by means of some English pilgrims who lost their way on the road to Jerusalem;[2] a hermit's vision of St Peter ordering Edward to restore Westminster;[3] Edward and Earl Leofric of Mercia at mass at Westminster seeing Christ in person;[4] the divine punishment of a fisherman who withheld tithe from Westminster;[5] and Edward's cure of an Irish cripple, Gillomichael, by carrying him on his back from his palace to the abbey on the orders of St Peter.[6]

About 1134, when Abbot Herbert was old and perhaps incapacitated, Osbert returned to Westminster as prior[7] and busied himself with the foundation of a house of canonesses at Kilburn, who, among their duties, were to pray for the soul of King Edward, founder of the church of Westminster, and for the souls of all its brethren and benefactors.[8] As Westminster was without an abbot from 1136 until the end of 1138, Osbert had a free hand. A popular cult of Edward had, apparently, already revived, especially among the lower classes (*rustica multitudo*), but seems to have been despised by the patricians.[9] Osbert did his best to make it respectable. He preached on Edward's anniversary,[10] and his labours were rewarded by a resumption of miracles – and among men and women of social standing. Most important, Osbert believed that after his attendance at a commemorative mass he himself was cured by Edward of a quartan fever. By 1138 Osbert had rewritten the *Vita Ædwardi Regis* as a saint's life, the *Vita beati Eadwardi regis Anglorum*, and composed Edward's three charters for the abbey. In 1138 or 1139 it was decided to petition for Edward's canonization.

On 13 December 1138 Innocent II's legate, Alberic, bishop of Ostia, opened an English legatine council in Westminster abbey,[11] and on

---

[1] Osbert, *Vita beati Eadwardi*, ed. Bloch, p. 75.

[2] Now only in Ailred, *Vita sancti Edwardi*, Migne, *PL*, cxcv, col. 769. It was an influential story: see below, p. 282, and H. G. Richardson, 'The coronation in medieval England', *Traditio*, xvi (1960), 136, 143. And see above, pl. 16(6).

[3] Osbert, *Vita beati Eadwardi*, p. 80.

[4] *Ibid.*, p. 91. And see above, pl. 16(5).   [5] *Ibid.*, p. 83.   [6] *Ibid.*, p. 82.

[7] In 1139 King Stephen, in a letter probably drafted by Osbert, wrote that Osbert had been prior for five years: *The Letters of Osbert*, no. 17 (p. 86).

[8] Armitage Robinson in *The Letters of Osbert*, pp. 16–17; *Flete's History of Westminster Abbey*, pp. 87–8.

[9] Ailred, *Vita sancti Edwardi*, col. 784; *VEdR*, pp. 124–8.

[10] See above, p. 265.

[11] Wilkins, *Concilia*, i. 413–18, Richard of Hexham, in *Chronicles of the Reigns of Stephen, Henry II, and Richard I*, ed. Richard Howlett (Rolls ser. 1886), iii. 167–76.

17 December he ordained as Herbert's successor Gervase of Blois, an illegitimate son of King Stephen.[1] Osbert gave Alberic a copy of his *Vita beati Eadwardi*, with a prefatory letter in which he asked that the lantern of his church, which had for so long been hidden in the dust, that is to say, Edward, God's anointed, as incorrupt in body as he had been virginally pure in mind, should be put on a candlestick.[2] Osbert must also have won over the new abbot,[3] for he wrote to Henry, bishop of Winchester, the abbot's uncle, asking for his support and drawing attention to Edward's many miracles and the bishop's relationship to the saint.[4] But the abbey seems to have made insufficient preparation, for when Osbert and his companions set out for Rome they had letters testimonial only from the king, Bishop Henry, and the chapter of St Paul's (as the see of London was vacant).[5] Moreover, the letters of the bishop and chapter were short and restrained. Henry of Blois had his own ambitions; London naturally had no interest in Westminster's schemes.[6] Only Stephen allowed an enthusiastic letter, drafted by Osbert, to go out in his name. It is doubtful whether he had political or any devious motives. He probably backed the move mainly for the sake of his son, the abbot, and, more generally, because it would do honour to England and its kings. He wrote to the pope that England's devotion to Rome was well known and was proved by the payment of Peter's

---

[1] For Gervase, see John of Worcester, *Chronica*, ed. J. R. H. Weaver (Anecdota Oxoniensia . . . med. and mod. ser. pt. xiii, 1908), p. 53; *Flete's History of Westminster Abbey*, pp. 88–91, 142–3; John of Hexham, 'Cont. Symeonis historia regum', *Symeonis Opera*, ed. J. Arnold (Rolls ser. 1882–5), ii. 330; H. Tillmann, *Die päpstlichen Legaten in England* (Bonn, 1926), p. 40; W. Holtzmann, *Papsturkunden in England* (Berlin, 1930), i, nos. 47, 68–70; H. G. Richardson and G. O. Sayles, 'Gervase of Blois, abbot of Westminster', *The Governance of Medieval England* (1963), pp. 413 ff.; Chaplais, *loc. cit.* The date of Gervase's ordination is given by John of Worcester: 'In dominica quae extiterat XVIᵒ kal. Jan.', Sunday 17 December. But 17 December 1138 was a Saturday; and Miss Tillmann corrected, rightly or wrongly, to 18 December.

[2] *The Letters of Osbert*, no. 14. Bernhard W. Scholz, 'The Canonization of Edward the Confessor', *Speculum*, xxxvi (1961), 39, suggests that Osbert hoped that the legate would canonize.

[3] Scholz, *op. cit.*, p. 44, for reasons which do not impress, holds that Gervase was uninterested in the venture.

[4] *The Letters of Osbert*, no. 15. Scholz, *op. cit.*, pp. 42–3, suggests, rather implausibly, that Henry and Stephen would realize that the promotion would be more advantageous to their Angevin rivals.

[5] *The Letters of Osbert*, nos. 16–18. Letter 21 (to his niece Margaret) was written when he was about to set off for Rome and letter 22 (to his niece Cecilia) probably on his return. But neither mentions the purpose of the journey.

[6] For the rival activities of St Paul's, see Scholz, *op. cit.*, pp. 40–1.

Pence; that the piety of English kings was famous; there had been martyrs and virgins, and among the latter Edward, who performed miracles in both life and death and whose body had been found after thirty-six years in the grave incorrupt; and that Edward, a generous benefactor of Westminster, was a relation of the king. Stephen hoped that the pope would listen to Osbert and accept his proofs.

Although the papal letters obtained by Osbert cannot be dated more exactly than 1139–42, there is every reason to think that the prior would have acted immediately.[1] As it turned out he was too late. By Christmas 1139 the pope had little reason to do a special favour for Stephen and his bastard. On 8 January 1139 Alberic consecrated Theobald of Bec to Canterbury, and the new archbishop set off to collect his pallium. Theobald was never a warm supporter of Stephen and Henry of Winchester. In the spring at the Lateran council the pope heard the Angevin charge that Stephen was a perjured usurper; and, although he took no action, he also avoided pronouncing sentence.[2] In the summer Stephen alienated the church and quarrelled with his brother when he broke the family of Roger, bishop of Salisbury. And in October the Empress Matilda and Robert of Gloucester invaded England. If it was December 1139 when the pope decided the Westminster case, he had every reason here again to defer a decision. In a letter to Abbot Gervase and the convent Innocent said that Osbert had made such an impression on him that if the prior had brought sufficient testimonials from bishops and abbots he would have canonized Edward. In the circumstances, on the advice of the cardinals, he was postponing action. Something which was to the honour and advantage of the whole kingdom should be requested by the whole kingdom; and the abbot and convent would have to decide whether they wanted to set about collecting the necessary testimonials and renew their petition.[3]

Innocent's letter was kind. He may have had unexpressed reservations. The promotion was associated too closely with Stephen's party, and the pope may have realized from Osbert's other petitions at the *curia* that all was not well at Westminster. The prior brought back

[1] Holtzmann, *Papsturkunden*, p. 249. Scholz, *op. cit.*, p. 43, *n.* 25, argues for 1139–40.

[2] R. L. Poole, *Ioannis Saresberiensis Historiae Pontificalis* (1927), pp. 108 ff. Marjorie Chibnall, *The Historia Pontificalis of John of Salisbury* (Nelson's Medieval Texts 1956), p. 83.

[3] *The Letters of Osbert*, no. 19; Jaffé-Wattenbach, *Regesta Pontificum Romanorum* (Leipzig, 1885–8), no. 8182; Migne, *PL*, clxxix, col. 568; cf. E. W. Kemp, *Canonization and Authority in the Western Church* (1948), pp. 76–8.

several letters intended to reform the state of affairs left by Herbert and protect Westminster from despoilers.[1] In one the pope ordered the monks to pay the abbot proper respect and the abbot to suppress murmurers and disorderly monks. The regalian insignia of the glorious King Edward, which were kept at Westminster, were to be preserved intact, and no one, of whatsoever order or dignity, was to have the right to take them away, sell them, or put them to any use outside that holy place, without the common assent of all the brethren.[2] It is not clear who was casting covetous eyes on Edward's crown and sceptre: it may be that Osbert was simply taking precautions. Nor is the letter proof that there was a division within the convent over Edward's sanctity. Innocent rejected Westminster's petition because it was defective in form, unconvincing in substance, and politically inopportune. Osbert had impressed the pope and could not have done more.

After this check we hear nothing of the cult for almost twenty years. Osbert seems to have quarrelled with Gervase, lost his office of prior, perhaps gone into exile again.[3] Without his drive the movement flagged. No miracles are reported between 1138 and 1163, when Ailred of Rievaulx rewrote Osbert's *Vita*. Nor does there seem to have been any great geographical expansion of the cult, for when Ailred wrote his *Genealogia regum Anglorum* in 1153-4, his chapter on Edward ignores the king's virginity, sanctity, and miracles.[4] But there remained supporters of the cause at Westminster; and it is possible that the diplomatic moves of 1138-9 at least had some propaganda value in the English church at large. In 1159 the claims made for Edward were less novel.

In November 1153 Stephen accepted Henry fitzEmpress as his heir; and immediately Osbert began to court the rising star.[5] About 1158 Gervase of Blois was deposed, presumably because he was Stephen's son, and replaced by Master Laurence, a Durham man, who, after a clerical career in the northern province, had become a monk at St Albans. Laurence had studied at Paris, was well acquainted with the

[1] Holtzmann, *Papsturkunden*, i, nos. 24-5; *The Letters of Osbert*, no. 20.

[2] *Papsturkunden*, no. 24. *Flete's History of Westminster Abbey*, pp. 90-1.

[3] *The Letters of Osbert*, p. 19. But Richardson and Sayles, *The Governance of Medieval England*, pp. 418-19, point out how obscure this period of Osbert's career is.

[4] Migne, *PL*, cxcv, col. 734. He also follows *Chron.* and not *VEdR* for the date of Edward's death. Cf. also *Aluredi Beverlac. Annales*, ed. T. Hearne (1716), p. 124.

[5] He wrote him an adulatory poem (*The Letters of Osbert*, no. 38), and letter no. 37 could be to Henry.

English Cistercian abbots, and clearly was a man of the new age.[1] In 1159 there was a double election to the papacy, with French and English opinion generally in favour of Roland Bandinelli, the papal chancellor, who took the title of Alexander III, against the imperial candidate, Octavian, Victor IV. We have an account of the events at Westminster from the pen of Richard of Cirencester, a monk of Westminster in the late fourteenth century, who made good use of his abbey's archives when compiling his *Speculum Historiale de Gestis Regum Angliae*.[2] We learn that it soon came to the new abbot's ears that some monks thought it shameful that Edward, a citizen of Heaven, distinguished by miracles, should still be concealed in a tabernacle of mortality, as though he was one of the dead. 'How much longer', they grumbled, 'is our precious treasure to lie hidden, buried in the earth?'[3] Richard of Cirencester does not name Osbert of Clare; but it is likely that we have here Osbert's usual attempt to get the support of a new abbot for his project.

Abbot Laurence acted with discretion, but also with vigour as the road opened before him. First he discussed Edward's life and miracles secretly with some senior brethren; and when he found these unanimous about Edward's sanctity, he raised the matter in chapter. The books written about Edward's life and miracles were produced and inspected, presumably the anonymous *Vita Ædwardi Regis*[4] and Osbert's *Vita beati Eadwardi*; and all the monks agreed that the abbey should again take public steps to get the king recognized as a saint. Timing, as the abbey knew from experience, was an important matter. In 1139 there had been schism in England, and it was the pope to whom the candidates had appealed. In 1159 there was a schism in the papacy, and it was the kings who had to decide which of the candidates they would recognize. An imperial council held at Pavia in February 1160 decided for Victor IV; councils held during the summer in England, Normandy, and France advised Henry II and Louis VII to recognize Alexander III. Henry used his 'ancestral' power to decide between rival claimants to the papacy to good diplomatic advantage before the weight of public

---

[1] *Flete's History of Westminster Abbey*, pp. 91–4. F. E. Croydon, 'Abbot Laurence of Westminster and Hugh of St Victor', *Mediaeval and Renaissance Studies*, ii (1950), 169–71; *VEdR*, p. 131.

[2] *Ricardi de Cirencestria Speculum Historiale de Gestis Regum Angliae*, ed. J. E. B. Mayor (Rolls ser. 1869), ii. 319 ff. Cf. also *Flete's History of Westminster Abbey*, pp. 92–4.

[3] Cf. below, p. 281.

[4] Richard of Cirencester himself twice borrowed passages from it, *op. cit.*, pp. 207–12, 291–2.

opinion forced him, in the latter part of the year, to make his formal recognition of Alexander.[1]

It was probably in the spring of 1160 that Laurence realized that this was Westminster's opportunity too. The abbey had Innocent II's instructions on procedure; and they were meticulously observed. A petition from the whole kingdom had to be organized. Laurence first enlisted the aid of the two archbishops, Theobald and Roger, and the bishop of London, Richard de Beaumeis. He then circularized the bishops and wrote also to many abbeys.[2] As we can see from the letters he obtained in support,[3] he made these points: there was overwhelming evidence, both written and oral, to prove Edward's sanctity; on the one hand were the king's virtues, on the other his miracles. Edward as king was mild and merciful; he ruled his kingdom with laws which tempered the harshness of the courts; he loved the church, founded and enriched Westminster abbey, was generous to many religious bodies, and greatly honoured St Peter and the church of Rome; although married he remained a virgin, and the integrity of his flesh was proved when, after thirty-five years in the tomb, his body was found to be incorrupt. Also, in life as in death, he worked wonders, cured the sick, and had the gift of prophesy.

The response to Laurence's circular must have been in general favourable. According to one of the petitions,[4] Archbishop Theobald and many of the bishops supported the cause. The thirteen letters, which have survived because they were copied and put into a book, are probably only a selection or chance gathering. Among the missing pieces are Westminster's own petition and all the associated documentation. Most of the letters were probably written in the late summer of 1160. Even if the abbey had started its campaign earlier, nothing official could be done until Louis VII of France and Henry agreed to recognize Alexander as pope. In the autumn Laurence went to Normandy to get the king's backing,[5] and then to Paris to enlist the support of Alexander's legates, the cardinals Henry and Otto.[6] He took with him

---

[1] W. Ohnsorge, *Die Legaten Alexanders III (1159–69)* (Berlin, 1928), pp. 15–38; F. Barlow, 'The English, Norman, and French Councils called to deal with the Papal Schism of 1159', *EHR*, li (1936), 264–8; *The Letters of Arnulf of Lisieux*, ed. Barlow (R. Hist. Soc. Camden 3rd ser., lxi, 1939), p. xl: Mary G. Cheney, 'The Recognition of Pope Alexander III, *EHR*, lxxxiv (1969), 474.

[2] Richard of Cirencester, ii. 320–1.   [3] See below, Appendix D.   [4] Below, p. 317.

[5] Richard of Cirencester, ii. 321. Henry spent the autumn in Normandy before moving to Touraine and then Le Mans for Christmas.

[6] Below, p. 311. As Liverani read *pariter* for *Parisius*, this fact has been generally unknown.

the vestment in which Edward had been wrapped, and which had been removed from the tomb in 1102, to prove the miracle of the incorruption of the body. The fabric was still whole, clean, and in no way faded.[1]

The king, flushed with the part he was playing in European diplomacy and his importance in ecclesiastical affairs, welcomed the Westminster plan.[2] The legates in their gratitude to Henry were enthusiastic.[3] Laurence may originally have intended to lead the delegation to Rome.[4] But it was possibly 13 November before he met the legates; and the difficulty of the journey in winter was at least an adequate excuse for withdrawing.[5] The fifteenth-century Westminster historian, John Flete, includes Osbert in the party which travelled to Anagni; but he must have been an old man and we may think it unlikely.[6] Two Westminster monks who obtained papal privileges at this time were the infirmarer, Roger, and the sacristan, Walter.[7] The one would have been able to give evidence about cures, the other about manifestations in the church. The pope discussed the matter thoroughly in a secret meeting with the delegation, was shown Innocent's letter, received the proofs, the book of miracles, presumably Osbert's, and the testimonial letters, which fulfilled Innocent's requirements, and, without great delay, authorized the bulls of canonization to be issued.[8] A brief letter dated Anagni, 7 February [1161] was sent in identical terms to the abbot and church of Westminster and to the whole English church. It states that, although it was usual to transact such difficult and sublime business in a solemn council, the pope, with the common consent of the cardinals, was pleased to agree to Henry's and Westminster's petition. It was, therefore, decreed that Edward should be canonized, inscribed in the catalogue of saints, and enrolled among the saints and confessors.[9] Alexander appointed a cardinal to celebrate the first mass of

---

[1] Below, pp. 311–12.

[2] Richard of Cirencester, ii. 321. His letter is printed below, p. 310.

[3] Below, p. 311.   [4] Below, p. 313.   [5] Below, p. 312.

[6] *Flete's History of Westminster Abbey*, pp. 91, 92. We know, however, that Osbert crossed the Channel after January 1156. In a letter, no. 42, to Adelidis, abbess of Barking, he refers to a visit to Ely in order to get St Ætheldreda's blessing before he went overseas to meet King Henry.

[7] Both obtained privileges dated at Anagni 7 February [1161], Holzmann, *Papsturkunden*, i, nos. 85–6.

[8] Richard of Cirencester, ii. 321–2, based largely on the bull.

[9] Printed below, p. 323. For the earlier, similar, but more complicated negotiations for the canonization of Henry II of Germany in 1146, see Renate Klauser, *Heinrichs- und Kunigundenkult*, pp. 55–6.

St Edward the Confessor.[1] He had repaid his debt to Henry with a most appropriate and welcome gift.

At Westminster Laurence held a joyful assembly at which, after the recital of the papal bull, the second mass of the saint was sung.[2] The translation, however, had to wait, for the king was still abroad.[3] This ceremony, based on Jesus's saying, 'No man, when he hath lighted a candle, putteth it in a secret place, neither under a bushel, but on a candlestick, that they which come in may see the light',[4] and commonly graced by a sermon on this text, was in its essence the raising of the body from below to above ground. The removal was both symbolic and also a matter of convenience: a relic placed on high could be adored, seen, even touched.[5] The translation allowed, too, an examination of the body and usually the construction of a more elaborate tomb. It was also a suitable occasion for the production of a new Life of the saint. The *Vita Ædwardi Regis* was not a saint's life and contained little of the twelfth-century collection of miracles, prophecies, and stories. Osbert's *Vita beati Eadwardi* was probably felt to have outlived its usefulness. It was written in an old-fashioned, unattractive style and was associated with schism in the abbey. Laurence turned to his kinsman, Ailred, abbot of Rievaulx, a distinguished English Cistercian with a graceful pen, and asked him to rewrite Osbert's work.[6] Ailred not only brought the legend up to date by including all the latest stories, but also strengthened the historical narrative, which Osbert had weakened, by taking material from the chronicles. This *Vita sancti Edwardi Regis* became the standard Latin Life; and the lections used at Westminster in the later Middle Ages were based on it.[7]

---

[1] Richard of Cirencester, ii. 323.   [2] *Ibid.*

[3] The translation of Henry II of Germany took place sixteen months after the canonization, a delay due partly to the death of the bishop of Bamberg, Klauser, *op. cit.*, p. 57.   [4] Luke xi. 33.

[5] Cf. Klauser, *op. cit.*, pp. 58–63. Moreover, better provision was made for the receipt of offerings. Coins were usually placed on top of the shrine or on a convenient ledge, for a common method of stealing was to remove coins in the mouth while kissing the tomb: cf. Symeon, *HDE*, pp. 96–7; Hermann, *De Miraculis S. Mariae Laudunensis*, Migne, *PL*, clvi, col. 985.

[6] *Chronicon Angliae Petriburgense* (saec. xiv), ed. J. A. Giles (Caxton Soc. 1845), p. 98; *Gesta abbatum monasterii S. Albani*, ed. H. T. Riley (Rolls ser. 1867), i. 159; see also F. M. Powicke, *Walter Daniel's Life of Ailred abbot of Rievaulx* (Nelson's Medieval Texts, 1950), pp. xlvii–xlviii. *Vita S. Edwardi Regis*, printed R. Twysden, *Hist. Anglic. Script. decem* (1652), i. 369 ff., reprinted Migne, *PL*, cxcv, coll. 737 ff.

[7] *Missale ad usum ecclesiae Westmonasteriensis*, ed. J. W. Legg (Henry Bradshaw Soc., 1891–7), iii. 1343–4, 1347–8.

Laurence probably found it harder to make arrangements with the king, and during 1163 waited for a suitable opportunity. In March Henry held a great council at Westminster to hear an ecclesiastical lawsuit, and we notice among the witnesses to the judgment not only Laurence but also Ailred of Rievaulx.[1] This may be the occasion on which the translation was discussed and seriously planned. According to Richard of Cirencester,[2] Laurence was advised to make a secret inspection of the tomb, but acted only after much hesitation and several false starts. It would have been awkward if the body, so recently proclaimed to be incorrupt, had in fact decayed. At last the abbot and prior and a few chosen monks, who had all prepared themselves by prayer and fasting, returned to the church towards daybreak, when the other monks had retired to bed after matins. The doors were locked against the lay servants, and, barefooted and dressed in albs, they held a short religious service. Then the abbot, prior, and two monks, leaving the others at the high altar in tears and prayers, advanced to the tomb, prised up the stone, and, raising their lanterns, peered in. They saw, a little obscured by the mortar and dust which had fallen down, the saint wrapped in a cloth of gold, at his feet purple shoes and precious slippers, his head and face covered with a round mitre, likewise embroidered with gold, his beard, white and slightly curled, lying neatly on his breast. Joyfully they called over the rest of the party, and as they cleared out the dirt from the tomb, they explored everything gently with their hands. To their relief nothing had changed. The body was still intact and the vestments were only a little dulled and soiled. Six of the monks lifted the body out, laid it on a carpet, wrapped it in a precious silk cloth, and placed it in a wooden coffin or feretory, which they had prepared. Everything they found with the body was transferred to the new shrine, except the ring (the one which St John had returned to Edward[3]), which Laurence removed to preserve as a memorial and as a sign of his personal devotion to the saint. Also, according to Flete,[4] three cloths were taken and made into embroidered copes.

[1] *The Registrum Antiquissimum of the Cathedral Church of Lincoln*, ed. C. W. Foster (Lincoln Record Soc., vol. 27), i (1931), no. 73, pp. 64–6. See also below, Appendix E, p. 326, *n*. 3.

[2] Richard of Cirencester, ii. 324–5. Symeon's account of the investigation of St Cuthbert's body in 1104 should be compared, *Symeonis Opera Omnia*, ed. T. Arnold (Rolls ser. 1882), i. 248 ff.

[3] See above, p. 274.   [4] *Flete's History of Westminster Abbey*, pp. 71–2.

On 1 October Henry held another great council at Westminster, at which ecclesiastical justice was discussed and the question raised whether the bishops would agree to the 'ancestral customs' of the realm.[1] And although the council ended with Henry's disgrace of Becket and departure from London, it must have been on this occasion that final arrangements were made for the translation of Edward on 13 October. On that day the assembly which had been so seriously divided less than a fortnight before gathered again in the abbey. Possibly because of the hostility between Canterbury and York (a rivalry which marred Edward's second translation in 1269) it was essentially a synod of the southern province only.[2] There were present Archbishop Thomas Becket and all his suffragans except Robert of Bath (Hereford and Worcester were vacant), three Norman bishops, Rotrou of Evreux, Achard of Avranches, and Arnulf of Lisieux (who had just crossed over to advise Henry on how to deal with Becket), four important abbots, and eight earls, about half their number. First the new feretory was opened, so that the king and others could see and, if they dared, handle the body;[3] then the chest was carried in procession through the cloisters on the shoulders of the king and the principal nobles. Finally it was placed within the shrine, the metalwork attributed to the Conqueror, that is to say in the same place, but now above instead of under the ground. Ailred of Rievaulx presented his new life of the saint and preached on the usual text.[4] 'The glorious lantern was put on a candlestick in the house of the Lord so that all who come in may see the light and be illuminated by it.'[5]

In the ceremony there was profit for all; and this is probably why they all temporarily sank their differences. Edward had at last received the honour due to him. Those Westminster monks who had supported Osbert of Clare's campaign had won a belated victory. Abbot Laurence acquired a valuable cult for his church.[6] The Cistercians, through

---

[1] See below, Appendix E.

[2] List in Richard of Cirencester, ii. 326; description of the ceremony, pp. 325–6.

[3] Cf. 1 John i. 1.

[4] *Walter Daniel's Life of Ailred*, ed. F. M. Powicke, pp. xlvii–xlviii, 41–2. *Chronicon Angliae Petriburgense*, p. 98, s.a. 1163, 'sanctus Alredus abbas huic translationi interfuit, offerens vitam regis et homeliam super *Nemo accendit lucernam* etc., ad laudem ejusdem sancti mirifice dictatam.'   [5] Richard of Cirencester, ii. 326.

[6] Some risk, however, was involved in creating a new official festival for the saint on a day different from the anniversary of Edward's death, the focus of the popular cult and traditionally celebrated with 'illegal' festivities. In the case of Henry II of Germany in 1146 the original intention was to translate the relics on the anniversary

Ailred of Rievaulx, displayed their patriotic spirituality. Henry II, now committed to a serious quarrel with his primate and many of his bishops, scored an important point. His *antecessor* was a saint who could work miracles; such a holy monarchy was specially fitted to rule the English church. And Becket, not yet, perhaps, aspiring to martyrdom, but steeling himself to an agonizing course, drew from the ceremony what consolation he could. As fee he asked not for a portion of the saint, but the gravestone to which Wulfstan's staff had adhered.[1] This was a relic which should protect him against the unjust decisions of a Westminster council; and he needed the support of good King Edward against a tyrannical king and his minions. He had also in a typically spirited way made preparations to answer Henry back. If Henry had an *antecessor* who was a saint, so had he. At the council of Tours in May 1163 he had asked the pope to canonize Anselm, archbishop of Canterbury, a primate who had suffered from unjust kings and treacherous bishops.[2] These manœuvres were not out of place round Edward's shrine. He was a saint for those interested in the secrets of political power. He never gained a large popular following. His Legend had little appeal to the refined or intellectual believer. When King Henry III became his most devoted admirer it was like calling to like.

Edward to the very end took all the credit for himself. The *Vita Ædwardi Regis* could have served equally well as a base for a campaign on behalf of Queen Edith. She shared her husband's chastity; she outdid him in charitable deeds and benevolence to the church; her modesty and virtue were an example to all women;[3] she was buried by Edward's side in the abbey. In the similar case of the Empress Kunigund of Germany, the wife was canonized, although not without difficulty, fifty-four years after the canonization of her husband.[4] But we have no

---

and so preserve continuity. See Klauser, *op. cit.*, pp. 57–8. Henry III of England, when he translated Edward again in 1269, wisely took the date of the 1163 translation. See below, Appendix E.

[1] Continuation of *Gesta Regum* in *The Historical Works of Gervase of Canterbury*, ed. W. Stubbs (Rolls ser. 1880), ii. 285. In 1218 Archbishop Stephen Langton took St Wulfstan's arm and in 1276 Robert Kilwardby took St Richard of Chichester's, *ibid.*

[2] Letter of Alexander III to Becket [9 June 1163], replying to the archbishop's request at the council of Tours for the canonization of Anselm on the evidence of a book of his life and miracles, and authorizing Becket, owing to the number of such petitions presented at Tours, to summon a provincial council with power to act, *Materials for the History of Thomas Becket*, v, 35. Becket seems to have abandoned the scheme. Probably too many of his bishops withheld their support.

[3] *VEdR*, pp. 41–2.   [4] Klauser, *op. cit.*, pp. 59–68.

evidence of any movement to get Edith recognized as a saint. We can only assume that there was never a popular interest in her relics or anniversary, that, as in the case of Kunigund, miracles were scarce, that the monks of Westminster did not honour her as a co-founder (in the *Vita* she is expressly dissociated from Westminster and shown as rebuilding Wilton in holy rivalry with her husband), and, possibly, that there was no enthusiasm to encourage the cult of a woman who was Anglo-Danish by birth. It could also be that the image of a holy royal pair, *sanctus rex, sancta regina*, had little attraction for a monastery. But it is not impossible, of course, that it was just what Edward and Edith had wished.

EPILOGUE

The place of Edward the Confessor in English history is not easy to define. He made no great impression on his contemporaries. After the Norman Conquest he stood for 'the good old times', yet it was the even more mythical Arthur who captured the romantic interest of the educated classes. The Confessor was Henry III's favourite saint; but Henry's son is known as Edward the First. In modern times he has generally been regarded with mistrust, as a devious and ambiguous man, a dubious patriot, a weak and irresponsible king, a doubtful saint. These attitudes are understandable. Because of his childlessness, because the Old-English dynasty ended with him, his reign easily assumes a provisional air and can be viewed as an interlude between the Danish and the Norman Conquests. Edward can also be seen as a complete failure, as a man who was always in the power of others, who never overcame any threat to his authority, who was throughout his life the victim of circumstances.

Although there is a measure of truth in all these views, they are superficial as well as uncharitable. A close analysis of Edward's problems and behaviour reveals his intelligence and resourcefulness if not good judgment and wisdom. He can be likened in some ways to Henry III, who in the course of a long reign recovered from a weak start and, despite many foolish and petulant actions, acquired in the end much respect and considerable authority. The achievements of a weak but persistent ruler, although often overlooked, or, if noticed, despised, are still achievements. At Christmas 1065 England was a rich and prosperous kingdom. Great political difficulties remained unsolved; the basic problem of the succession to the throne was not yet settled; but there was a valuable and coherent inheritance awaiting the heir. Nor can it be asserted incontrovertibly that Edward planned to no avail. Unless it is thought that he wanted Tostig or Edgar Ætheling to succeed him, he either successfully transferred the kingdom to Harold, who rashly threw the bequest away, or made it possible for William, despite all hindrances, to obtain his rightful inheritance. In any case only limited responsibility should be attributed to Edward for events which occurred after his death.

Most judgments on Edward are based on interpretations of his political aims, which it is impossible to substantiate, or are derived from attitudes towards the Norman Conquest, which can hardly be justified. His real achievement is often ignored. His kingdom passed entire to Harold and then to William; and that kingdom he had helped to fashion. Edward's reign of close on a quarter of a century should not be regarded as a provisional interlude: it was a period in which many threads were firmly tied together, so that a recognizable and lasting English contribution passed into, and through, the Anglo-Norman state.

Since Alfred there had been great changes in every aspect of English life. All sorts of kings, both English and Danish, had made their individual contributions. Scandinavian settlers had been assimilated, a variety of foreigners had entered the aristocracy. There had been much experiment in local government and a major reform in the church. These alterations in the pattern of society must have had far-reaching consequences and must often have been deeply disturbing, making for unrest, for social and political instability. Against this background Edward's reign can be seen as a period of consolidation, of growing Anglo-Danish concord. Edward had not the power to govern arbitrarily, to re-design what he found, to introduce many novelties. But he was not so weak as to remain a mere plaything of existing forces. Throughout his reign he struggled to recover and preserve his rights, to achieve a balance in the realm which he could manipulate in his favour. He acquired an empire in the British Isles without much fighting. Like Edgar and Cnut he gave England peace.[1] Much of the machinery of local government, which had been adapted from military administration, acquired a more legitimate air. By 1066 the kingdom had more organic unity than it had possessed in 1042. It had shaken down into a polity which could absorb the shocks administered to it in 1051–2 and 1065. Despite the crudities and the undeniable tensions it was comparatively mature.

[1] The hiding of money in the ground indicates lawlessness and insecurity. For the whole of Edward's reign only three hoards have been recorded, and one of these comes from the very beginning. J. D. A. Thompson, *Inventory of British Coin Hoards A.D. 600–1500* (Royal Numismatic Soc. 1956), nos. 270, 294, 374. The last, although dated by Thompson *c.* 1050, contains coins of Harthacnut but not of Edward: a date *c.* 1042 is to be preferred. After Edward's death and throughout William I's reign deposits were much more frequent.

Edward's kingdom had to face the buffetings of the Norman Conquest, of the rebellions, and of renewed Danish invasions in 1069–70. That it came through largely intact is a tribute not only to Norman military tenacity, but also to the integrity of the fabric. If Edward had left behind a discordant, incoherent, ill-governed kingdom, the effects of the Norman Conquest would have been very different. Later generations did right to appeal to the good old laws of King Edward. He had become a symbol of a way of life which refused to die and which in part came into its own again.

Edward was also a transitional figure who helped to reconcile the various national cultures in eleventh-century England. A descendant of Cerdic and Rollo, he was not without honour in Scandinavia and had found a home in Normandy. He was the first English king since Egbert of Wessex to have direct knowledge of Frankish customs. His court was probably as cosmopolitan as that of the king of Germany. After the Norman Conquest his memory had an appeal to both nations. He was William's cousin, benefactor, *antecessor*. The position the Normans gave him both legitimized their rule and also worked to restrain their behaviour. When the English petitioned William to take the crown they were inviting him to ascend Edward's throne and accept, and be content with, Edward's rights. Edward's cult had a part to play in the reconciliation of the races and can also be seen as a straw in the wind. When Laurence of Westminster, Ailred of Rievaulx, Thomas Becket, and Henry II joined together to celebrate the canonization of the royal confessor, it was a sign that a new Anglo-French kingdom had been formed, unashamed of its English past. Edward had made the barbarous 'pre-history' of England more respectable.

APPENDICES

Appendix A

THE PURPOSE OF THE
VITA ÆDWARDI REGIS

Controversy over the date of the *Vita* and its hagiographical aspect has hindered its appreciation as a political work of its own time. If, however, we allow that Book I could have been started before Edward's death or, at the latest, before Tostig and Harold were dead,[1] an exercise based on that assumption is worth while.[2] Not only may it provide the correct interpretation of the book, it may also help in the argument over its date.

The author maintains consistently that his aim was to please and honour Queen Edith. The two books of the work are dedicated to her; and it seems from both prologues that the project was started under her patronage, possibly at her instigation. Even though the Muse, who in a dialogue with the Poet dictates the plan, is not Edith, to some extent she must represent her: she is the woman who inspires the Poet to write. We are immediately reminded of the *Gesta Cnutonis* or, as it is now called, the *Encomium Emmae Reginae*, an historical tract written for Queen Emma during the reign of her son, Harthacnut (1040–2),[3] although possibly commissioned while she was in Flanders waiting for Harthacnut to invade. Dr Sten Körner has argued persuasively that the political purpose of this work was to demonstrate Harthacnut's right to the English throne against other pretenders, especially Edward.[4] It is possible that in 1065–6 Edith had a similar scheme in mind.

---

[1] Barlow, *VEdR*, pp. xxv ff.

[2] Körner, *Battle of Hastings*, pp. 36–7 n., rejects my 'suggestion that the work was written before Edward's death' and makes no special investigation of motive. But Karl Schnith, 'Die Wende der englischen Geschichte im 11. Jahrhundert', *Historisches Jahrbuch*, 86 (1966), 34–9, makes a most interesting appreciation of purpose. His basic view, however, that the *Vita* was commissioned by the house of Godwin so as to prepare the ground for the accession of a new dynasty, and that the programme was completed when Harold ascended the throne, although certainly tenable, is not in my opinion the likeliest explanation.

[3] Campbell, *Encomium Emmae*, p. xxi.

[4] Körner, *Battle of Hastings*, pp. 47 ff.

The author of the *Vita Ædwardi Regis*, because he was very proud of his technical skill, informs his readers about the mechanics of the composition. Several times he refers to what the grammarians would term the *inventio*, the purpose of the work, and, although the explanations are not wholly consistent, they can always be harmonized and can be considered either as aspects of his project, or as fluctuating emphases. He usually then mentions how he is going to carry the *inventio* out, his plan (*dispositio*). In the prologue to Book I he tells us that he is writing a hymn of praise (*laudes*) in honour of Edith,[1] and his plan is to laud her family, her husband, Edward, her father, Godwin, and Godwin's four sons, apparently Harold, Tostig, Gyrth, and Leofwine. He intends to treat of them one by one.[2] And he also informs us about the style (*elocutio*) he has chosen for the work. Later he writes that his purpose was to ensure that the sterling qualities (*probitas*) of Godwin's children were not forgotten by future generations,[3] and so he proposed to describe the life, habits, and deeds of Harold and Tostig.[4] He wished to present them as models to be imitated by posterity.[5] It is possible that we can discern here a change from a political to a memorial purpose; but not necessarily, for we are sure that Edith, who is one of those explicitly designated as worthy of imitation, was still alive when the author was writing.

If we cast a general glance over Book I we shall hardly doubt that the author was honest in his statements. He may not indicate the secret purpose in his patron's mind; but he was probably unaware of it. He may not always keep exactly to his plan; but this is the way of authors. By and large he does Edith and her family proud. Throughout the work he stresses the loyal and valuable services which the house of Godwin rendered to the English monarchy. Godwin served both Cnut and Edward devotedly, despite the latter's ingratitude. He had his children educated with royal service in mind; he wanted them to follow him as the kingdom's protectors,[6] *regni nutricii*,[7] pillars of the realm.[8] Their military prowess guaranteed Edward's peaceful reign.[9] At court was Edith, a sort of governess, *in omnibus regalibus consiliis moderatrix*, the king's wisest, most disinterested counsellor.[10] She was always at his side like a devoted daughter, seeing to his comfort and

---

[1] *VEdR*, pp. 2–3, 59.　　[2] *Ibid.*, pp. 4, 6.　　[3] *Ibid.*, p. 6.
[4] *Ibid.*, p. 31.　　[5] *Ibid.*, pp. 31, 42.　　[6] *Ibid.*, p. 6.
[7] *Ibid.*, pp. 42, 79. Godwin, too, was the *nutricius* of the people and the kingdom, p. 30. Cf. Schnith, 'Die Wende', p. 36.
[8] *VEdR*, p. 37.　　[9] *Ibid.*, pp. 32–3; cf. 15.　　[10] *Ibid.*, p. 23, cf. 54.

interests.[1] Naturally when Edward took the advice of this family, all was well. When he listened instead to bad counsellors things went wrong.[2] Godwin married Cnut's 'sister' and Edith Edward; so close was this clan to the throne that in the end the author can call Godwin's sons, 'these boys of royal stock'.[3]

But, although the author's general intention is clear enough, there are ambiguities when we come to details. Godwin's children are likened to the four streams out of paradise, but are never positively identified. A poem on the children is totally obscure.[4] In practice the author almost confines his attention to two sons, Harold and Tostig; and an impression that he wavers in his preference makes it hard to get his attitude in sharp focus. Moreover, before he has finished writing both are dead – and the other two brothers as well. The whole purpose of the book, as the author recognizes in the prologue to Book II, has been destroyed.[5] Nor is the stated plan, to devote successive chapters to members of the family, carried out exactly. The failure to give suitable space to Gyrth and Leofwine could be explained by their unexpected unimportance in the story, either because Harold had taken the throne, or because they had all been killed.

We get the impression that the original plan, perhaps even the original purpose, has been modified while the book was being written. Nevertheless, a summary of the chapters shows that the author always had the intention to please the queen, and wrote what he thought would do her honour. In Chapter I Earl Godwin, described as the father of the English people, secures the throne for Edward after Cnut's death. There are tributes to the administrative skill and passion for justice of both Godwin and Edward; and there are here some of the most enthusiastic passages about Edward, presumably because he is the ruler whom both God and Earl Godwin (correctly interpreting the will of God) have chosen for the English. Although later Edward goes astray, in 1042 he is a paragon of virtue. In this chapter is Bishop Beorhtweald's vision at Glastonbury not only of Edward's future coronation, but also of how a successor to a celibate king was to be found. St Peter told Edward, 'The kingdom of the English is the kingdom of God; and after you he has already provided

---

[1] *VEdR*, pp. 15, 41–2, 79.   [2] *Ibid.*, pp. 17 ff.
[3] *Ibid.*, p. 50. Although they were through their mother the great-great-grandsons of King Harald Bluetooth of Denmark, it is unlikely that it was this which was in the author's mind.
[4] *Ibid.*, pp. 15–17.   [5] *Ibid.*, pp. 56 ff.

a king according to his will.' This is a point at which many important themes of the *Vita* meet. There is the view of Edward as the childless king served by the children of Godwin: they 'adopt' Edward as their father. It is possibly an answer to (is certainly the reverse of) the Norman story that Edward adopted William as his son. There is the thesis that Godwin and his family were patient and prepared to wait. The author possibly believed that they were tempted in 1052 to dethrone Edward, but, like David, spared Saul and waited 'for things to subside or die of themselves'.[1] There is also the underlying assumption that man's first political duty is to ascertain and carry out the will of God.[2] And here we have the only direct reference in Book I to the problem of the succession. Just as Edward had been declared beforehand by a sign from God to be the future king of England,[3] so now someone (unnamed and still to be recognized) was being indicated by St Peter to the faithful as Edward's successor. Until January 1066 God's choice remained unknown. On 6 January it was seen to be Harold. Not before 14 October could there have been real doubt that God's will might have been misunderstood.

The poem which follows Chapter I is devoted to Godwin's gift of a ship to Edward, and Chapter II, which has been lost, probably dealt largely with his provision of a wife for the king. Edith, Godwin's eldest daughter, was, we gather, famous for her beauty, her learning and culture, and her skill with the needle. There was probably also some reference to her brothers (we know that Gyrth was mentioned[4]); and the next poem praises in obscure metaphor the earl's children and also gives the first foreboding of disasters due to envy and failure to observe agreements. Here there may be an allusion to the rivalry between Godwin's sons; but, more probably, we are being introduced to the next theme: Edward's repudiation of his pact with the family and the chaos which resulted. At the beginning of Chapter III Edward is described as *beatae memoriae*; but this could be the result of textual revision, and we do not have to believe that the king was dead when the chapter was first written.[5]

In Chapter III Edward, misled by evil counsellors (especially Robert of Jumièges), allows Godwin and his family to be destroyed by

---

[1] *VEdR*, pp. 19, 28–30, 32. Cf. Schnith, 'Die Wende', p. 37. Just as Godwin was a king-maker, so he could have unmade the king.

[2] Schnith, *op. cit., passim.*   [3] *VEdR*, pp. 7, 60.   [4] *Ibid.*, p. 33.

[5] Körner, *Battle of Hastings*, p. 37 *n.*, will not accept this.

enemies. The earl, as the following poem proclaims, was completely innocent of any crime. But it was the relegation of Queen Edith to Wilton abbey which caused the most sorrow at court. She was a woman of complete integrity who looked only to the king's profit and honour (rather than, we should understand, her own family's). Chapter IV is concerned with the house of Godwin's recovery of power. Godwin's return is popular: he is still the father of the people; he dissuades his army from acts of vengeance; he shows the utmost moderation, treats the king with respect, and merely observes that his enemies have fled before him. The earl has destroyed a great evil without spilling a drop of blood: he was, as the next poem demonstrates, another David who spared another Saul. The queen, amid general rejoicing, was restored to the king's bedchamber.

After this historical interlude we return to the plan. Chapter V is devoted to Harold and Tostig. 'No age and no province has reared two mortals of such worth at the same time.' Gyrth is again mentioned; but Leofwine, noticed in the previous chapter, has dropped out of the story. It is difficult to say which of the two elder brothers the author prefers here. At the beginning of the chapter he seems to favour Harold,[1] by the end he is neutral. Harold returned safely from Rome, 'by God's grace . . . passing with watchful mockery through all ambushes, as was his way.' In Tostig's case, 'God . . . leads forth and brings back those of His people who trust in His keeping.' The following poem passes quickly to the rivalry of Harold and Tostig. It is not quite clear whether all is lost, whether both brothers have already fallen, or whether, as the last lines suggest, there is still a chance of peace. Chapter VI, however, does not move on to Gyrth and Leofwine, as it could, perhaps should, have done. It starts with Edward and Edith, passes to Harold and Tostig's achievements against Wales and Scotland, and then returns to the king and the queen – 'the illustrious mistress whom we chiefly serve in this present account' – and their church-building. The most baffling thing in this section is the author's promise to tell us more on a later occasion about Harold's and Tostig's campaigns. At this point he could not do full justice to the subject: it needed more investigation and a fuller treatment.[2] There are also,

---

[1] Harold, when he succeeds his father as earl of Wessex, is 'filius eius maior natu et sapientia', *VEdR*, p. 30.

[2] The verses on the Welsh campaign in the prologue to Book II, *ibid.*, pp. 57–8, are another confession of failure, not a fulfilment of this promise.

besides the author's reference to his special obligation to Edith, remarks about his indebtedness to her brothers. He has promised to
describe Harold in this book because of the earl's great undertakings.
He is much indebted to the earls because of their outstanding merit.
The author no longer seems to know exactly what he should be doing.

With Chapter VII, however, we come to the end of the story: the
rebellion in Northumbria against Tostig, Harold's failure to help his
brother, Edward's desertion by his vassals, Edith's powerlessness,
Tostig's exile, and Edward's death. Here the author's sympathies seem
to lie with the younger brother; and the most significant feature in this
chapter is the omission of Harold's accession to the throne. Nowhere in
the book is that event explicitly mentioned; and it is only the *reges
equivoci* (the two Harolds who fought at Stamford Bridge)[1] of the
introductory poem to Book II which proves that the writer was aware
of the fact. The author confesses in the poem that a description of the
battles of 1066 would hardly please the queen. He may well have
thought the same about Harold's coronation.

If we accept the writer's plain statement that the disasters of 1066
had destroyed the purpose of the book, we must, when attempting to
define that purpose, allow for dislocation and some later revision of the
text. We can start with a certainty: the original intention of the writer,
probably on Edith's instructions, was to show that Earl Godwin's
family was specially well equipped to direct the kingdom's affairs. We
can, of course, leave the matter there, and suggest that Edith commissioned the work, when her family was at the height of its power, for the
simple glorification of herself and her relatives. But could Edith in
1065 have been so simple, so politically naive? Is it not likely that there
was at least an ulterior motive? That she had in mind the situation on
Edward's death?

Hidden aims are not always easy to discern. And with our ignorance
of the political scene at the end of Edward's reign no confident answer
can be given to the question what were Edith's real motives. Nevertheless the subject can be discussed with profit. In comparison with the
Encomium Emmae Reginae it is difficult to see against whom, against what
rival, the *Vita Ædwardi Regis* was written. In the former we are told that
Harold Harefoot was supposititious, Edward Æthelredsson uninterested in the crown.[2] In the latter work, so far as we can see, no living
enemies, no possible rivals of the house of Godwin are mentioned.

[1] *VEdR*, p. 58.　　　　　　　　　　[2] *Encomium Emmae*, pp. 38–41, 48.

William of Normandy, Harald Hardrada, Svein Estrithson, Edgar Ætheling are not named. The king of Denmark is shown in the first chapter becoming Edward's vassal;[1] but this seems to be too casually inserted to bear on the point at issue. Even Eadwine and Morkere are unnamed – they appear as the sons of Earl Ælfgar[2] – and, although they are denounced for leading the revolution against Tostig, they are not traduced or treated as a rival power. The author knew that he could attack Robert of Jumièges and other Normans for their behaviour in the first part of the reign: but he was not required to pursue this matter. It is quite clear that he was not instructed to write against any specific rival interest.

It is possible, therefore, that when the book was commissioned Edith's ambitions were not precisely formulated. By producing an encomium of herself and her four brothers she gained propaganda material that could suit most eventualities. But a recurrent theme in the book is that the breaking of pacts leads to chaos and disaster.[3] This suggests that at one point Edith and her brothers had agreed to share the spoils. But what was the pact? Karl Schnith has argued that the whole purpose of the *Vita* was to justify a change of dynasty, to prepare for the transfer of the crown from the house of Cerdic to the house of Godwin (as from the Merovingians to the Carolingians) and that there was agreement in the family after 1053 that Harold, 'the eldest and wisest', should succeed not only to Wessex, but also in fullness of time to England.[4]

The most obvious objection to this theory – that Harold's coronation and reign are ignored by the *Vita* – is not insuperable. The omission may simply be the result of the battle of Hastings. The author when attempting to salvage his work after the death of his lords, could not afford to include this politically unacceptable episode and either left or cut it out. In any case, with William on the throne, it could serve no useful purpose. We can also explain the author's picture of Edith's grief at Tostig's banishment in 1065 not as showing that the queen sympathized with Tostig and condemned Harold, but as evidence of her foresight. He probably believed that the quarrel between the brothers not only led to Stamford Bridge, but also directly caused Harold's failure at Hastings: and so Edith 'showed by her tears her foreknowledge of future disasters.'[5]

---

[1] *VEdR*, pp. 10–11.   [2] *Ibid.*, p. 50.   [3] *Ibid.*, pp. 15–16, 37–40; cf. 56–7.
[4] 'Die Wende', pp. 37–8.   [5] *VEdR*, p. 54.

A far more serious difficulty is that it can be argued that Tostig is the real hero of the story. E. A. Freeman wrote,[1] 'it is clear that, whether from his own actual convictions or from a wish to please his patroness, the Lady Eadgyth, it is Tostig rather than Harold whose partizan he is to be reckoned, and it is Tostig whose actions he is most anxious to put in a favourable light.' Certainly there is much more in the book about Tostig than about Harold: and if its purpose was to promote Harold's claim to the throne, the author went a strange way about it. Even when the two brothers are balanced, Tostig often comes out better. Although Harold could have been described as the founder of Waltham minster,[2] he is shown as less interested in the church than Tostig (and far less interested than Edward and Edith). And the author seems definitely to warm towards Tostig as the story proceeds. Tostig at the time of his banishment is clearly presented as the favourite of the court. As Tostig died before Harold there is no question of transferring support to the survivor.

All the same, it is possible that Edith instructed the author to keep an equal balance between Harold and Tostig, and that it was a combination of the author's inability and changes in the actual situation which gave the extant version its apparent bias in favour of Tostig. Certainly in the plan there is marked symmetry. We start with four brothers and are left with the leading pair. Both of these go to Rome; both fight against England's enemies; the one guards the south, the other the north. The two are compared and contrasted in a celebrated set-piece. An important theme is the equality, the twinship of the brothers. There is the promise of harmony and stability in their balanced division.[3] And, it can be argued, in order to show Harold and Tostig as equals the author has to give Tostig something to make up for his being the junior by birth. But it also seems that the biographer

[1] *NC*, ii. 379. Because Freeman idolized Harold, he exaggerated the coldness of Harold's portrait in the *Vita*.

[2] Freeman, *NC*, ii. 442, no doubt exaggerates the importance of Harold's benefaction: 'In truth, of the two great foundations of this reign, Earl Harold's College at Waltham stands in distinct opposition, almost in distinct rivalry, to King Eadward's Abbey at Westminster.' But the author of the *Vita* does not trouble to make Harold even respectably religious. If he was connected with Christ Church, Canterbury, he could have been offended by Harold's burial there of one of his children, said to be unbaptized. See Osbern, *Miracula S. Dunstani* in *Memorials of St Dunstan*, ed. W. Stubbs (Rolls ser. 1874), pp. 141–2. But if it was his task to portray Harold as worthy of the throne, he was carrying out his commission incompetently.

[3] *VEdR*, pp. 31–40, 42–3, 56–8.

found information about Tostig more easy to come by, and that in the end, perhaps influenced by the story he was telling, he became a partisan of the younger brother. He did not, however, go completely off the rails. As late as the prologue to Book II he is still concerned more with the whole family than with any individual: 'a miserable wretch, bereaved of all those famous lords', he turns to his new task – the glorification of King Edward – with a regret which is in deliberate contrast to the joy with which he accepted the original commission.[1]

If the brothers cancelled each other out, the sister was left pre-eminent. Edith was the gem in the middle of the kingdom;[2] and it is possible that the special aim of the *Vita* was to justify a claim that Edith was Edward's heiress. English queens in the tenth and eleventh centuries were not innocent of political ambition; and we can picture Edith as not entirely unlike her mother-in-law, Emma. We notice the insistence in the *Vita* that Edith had the status of a daughter. Edward is reported as saying on his deathbed, 'She has served me devotedly and has always stood close by my side like a beloved daughter.'[3] This theme was later understood as implying a chaste marriage and was incorporated into the legend. But it is more likely that the author had in mind the important rule of Roman law that a will was automatically revoked by marriage and that a wife acquired the status of a daughter and became her husband's self-successor.[4] If Edith was Edward's daughter she was clearly his heiress. Edward's other dying words concerning Edith can also be held to support this view: Edith would continue to rule as queen; Harold should honour her as his lord (*domina*) and sister, and serve her faithfully.[5] In 1066 Edith was under forty-six years of age and could even have been in her late thirties. Obviously, like Emma, she could have made a second marriage. It is equally obvious to us that, since it is unlikely that she would have borne a child, this plan would not have solved the political problem. But it may have been a long-standing ambition of Edith's which she was reluctant completely to abandon; and she may have come to the view that in any case after her time one of her brothers could follow on the throne. This is where the vaunted patience of the family would have been so useful.

[1] *VEdR*, pp. 5, 60. [2] *Ibid.*, p. 15.

[3] *Ibid.*, p. 79; cf. 15, 41–2. It is also characteristic of the author's vocabulary: Godwin is a father-figure; cf. the use of *nutricius*.

[4] 'Idem iuris est si cui post factum testamentum uxor in manum conveniat . . .; nam eo modo filiae loco esse incipit et quasi sua.', *Gai Institutiones*, II, 139; Inst. 2, 17, 2. [5] *VEdR*, p. 79.

If this was the plan, it was wrecked when Harold failed to support Tostig and then took the throne. There is in the book tacit condemnation of both these actions. The book was not written to justify Harold's seizure of the crown. Yet the significance of Bishop Beorhtweald's vision is that God had provided some mysterious successor to Edward. Strictly speaking it would have been contrary to God's will for no one to succeed; it would also have been a most unusual situation. It is possible, therefore, that we should not push the theme of throne-worthiness too hard, that the true purpose of the *Vita* was to portray the family not as Edward's heirs but as king-makers, statesmen specially equipped to interpret the will of God. If so, we must imagine that the family had a candidate in mind, suitable for raising to the throne and in whose name they would continue to govern. The obvious candidate is Edgar the aetheling; and such a plan is plausible enough. The difficulty about this interpretation is that it has no positive foundation in the *Vita*. If Edith had a successor in mind, we would have expected to find some reference to him in the tract written to support the scheme. But it is possible that in 1065 Edith and her brothers had not decided whom to make king. They could make a deal with a foreign prince, as they may have believed Godwin had come to terms with Edward, or they could promote Edgar. Their hands were free; the *Vita* kept them free and justified their claim to be king-makers. If this was their plan in 1065, it was possibly a casual opportunity for Harold – the rebellion in Northumbria – which destroyed the family pact and caused, as the author of the *Vita* recognized, the ruin of them all.

Owing to the change in the author's plan it is impossible to be sure exactly what was the original political purpose of the *Vita*. The safest view is that when Edith commissioned the work she was preparing for the future, but was not committed, or did not wish to be committed, to any one scheme. Accordingly, she told the author to write in praise of her family. It was this general commission which allowed the author to change his emphasis as the political situation altered and so to produce a work which we now find most difficult to understand.

Appendix B

HOSTAGES TAKEN FROM EARL GODWIN'S FAMILY

From William of Poitiers, archdeacon of Lisieux, who wrote probably after 1073 or 1076 and several twelfth-century English and Norman writers we learn something of members of the house of Godwin in the hands of William of Normandy. We also get the impression that we are concerned with a rumour, perhaps based on fact but unreliable in detail, repeated from one circle to another.

The earliest authority, William of Poitiers, informs us that Edward confirmed his grant of the succession of the throne to William by surrendering two hostages, a son and *nepos* of Earl Godwin.[1] The latter, described as Earl Harold's *fratruelis*, was released by William to Harold, on his visit to Normandy in 1064 or 1065, as an act of grace.[2]

The word *nepos*, originally meaning 'grandson',[3] was used by later Latin writers in the sense of 'nephew', and also always had the general meaning of 'a descendant'. All three usages can be exemplified from the *Gesta Guillelmi*: the meaning is usually clear from the context. One of Duke William's captains at the battle of Hastings was Robert, son of Roger of Beaumont and *nepos et haeres* of Hugh, count of Meulan, who had married Adeline, Roger's sister.[4] Here *nepos* undoubtedly means 'nephew'. But it is the one and only case in William of Poitiers. The other two senses cannot be completely separated. The archdeacon predicted that King William's *liberi atque nepotes* would rule by hereditary descent over England.[5] The father of Adela, countess of Flanders, was Robert (I), king of France, who, *filius et nepos regum*, himself engendered kings.[6] In these cases *nepos* could be either a grandson or a descendant. But in two other texts the word is best translated 'grandson'. Bishop Hugh of Lisieux was the *nepos* of Count Richard I of Normandy

---

[1] William of Poitiers, pp. 30–2, 176.   [2] *Ibid.*, pp. 100, 114.
[3] Cf. Isidore of Seville, *Orig.* 9, 5, 26, 'Nepos est, qui ex filio natus est. . . . Hinc et posteritas, quasi postera aetas.' See also 9, 6, 23.
[4] William of Poitiers, p. 192.   [5] *Ibid.*, p. 222.   [6] *Ibid.*, p. 50.

through the count's *filius*, William, count of Eu.[1] The Emperor Henry (IV) was the *filius* of the Emperor Henry (III) and the *nepos* of the Emperor Conrad (II).[2] Nor was William of Poitiers unique. Although the historian Orderic Vital seems always to have employed *nepos* in the sense of 'nephew' or 'descendant',[3] his contemporary, William of Malmesbury, used it for 'grandson'.[4] Dr Sten Körner is, therefore, mistaken in thinking that it is almost certain that William of Poitiers meant a nephew of Earl Godwin.[5] Körner, however, did not notice the archdeacon's description of Godwin's *nepos* as Harold's *fratruelis*. Here he would have been on safer ground in maintaining that, although *fratruelis* could stand for 'nephew', it was defined by Isidore, *Orig.* 9, 6, 15, thus: 'fratrueles filii materterae sunt', that is to say, cousins on the maternal side, strictly, the offspring of two sisters. Unfortunately we cannot demonstrate from other passages what William of Poitiers meant by the word.

On this evidence it cannot be decided what relationship William of Poitiers intended to convey. It is quite possible that, as Körner maintains, he was in the dark; in which case the ambiguous *nepos* should be translated 'relation'. But Eadmer, the English writer, believed that the second hostage was Godwin's grandson;[6] and even if he were merely expounding William of Poitiers, it is a warning not to reject this interpretation out of hand. Körner, having rejected it, maintained that Godwin had no brothers or sisters, and that therefore the archdeacon's story was absurd. If, however, he had looked for relations on the spindle side he would have found nephews of the greatest distinction. Godwin's wife, Gytha, was the sister of the Danish noblemen, Eilifr and Ulf; and among her nephews was Svein Estrithson, king of Denmark.

It is clear that the Norman account of Anglo-Norman diplomacy cannot be dismissed by ridiculing the section on the hostages, as Körner attempts to do. William of Poitiers was not incompetent. Nevertheless his story of the hostages is his own contribution and lacks corroboration. He added it to the version of this affair which he found in William of Jumièges, and it is likely that his source was hearsay. Moreover, when Orderic Vital in his turn came to write of the two

---

[1] Poitiers, p. 136.   [2] *Ibid.*, p. 154.   [3] See below, p. 307.
[4] Cf. Malmesbury, *GR*, i. 238: Edward was the son of Æthelred and the *nepos* of Edgar; also 'nepos Aldredi comitis, comes Waltheof, erat enim filius filiae illius', *De obsessione Dunelmi*, in *Symeonis Monachi Opera Omnia*, ed. T. Arnold (Rolls ser. 1882), i. 219.   [5] Körner, *Battle of Hastings*, pp. 126 ff.   [6] See below, p. 303.

episodes in his *Historia Ecclesiastica*, although he was familiar with, and made great use of, William of Poitiers' work, he omitted all mention of the hostages.[1] This is not because he did not believe that the duke had held captive members of the house of Godwin.[2] It is probably because by 1114–24, when he wrote Book III of his History, another, discordant, version of the story was in circulation, and Orderic decided to play safe.

By the twelfth century it was probably widely known that Wulfnoth, a son of Earl Godwin, had been one of William's prisoners, presumably because he was one of those whom the dying king had ordered to be released in 1087.[3] Orderic, when revising William of Jumièges about 1109, inserted into the account of Harold's visit to Normandy the information that the duke retained Wulfnoth as a hostage,[4] and this information also appeared in English historical tradition from about 1112. Although we may be fairly sure that Wulfnoth Godwinesson was indeed one of the Conqueror's prisoners, this fact does not prove the truth of any of the stories of how he fell into William's hands.

The second hostage was identified about the same time. According to Eadmer, monk of Christ Church, Canterbury, he was Hakon, son of Swegn Godwinesson, Godwin's grandson, Harold's nephew.[5] This identification was adopted, probably always by copying, by other twelfth-century Anglo-Norman historians.[6] It is by no means impossible that Eadmer is simply expanding William of Poitiers and believed that of Godwin's sons only Swegn had children in 1052. But where he learned that Swegn had a son named Hakon we do not know. Swegn's only recorded 'matrimonial' adventure is his abduction of Eadgifu, abbess of Leominster, in 1046.[7] But a child of that union is unlikely to have been called Hakon, and, unless Godwin and Gytha had adopted the boy, a five year old orphaned bastard would hardly be the most desirable sort of hostage. If the second hostage was indeed Swegn's son, Hakon, he was probably the offspring of an earlier liaison, most likely with an Anglo-Norwegian girl.[8]

---

[1] The parallel passages are displayed in Barlow, 'Edward the Confessor's Early Life', *EHR*, lxxx (1965), 242–3.

[2] See below, *n.* 4.   [3] Florence, ii. 20.

[4] William of Jumièges, p. 191.   [5] Eadmer, *Historia Novorum*, pp. 6, 8.

[6] Cf. Symeon, *HR*, ii. 183.   [7] See above, p. 91.

[8] The name occurs in Scandinavian dynasties; but, although it was sometimes asserted that Earl Hakon married a niece of Cnut – which would bring the name into a family related to Godwin – it is probably a mistake: Campbell, *Encomium Emmae*, pp. 71, 85. We would expect that Earl Swegn would call one of his sons Cnut: see above, p. 90.

Eadmer not only provided names for the hostages, he also produced a new explanation of how and why they fell into William's hands.[1] For the events of 1051–2 he followed English sources, but added that when Godwin and his family returned to England in 1052 they had to surrender Wulfnoth and Hakon as hostages to Edward; and Edward sent them to Normandy for safe custody. Here, presumably, he is expanding the *E* version of the Chronicle. This Canterbury recension is alone in giving the terms of the truce, arranged on 14 September 1052, which led to the reconciliation of the king and the outlaws on the following day. We are told that the intermediaries, led by Stigand, agreed that hostages 'should be arranged for both sides. And so it was done.' Whereupon Archbishop Robert and the other Frenchmen fled. What Eadmer has done is to name Godwin's hostages and imply that Robert conveyed them out of the country. This may have been Canterbury tradition; but whether it is sound is another matter. The *E* version does not convincingly support Eadmer's extensions. It does not state explicitly that hostages were actually exchanged: if the foreigners fled immediately they heard of the truce, the deserted king may have lost the power to enforce the conditions. If the French had snatched the hostages almost out of Godwin's hands, it was a coup that the chronicler would hardly have passed over in silence. And the whole incident does not fit very well into the general picture presented by the Chronicle.[2] All versions agree that the entire family was taken back into favour: all causes of discord were removed. It is also clear that the earls returned from exile as victors, not as suppliants. They were in no mood to be tricked.

It is likely that Eadmer is being quite as arbitrary as William of Poitiers in his use of the hostages. He describes the events of 1051–2 as a prologue to his account of Harold's visit to Normandy, which, although probably based on William of Poitiers, for the basic pattern remains, is much altered. Eadmer wanted to dissociate the hostages from Edward's appointment of William as his heir. So he not only made Godwin give the hostages in 1052 and to Edward, but also asserted that Edward made his promise to William while he was still an exile in Normandy. After this preparation Eadmer could treat Harold's Norman visit quite differently: the earl insisted on going to Normandy, against Edward's wishes and despite his forebodings, solely in order to release his brother and nephew; and William craftily took advantage

[1] *Historia Novorum*, pp. 5–6.   [2] See above, p. 124.

of Harold's foolishness. Thus the episode was still connected, although quite differently, with the Norman Conquest; and it could also illustrate Edward's spirit of prophecy.

Eadmer's story of Harold's visit to the duchy is even more legendary in tone than the archdeacon's. We are asked to believe that Edward seriously promised a boy of thirteen the succession to a throne which he himself had still to acquire. We are given an unlikely scene at Edward's court. And we have the hostages in a new setting. We can hardly doubt that we are concerned with an imaginary and partisan reconstruction of an original which may itself be hardly less fictitious and no less biased in the other direction.

No light can be thrown on these episodes from other quarters. Wulfnoth scarcely exists, and Hakon does not occur outside this context. Other twelfth-century writers had little of value to contribute to the stories already current.[1] Yet it is possible, by taking elements from the two basic accounts of the hostages, to construct an explanation which at least harmonizes with the view of events presented by the Anglo-Saxon Chronicle. According to this source, it was in the autumn of 1051, between the abortive rebellion of Godwin and his sons and their banishment, that Edward demanded hostages;[2] and this would indeed seem the likeliest moment for Godwin and Swegn Godwinsson each to surrender a son. Then, after the sentences of outlawry and before the earl's return by force (October 1051–June 1052), Edward could have transferred the hostages to Normandy, possibly by means of the duke himself if he indeed visited England at this time. The reason could have been either to put them beyond the reach of the returning earls or to provide security in some diplomatic scheme. But the first reason could have been succeeded by the second, or William could have refused to part with his valuable acquisition.

This proposed rectification of the story of the hostages would not invalidate William of Poitiers' view of the events of 1051–2, although it weakens its coherence and casts doubt on the writer's trustworthiness. Nor would it necessarily harm Eadmer's explanation of why Harold visited Normandy in 1064/5. The value of these accounts has to be

[1] Symeon, *HR*, ii. 183, 214, copies Eadmer and Florence. Florence, ii. 21, contributes the information that another member of the house of Godwin, Ulf Haroldsson, was in Robert Curthose's hands in 1087. William of Malmesbury, *GR*, i. 245, tells us that in the Conqueror's reign Wulfnoth was kept in chains at Salisbury, and Orderic (ed. Chibnall), ii. 178, that Wulfnoth died as an old man at Salisbury.

[2] See above, pp. 112–13.

judged in other ways. But the ease with which the story of the hostages can be manipulated is detrimental to the credit of both. All, however, is not loss. By putting the hostages into what seems to be a truer historical setting, we get a version which is not only satisfactory in itself, but which could easily have been perverted into the other forms. We may, at least here, be getting nearer historical truth.

Appendix C

THE DESCENDANTS OF EUSTACE OF BOULOGNE AND GODGIFU

It is common knowledge that Eustace II, count of Boulogne, married, first, the widow Godgifu or Goda, Edward the Confessor's sister, and, second, Ida of Lorraine or of Bouillon. It is generally believed that, although Godgifu had three sons by her first husband and Eustace as many from his second wife, no children survived from the marriage of Eustace and Godgifu. Accordingly Eustace had no direct interest in the descent of the English throne, and his interventions in English affairs in 1051 and 1067 have to be explained in some other way. But it is possible that Eustace and Godgifu raised at least one daughter who married and produced a son.[1] This grandson would have been the great-grandson of King Æthelred and the great-great-grandson of Count Richard I of Normandy.

Eustace, according to William of Poitiers, gave William of Normandy a son as hostage in 1066,[2] and in the following year, after the Conqueror had returned to the duchy, invaded Kent and tried to capture Dover.[3] The attack was repulsed and in the retreat a squire of high birth (*nobilissimus tiro*), Eustace's *nepos*, was captured. Orderic Vital repeated this information without comment.[4] Both Professor Foreville and Mrs Chibnall translate *nepos* as 'nephew'. It is true that Orderic usually uses *nepos* in that sense or in the wider sense of descendants or kinsmen;[5] but here he was copying William of Poitiers, and the Norman usually meant 'grandson' or 'descendant'.[6] If Eustace had indeed a grandson of near-military age – perhaps thirteen or fourteen – in 1067, the

---

[1] I owe the suggestion to Miss Hope Muntz and Miss Catherine Morton, who also drew my attention to Edmond Rigaux, 'Recherches sur les premiers Comtes de Boulogne', *Bulletin de la Société académique de l'arrondissement de Boulogne-sur-Mer*, v (1894), 151–77. I am grateful to them.   [2] Poitiers, p. 264.
[3] *Ibid.*, p. 266.   [4] Orderic, ii. 175 (ed. Chibnall, ii. 206).
[5] Cf. Orderic, ed. Chibnall, ii. 30, 48, 74, 104, 148, 158; 30, 56, 152.
[6] See above, pp. 301–2.

grandmother, if the descent was legitimate, must have been Godgifu.

The date of her marriage to Eustace is unknown. She was born between 1003 and 1014 and widowed in 1035, when Drogo died on Count Robert of Normandy's pilgrimage to Jerusalem. As Eustace had a son by Ida in 1066 both marriages took place in the period 1036–64. He succeeded his father as count about 1047 and in 1049 was excommunicated at the council of Rheims for an incestuous marriage.[1] This can hardly be an indication of when he married Godgifu, who would have been about forty at the time: the sentence marks either the end of that union or the beginning of his marriage to Ida.[2] In any case, if we allow time for Eustace's marriage to Godgifu, no son or daughter of Eustace and Ida could have produced a boy of near-military age by 1067. If Eustace had such a legitimate grandson in 1067 he must have married Godgifu in, or shortly after, 1036,[3] when she was about thirty. A daughter born in 1037 could have married in 1049 at twelve; and a son born to her in 1052 would have been fifteen in 1067. It is a fairly tight, but by no means unlikely timetable; and there are no obvious objections to it.

If this reconstruction is correct, Eustace's interest in England must be reassessed. In 1051 he may have wished to consult Edward about the girl's marriage or about its consequences, for her son would be Edward's great-nephew and a possible heir to the throne. In 1067 he took a pretender to the crown with him to England. This *nepos* was captured at Dover. And, although William and Eustace were reconciled shortly before 1074, it is not surprising that we hear nothing more of the boy. The Conqueror liked to hold hostages and felt happy when dynastic rivals were inside his castles.

---

[1] Anselm's account of the council, Mansi, *Concilia*, xix. 742.

[2] Rigaux, pp. 166–70, argues in favour of the latter. An interesting argument is that Eustace and Ida founded monasteries, which, like William of Normandy's, could have been in atonement for incest.

[3] Rigaux, pp. 164–5, refers to *Encomium Emmae*, p. 43, where we learn that Alfred, Godgifu's brother, about to invade England in 1036, refused men from Flanders and took companions from Boulogne.

Appendix D

CORRESPONDENCE CONCERNING
EDWARD'S CANONIZATION

On three pages of a Vatican Library manuscript, latin 6024, ff. 150ᵛ–1ᵛ, are copied fourteen letters, thirteen to Pope Alexander III and one in reply, concerned with Edward's canonization.[1] They were printed, but not together, and rather unsatisfactorily,[2] by Francesco Liverani, *Spicilegium Liberianum* (Florence, 1863). This group of letters is a sub-section of a larger collection, written on a double quire (ff. 140–54), which Z. N. Brooke believed had been made by, or under the direction of, Master David of London, a clerk prominent in Henry II's reign and engaged in important diplomacy, especially at the papal court.[3] However that may be, they seem to have been preserved as a formulary, for proper names are mostly reduced to initials, and, as can be demonstrated in one case,[4] the editor excised as much extraneous matter as possible. The reduction of the contents was probably a fairly drastic operation: the belated recognition of a pope was not only a time for congratulations but also an opportunity for transacting business. Nor is the collection complete. There is, for example, no letter from Archbishop Theobald of Canterbury. Although the archbishop was close to death, a letter could have issued from his household, and there is a reference to his support in Nigel of Ely's missive.[5]

No stray pieces from the dossier have as yet been noticed. Nor can more than one of the mutilated letters be reconstructed. But the identity of all except the humblest correspondents presents no difficulty, and

---

[1] The MS has been described by Paul Ewald, 'Reise nach Italien im Winter von 1876 auf 1877', *Neues Archiv der Gesellschaft für ältere deutsche Geschichtskunde*, iii (1878), 150–1; R. Poupardin, 'Dix-huit lettres inédites', *Bibl. de l'Ecole des Chartes*, lxiii (1902); Z. N. Brooke, 'The Register of Master David of London and the part he played in the Becket Crisis', *Essays in History presented to R. L. Poole*, ed. H. W. C. Davis (1927), pp. 227 ff.; F. Barlow, *The Letters of Arnulf of Lisieux* (R. Hist. Soc. Camden 3rd ser. lxi, 1939), pp. lxxiii, lxxxii–lxxxiii.

[2] There are errors of transcription in every letter; but only one (below, p. 311, *n.* 2) is of any importance. Liverani also misled by extending initials, sometimes wrongly.

[3] 'The Register of Master David', pp. 232–3, 235–6.

[4] Below, no. 5.   [5] Below, p. 317.

the letters can be dated closely enough. Although Westminster may have canvassed support for its scheme before the kings of France and England decided between the rival claimants to the papacy, no official approach could have been made to Alexander before the decision, and, since most letters congratulate him on his recognition, these at least date from the autumn of 1160. The letter from Alexander's legates in France may have been written in the second half of November;[1] and this is probably the *terminus ad quem* for all the petitions. The papal bull can be dated from other copies 7 February 1161.

THE LETTERS

1. *King Henry II to Pope Alexander III*

[*fo. 150ᵛ*] Domino pape rex Anglorum H. Gratum mihi est et deo gratias refero quod, summi pontificatus honore sullimatus, suscepistis regimen universalis ecclesie, salubriter annuente domino vestra discretione dispensand*um*. Et mihi quidem cordi est matrem nostram sanctam Romanam ecclesiam sincera semper affectione diligere, officiis colere, ac personam vestram pura indesinenter amplecti devotione. Universos quoque quos divina dignata est gratia mee potestati subicere, volo apostolicam sedem ad instar divini numinis honorare*ᵃ* ac debitam ei obedientiam mecum pariter exhibere. Inde est quod apostolatui vestro confidentius preces offero, obnixe deposcens, sicut tota deposcit Anglorum ecclesia, ut gloriosum regem Eduardum in cathalogo sanctorum iubeatis ascribi et in ecclesia sanctorum canonizari. De cuius sanguine propagatum me, licet indignum, dignatus est dominus sua dispositione in solio regni eiusdem regis sullimare, sicut datum fuerit desuper pro tempore regnaturum. Nec in hac re oportet experientiam vestram, ut estimo, hesitare, cum multi religiosi ac discreti viri, sicut litteris illorum vobis intimatur, attestentur huius sancti sanctitatem signis ac virtutibus sepenumero fuisse declaratam. Quorum spes est quod adiciet misereri deus, statuens ut complacitior sit adhuc populo suo per merita confessoris sui, vestra si placet auctoritate glorificandi.

ᵃ adorare *expunged*

1. Henry congratulates Alexander on becoming pope and professes his devotion to the Roman church. He joins with the whole English

[1] Below, no. 2.

church in requesting the canonization of King Edward, his kinsman and predecessor on the throne. The proofs of Edward's sanctity, as will be seen from the letters testimonial of many religious and discreet men, leave no room for hesitation.

2. *Cardinals Henry and Otto to Pope Alexander III*[1]

Sanctissimo patri et domino Alex., dei gratia summo et universali pontifici, H. et O., eadem gratia sancte Romane [ecclesie] cardinales, obedientiam tam debitam quam devotam. Gloria nostra hec est, pater, testimonium conscientie nostre quo iudice confidenter quod scimus loquimur, et quod indubitanter verum esse credimus constantissime nuntiamus. Credimus quidem, propter et*a* loquimur, et testimonium nostrum per gratiam dei recipitur, quoniam verum esse creditur et speratur. Negotium ecclesie faciente domino prosperatur et recurritur ad sacrosanctam matrem nostram Romanam ecclesiam et ad vos, atque illorum testimonio sanctitatis vestre favor postulatur et gratia, qui creduntur vobis non nisi vera debere aliqua ratione intimare. Venit ad nos karissimus frater noster, Laur., Westm. ecclesie abbas, Parisius,[2] et de sancta ac laudabili vita, de obitu etiam et miraculis gloriosi regis Angl. Eduardi, qui beate memorie Nicholao, predecessori vestro, et per eum beato Petro et Romane ecclesie, regnum quod optinebat pia devotione contradidit, multa nobis et magnifica enarravit. Inter que unum nobis miraculum oculata fide de supradicto viro ostendit, quod tanto specialius paternitati vestre intimare decrevimus, quanto et que oculorum fidei sunt subiecta melius credimus, et a pluribus archiepiscopis et episcopis Anglie attestantur, confidentius enarramus.*b* Ostendit siquidem nobis pallii casulam in quo, cum iamdicti regis corpus iuxta supradictorum testimonium per annorum multa remansisset curricula involutum, nullam tamen lesionem invenimus vel etiam coloris

[1] Liverani extended the initials to *Hyacintus* and *Otho*, identifying the former as cardinal-deacon of St Mary in Cosmedin. Bernhard W. Scholz, 'The Canonization of Edward the Confessor', *Speculum*, xxxvi (1961), 49, follows, although, p. 52, *n.* 68, he expresses doubts. For the legation of Henry, c.-p. of St Nereus and Achilles, and Otto, c.-d. of St Nicholas in Carcere Tulliano, to France, 1160–62, see Werner Ohnsorge, *Die Legaten Alexanders III im ersten Jahrzehnt seines Pontifikats (1159–1169)* (Berlin, 1928), pp. 15 ff.

[2] Liverani read 'pariter' and so concealed this important fact. The occasion was possibly 13 November 1160, when Louis VII's new wife, Ada, was crowned queen at Paris by Hugh, archbishop of Sens, in the presence of the papal legates, Henry, Otto, and William, c.-p. of St Peter ad vincula, Ohnsorge, *op. cit.*, p. 36.

obfuscationem potuimus denotare. Fulget enim eiusdem casule pannus ita specie ac colore ut merito divina virtute credatur servatum illesum, quod humani corporis menbra, nisi adesset miraculum, debuerant penitus consumpsisse. Qua de re, pater sanctissime, supplicamus et nos cum iamdicto abbate, qui ad pedes vestros, nisi vie difficultas obstitisset, utique corruisset, supplicamus, inquam, ut preces iustas ipsius et illustris regis Anglorum atque archiepiscoporum et episcoporum, qui super hoc vobis scribunt, exaudire dignemini et remittere nuntios eius ad propria cum gaudio et fine debito negotii quod apportant. Exaudi-endus est quippe memoratus filius vester abbas in iustis postulationibus suis, quoniam honestate ac prudentia est, prout novit fere universa ecclesia, redimitus, et contra scismaticos tanquam vir catholicus exstitit ferventissimus decertator.

^a *text corrupt*; propter quod et *L*; ? *amend to* quapropter et
^b *the text is defective*

2. The legates are in duty bound to declare what they believe to be true. They have been visited at Paris by Laurence, abbot of West-minster, who told them much about the holy life and the death and miracles of Edward, the glorious king of the English who handed over his kingdom to Pope Nicholas [II], St Peter, and the Roman church. Laurence also showed them the pall in which Edward's corpse had been wrapped and which, despite its long sojourn in the grave, had remained intact, unfaded, and unstained. Laurence is prevented from visiting Rome in person because of the difficulty of the journey; and the legates beg the pope to give a favourable answer to the petition presented by the abbot, the king, and the archbishops and bishops. The abbot is an honest and prudent man and has been a great supporter of the pope against the schismatics.

3. [*Roger of Pont l'Evêque,*] *archbishop of York, to Pope Alexander III*
Domino pape Eborac. archiepiscopus. Quotiens amicorum precibus pulsatus, pater sancte, vobis scribere presumo, aggravatur dolor meus et exitus aquarum deducunt oculi mei, quoniam non datur videre quem diligit anima mea. Interim, donec conteratur draco iste, qui sibilat in Italia, formatus a domino ut illudatur ei, muti litterarum apices vive vocis vicem aput discretionem vestram in his, que ad me vel amicos

meos spectant, optineant, nec honestis petitionibus deroget absentia
mea, quam excusare facile potest necessitas. Ecce prostratus ad pedes
sanctitatis vestre devotus filius vester, Laur., abbas Westm., con-
supplicat cum fratribus suis, quatenus auctoritate vestra rex Eduardus,
eiusdem monasterii fundator, inter sanctos conscribatur, ad ecclesie
Romane honorem, quam, dum erat in terris, pre cunctis temporis sui
regibus dilexit, et populi regni Anglorum devotionem. Hic in regni
sullimatus fastigio iuxta divinarum legum sancionem regni adminis-
travit negotia, sed regni nequaquam secutus delicias, in carne vivens
carnis vehementer persecutus est voluptates. Predicti abbatis petitioni
cleri principis tocius regni commune votum accedit. Inter quos saltem
ultimum locum dominus meus servo suo reservet, ut facilius interventu
meo possit impetrari quod apostolica mansuetudo publico non negabit
desiderio.

3. Roger grieves that he is unable to visit the pope in person. He
commends Laurence's petition for the canonization of Edward, the
founder of his monastery. Edward loved the Roman church. He
governed his kingdom in accordance with the precepts of divine law,
and when living in the flesh repressed all the pleasures of the flesh.
The petition is supported by the whole kingdom.

4. [*Henry of Blois,*] *bishop of Winchester, to Pope Alexander III*
Domino pape episcopus Winton. Devotus filius vester Laur. ad vos
ire sive mittere disposuit. Eapropter humiles preces paternitati vestre
porrigimus, quatenus ipsum et suos benigne suscipere et in iustis
petitionibus suis exaudire dignemini. Valeat sanctitas vestra in domino.

4. Laurence is about to go or send nuncios to the pope. Henry
commends them and their business.

5. [*Gilbert Foliot,*] *bishop of Hereford, to Pope Alexander III*[1]
Domino pape Hereford. episcopus.[a] Qui nube tristicie nuper obducti,
matre nostra sancta Romana ecclesia[b] gravi scismatis errore concussa,

[1] This is a shortened version of the letter printed *Materials for the History of Thomas
Becket*, ed. J. C. Robertson (Rolls ser. 1881), v. 16 ff.; collated here as *R*.

altius ingemendo^c doluimus, luce veritatis bonorum cordibus illuces-
cente, tota gaudii plenitudine, in christo dilecte pater, exultavimus,
cum munere divino procella nobis in auram statuta est, et post noctem
dies nobis tam profecto grata quam serena resplenduit.^d Celitus^e itaque
collato vobis honori, pater, ut Anglorum plenius applaudat ecclesia, in
uno devotissime beatis^f auspiciis vestris postulat exaudiri, ut beati regis
Eduardi corpus liceat fidelissimo filio vestro, Westm. abbati, L., prout
eius expetit sanctitas, honorare, et a terra levatum et condigna theca
repositum in publicas tocius populi gratulaciones in ecclesia sullimare,
quam a fundamentis erectam construxit,^g et amplissime dotatam
omnibus, que ad honorem^h domus dei sunt, in honorem dei et beati
Petri nobilitatemⁱ beatissime consummavit. Hoc quidem corpus, ut ab
his, quibus ut credimus fides^j habenda est, frequenter audivimus, a
xxxv^k annis usque nunc integrum incorruptumque cum visitaretur
inventum est, et qui, licet in coniugio positus, animi tamen summa
virtute toto^l vite sue curriculo, ut predicatur ab omnibus, virgo perman-
sit,^m post mortem etiam beata sui [corporis]ⁿ incorruptione donatus est.
Hunc prophetie spiritum habuisse, / [*fo. 151*] et in carne degentem
futura, domino revelante, predixisse constanter affirmant. Mitem^o
misericordem^o mansuetum super omnes, et beato Petro tam devotum
fuisse commemorant, ut diem qua ipsius ecclesie nichil contulerat, se
prorsus amisisse deploraret. Eius adhuc leges aput nos iudicia temperant,
et regni sui pauperes usque hodie in multis illesos provida ipsius
circumspectione conservant. Honore[m] vero qui sanctis exhibetur
quia domino placere non ambigimus, in hoc communi voto serenitati
vestre supplicamus, ut regnum Anglie, apostolice semper sullimitati
devotissimum, honoretis, et fidelem populum regi suo, quem ob multa,
que epistolaris brevitatis^p non capit angustia, vere sanctum existimant,
debitum sanctis honorem et reverentiam exhibere concedatis.^q

^a Patri suo et domino summo pontifici A. frater G., Herefordiensis ecclesiae
minister, devotum et debitum caritatis et obedientiae famulatum *R*   ^b *om.* s. *R.*
eccles. *R*   ^c ingemiscendo *R*   ^d *about 450 words of R are omitted here*   ^e Divini-
tus *R*   ^f in beatis his *R*   ^g constituit *R*   ^h decorem *R*   ⁱ nobilitatam *R*
^j fid. ut cred. *R*   ^k a centum iam *R*   ^l virtut *expunged MS*   ^m *add* et *R*
ⁿ corporis *R, om. MS*   ^o *add* et *R*   ^p *altered from* brevitastiis *MS, om. R*   ^q *add*
Conservet vos incolumem in longa tempora divina virtus, in Christo dilecte pater *R*

5. Gilbert rejoices that Alexander is emerging victorious from the
schism, and at this time of rejoicing and congratulation commends

the wish of Laurence and the whole English church to translate the body of Edward, the king who built and amply endowed Westminster. Edward's body was found incorrupt after thirty-five years in the tomb, for although married, he remained a virgin. He had the gift of prophecy and could foretell the future. He was gentle and merciful and so devoted to St Peter that he counted the day lost on which he gave nothing to the apostle's church. Edward's laws still temper the harshness of the law courts and take care of the kingdom's poor. By canonizing Edward the pope will honour the kingdom which has always been the most devoted to the Roman church.

6. [*Hilary,*] *bishop of Chichester, to Pope Alexander III*
Domino pape episcopus Cicestr. Ut ecclesiarum salus salva consistat, omnino, domine, nos viros venerari expedit quos, tormentorum cruciatibus aut triumphis confessionis sue mirabilibus examinatos, dominus tulit de area et in horreo taxari sua miseratione donavit. Quorum collegio associatum, et angelorum cetibus admixtum, gloriosum regem Eduardum multa religiosorum turba probabiliter asseverat. Aiunt enim quod in carne vivens carnis illecebras cavere satagebat, abduci blandiciis, seduci fallaciis, trahi deliciis, iniuriisve frangi vel adversis fatigari, semper attendens 'principem te constituerunt; esto in illis quasi unus ex illis.' Spiritu quoque prophetie claruit signisque choruscans, in usus pietatis opes regias indesinenter erogare invigilavit. Multo quidem tempore coniugatus virgo senex obiit, et sine lesionis indicio post vii lustra caro eius de tumulo incorrupta apparuisse memoratur. Quia ergo non minus pium quam iustum esse viditur, ut magnus magnificetur adhuc, cum venerabili viro devoto filio vestro, abbate Westm., L., eiusque fratribus, discrecionis vestre mansuetudinem deposco, quatenus virum a domino mirificatum regem iamdictum in cathalogo sanctorum conscribi iubeatis et canonizari, ut sicut aput nos celo et terra teste sanctus asseritur, ita et in ecclesia sanctorum auctoritate vestra celebris habeatur. Sic, sic, pater, sic ecclesie sic regi et regno, nuper ut semper ecclesie Romane fideliter obsequenti, celeberrima gaudia suscitabitis, et in memoria eterna erit cum iusto opus apostolice consum[m]ationis.

6. Hilary reports that there is general belief that Edward is a saint: it is said that when living in the flesh he avoided the temptations of

the flesh, that he had the gift of prophecy, that he was distinguished by miracles, and that he tirelessly gave away his wealth in good causes. Long married, he died in old age a virgin, and after thirty-five years in the tomb his flesh was found incorrupt. Hilary supports the petition for Edward's canonization. The pope is in a position to give great pleasure to a church, king, and kingdom which has been recently, as always, faithful to the Roman church.

7. *[William de Turbe,] bishop of Norwich, to Pope Alexander III*
Domino pape Norwic. episcopus. Quam gratus quamque deo acceptus existat gloriosissimus rex Eduardus et vite meritis et celestibus declaratur oraculis. Quippe dum in tabernaculo carnis rex regi, adleta imperatori, victoriosissime militaret, tam de mundi periculis quam de blandientis regni lenociniis semper gloriosum reportavit triumphum. Et licet in etatis lubrico et splendidissime regine capistratus esset coniugio, perpetuam tamen virginitatem virgo virginis filio creditur consecrasse et in fructu centesimo domino plurimum placuisse. Cuius tota intentio actus et opus solus semper erat Christus. Sed ne de stola glorificationis ipsius mentibus Anglorum aliquis scrupulus dubitationis possit occurrere, tam mira quam magnifica que circa corpus ipsius cotidie coruscant miracula manifeste declarant regem regio cursu ad bravium eterne beatitudinis gloriosissime pervenire. Favore igitur et gratia tanti regis vestre sanctitatis genibus provoluti, cum venerabili fratre nostro Laur. Westm. abbate preces propensiores prosternimus, constantissima devotione obsecrantes, quatenus regem mirificum in sanctorum cathalogo conscribi et consignari faciatis.

7. Edward's dearness to God is proved both by his meritorious life and by his miracles. As king he fought victoriously for the heavenly king, and, although in the prime of life and married to a brilliant queen, remained, it is believed, a virgin. The miracles which occur at his tomb prove him to be a saint. William joins with Laurence in petitioning for Edward's canonization.

8. *Nigel, bishop of Ely, to Pope Alexander III*
Alex., dei gratia summo pontifici, domino et patri spirituali, Nigellus, Elyensis ecclesie humilis minister, salutem et debitam in omnibus cum **omni** devotione subiectionem. Conditori ac redemptori omnium, licet

insufficientes, gratiarum referimus actiones, qui, mundi principe potenter adacto, menbra ipsius in ipso dampnavit capite, et ecclesie unitatem, quam suo redemit sanguine, servavit illesam. Prebuit immaculate sponse sue, quasi parturienti, post lamenta letitiam, et pro votis omnium te pastore suscepto, pressure preterite fecit immemorem. Eiecta est iterum de domo patris ancilla cum filio suo, et ipsum auctorem scelerum caput sibi constituit ecclesia malignantium. Verum libera in patris hereditate sponso suo fetus producit multiplices, et egregii piscatoris navicula, tanto rectore secura, nec minas equoris nec fluctus pertimescit invidie. Valeat igitur in multo tempore rector iste cum navi cui presidet, et in eternitatis littore videre mereatur appulsam. Te, sanctissime pater, omnium tam cleri quam populi vota susceperunt, et precipue sedi Romane devotissima Anglorum ecclesia, cui tempore administrationis tue et pax pristina restauratur et diu sopita iura restituuntur, ut etiam apostolatus tui tempore, cui hoc divino nutu servatum est eidem ecclesie spiritualis iocunditas prestetur uberior, preciosam margaritam, in ecclesia beati Petri apostolorum principis reconditam, corpus scilicet beati Eduardi quondam Anglorum regis ibidem humatum, de terra levare et condigna theca collocare fidelis devotio disposuit. Hic, ut scripturarum testimonio et veridicorum relatione didicimus, ab ineunte etate sanctissime degens, et regni tempora, quod iure hereditario adeptus est, inoffense, legibus, quas ipse condiderat, permoderans, mente et corpore virgo permanens, denique*a* functus est, et in ecclesia beati Petri aput*b* Westm., quam a primis fundamentis construxerat, magnifice collocatus, ubi eius intervenientibus meritis multis innumera prestari creduntur beneficia. Tibi igitur, pater sanctissime, una cum patre nostro spirituali, T. Cant. archiepiscopo,[1] et aliis coepiscopis nostris cum omni precum instantia supplicamus, ut quod de glorioso et incorrupto eius corpore levando fideles in Christo fratres nostri, eiusdem loci abbas et monachi, fideliter conceperunt, annuatis, et beati Petri apostolorum principis, cuius sedem tenetis, patrimonium sic sullimari concedatis.

a the MS seems to read deē [?deest]; *but* denique *makes good sense*   *b* apostolici *L*

8. Thanks be to God for preserving the unity of the church! Alexander has been victorious and the English church has, as always,

[1] Theobald, who died on 18 April 1161. Liverani printed *Thoma* (Thomas Becket), which misled concerning the date.

been loyal to the Roman see. Typical of its devotion is its wish to translate King Edward. Nigel knows from written and oral testimony that Edward always lived a religious life, ruled his kingdom according to good laws which he established, and lived in mind and body a virgin. Buried at Westminster, which he built and richly endowed, he still confers benefits. Nigel joins with Archbishop Theobald and his fellow bishops in begging for the translation of Edward's incorrupt body.

9. [*Jocelin de Bohun*,] *bishop of Salisbury, to Pope Alexander III*

Domino pape Saresb. episcopus. Celebris fame testimonio et miraculorum manifestatione didicimus gloriosum regem Eduardum huius mundi caduca respuisse et summo regi fideliter ministrasse. Preces itaque devotas vestre facimus sanctitati, quatinus regi regum dum vixit servientem in sanctorum cathalogo consignari faciatis, et stolam glorificationis ipsius, multis declaratam miraculis, Anglorum mentibus cum omni devotione recolendam, per apostolica suggeratis rescripta, ut tota Anglorum ecclesia de meritis gloriosi regis gaudeat, et de eius implorato patrocinio, gratia dei et vestre sancto sanctitatis assensu et exhortatione, confidere valeat.

9. Joscelin has learned from Edward's life and miracles that the king always despised the world and served God. He begs for Edward's canonization, so that the whole English church may rejoice in the merits of the glorious king.

10. *Abbot* [*Roger*][1] *and the convent of Reading to Pope Alexander III*

Domino pape abbas et conventus Rading. Benedictus dominus qui iuxta proprie promissionis tenorem suorum tristiciam convertit in gaudium, cum post noctis tetre caliginem lucem splendidam ecclesie sue restituit, auctoresque scismatis et fautores de navicula Petri tam potenter quam et clementer exturbans, vestis sue integram conservare studuit unitatem. Hinc deum in veritate querentibus novum gaudium, honor, tripudium oriri visum est, magnorum quoque de reliquo certior

[1] Scholz, *op. cit.*, p. 49, identifies the abbot as William. He was Roger (1158–65), *The Heads of Religious Houses*, ed. D. Knowles, C. N. L. Brooke, Vera London (1972), p. 63.

et solidior spes gaudiorum. Anglorum proinde ecclesia, sancte sedi apostolice speciali quadam devotione ab ipsis fidei rudimentis semper obnixa, speciali nichilominus exultatione indulto vobis celitus applaudit honori, sperans et obsecrans suam quoque gloriam in huius sancti gaudii plenitudine per vos, pie pater, dilatari. In qua et cum qua nostra quoque apostolice maiestati vestre supplicare presumit humilitas, ut viri religiosi fidelis filii vestri L. abbas Westm. et fratrum sub ipso pastore agentium preces dignanter exaudiatis, desiderium compleatis; liceatque eis ad honorem dei et sanctorum eius tociusque regni gloriam et exultationem beati regis Eduardi corpus condigno et debito sanctis honore in ecclesia sullimare. Ipsius siquidem regis et vitam laudabilem et mortem in conspectu domini preciosam, sicut a multis et fide, ut arbitramur, dignis relatoribus predicatoribus insuper et scriptis traditum reperitur, tam pia virtutum opera quam miracula crebra testantur. Conservet sanctitatem vestram ad honorem et pacem unice sponse sue omnipotens dominus.

10. The abbot rejoices at the end of the schism. The English church, from its beginning specially devoted to the apostolic see, is especially gladdened by Alexander's success. He joins with Laurence in begging for the canonization of Edward, where closeness to God is proved by his good deeds and miracles.

11. *H., minister of St N.,*[1] *to Pope Alexander III*
Reverendo domino suo et omnium ecclesiarum Christi patri et pastori Alex., H. beati N. minister humilis, salutem et omnem cum reverentia obedientiam. Exultat celsitudinis vestre servus humilis, exultat et Anglorum omnis ecclesia, quod mater noster post tantos sudores respirat, post tenebras erroris refulget, post scismata redintegratur, et, inexpleta pravorum cupiditate sauciata, cotidie proficiendo iam convalescit. Pastor ille bonus lacrimosa gregis suscepit suspiria et vota devotorum misericorditer implevit; a lupi faucibus potenter nos eruit, et secundum cor suum pastorem nobis prebuit, qui novit compati

---

[1] Liverani went no further than to suggest a bishop or abbot. Brooke, 'The Register of Master David', p. 232, suggested Herbert, prior of St Neots (Hunts.), which was a cell of Bec, who occurs *ante* 1158–*post* 1189: *Heads of Religious Houses*, p. 108.

infirmitatibus nostris et salutem querit animarum nostrarum. Regi summo gratias, in cuius manu corda sunt regum, qui pridie ad idolatriam trahi verebamur, iam vestre ditioni obedire precipimur. Iugum istud suave nobis est et onus leve. Misericordiam enim vestram alias audivimus, et quicquid postulare ausi sumus a pietate vestra leti suscepimus. Caritatis illius vestre copia fiduciam prestat sperandi maiora. Imploramus igitur maiestatem vestram, pater sancte, quatenus virum venera / [*fo. 151ᵛ*] bilem et vere religiosum, Westm. abbatem L., semper vestrum, in tam honestis petitionibus misericorditer exaudiatis, et, beatum regem E. honorando, universam Anglorum ecclesiam magno gaudio letificetis. Placeat serenitati vestre quatenus rex tante sanctitatis auctoritate vestra honoretur in terris, quem inter eos, qui secuntur agnum quocumque ierit, indubitanter credimus honoratum in celis. Ego sanctitatis vestre servus in prefato monasterio, ubi tanti regis corpus iacet incorruptum, a cunabulis usque ad hec fere tempora sum educatus, perfecteque didici ex virtutum frequentia quantum refulgeat in Christi presentia. Felicitatis eius argumentum est et spiritus prophetie, quo magnifice claruit, et iuncti coniugio vera virginitas, quam carnis integritas adhuc ostendit. Protestantur eius devotionem fere omnia Anglie loca religiosa, que largitionibus suis habunde ditavit, dignitatibus honoravit, sacris legibus communivit. Honorate igitur quem honorat dominus, et supplicum vestrorum preces admittite, qui sola que dei sunt a sanctitate vestra querimus impetrare. Valeat semper dominus meus. Sit dominus inimicus inimicis vestris. Qui autem diligunt vos, sicut sol in ortu suo splendet, ita rutilent. Litteras reverentie vestre cum omni reverentia suscepimus, imperiumque vestrum effectui mancipantes, proprios nuntios vobis mittere maturabimus.

11. A humble slave of the pope, he rejoices with the whole English church at Alexander's victory in the schism. He begs the pope to listen favourably to Laurence's petition for Edward's canonization. As he has been from childhood until recently a member of the community at Westminster he can give evidence on Edward's behalf. The king's spirit of prophecy and his virginity in marriage – proved by the incorruption of his body – are proof of his devotion to God. The writer has received Alexander's letters, will carry out the pope's instructions, and will report back by his own messengers.

12. *Abbot Gregory (?) of Malmesbury to Pope Alexander III*

Amantissimo patri et domino Alex., dei gratia summo pontifici, frater E.,[1] humilis minister Malmesb. ecclesie, devotam ut patri reverentiam, humilem ut domino subiectionem. Religiosis desideriis et piis affectibus apostolica clementia benigne consuevit occurrere, precipue in his que magis solent sancte matris ecclesie decus et gloriam augmentare. Que nimirum, licet in capite suo superhabundanter habeat unde proficiat, solet tamen et de suorum menbrorum glorificatione profectum adquirere et in magni decoris celsitudinem expensa eisdem reverentia excrescere. Cum igitur corporibus sanctorum, de quorum frequenti patrocinio regio nostra letatur, debitus passim honor impenditur, aptissimum valde esset si apostolica excellentia vestra dignum duceret, ut eiusdem honoris reverentia bono et glorioso regi Eduardo exhiberetur, cuius gloriosissimum corpus in monasterio Westm. requiescere dinoscitur. Cuius profecto mirabilis sanctitatis eminentiam, cum ante et post obitum numerosa et preclara miracula oculatis testimoniis efferant, integritas tamen illibati et virginei etiam post coniugium corporis, post tricesimum sextum sepulture annum cum omni vestimentorum integritate inventi, etiam si cetera sileant, sufficienter poterit commendare. Concurrunt preterea in huius veritatis assertionem copiose virtutis indicia, etiam sub nostris temporibus exhibita, que vel oculis nostris, utpote peculiaris huius gloriosissimi alumpnus, vidi vel ab his qui viderunt audivi, tam in frequenti languent[i]um curatione quam in febricitancium refocillatione, que epistolaris brevitas comprehendere non poterit. Securus igitur de tanti viri preclaris meritis, pietati vestre humiles preces offero, quatinus inter eos, qui pro huius sancti veneratione maiestati vestre supplicant, me quoque, licet minimum et abiectum vestre sanctitatis servum, exaudire dignemini, ut videlicet auctoritatis vestre precepto et assensu natalicius [transitus eius dies cathalogo sanctorum insertus, ecclesiastica devotione in terris decetero celebretur, cuius nomen in libro vite scriptum multimoda miracula contestantur. Ex quo profecto excellentie vestre plurimum gratie accedet, si videlicet sub apostolatus vestri temporibus quod hactenus latuit, in multorum provectum prodeat, unde et sancte matris ecclesie

[1] The initial would seem to be *E* rather than *G*; but the two are easily confused. Liverani suggested that we were concerned with William of Malmesbury, the historian; but there is no evidence that he lived after 1142: see W. Stubbs, Malmesbury, *GR*, i, p. xliii, ii, p. cv. Brooke, p. 232, gives 'G. abbot of Malmesbury'; Scholz, p. 49, 'a brother William from the abbey of Malmesbury'. Gregory was abbot ?1159–68, *Heads of Religious Houses*, p. 55.

gaudia cumulentur, integritas fidei roboretur, patrocinium accrescat devotioni fidelium. Sanam et incolumem sanctitatem vestram longis temporibus deus omnipotens custodiat.

12. England rejoices in the patronage of many saints, and it would be fitting if the pope would canonize Edward. The king's sanctity is proved by the miracles he performed both before and after death and by the incorruption of his virgin body found with all vestments intact after thirty-six years in the tomb. There are also all those cures of the sick and sufferers from fever which the writer had himself witnessed when he was a Westminster monk or which he has heard of from eye-witnesses. Edward's canonization would be advantageous to all parties.

13. *R[eginald], prior of St A[ndrew's], R[ochester]* (?), *to Pope Alexander III*
Alex., dei gratia summo pontifici, patri amantissimo et domino, frater R. sancti A. de R. presbiter*a* licet indignus,[1] salutem et plenam cum devotione obedientiam. Quoniam in postulatione quam facio, quamvis indignus, non solus tamen invenior, multis et magnis sociatus, aput clementiam vestram pietatis affectu confidentius ago, quatenus quod celum gaudet, terra testatur, per mean quoque parvitatem excellentie vestre auctius innotescat. Celebre enim et notum habet Anglorum populus et ecclesia tota quod gloriosus eorum rex Eduardus, dum adhuc in carne viveret, carnem omnimode servavit, et, cum regiam foris suscepisset potestatem, sic regni sceptra exterius gubernabat ut de sui cordis regimine nullatenus sibi quicquam deperiret. Unde cum de mundanis affectibus incessanter Christo militans, victor coram deo gloriosus haberetur, sicut scriptorum declarant monita et asserit probabiliter religiosorum turba copiosa, spiritu enituit prophetico, pietate clarus, signis admirandus, humilitate conspicuus, beneficentia largissimus, fidei et iusticie intentus cultor. Et cum per tempora multa uxori coniugatus vixisset, plenus dierum purus immaculatus et virgo ex hac luce decessit. Unde non immerito, ut asserunt, cum caro eius tam

---

[1] Liverani printed 'R. sancti Asaph de R.', which Scholz, p. 49, turned into 'R. of St Asaph'. As the letters are presented in order of rank, we can assume that R. was the lowest in dignity. Reginald occurs as prior in 1155, *Heads of Religious Houses*, p. 64.

munda tam sancta annis ferme xl in tumulo quievisset, sana et incorrupta inventa est. Si quid igitur aput tantum vestre sanctitatis iudicium parvitatis mee preces possunt, ego una pietate et eadem devotione sed merito dissimilis, vestre supplico gloriose maiestati, una cum dignissimo viro devoto filio vestro Laur. abbate Westm., quatenus regem, tantis meritis gloriosum, sanctorum cathalogo conscribi faciatis, ut qui aput nos gloriosis fulget miraculis, vestra canonizatus auctoritate, glorie sanctorum, ut creditur, adunatus in celis, digne per vos honoretur in terris.

a p'sbr'o *MS.? Amend to* prior et presbiter.

13. Although unworthy, he is not alone in petitioning for Edward's canonization. It is well known in England that Edward lived and ruled piously. There is evidence, both written and oral, that he had the gift of prophecy, was religious, humble, generous, and a lover of justice, and that he performed miracles. Although married, he died in old age a virgin, and so, after he had lain for almost forty years in the tomb, his clean and holy flesh was found incorrupt. The writer supports Laurence's petition.

14. *Pope Alexander to Abbot Laurence and the chapter of Westminster*[1]
[7 February 1161]
Alex., episcopus, servus servorum dei, dilectis filiis Laur. abbati et universo capitulo Westm.,*a* salutem et apostolicam benedictionem. Illius devotionis constantiam et fidei firmitatem, quam circa matrem vestram sacrosanctam Romanam ecclesiam exhibetis, diligentius attendentes, in id propositi et*b* voluntatis adducimur,*c* ut vos sicut karissimos*d* et speciales ecclesie filios sincera caritate in domino diligamus, propensius honoremus, et postulationes vestras, quantum cum deo possumus, libenti animo admittamus. Inde utique fuit quod super petitione, quam de Eduardo glorioso quondam rege Anglorum canonizando et in sanctorum cathalogo ascribendo tam karissimus in Christo filius noster H. illustris Anglorum rex*e* quam vos ipsi nobis instantius porrexistis, sollicitam cum fratribus [nostris] deliberationem habentes,

[1] Other versions of the letter are in *The History of Westminster Abbey by John Flete*, ed. J. Armitage Robinson, p. 93 (*F*), Mansi, Concilia, xxi. 871 (*M*), and Richard of Cirencester, *Speculum Historiale*, ed. J. E. B. Mayor (Rolls ser. 1869), ii. 322–3 (*RC*), and an extract is in Diceto, *Opera Historica*, ed. W. Stubbs (Rolls ser. 1876), ii. 238.

libro miraculorum inspecto, que, dum in carne mortali[f] viveret et
postquam de presenti seculo est assumptus, omnipotens dominus per
suam misericordiam declaravit; visis etiam litteris antecessoris nostri
pie recordationis[g] Innocentii pape, vestris quoque testimoniis inde
receptis; quamvis negotium tam[h] arduum et sullime non frequenter
soleat[i] nisi in sollempnibus conciliis de more concedi, de communi
tamen[j] fratrum nostrorum consilio, iuxta votum et desiderium predicti
filii nostri regis ac vestrum, corpus ipsius confessoris ita glorificandum
censuimus, et debitis[k] preconiis honorandum[l] in terris, sicut eundem
confessorem dominus per suam gratiam glorificavit in celis, ut[m] videlicet
inter sanctos confessores decetero numeretur, qui[n] hoc ipsum aput deum
signis meruit et virtutibus optinere. Quia igitur decet honestatis vestre
prudentiam eum pie colere et toto studio venerari, quem auctoritate
apostolica[o] venerandum vestra postulavit devotio et colendum, univer-
sitatem vestram per apostolica scripta monemus et exhortamur in
domino, quatenus ita eum[p] deinceps studeatis debitis obsequiis[q]
honorare, ut ipsius intercessionibus aput districtum iudicem mereamini
veniam optinere et gloriosum in eterna beatitudine premium invenire.[r]

[a] venerabilibus [fratribus RC] archiepiscopis, episcopis, et dilectis filiis abbatibus,
prioribus et aliis/aliisque RC/ecclesiarum praelatis per Angliam constitutis M, RC
[b] propositum M   [c] adducuntur RC   [d] add fratres M; add fratres nostros RC, F
[e] Ang. ill. rex RC   [f] mortali carne RC, F   [g] memorie M   [h] om. M   [i] soleat
after conciliis MS   [j] om. F   [k] delatis RC   [l] adorandum M   [m] Unde M
[n] quod M   [o] om. honestatis vestre . . . apostolica RC   [p] eum ita M; ita deinceps
eum RC   [q] obsequiis M, RC, F; exequiis MS   [r] add Datum Anagniae septimo
Idus Februarii M, RC, F

14. The pope is happy to reward the constant devotion and firmity of
faith which Laurence and the chapter of Westminster have shown
towards the Roman church. In the matter of the petition for the
canonization of Edward, submitted by King Henry and Westminster,
the pope has conferred with the cardinals, inspected the book listing
the miracles which Edward worked before and after death, referred
to the letters of his predecessor, Pope Alexander II, received the
letters testimonial, and, although such sublime and difficult business
should normally be done only in a solemn council, grants with the
common counsel of the cardinals that Edward shall be numbered
among the holy confessors. Westminster should pay the new saint
all due honour.

Appendix E

THE DATE OF THE
FIRST TRANSLATION

Richard of Cirencester, writing in the late fourteenth century, dated Abbot Laurence's translation of Edward Sunday, 13 October (3 Ides October) 1163, the ninety-seventh year since the burial, the fourth year of Alexander III and the ninth of Henry II. There is nothing much wrong with this dating clause.[1] He also gives a list of the notables present at the ceremony, and names, besides the king, Archbishop Thomas, and Laurence, ten English, one Welsh, and three Norman bishops, four abbots, and eight earls. There is no obvious fault in the list, and the inclusion of Arnulf of Lisieux and the other Norman bishops is a strong point in its favour. Stubbs, however, followed by Eyton,[2] found it difficult to fit this event into the king's itinerary; and there are indeed obvious difficulties here which must be met. But the ways in which Stubbs and Eyton tried to discredit the date are not persuasive.

Stubbs pointed out that Henry III translated Edward to his new tomb in the rebuilt Westminster abbey on 13 October 1269; and suggested that Richard of Cirencester took the day and month from the later ceremony.[3] But in fact the later date confirms the other. Henry III chose 13 October precisely because it was St Edward's day. He wrote to Llewelyn ap Gruffydd, prince of Wales, that he was about to celebrate the feast of the translation of St Edward in the new church at Westminster on the feast day of that saint, that is to say the quindeme of St Michael (13 October), and invited him to be present.[4] Eyton claimed to prefer Herbert of Bosham's chronology. Herbert, the sole contemporary witness to the event, includes it in the happenings (all undated by him) which led to, or preceded, the quarrel between

[1] *Speculum Historiale de gestis regum Angliae*, ed. John E. B. Mayor (Rolls ser.), ii (1869), 326–7. The year 4 Alexander III was September 1162–September 1163.

[2] R. W. Eyton, *Court, Household, and Itinerary of King Henry II* (1878), p. 71.

[3] *The Chronicle of . . . Benedict of Peterborough* (Rolls ser.), ii (1867), p. cxxxiv.

[4] *Close Rolls 1268–72*, p. 71.

Henry and Becket.[1] He mentions that Roger was elected to Worcester and that Thomas consecrated Robert to Hereford and also Roger (March, 22 December 1163, and 23 August 1164 respectively). Thomas then dedicated Reading abbey in the presence of the king. This was on Sunday 19 April 1164. In the same year, Herbert continues, Thomas, in the presence of the king, translated Edward at Westminster. So far the king and archbishop had been friends; but quarrels began, and Henry convoked a council of the province of Canterbury to Westminster. Herbert describes what took place at this council; and the next certain point in his narrative is the council of Clarendon, January 1164. It is obvious that Herbert, far from giving events in chronological sequence, is jumping about from subject to subject; and although it could be argued that he thought that the translation of Edward took place in 1164 – in which case it certainly cannot be dated 13 October[2] – it must also be accepted that he put it before the council of Clarendon, if not before the council of Westminster.

It is tempting, of course, to associate the translation with the council of Westminster. And it is this which caused Stubbs and Eyton trouble. Most of Becket's biographers mention, always without a date and usually unidentified as to place, a council which preceded the council of Clarendon, 13–28 January 1164, and at which the first general and public debate over criminous clerks occurred.[3] This seems to be the council of Westminster or London, dated 1 October 1163 in the *Summa causae inter regem et Thomam*,[4] although there are details in the *Summa* which are at variance with the other accounts. A date in October for this council seems reasonable enough in view of the events which the writers put between the two councils. But all authorities agree that the council of Westminster ended with the king disgracing Becket because of the archbishop's opposition and leaving London secretly and abruptly; and they do not bring him back to London before the council of Clarendon, but refer to events in the midlands and north. Yet we are expected to believe, on Westminster evidence, that, a fortnight after

[1] 'Vita S. Thomae', *Materials for the History of Thomas Becket*, ed. J. C. Robertson (Rolls ser.), iii (1877), 258–61.

[2] On 13 October 1164 Henry and Becket were at Northampton, Eyton, *op. cit.*, p. 74.

[3] Herbert of Bosham, *Materials*, iii. 266–75; Anon. I, *ibid.*, iv. 25–7; Anon. II, *ibid.*, iv. 95–7. For the council, see David Knowles, *The episcopal colleagues of Archbishop Thomas Becket* (1951), pp. 56 ff. The judgment in the lawsuit mentioned by Knowles (and see above, p. 282) is dated by Eyton, *op. cit.*, p. 59, 8 March 1163.

[4] *Materials*, iv. 201.

this angry scene, Henry, Becket, almost all the bishops of the southern province, and half the earls reassembled at Westminster for the celebration, an event ignored by all Becket's biographers save Herbert of Bosham.

Nevertheless it is possible. On Sunday 19 April 1164, when the quarrel was even more bitter, Thomas with ten of his bishops consecrated the monastic church of Reading in Henry's presence. All the same, it would be easier if we could conflate the two Westminster ceremonies. As the date 13 October for the translation seems unimpeachable and much better attested than the date of the council, we could move the council forward. But in order to hold that the council described by Becket's biographers opened with Edward's translation we have to accept that most contemporary writers either forgot the ceremony or considered it irrelevant to their story. Moreover, although there is disagreement over what sort of a council met at Westminster, it seems to have been attended by the archbishop of York, who is not on Richard of Cirencester's list. And if there were two separate occasions, we may as well accept the two dates which we have been given. We must assume that arrangements for the second ceremony were made at the first and, despite what subsequently happened, rather surprisingly honoured by all.

SOME UNPUBLISHED
ROYAL CHARTERS

1. *Æthelred books land at Hallam (Derbys) to his thegn, Elmod [? Æthelnoth].*
IOII.
Aberystwyth, N. L. W. MS. Peniarth 390 (saec. xiv), pp. 364–5;
Sawyer, no. 923.

This Burton abbey document, a record of Æthelred's sale of land to a
royal thegn, is hardly in unblemished condition. Some very difficult
Latin has not been successfully transmitted. There also has been a loss
of material besides the indicated omissions, for we have an unrelated
reference to 'an above-mentioned woman' who had, apparently, lost her
estates to Æthelred. Moreover, the payment mentioned, 21 gold
pounds, seems too large for the single estate named in the charter which
is rated at two hides. There are, however, no obvious anachronisms in
the charter and the witness list is sound.

Carta Æthelredi Regis de Burhalim. anno domini MoXIo.[a]

Summe[b] vereque bonitatis deum solum. substantia simplum. personis
triplum, constare nemini ratione vigentium hesitandum est. qui sue
incircumscripte diuamia*[c] maiestatis circumscripta queque quasi
pugillo continet chirali*, cunctaque que sunt eius bonitate bona sunt,
non tamen condita per se, set quia a summo bono essendi ceperant
formam, bona sunt. Quam ob causam eiusdem summe bonitatis bona
perpetualiter siquidem permanenda. viuati mentis intencione iugiter
appetenda sunt, quibus quippe adeptis, nichil desiderabilius excel-
lentiusve requiri quibit. Hinc etenim ego Ethelredus tocius rector
archosque Bryttannie, regalis potentie dignitatibus dei dapsilitate
inpensi[ssi]ma fauente preditus opum largitione caducarum transi-
toriarumque, bona haut caduca hautque defectiua adipisci omnimodo
exoptans inter cetera bonorum studia largiendorum quibus me minime
deficientis agalliasinata* [? agalhasmata*] regni adepturum esse spero,
terre particulam quandam duas videlicet cassatas Elemod ministro

gratissimo libens hilarisque impartior, ob ipsius siquidem in/defessi obsequia famulatus. Que quidem terra agnoscitis patrie accolis Burhhalim nuncupatur, Eandem denique terram quamdiu spiramine attrahendo uel emittendo frui valeat. totius alitnus*[d] conflictus securus possideat. dumque se viuans [h]alitum flaminis amissum ire perspexerit, arbitrium ei liberum assistat cui successorum eius. alieno scilicet uel propinquo eandem terram subigat possidendam. Matronae autem suprascripte tam naturales quam legittimas villas michi iure decretario assignatas ministro prememorato Elemodo viginti et unius librarum appensibus aureis michi concessis alacriter condonaui. Itaque hoc nostre largitionis donum in ipsius arbitrio tuta semper valletur libertate cum cunctis ad ipsam rite pertinentibus terram. campis videlicet etcetera. Tribus causis exceptis etcetera. Sit ergo terre istius libertas vndique solida et imunita.[e] Et antiquioris uel futuoris libri quocunque modo prolati nullo modo contradictioni subiaceat. set magis omnibus hostibus deuictis proprie potestatis ditione floreat. Istis terminibus predicta terra circumgirata est etcetera. MºXIº.

+Ego Æthelred rex tocius Brittannice telluris hanc libertatem confirmaui.

+Ego Ælfheagus Dorob' ecclesie archiepiscopus consignaui.

+Ego Wulstanus Ebor' ecclesie archiepiscopus consensi.

+Ego Ælfgyuu collaterana eiusdem regis hoc michi placere professa sum.

+Ego Æthelstanus	clyto confirmaui	+Ego Lyuingc episcopus communeraui.
+Ego Eadmund	clyto consignaui.	+Ego Æthelric episcopus consensi.
+Ego Eadred	clyto corroboraui.	+Ego Ælfwold episcopus conclaui.
+Ego Eadwig	clyto conniui.[f]	+Ego Athulf episcopus confixi.
+Ego Eadweard	clyto consolidaui.	+Ego Godwine episcopus confirmaui.
+Ego Ælfhun	episcopus conquieui.	+Ego Eadnoth episcopus coadunaui.
+Ego Æthelwold	episcopus coniungaui.	+Ego Ælfmaer episcopus consolidaui.

Et ceteri abbates sex. duces quattuor. et ministri viginti et tres.

2. *Edward confirms a grant of Earl Leofric to Evesham abbey.* Spurious. London, Br. Mus. MS. Cott. Vesp. B. xxiv (saec. xii), fo. 30ᵛ; Sawyer, no. 1053.

The first piece is completely irregular in form and has an inconsistent witness list. Bishop Lyfing [of Worcester] died in 1046 and Bishop Ælfweard [of London] in 1044; but the list ends with Bishop Heca [of Selsey], appointed in 1047. The second piece is likewise irregular and also is written in (?deliberately) barbarous Latin.

Hampton (Worcs.), according to the Evesham chronicler, was granted by King Æthelbald of Mercia to the first abbot, Egwin, and subsequently was several times lost and recovered. Cnut granted it to Leofric when he made him earl, apparently among other estates which had belonged to Leofric's brother, Norman. Leofric restored it to Evesham. It is also stated that Hampton was among those estates which Abbot Æthelwig recovered, largely at his own expense, from King Edward and other good men. *Chronicon abbatiae de Evesham*, ed. W. D. Macray (Rolls ser. 1863), pp. 72, 84–5, 94. As there is in this charter an irregular formula concerning the common burdens – they are to be paid to no one except Edward and his successors – the purpose of the fabrication was probably to prevent someone else, either the earl, or more likely, the bishop of Worcester, from exacting military service in respect of this estate.

Ego Eadwardus totius anglie basileus. demonstro cunctis fidelibus mei regni quod Leofricus dux fidelis meus dedit quandam terram que uocatur Heamtun ad monasterium in Eouesham pro salute anime mee. et pro sua et suorum. Et ego concedo ut fratres et monachi eiusdem monasterii habeant hanc elemosinam in hereditate perpetua. ad uictum suum cum omnibus reditibus qui pertinent ad eandem terram. Ipsa uero terra in iura antecessorum meorum per iudicium uenit. et uolo et concedo ut sicut antecessores liberam eam habuerunt. et dederunt cui uoluerunt. ita abbas eiusdem monasterii et successores sui liberam eam habeant. neque de aliqua lege uel de expeditione arcis pontisue constructione. neque de tributis exsoluendis. alicui homini respondeant nisi mihi et successoribus meis. Quicumque hanc nostram donationem seruauerit. seruet illum deus ad uitam eternam. Qui uero excidere uoluerit aut temptauerit. excidatur de gloria paradisi. et detrudatur in penas inferni. nisi resipuerit et ad emendationem uenerit.

Ego EADWARDUS Rex confirmaui. et mea manu corroboraui. Ego Edsinus archiepiscopus confirmaui. Ego Ælfricus archiepiscopus consensi. Ego Stigandus episcopus consensi. Ego Eadnoth episcopus consensi. Ego Lifingus episcopus consensi. Ego Wulsinus episcopus consensi. Ego Ælfwardus episcopus consensi. Ego Hecha episcopus consensi.

Ego EADWARDUS Rex manifesto in isto breui omnibus dei amicis cum testimonio Liuingi episcopi, quod Leofricus comes habet donatam illam terram de heamtun in monasterio de Eouesham. et ego uolo ut illa terra iaceat in illo monasterio hoc sunt quinque hyde tam plene et tam firme, sicut aliqua terra que melius iacet in illo monasterio. Ego uolo etiam ut ille sanctus locus qui diu stetit desertus habeat suam libertatem, sicuti melius et plenius habuit.

3. *Edward books land at Millbrook (Hants) to Earl Godwin.* 1045. Fabricated.
London, Br. Mus. MS. Add. 15350 (saec. xii), fos. 78ᵛ–79ᵛ; Sawyer, no. 1009.

This charter is, except for the name and style of the grantee, identical with *KCD*, no. 781 (Sawyer, no. 1008), a grant of Edward's to Ælfwine, bishop of Winchester. In place of 'cuidam episcoporum meorum perpetualiter trado, Ælfwino uidelicet Wentane ciuitatis episcopo', has been substituted, 'cuidam ministrorum meorum perpetualiter trado. Godwino uidelicet occidentalium saxonum duci', a phrase containing almost exactly the same number of letters. H. P. R. Finberg, *The Early Charters of Wessex* (1964), p. 64, classifies the grant to the bishop (no. 163) as 'original charter, authenticity not in doubt', and the grant to the earl (no. 164) as 'charter available only in later copy or copies, authenticity not in doubt'. But although it is difficult to see why a sound charter in favour of the bishop should have been altered in this way, especially as Godwin's possession of an estate could hardly have improved anyone's title after 1066, this is clearly what has happened. The formula in the grant to the bishop is perfectly regular and has been adapted in a most irregular manner to fit an earl. An earl is not one of the king's *ministri*, thegns, and it was not usual to give him a territorial title. We can compare the following examples from the reigns of Æthelred, Cnut, and Edward: 'cuidam meo fideli duci nomine Æthelmero', 'cuidam familiari duci meo Godwino', and 'uni meo fideli duci nuncupato uocamine Godwino' (*KCD*, nos. 638, 752, 793; Sawyer, nos. 846, 970, 1022).

4. *Edward books land at 'Berghe' to his earl [?thegn] Tofig.* 1048.
Aberystwyth, N. L. W. MS. Peniarth 390 (saec. xiv), p. 368; Sawyer, no. 1017.

Like no. 1, this is a Burton abbey charter, and is as dilapidated as the other. *Berghe* has not been identified, although most of the abbey's estates were in Derbyshire and Staffordshire. No earl Tofig is known; but there were thegns with this name, including Tofig 'the Proud'. Probably 'min.' has been mis-copied as 'com.' The witness list is sound. Abbot Oswig signs no other charter.

Carta sancti Eadwardi regis et confessoris. patroni Westm' de Berghe. anno domini MᵒXLVIIIᵒ.

Adstipulatione siquidem sacri spermatis herilis promulgando intonat buccina mestiferam tremendi examinis ymeram perpeti fore subreptione occursuram glomeratis terrigenum uniuersalis ubi astabit cuneus ac cuncti tonantis almifluo alti*ᵃ* throni*ᵇ* clangente diathemate ac in diecula*ᶜ* palatinis raptim collegio addicti contubernialibus luci comi nasciscuntur poli ciuilia acta quorum lanx trutinando*ᵈ* fore probat faustissima quorumque eneruit*ᵉ* studia probis actionibus extant classia* [*or* classca*] imperpetua ceu cleronomi multabuntur erumpna*.ᶠ* ac pro talione infanda*ᵍ* gehennalis Stycgie sine meta haurient infernalia. Quapropter ego Eadweard tocius Albionis basileos mee donationis arte libere fruens quandam telluris particulam. ii. videlicet territoria in loco qui ab incolis Berghe cognominatur cuidam michi fideli comiti Touig' vocitamine in perpetuam hereditatem donata*ʰ* concedo. ut habeat ac possideat quamdiu vitali calore arctus caluerint. et post uite sue terminum cuicumque sibi libuerit sine aliquo scrupulo in hereditariam libertatem concedat. Tellus autem predictum [*sic*] sit cum omnibus ad eandem rite pertinentibus. campis. pascuis. siluis. aquarum riuulis ab omni mundiali obstaculo liberum [*sic*]. tantum expedicione. pontis arcisue restauratione exceptis. Quod si quispiam hanc nostre donacionis libertatem inuidie face turgens euertere conatus fuerit, cum Pilato et Juda Scariothen. Caypha quoque eorumque commanipularibus eternaliter ac Herontica combustione trudatur, nisi ante mortis articulum satisfactione penituerit congrua quod nostre donacionis presumpsit violare quod absit statuta. Hiis nempe metis rus antescriptum circumcingitur etcetera.

Acta est autem hec mea donacio anno ab incarnacione domini nostri Ihesu Christi M⁰XLVIII Indictione ii. Hiis testibus consentientibus quorum nomina hic inferius karraxantur.ⁱ

+Ego Eadweard rex Anglorum cum triumpho sancte Crucis hoc donum immobile corroboraui.

+Ego Ea[ds]i archiepiscopus regie roborator donationis agye triumphale crucis signaculum depinxi.

+Ego Ælfric archiepiscopus triumphale tropheum agye crucis suppressi.

+Ego Æthelstan episcopus consolidaui.	+Ego Leofstan abbas	+Ego Leofwine minister
+Ego Eadnoth episcopus consummaui.	+Ego Leofsig abbas	+Ego Tostig minister
+Ego Stigandus episcopus confeci.	+Ego Earnwig abbas	+Ego Ælfstan minister
+Ego Aldred episcopus adquieui.	+Ego Oswig abbas	+Ego Ælfgar minister
+Ego Duduc episcopus subscripsi.	+Ego Godwine dux	+Ego Odda minister
+Ego Rodbeard episcopus consensum prebui	+Ego Leofric dux	+Ego Ordgar minister
+Ego Ægelweard abbas	+Ego Siward dux	+Ego Ordulf minister
+Ego Wulfric abbas	+Ego Harold dux	+Ego Brihtric minister
+Ego Ælfwine abbas	+Ego Beorn dux	+Ego Ælfwine minister

---

a alteri *MS*   *b glossed* dei   *c glossed* diu . . .   *d glossed* liberando   *e glossed* sine viribus (?)   *f glossed* id est heredes quod . . .   *g illegible gloss*   *h* donant' *MS*
i glossed ? scribuntur

5. *Edward books land at Wheathamstead (Herts) to Westminster Abbey.* 1060. Hertfordshire Record Office, Accession No. 1175; Sawyer, no. 1031.

When Mr Sawyer produced his List this charter was known only from a fourteenth-century Westminster Abbey Muniment Book, 11, fo. 204. Recently, however, he has discovered what seems to be the original and very kindly drew my attention to it. It appears to be an eleventh-century parchment; but the text is unusual in that the estate granted is freed from the common burdens – usually a clear sign of forgery. But as Edward was a great benefactor of Westminster he may have given it exceptional privileges.

The bounds are discussed, J. E. B. Gover, Allen Mawer, and F. M. Stenton, *The Place-Names of Hertfordshire* (English Place-Name Society, xv, 1938), p. 54, *n*.

Regnante*a* inperpetuum domino nostro ihesu christo. Status mundi huius in uolubilitate fatescet [*sic*]. atque citanter in uelocitate deficiet. Ideoque totis festinandum est uiribus sub ipsius regimine manentibus. ut dum in hac labilis uitę dilatione tempus mercandi fuerit. labentibus rebus aeterna regna incessabili mentium conamine adquirere non destinant. Haec itaque reminiscens ego EADWARDUS. telluris Bryttanice totius largiflua dei gratia rex et gubernator. ad promerenda et impetranda salutifera mihi siderei suffragia clauiger(i Pe)tri scilicet apostoli. et ad supplendam utilitatis cuiuslibet amminiculationem uerę petrę christo iugi seruitio famulantibus in coenobio quod westmynstre uocatur quampiam ruris particulam id est.x.mansas in communi tamen terra collocatas in loco uidelicet quem solicolę soli ipsius hwaetham-stede proprio nuncupant uocabulo ad possidendum in sempiternum iure hereditario libens ac largus impendo. Maneat autem istud donum ab omni seculari seruitio exinanitum cum omnibus ad se rebus perti-nentibus. campis. pratis. pascuis. siluarumque densitatibus. ita ut nullis sit umquam grauatum honeribus. scilicet nec expeditionis nec pontis et arcis edificamine. nec iuris regalis fragmine. nec furis aprehen-sione. Et ut omnia simul comprehendam. nil debet exsolui. uel regis preposito. uel episcopi. uel ducis. uel ullius hominis. sed omnia debita exsoluant iugiter. qui in ipsa dominatione fuerint. ad supradictum sanctum locum. Siquis autem nostre munificentię donationem augere uel amplificare uoluerit. augeat illi omnipotens deus et in hoc seculo et in futuro aeternam felicitatem. Si uero econtra quis quod non optamus hoc cyrographi decretum in aliud quam constituimus infringere temptauerit. seu ueteres uel nouos apices ostenderit. sciat se anathematis interdictionum nexibus obligatum et a regno dei separatum. nisi hic antea emendauerit.

This syndon thá land gemaeru into hwaethamstede. fram maerforde to thaere headic. & fram thaere headic aefter daene into deorleage. fram deorlege & langhecge thaet hit cymth to lippelane. fram lippelane to secgham & fram secgham to pobbenaettoce. & fram bobbenaettoce to herpedene. fram herpedene to tham aesce to thaec forde. fram tham aesce to plu(mstigele. & fram) plumstigele to tham hole beame. fram than hole beame to gilmere. fram gilmere to thaes ealdermannes mere. fram thaes ealdermannes mere into merdene & swa (into m)erforde. Peracta est ergo huius dapsilitatis larga distributio dominicę incarnationis anno. post mille.lx. indictione.xiii. his testibus consentientibus. quorum nomina hic infra habentur.

+Ego EADWEARDUS rex totius Brittanie pręfatam meam donationem cum sigillo sanctę crucis regali stabilimento affirmaui.

+Ego EADGYTH eiusdem regis conlaterana hanc regalem donationem gaudenter stabiliui.

+Ego Stigandus archiepiscopus triumphalem agie crucis tropheum hic regio munere gaudenter inpressi.

+Ego Kynsinus archipresul hanc territoriam scedulam signo sanctę crucis diligenter adsignare curaui.

+Ego Heremannus.   +Ego Harold. dux.   +Ego Huglin minister.
    episcopus. consolidaui.

+Ego Leofricus.   +Ego Tosti. dux.   +Ego Esgar minister.
    episcopus. coadunaui.

+Ego Ealdredus.   +Ego Ælfgar. dux.   +Ego Rauulf minister.
    episcopus. corroboraui.

+Ego Vulfwius.   +Ego Gyrth. dux.   +Ego Rodbeard minister.
    episcopus. confirmaui.

^a *In the top left-hand margin are a cross and the letters alpha and omega*

LIST OF RULERS

1. KINGS OF WESSEX

Alfred	871–899
Edward the Elder	899–924
Athelstan	924–939
Edmund	939–946
Eadred	946–955

2. KINGS OF ALL ENGLAND

Eadwig	955–957/9
Edgar	957/9–975
Edward 'the Martyr'	975–978/9
Æthelred	978/9–1016
Svein 'Forkbeard'	1013–1014
Edmund 'Ironside'	1016
Cnut	1016–1035
Harold 'Harefoot'	1037–1040
Harthacnut	1040–1042
Edward 'the Confessor'	1042–1066
Harold	1066
William I	1066–1087

3. PRINCES IN WALES

GWYNEDD

Gruffydd ap Llewelyn	1039–1063
Bleddyn ap Cynfyn	1063–1075

DEHEUBARTH

Hywel ab Edwin	c. 1035–1044
Gruffydd ap Rhydderch	1044–1055
Gruffydd ap Llewelyn	1055–1063
Maredudd ab Owain	c. 1063–1072

4. KINGS OF SCOTLAND

Malcolm II	1005–1034
Duncan I	1034–1040
Macbeth	1040–1057
Lulach	1057–1058
Malcolm III 'Canmore'	1058–1093

5. KINGS OF DENMARK

Harald 'Bluetooth'	*c.* 930–*c.* 988
Svein 'Forkbeard'	*c.* 988–1014
Harald	1014–*c.* 1018
Cnut	*c.* 1018–1035
Harthacnut	1035–1042
War of succession between Magnus of Norway and Svein Estrithson	1042–1047
Svein Estrithson	1047–1074

6. KINGS OF NORWAY

Harald 'Fairhair'	*c.* 872–*c.* 930
Eric 'Blood-axe'	*c.* 930–*c.* 935
Hacon I 'the Good'	*c.* 935–961
petty kings and rulers	961–995
Olaf Tryggvason	995–1000
Jarls Eric and Svein Hakonarson	1000–1015
Olaf Haraldsson (St)	*c.* 1015–1030
Svein Alfifasson (Cnut's son and deputy)	1030–1035
Magnus 'the Good'	1035–1047
Harald Sigurdsson (Hardrada)	1047–1066
Magnus II	1066–1069
Olaf Haraldsson 'the Peaceful'	1067–1093

7. KINGS OF SWEDEN

Anund (James)	1022–1056
Edmund Gamul	1056–1060

8. COUNTS OF FLANDERS

Baldwin IV 'the Bearded'	989–1034
Baldwin V 'of Lille'	1034–1067

9. COUNTS OF NORMANDY

Richard I	942–996
Richard II	996–1026
Richard III	1026–1027
Robert I	1027–1035
William	1035–1087

10. KINGS OF FRANCE

Robert II	996–1031
Henry I	1031–1060
Philip I	1060–1108

11. KINGS OF GERMANY

Otto III	983–1002
Henry II	1002–1024
Conrad II	1024–1039
Henry III	1039–1056
Henry IV	1056–1106

12. POPES

Benedict IX	1033–1045
Gregory VI	1045–1046
Clement II	1046–1047
Damasus II	1048
Leo IX	1048–1054
Victor II	1055–1057
Stephen IX	1057–1058
(Benedict X	1058–1059)
Nicholas II	1059–1061
Alexander II	1061–1073

SCHEDULE OF SELECTED DATES

979	(18 March) Murder of King Edward 'the Martyr'; accession of Æthelred to the throne.
991	Battle of Maldon.
1001	Visit of the Icelandic poet, Gunnlaug 'Serpent's Tooth', to Æthelred's court.
1002	(spring) Marriage of Æthelred to Emma of Normandy.
1003/4	Gunnlaug's second visit.
1005?	Birth of Edward
1006–7	Viking invasion.
1008–12	Viking invasion under Thorkell Hávi (the Tall)
1012?	Death of Æthelstan, Edward's eldest half-brother.
1013	Invasion of King Svein Forkbeard of Denmark and his son, Cnut.
	(autumn) Queen Emma, her sons Edward and Alfred, and King Æthelred flee to Normandy.
1014	(3 February) Death of King Svein.
	(spring) Edward negotiates in England for Æthelred's return.
	(after Easter) Cnut returns to Denmark.
1015	Edmund Ironside assumes power in the E. Midlands; Cnut invades England.
1016	(23 April) Death of Æthelred.
	Edmund Ironside chosen king.
	War between Edmund Ironside and Cnut.
	(18 October) Battle of *Assandun*.
	Treaty of Alney: England divided between Edmund and Cnut.
	(30 November) Death of Edmund Ironside; accession of Cnut to the whole kingdom.
	(25 December) Edward grants a charter to Ghent; beginning of his exile.
1017	(July) Marriage of Cnut to Emma, Æthelred's widow.
1027	Cnut's pilgrimage to Rome.
1030	Battle of Stiklestad: St Olaf killed; Harald Sigurdsson (Hardrada) wounded.

339

1035   Edward's sister widowed by the death of Count Drogo of the Vexin – she takes as second husband Eustace of Boulogne. Death of Count Robert I of Normandy on pilgrimage – succeeded by his son, William 'the Bastard'.

                (12 November) Death of Cnut – in the absence of Harthacnut in Denmark, Harold Harefoot *de facto* king of England.

1036   Edward's 'invasion' of England up Southampton Water.

                Alfred's fatal 'invasion' via Dover.

1037   Harold Harefoot recognized as king of all England.

                (autumn) Queen Emma expelled to Bruges.

1038?   Edward visits his mother at Bruges.

1039   Peace Treaty between Harthacnut, king of Denmark, and Magnus, king of Norway; Harthacnut joins his mother at Bruges.

                Gruffydd ap Llewelyn ambushes Mercian forces at Rhydd y Groes.

1040   (17 March) Death of Harold Harefoot.

                (summer) Harthacnut recognized as king of England.

1041   Edward joins Harthacnut and Emma in England.

1041–2   *Encomium Emmae* written at St Omer.

1042   (8 June) Death of Harthacnut.

                Edward recognized as king.

1043   (Easter) Edward's coronation.

                Earl Godwin's sons, Swegn and Harold, made earls.

                Stigand appointed bishop of East Anglia.

                (16 November) Edward temporarily disgraces his mother and Stigand.

1044   Edward in command of the fleet at Sandwich.

                Edward banishes Gunnhildr, Cnut's niece, and her children.

1045   (23 January) Marriage of Edward and Edith, Godwin's daughter.

                Edward again in command of the fleet at Sandwich.

                Beorn Estrithson, Godwin's nephew, made earl.

1046   Earl Swegn invades Wales and abducts the abbess of Leominster.

                Magnus of Norway conquers most of Denmark from Svein Estrithson.

                Edward banishes Osgot Clapa.

1047   Stigand promoted to the bishopric of Winchester.

Earl Swegn banished; Ralf of Mantes promoted earl.

Edward refuses to send help to Svein Estrithson.

(25 October) Death of Magnus of Norway – succeeded by Harald Sigurdsson (Hardrada).

1047–9   Lotharingian rebellion against Emperor Henry III.

1048   Edward again refuses to send help to Svein Estrithson.

South-East England raided by the Vikings, Lothen and Yrling.

1049   Edward, in alliance with the Emperor Henry, blockades Flanders from Sandwich.

(summer) Return from exile of Earl Swegn.

(summer) Bishop Ealdred of Worcester defeated by Irish Vikings and Gruffydd ap Rhydderch.

(autumn) Swegn murders Earl Beorn and is again banished.

(October) Leo IX's council at Rheims – William of Normandy's marriage to Matilda of Flanders prohibited.

1050   (mid-Lent) Royal council in London – 9 of the 14 mercenary ships paid off.

(Easter) Leo IX's council at Rome.

(summer) Earl Swegn pardoned.

(29 October) Death of Eadsige, archbishop of Canterbury.

King Macbeth of Scotland visits Rome.

1051   (mid-Lent) Royal council in London – Robert of Jumièges promoted to Canterbury; the last of the mercenary fleet dismissed.

(spring) Treaty made with William of Normandy.

(summer) Marriage of Earl Tostig and Judith of Flanders.

(September) Visit of Eustace of Boulogne to Edward's court.

Earl Godwin's abortive rebellion and banishment.

(winter) ? Visit of William of Normandy to Edward's court.

1052   (6 March) Death of Emma, the queen-mother.

Gruffydd ap Llewelyn invades Herefordshire.

(late summer) Return of Earl Godwin and his sons by force; peace made on 15 September.

Stigand promoted to the archbishopric of Canterbury.

(September) Death of Earl Swegn.

(?) Marriage of William of Normandy to Matilda of Flanders.

1053   (15 April) Death of Earl Godwin – succeeded by Harold.

Gruffydd ap Rhydderch raids Westbury on Severn.

1054   (summer) Earl Siward invades Scotland and defeats Macbeth on 27 July.

(late summer) Embassy of Bishop Ealdred to Germany.

(December) Visit of John, abbot of Fécamp, to England.

Death of Osgot Clapa.

1055   (early) Death of Earl Siward of Northumbria – succeeded by Tostig.

Earl Ælfgar of E. Anglia exiled.

Return of Bishop Ealdred from Germany.

Gruffydd ap Llewelyn becomes ruler of all Wales.

(24 October) Earl Ralf defeated at Hereford by Ælfgar and Gruffydd.

Peace of Billingsley.

1056   (June) Bishop Leofgar of Hereford defeated and killed by the Welsh.

(31 August) Death of Earl Odda.

(5 October) Death of the Emperor Henry III.

(November) Earl Harold at St Omer.

1057   Edward 'the Exile' returns to England.

(autumn) Death of Earl Leofric of Mercia – succeeded by Ælfgar.

Ælfgar outlawed for treason.

(21 December) Death of Earl Ralf.

Malcolm of Scots defeats and kills Macbeth.

1058   Malcolm of Scots kills Lulach.

Earl Ælfgar returns from exile with the help of Gruffydd ap Llewelyn.

A Viking fleet under Magnus, son of Harald Hardrada, operating off Wales.

Stigand receives a pallium from Pope Benedict X.

Bishop Ealdred visits Jerusalem.

(?) Goscelin of St Bertin joins Bishop Herman of Wiltshire.

1059   (? Christmas) Malcolm of Scots visits Edward's court.

1060   (December) Bishop Ealdred of Worcester promoted to York.

1061   Embassy of Earl Tostig and Archbishop Ealdred to Rome.

Invasion of Malcolm of Scots.

1062   No entry in the Anglo-Saxon Chronicle.

? Earl Ælfgar dies – ? succeeded by son Eadwine.

Battle of Nissa: defeat of Svein of Denmark by Harald of Norway.

(Christmas) Earl Harold raids Rhuddlan.

1063 (May) Earls Harold and Tostig invade Wales.

(5 August) Gruffydd ap Llewelyn killed.

William of Normandy conquers Maine.

1064 No entry in the Anglo-Saxon Chronicle.

(?) Death of Walter III, count of Mantes.

Peace treaty (at Gota) between Svein of Denmark and Harald of Norway.

(early summer) (or 1065) Earl Harold in Normandy.

(28 December) Gospatric killed at the king's court.

1065 (spring) Earl Harold invades South Wales.

(summer) Proposed visit of Edward to Portskewet.

(summer) Dedication of Wilton.

(?) Writing of the *Vita Ædwardi Regis* begun.

(24 August) Caradog ap Gruffydd destroys Portskewet.

(autumn) Edward and Tostig go hunting in Wiltshire.

(3 October) Outbreak of the Northumbrian rebellion.

(28 October) Earl Harold negotiates with the rebels at Oxford.

(November) Exile of Tostig.

(24 December) Edward becomes ill.

(28 December) Dedication of Westminster abbey.

1066 (4/5 January) Death of Edward.

(6 January) Burial of Edward in Westminster abbey; coronation of Harold.

(20 September) Battle of Gate Fulford.

(25 September) Battle of Stamford Bridge.

(14 October) Battle of Hastings.

(25 December) Coronation of William.

1067? *Vita Ædwardi Regis* completed.

1075 (18 December) Death of Edith, Edward's widow.

1100? Date of existing copy of *Vita Ædwardi Regis* (London, B.M. MS Harl. 526).

1102 Inspection of Edward's grave.

1125 William of Malmesbury finishes his *Gesta Regum Anglorum* and *Gesta Pontificum Anglorum*.

1134? Miracles start again at Edward's tomb.

1138	Osbert of Clare writes *Vita beati Eadwardi regis Anglorum*.
	(17 December) Gervase of Blois ordained abbot of Westminster.
	Westminster petitions the pope for Edward's canonization.
1139?	(9 December) Innocent II defers a decision on Edward.
1158?	Laurence appointed abbot of Westminster.
1159?	Westminster decides to make a new approach to the papacy.
1160	(autumn) Abbot Laurence secures Henry II's support.
	(? 13 November) Laurence meets the papal legates in Paris.
1161	(7 February) Pope Alexander III canonizes Edward.
1161–3	Ailred of Rievaulx writes *Vita Sancti Edwardi Regis*.
1163	(13 October) Translation of Edward's body at Westminster.
1269	(13 October) Edward's second translation in Henry III's rebuilt Westminster abbey.

SELECT BIBLIOGRAPHY

The lists which follow are not to be regarded as a full bibliography for the history of Edward the Confessor and his times. They serve to give further precision to the citations in the footnotes of this book and to give some indication of the author's indebtedness to other scholars.

I. PRIMARY SOURCES

Abingdon: *Chronicon Monasterii de Abingdon*, ed. J. Stevenson, Rolls ser., 1858.

Adam of Bremen: *Magistri Adam Bremensis Gesta Hammaburgensis ecclesiae pontificum*, ed. B. Schmeidler, Scriptores rerum Germanicarum in usum scholarum, 3rd ed. Hannover and Leipzig, 1917.

Ælfric, *Life of St Swithun*, *EHD*, i. 853.

—— *Lives of Saints*, ed. W. W. Skeat, Early English Text Soc., vols. 76, 82, 94, 114 (1881–1900).

—— *The Old English Version of the Heptateuch, Ælfric's Treatise on the Old and New Testament, and his Preface to Genesis*, ed. S. J. Crawford, Early English Text Soc., 160 (1922).

Ailred of Rievaulx, *Genealogia regum Angliae et regis David Scotiae* in Migne, *PL*, cxcv. 739.

—— *Vita Sancti Edwardi*, in *Historiae Anglicanae scriptores X (q.v.)* i. 369, reprinted Migne, *PL*, cxcv. 737.

—— *The Life of Ailred of Rievaulx by Walter Daniel*, ed. F. M. Powicke, Nelson's Medieval Classics, 1950.

Anglia Sacra, ed. H. Wharton, 1691.

Anglo-Saxon Charters, ed. and trans. A. J. Robertson, Cambridge Studies in English legal history, 1956.

Anglo-Saxon Charters: *Codex Diplomaticus Aevi Saxonici*, ed. J. M. Kemble, vols. iii, iv, vi, 1845, 1846, 1848.

Anglo-Saxon Charters: an annotated List and Bibliography, ed. P. H. Sawyer, Royal Hist. Soc., 1968.

Anglo-Saxon Chronicle, ed. D. Whitelock with D. C. Douglas and S. I. Tucker, *EHD*, vol. i, and independently 1961.

Anglo-Saxon Laws: *Die Gesetze der Angelsachsen*, ed. F. Liebermann, Halle, 1903.

Anglo-Saxon Poetry, ed. and trans. R. K. Gordon, Everyman, 1926.

Anglo-Saxon Poetry: *Bibliothek der Angelsächsischen Poesie*, ed. C. W. M. Grein and R. P. Wulcker, 1883–98.

Anglo-Saxon Poetry: *The Earliest English Poems*, trans. M. Alexander, Penguin Classics, 1966.

Anglo-Saxon Wills, ed. and trans. D. Whitelock, Cambridge Studies in English legal history, 1930.

Anglo-Saxon Writs, ed. F. E. Harmer, 1952.

Anglo-Saxon Writs: *Facsimiles of English Writs to A.D. 1100*, ed. T. A. M. Bishop and P. Chaplais, 1957.

Annales Cambriae, ed. John Williams ab Ithel, Rolls ser. 1860.

Annals of the Kingdom of Ireland by the Four Masters, ed. J. O'Donovan, Dublin, 1854; New York, 1966.

Anonymi Roskildensis Chronicon Danicum, ed. J. Langebek, in *Scriptores Rerum Danicarum Medii Ævi*, i, Copenhagen, 1772.

Archpoet: *Die Gedichte des Archipoeta*, ed. M. Manitius, Münchener Texte, nr. 6, 2nd ed. 1929.

Arnulf of Lisieux: *The Letters of Arnulf of Lisieux*, ed. F. Barlow, Royal Hist. Soc., Camden 3rd ser. lxi, 1939.

Ashdown, M., *English and Norse Documents relating to the Reign of Ethelred the Unready*, 1930.

Bayeux Tapestry, ed. F. M. Stenton and others, Phaidon, 1957.

Beowulf, trans. D. Wright, Penguin Classics, 1957.

Bury St Edmunds: *Feudal Documents from the Abbey of Bury St Edmunds*, ed. D. C. Douglas, Br. Acad. 1932.

Calendar of Documents preserved in France, ed. J. H. Round, i, 1899.

Chronicles of the Reigns of Stephen, Henry II, and Richard I, ed. R. Howlett, Rolls ser. 1886

Chroniques Anglo-Normandes, ed. F. Michel, Rouen, 1836.

Domesday Book, ed. Record Commission, 1783–1816.

Durham: *De Obsessione Dunelmi* in *Symeonis Monachi Opera Omnia*, ed. Arnold (*q.v.*)

Durham: *Annales Dunelmenses*, ed. G. H. Pertz in *Monumenta Germaniae historica*; Scriptores xix, Hannover, 1866.

Durham: *Historia translationum S. Cuthberti*, ed. H. Hinde, Surtees Soc. li, 1868.

Eadmer, *Historia Novorum in Anglia*, ed. M. Rule, Rolls ser. 1884.

Ely: *Liber Eliensis*, ed. E. O. Blake, Royal Hist. Soc., Camden 3rd ser. xcii, 1962.

Encomium Emmae Reginae, ed. A. Campbell, Royal Hist. Soc., Camden 3rd ser. lxxii, 1949.

English Coronation Records, ed. L. G. W. Legg, 1901.

English Historical Documents, ed. D. C. Douglas, i, 1955, ed. D. Whitelock.

Evesham: *Chronicon Abbatiae de Evesham*, ed. W. D. Macray, Rolls ser. 1863.

Exeter Book, ed. G. P. Krapp and E. Van Kirk Dobbie, 1936.

Facsimiles of Anglo-Saxon Manuscripts, ed. W. B. Sanders, Ordnance Survey, 1881.

Florence of Worcester, *Chronicon ex chronicis*, ed. B. Thorpe, Eng. Hist. Soc., 1848–9.

Gaimar, *Lestorie des engles*, ed. T. D. Hardy and C. T. Martin, Rolls ser. 1888–9.

Gervase of Canterbury: *The Historical Works of Gervase of Canterbury*, ed. W. Stubbs, Rolls ser. 1880.

Ghent: *Chartes et documents de l'abbaye de Saint-Pierre au Mont-Blandin à Gand*, ed. A. Van Lokeren, i, Ghent, 1869.

Giraldus Cambrensis, *Descriptio Kambriae* in *Opera Omnia*, ed. J. F. Dimock, Rolls ser. 1868.

Goscelin of St Bertin: 'La Légende de Ste. Edith en prose et vers par le moine Goscelin', ed. A. Wilmart, *Analecta Bollandiana*, lvi, 1938.

—— 'The Liber confortatorius of Goscelin of Saint Bertin', ed. C. H. Talbot, *Studia Anselmiana*, fasc. xxxvii = *Analecta Monastica*, 3rd ser., Rome, 1955.

—— *Historia translationis S. Augustini episcopi* in Migne, *PL*, clv.

—— 'The Life of Saint Wulsin of Sherborne by Goscelin', ed. C. H. Talbot, *Revue Bénédictine*, lxix, 1959.

—— *Vita S. Vulfhilde*, ed. M. Esposito, *Analecta Bollandiana*, xxxii, 1913.

Gunnlaug's Saga Ormstungu, ed. M. Ashdown (*q.v.*)

Guy of Amiens: *The Carmen de Hastingae Proelio of Guy bishop of Amiens*, ed. Catherine Morton and Hope Muntz, Oxf. Med. Texts, 1972.

Harald Sigurdsson (Hardrada): *King Harald's Saga*, trans. M. Magnusson and H. Pálsson, Penguin Classics, 1966.

Helgaud, *Epitoma vitae regis Roberti pii*, in Migne, *PL*, cxli.

Hemingi Chartularium ecclesiae Wigorniensis, ed. T. Hearne, 1723.

Herman, *Miracula S. Eadmundi* in Liebermann, *Ungedruckte* (*q.v.*)

Henry of Huntingdon, *Historia Anglorum*, ed. T. Arnold, Rolls ser. 1879.

Historia Norwegiae, ed. G. Storm in *Monumenta Historica Norvegiae*, Christiana, 1880.

Historiae Anglicanae scriptores X, ed. R. Twysden, 1652.

Holtzmann, W., *Papsturkunden in England*, Berlin, 1930.

Hugh Candidus: *The Chronicle of Hugh Candidus, a monk of Peterborough*, ed. W. T. Mellows, 1949.

John Flete: *The History of Westminster Abbey by John Flete*, ed. J. A. Robinson, 1909.

Johannes de Fordun, *Chronica Gentis Scotorum*, ed. W. F. Skene, 1871.

John of Salisbury: *Ioannis Saresberiensis Historia Pontificalis*, ed. R. L. Poole, 1927.

—— *The Historia Pontificalis of John of Salisbury*, ed. M. Chibnall, Nelson's Medieval Texts, 1956.

—— *Johannis Saresberiensis episcopi Carnotensis Policraticus*, ed. C. C. J. Webb, 1909.

John of Worcester, *Chronica*, ed. J. R. H. Weaver, Anecdota Oxoniensia . . . med. and mod. ser., pt. xiii, 1908.

Kalendars: F. Wormald, *English Kalendars before A.D. 1100*, Henry Bradshaw Soc. lxxii, 1933; *English Benedictine Kalendars after A.D. 1100*, Henry Bradshaw Soc., lxxvii, lxxxi, 1938, 1943–4.

Laws of the Kings of England from Edmund to Henry I, ed. and trans. A. J. Robertson, 1925.

Leofric Missal, The, ed. F. E. Warren, 1883.

Liebermann, F. (ed.), *Ungedruckte Anglo-Normannische Geschichtsquellen*, Strassburg, 1879.

Lincoln: *The Registrum Antiquissimum of the Cathedral Church of Lincoln*, ed. C. W. Foster, Lincoln Record Soc., vol. 27, i, 1931.

Lives of the Cambro-British Saints, ed. W. J. Rees, Welsh MSS Soc., 1853.

Maldon: *The Battle of Maldon*, ed. M. Ashdown (*q.v.*)

Mansi, J. D. (ed.), *Sacrorum Conciliorum nova et amplissima Collectio*, 1759 ff.

Map, Walter, *De Nugis Curialium*, ed. T. Wright, Camden Soc., vol. 50, 1850.

Materials for the History of Thomas Becket, ed. J. C. Robertson, Rolls ser. 1881.

Mathew Paris, *Historia Anglorum*, ed. Sir F. Madden, Rolls ser. 1866.

—— *Historia Majora*, ed. H. R. Luard, Rolls ser. 1874.

Missale ad usum ecclesie Westmonasteriensis, ed. J. W. Legg, Henry Bradshaw Soc., 1891–7.

Monasticon Anglicanum, ed. W. Dugdale, rev. by Caley, Ellis, and Bandinel, 1817–30.

Norman Anonymous [also known as The Anonymous of Rouen/York]: *Die Texte des normannischen Anonymus,* ed. K. Pellens, Wiesbaden, 1966.

Olafsdrapa, ed. M. Ashdown (*q.v.*)

Olafs Saga Helga, ed. M. Ashdown (*q.v.*)

Olafs Saga Tryggvasonar, ed. M. Ashdown (*q.v.*)

Ordericus Vitalis, *Historia Ecclesiastica libri tredecim,* ed. A. Le Prévost, Paris, 1838–55; Books III–XIII, ed. Marjorie Chibnall, Oxford Medieval Texts, 1969–78.

Osbern, *Miracula S. Dunstani* in *Memorials of St Dunstan,* ed. W. Stubbs, Rolls ser. 1874.

—— *Vita S. Elphegi* in *Anglia Sacra,* ii, 1691.

Osbert of Clare: 'La vie de S. Edouard le Confesseur par Osbert de Clare', ed. M. Bloch, *Analecta Bollandiana,* xli, 1923.

—— *The Letters of Osbert of Clare,* ed. E. W. Williamson, 1929.

Patrologiae cursus completus: Patrologia latina, ed. J. P. Migne, 1844 ff.

Peterborough: *Chronicon Angliae Petriburgense,* ed. J. A. Giles, Caxton Soc., 1845.

Ramsey: *Chronicon abbatiae Rameseiensis,* ed. W. D. Macray, Rolls ser. 1886.

Recueil des Actes Ducs de Normandie de 911 à 1066, ed. M. Fauroux, Société des Antiquaires de Normandie, 1961.

Recueil des Historiens des Gaules et de la France: Bouquet, M., *Rerum Gallicarum et Francicarum scriptores,* Paris, 1738–1876.

Regesta Pontificum Romanorum, ed. Jaffé-Wattenbach, Leipzig, 1885–8.

Richard of Cirencester: *Ricardi de Cirencestria Speculum Historiale de Gestis Regum Angliae,* ed. J. E. B. Mayor, Rolls ser. 1869.

Roger of Wendover, *Flores Historiarum,* ed. H. O. Coxe, Eng. Hist. Soc., 1841–4.

Rouleau Mortuaire du B. Vital, abbé de Savigni, ed. L. Delisle, Paris, 1909.

St Albans: *Gesta abbatum monasterii S. Albani,* ed. H. T. Riley, Rolls ser. 1867.

Saint Riquier: Hariulf, *Chronique de l'abbaye de Saint-Riquier,* ed. F. Lot, Paris, 1894.

Saints: *Die Heiligen Englands,* ed. F. Liebermann, Hannover, 1889.

Saxonis Grammatici Gesta Danorum, ed. A. Holder, Strassburg, 1886.

Scriptores Rerum Gestarum Willelmi Conquestoris, ed. J. A. Giles, 1845.

Select Charters of English Constitutional History, ed. W. Stubbs and H. W. C. Davis, 9th ed., 1911.

Snorre Sturlason, *Heimskringla*, trans. E. Monsen and A. H. Smith, 1932.

'Sulcard of Westminster: "Prologus de Construccione Westmonasterii" ', ed. B. W. Scholz, *Traditio*, xx, 1964.

Symeon of Durham: *Symeonis Dunelmensis opera*, ed. J. H. Hinde, Surtees Soc., li, 1868.

—— *Symeonis Monachi Opera Omnia*, ed. T. Arnold, Rolls ser. 1882.

—— *Historia Ecclesiae Dunhelmensis*, ed. T. Arnold, Rolls ser. 1885.

Theodrici monachi historia de antiquitate regum Norwagiensium, ed. G. Storm, in *Monumenta Historica Norvegiae*, Christiana, 1880.

Tigernach: 'The Annals of Tigernach: the fourth fragment A.D. 973–A.D. 1088', ed. W. Stokes, *Revue Celtique*, Paris, xvii, 1896.

Ungedruckte Anglo-Normannische Geschichtsquellen, ed. F. Liebermann, Strassburg, 1879.

Vita Ædwardi Regis (The Life of King Edward), ed. and trans. F. Barlow, Nelson's Medieval Texts, 1962.

Vita Haroldi, ed. W. De Gray Birch, 1885.

Vita Sancti Gundleii in *Lives of the Cambro-British Saints* (*q.v.*) and *Vitae Sanctorum Britanniae et Genealogiae* (*q.v.*).

Vita S. Henrici [II of Germany], auct. anon. in Migne, *PL*, cxl.

Vita S. Margaretae Scotorum reginae in *Symeonis Dunelmensis opera*, ed. J. H. Hinde (*q.v.*)

Vita Sancti Oswaldi, by a monk of Ramsey, *HCY*, i.

Vita Wulfstani of William of Malmesbury, ed. R. R. Darlington, Royal Hist. Soc., Camden 3rd ser., xl, 1928.

Vitae Sanctorum Britanniae et Genealogiae, ed. and trans. A. W. Wadel Evans, 1944.

Walter Daniel: *Walter Daniel's Life of Ailred of Rievaulx*, ed. F. M. Powicke, Nelson's Medieval Classics, 1950.

Waltham: *The Foundation of Waltham abbey*, ed. W. Stubbs, 1861.

Wells: *Ecclesiastical Documents: A brief History of the Bishoprick of Somerset*, ed. J. Hunter, Camden Soc., 1840.

William of Jumièges: Guillaume de Jumièges, *Gesta Normannorum Ducum*, ed. J. Marx, Rouen and Paris, 1914.

William of Malmesbury, *De Gestis Pontificum Anglorum*, ed. N.E.S.A. Hamilton, Rolls ser. 1870.

—— *De Gestis Regum Anglorum*, ed. W. Stubbs, Rolls ser. 1887–9.

—— *Historia Novella*, ed. K. R. Potter, Nelson's Medieval Texts, 1955.

William of Poitiers, *Gesta Guillelmi*, ed. and trans. R. Foreville, Les classiques de l'histoire de France au moyen âge, Paris, 1952.

Winchcombe: *Ann. Winchcombe*, ed. R. R. Darlington, in *A Medieval Miscellany for Doris Mary Stenton*, ed. P. M. Barnes and C. F. Slade, Pipe Roll Soc. 1962.

Winchester: *Annales de Wintonia* in *Annales Monastici*, ii, ed. H. R. Luard, Rolls ser. 1865.

Wulfstan: *Die 'Institutes of Polity, Civil and Ecclesiastical': Ein Werk Erzbischof Wulfstans von York*, Swiss Studies in English, vol. 47, Bern, 1959.

—— *The Homilies of Wulfstan*, ed. D. Bethurum, 1957.

—— *Sermo Lupi ad Anglos*, *EHD*, i. 855–8.

York: *The Historians of the Church of York and its Archbishops*, ed. J. Raine, Rolls ser. 1879–94.

II. SECONDARY AUTHORITIES

Anglo-Saxon Coins: studies presented to F. M. Stenton, ed. R. H. M. Dolley, 1961.

Barlow, F., *The Feudal Kingdom of England*, 1961.

—— *Edward the Confessor and the Norman Conquest*, The Hastings and Bexhill Branch of the Historical Association, 1966.

—— *William I and the Norman Conquest*, 1965.

—— 'Two Notes: Cnut's Second Pilgrimage and Queen Emma's Disgrace in 1043', *EHR*, lxxiii, 1958.

—— 'Edward the Confessor's Early Life, Character and Attitudes', *EHR*, lxxx, 1965.

—— 'The Vita Ædwardi (Book II); The Seven Sleepers: some further evidence and reflections', *Speculum*, xl, 1965.

—— 'The English, Norman, and French Councils called to deal with the Papal Schism of 1159', *EHR*, li, 1936.

—— *The English Church 1000–1066*, 1963, reprinted 1966, 2nd edn. 1979.

—— 'The Carmen de Hastingae Proelio' in *Studies in International History*, ed. K. Bourne and D. C. Watt, 1967.

Bigelow, M. M., *History of Procedure in England from the Norman Conquest*, 1880.

Bloch, M., *La société féodale*, Paris, 1939–40.

—— *Les rois thaumaturges*, Strasbourg, 1924.

Brand, J. D., 'Meretricious Metrology', Spink and Son Ltd., *The Numismatic Circular*, lxxv, 1967.

Brooke, G. C., *English Coins*, 3rd ed., 1950.

—— *Sylloge of Coins of British Isles*, British Academy, 1958 ff.

Brooke, Z. N., 'The Register of Master David of London and the part he played in the Becket Crisis' in *Essays in History presented to R. L. Poole*, ed. H. W. C. Davis, 1927.

Brown, R. A., *The Normans and the Norman Conquest*, 1969.

Brown, R. A., Colvin, H. M., and Taylor, A. J., *The History of the King's Works: i, The Middle Ages*, 1963.

Bullough, D. A., 'Anglo-Saxon Institutions and Early English Society', *Annali della Fondazione italiana per la storia amministrativa*, Milan, 2, 1965.

Burrows, M., *Historic Towns: Cinque Ports*, 1888.

Chaplais, P., 'The original charters of Herbert and Gervase abbots of Westminster' in *A Medieval Miscellany for Doris Mary Stenton*, Pipe Roll Soc., 1962.

—— 'The Anglo-Saxon Chancery: from the Diploma to the Writ', *Journal of the Soc. of Archivists*, iii, 1966.

Colgrave, B., 'The post-Bedan miracles and translations of St Cuthbert' in *The Early Cultures of North-West Europe*, ed. C. Fox and B. Dickins.

Corbett, W. J., 'England from A.D. 954 to the death of Edward the Confessor', *Cambridge Medieval History*, iii, 1922.

Croydon, F. E., 'Abbot Laurence of Westminster and Hugh of St Victor', *Mediaeval and Renaissance Studies*, ii, 1950.

Darlington, R. R., 'The last phase of Anglo-Saxon History', *History*, xxii, 1937.

David, M., 'Le serment du Sacre', *Revue du Moyen Age latin*, li, 1950.

Davis, H. W. C., 'Cumberland before the Norman Conquest', *EHR*, xx, 1905.

Davies, R. H., *The lands and rights of Harold, son of Godwine, and their distribution by William I: A study in the Domesday evidence*, unpublished M.A. dissertation, University College, Cardiff, 1967.

Dhondt, J., 'Henri Ier, L'Empire et L'Anjou (1043–1056)', *Revue Belge de Philologie et d'Histoire*, xxv, 1946.

Dickins, B., *Leeds Studies in English and Kindred Languages*, vi, 1937.

Dickinson, W. C., *Scotland from the Earliest Times to 1603*, 1961.

Dolley, R. H. M., *Anglo-Saxon Pennies*, British Museum, 1964.

—— 'New light on the order of the early issues of Edward the Confessor', *British Numismatic Journal*, xxix, 1960.

—— 'The Unpublished 1895 Find of coins of Edward the Confessor from Harewood', *Yearbook of the British Association of Numismatic Societies*, 1961.

Dolley, R. H. M., and Jones, F. E., 'A new suggestion concerning the so-called "Martlets" in the "Arms of St Edward" ' in *Anglo-Saxon Coins* (*q.v.*)

—— 'Some Remarks on BMC Type VII var. *B* of Edward the Confessor', *Numismatic Chronicle*, 6th ser., xx, 1960.

Dolley, R. H. M., and Metcalf, D. M., 'The reform of the English coinage under Eadgar', in *Anglo-Saxon Coins* (*q.v.*)

Douglas, D. C., 'Robert de Jumièges et la Conquête de l'Angleterre', *Jumièges – XIIIe centenaire.*

—— 'Edward the Confessor, Duke William of Normandy and the English Succession', *EHR*, lxviii, 1953.

—— 'Odo, Lanfranc, and the Domesday Survey' in *Historical Essays in Honour of James Tait*, ed. Edwards, Galbraith, Jacob, 1933.

—— *William the Conqueror*, 1964.

Ewald, P., 'Reise nach Italien im Winter von 1876 auf 1877', *Neues Archiv der Gesellschaft für ältere deutsche Geschichtskunde*, iii, 1878.

Eyton, R. W., *Antiquities of Shropshire*, 1854–60.

—— *Court, Household, and Itinerary of King Henry II*, 1878.

Fest, S., 'The Sons of Eadmund Ironside, Anglo-Saxon king at the Court of St Stephen', *Archivum Europae Centro-Orientalis*, Budapest, iv, 1938.

Finn, R. W., *The Domesday Inquest*, 1961.

—— *An Introduction to Domesday Book*, 1962.

—— *The Liber Exoniensis*, 1964.

—— *The Eastern Counties*, 1967.

Folz, R., 'La chancellerie de Frédéric Ier et la canonisation de Charlemagne', *Le Moyen âge*, lxx, 1964.

Foreville, R., 'Aux origines de la renaissance juridique: Concepts juridiques et influences romanisantes chez Guillaume de Poitiers, biographe du Conquérant', *Moyen âge*, lviii, 1952.

Freeman, E. A., *The History of the Norman Conquest of England*, i, ii, 2nd ed. 1870; iii–v, 1st ed. 1869–75.

Galbraith, V. H., *Studies in the Public Records*, 1948.

—— *The Making of Domesday Book*, 1961.

—— 'Who wrote Asser's Life of Alfred' in *An Introduction to the Study of History*, 1964.

Ganshof, F. L., *Le Moyen Age* in *Histoire des Relations Internationales*, ed. P. Renouvin, vol. i, Hachette, 1953.

Glover, R., 'English Warfare in 1066', *EHR*, lxvii, 1952.

Grierson, P., 'A visit of Earl Harold to Flanders in 1056', *EHR*, li, 1936.

Griesron, P., 'Sterling', in *Anglo-Saxon Coins* (q.v.)

Harmer, F. E., 'A Bromfield and a Coventry Writ of King Edward the Confessor' in *The Anglo-Saxons*, ed. P. Clemoes, 1959.

—— 'Three Westminster Writs of King Edward the Confessor', *EHR*, li, 1936.

—— '*Chipping* and *Market*: a lexicographical investigation' in *The Early Cultures of North-West Europe*, H. M. Chadwick Memorial Studies, ed. Sir C. Fox and B. Dickins, 1950.

Hart, C., 'The site of Assandun', *History Studies*, i, 1968.

Harvey, S., 'Royal Revenue and Domesday Terminology', *Ec. Hist. Rev.*, 2nd ser., xx, 1967.

Henry, P. L., *The Early English and Celtic Lyric*, 1966.

Hollister, C. W., *Anglo-Saxon Military Institutions*, 1962.

Hurnard, N. D., 'The Anglo-Norman Franchises', *EHR*, lxiv, 1949.

John, E., *Land Tenure in Early England*, 1960.

—— *Orbis Britanniae*, 1966.

Jolliffe, J. E. A., *Angevin Kingship*, 1955.

Jost, K., 'Wulfstan und die angelsächsische Chronik', *Anglia*, xlvii, 1923.

Kemp, E. W., *Canonization and Authority in the Western Church*, 1948.

Ker, N. R., *Medieval Libraries of Great Britain*, Royal Hist. Soc., 1964.

Kienast, W., *Untertaneneid und Treuvorbehalt in Frankreich und England*, Weimar, 1952.

Klauser, R., *Der Heinrichs- und Kunigundenkult im mittelalterlichen Bistum Bamberg*, Bamberg, 1957.

Knowles, D., *The episcopal colleagues of Archbishop Thomas Becket*, 1951.

Körner, S., *The Battle of Hastings, England and Europe, 1035–1066*, Lund, 1964.

Lanfry, G., *L'abbaye de Jumièges, Plans et documents*, Rouen, 1954.

—— 'Fouilles et découvertes à Jumièges: le déambulatoire de l'église romaine', *Bulletin Monumental*, lxxxvii, 1928.

Larson, L. M., *The King's Household in England before the Norman Conquest*, 1904.

Leclercq, J., *The Love of Learning and the desire for God*, Mentor Omega Book, 1962.

Leclercq, J., and Bonnes, J-P., *Un Maître de la Vie Spirituelle au XIᵉ siècle, Jean de Fécamp*, Etudes de Théologie et d'Histoire de la spiritualité, Paris, 1946.

Lemarignier, J-F., *Autour de la royauté française du IXᵉ au XIIIᵉ siècle*, Bibl. de l'Ecole des Chartes, cxiii, 1955.

—— 'Structures monastiques et structures politiques dans la France de la fin du Xe et des débuts du XIe siècle', *Settimane di studio del Centro italiano di studi sull' alto medioevo*, Spoleto, 8–14 apr., 1956, iv.

Lethaby, W. R., *Westminster Abbey re-examined*, 1925.

Lloyd, J. E., 'Wales and the coming of the Normans', *Cymmrodorion* 1899–1900, 1901.

—— *A History of Wales*, 3rd ed., 1939.

Loyn, H. R., 'Gesiths and thegns in Anglo-Saxon England from the Seventh to the Tenth Century', *EHR*, lxx, 1955.

—— 'Boroughs and Mints A.D. 900–1066' in *Anglo-Saxon Coins* (*q.v.*)

Lyon, B. D., 'The money fief under the English kings, 1066–1485', *EHR*, lxvi, 1951.

Lyon, C. S. S., 'A round halfpenny of Edward the Confessor', *British Numismatic Journal*, xxiv, 1966.

Maitland, F. W., *Domesday Book and Beyond*, 1897; refs. are to the reissue: Fontana Library, 1960.

Markland, M. F., 'Boethius, Alfred, and Deor', *Modern Philology*, lxvi, 1968.

Matthew, D., *The Norman Monasteries and their English Possessions*, 1962.

North, J. J., *English Hammered Coinage*, Spink and Son, 1963.

Ohnsorge, W., *Die Legaten Alexanders III im ersten Jahrzehnt seines Pontifikats (1159–1169)*, Berlin, 1928.

Oleson, T. J., *The Witenagemot in the reign of Edward the Confessor*, 1955.

—— 'Edward the Confessor's promise of the throne to Duke William of Normandy', *EHR*, lxxii, 1957.

—— 'Edward the Confessor in History', *Transactions of the Royal Soc. of Canada*, vol. lii, ser. iii, June 1959.

Plummer, C., and Earle, J., *Two of the Saxon Chronicles Parallel*, vol. ii, 1899.

Poupardin, R., 'Dix-huit lettres inédites', Bibl. de l'Ecole des Chartes, lxiii, 1902.

Richardson, H. G., 'The English Coronation Oath', *Speculum*, xxiv, 1949.

—— 'The coronation in medieval England', *Traditio*, xvi, 1960.

Richardson, H. G., and Sayles, G. O., *The Governance of Medieval England from the Conquest to Magna Carta*, 1963.

Ritchie, R. L. G., *The Normans in Scotland*, 1954.

Robinson, J. Armitage, 'Westminster in the twelfth century: Osbert of Clare', *Church Quarterly Review*, lxviii, 1909.

—— *Gilbert Crispin, abbot of Westminster*, 1911.

Round, J. H., 'The attack on Dover, 1067', *The Antiquary*, xii, 1885.
—— *Feudal England*, 1895.
Russell, J. C., *British Medieval Population*, Albuquerque, New Mexico, 1948.
Sawyer, P. H., 'The density of the Danish Settlement in England', *University of Birmingham Historical Journal*, vi, 1957–8.
Schnith, K., 'Die Wende der englischen Geschichte im 11. Jahrhundert', *Historisches Jahrbuch*, 86, 1966.
Scholz, B. W., 'The Canonization of Edward the Confessor', *Speculum*, xxvi, 1961.
Schramm, P. E., 'Die Krönung bei den Westfranken und Angelsächsen von 878 bis um 1000', *Zeitschrift der Savigny-Stiftung für Rechtsgeschichte*, liv, kan. abt. xxiii, Weimar, 1934.
—— 'Die Krönung in Deutschland bis zum Beginn des Salischen Hauses (1028)', *Zeitschrift der Savigny-Stiftung für Rechtsgeschichte*, lv, kan. abt. xxiv, Weimar, 1935.
—— *A History of the English Coronation*, trans. L. G. W. Legg, 1937.
—— *Herrschaftszeichen und Staatssymbolik*, Schriften der Monumenta Germaniae historica, 1954–6.
Schütt, M., 'The Literary form of Asser's "Vita Alfredi" ', *EHR*, lxxii, 1957.
Seaby, P., 'The sequence of Anglo-Saxon coin types, 1030–50', *British Numismatic Journal*, 1955–7, xxviii, 1958.
Smith, R. A. L., 'The place of Gundulf in the Anglo-Norman church', *EHR*, lviii, 1943.
Southern, R. W., 'The First Life of Edward the Confessor', *EHR*, lviii, 1943.
—— *The Place of Henry I in English History*, The Raleigh Lecture on History, British Academy, 1962.
Stanley, E. G., 'Old-English poetic diction and the interpretation of the Wanderer, the Seafarer, and the Penitent's Prayer', *Anglia*, lxxiii, 1955–6.
Stenton, D. M.: *A Medieval Miscellany for Doris Mary Stenton*, ed. P. M. Barnes and C. F. Slade, Pipe Roll Soc. 1962.
Stenton, F. M., *Anglo-Saxon England*, 1943.
Tanner, L. E., and Clapham, A. W., 'Recent discoveries in the Nave of Westminster Abbey', *Archaeologia*, lxxxiii, 1933.
Taralon, J., *Jumièges*, Nefs et Clochers: les éditions du Cerf, 1955.
Tillmann, H., *Die päpstlichen Legaten in England*, Bonn, 1926.

Vinogradoff, P., *English Society in the Eleventh Century*, 1908.

Von Feilitzen, O., *The Pre-Conquest Personal Names of Domesday Book*, Nomina Germanica, 3, Uppsala, 1937.

Whitelock, D., 'The Interpretation of *The Seafarer*', in *The Early Cultures of North-West Europe*, H. M. Chadwick Memorial Studies, ed. Sir Cyril Fox and Bruce Dickins, 1950.

Whitting, P. D., 'The Byzantine Empire and the Coinage of the Anglo-Saxons', in *Anglo-Saxon Coins (q.v.)*

Widmore, R., *Enquiry into the time of the first foundation of Westminster Abbey*, 1751.

Wilkinson, B., 'Northumbrian separatism in 1065 and 1066', *EHR*, xxxii, 1936.

—— 'Freeman and the Crisis of 1051', *Bull of the John Rylands Library*, xxxiv, 1938.

Wright, C. E., *The Cultivation of Saga in Anglo-Saxon England*, 1939.

Young, J. I., 'Ungloomy Aspects of Anglo-Saxon Poetry' in *The Early Cultures of North-West Europe*, H. M. Chadwick Memorial Studies, ed. Sir Cyril Fox and Bruce Dickins, 1950.

The English Earldoms in
1045
(after E.A.Freeman)

MACBETH

THORFINN ?

Hexham

Carlisle · Durham

SIWARD

Lancaster · York

LEOFRIC

Chester · Lincoln

BEORN

Stafford Derby · Nottingham

Shrewsbury Leicester Stamford

Lichfield · Norwich

Coventry

RALF SIWARD

Worcester Huntingdon HAROLD

Hereford Northampton Bedford Cambridge

GRUFFYDD ap Llewelyn

GRUFFYDD ap Rhydderch

BEORN

Gloucester Oxford

Beverstone SWEGEN

London

Southwark Sandwich

Wells Salisbury Canterbury

Winchester Dover

Exeter GODWIN Hastings

358

The English Earldoms in
1065
(after E. A. Freeman)

MALCOLM

OSWULF
Hexham
Carlisle
Durham

GODRED

MORKERE
Lancaster
York

Chester
Lincoln

EADWINE
Derby
Nottingham

Stafford
Leicester
Stamford
Norwich
Shrewsbury
Lichfield

BLEDDYNN & RHIWALLON

Coventry
WALTHEOLF
Huntingdon
H
Worcester
Cambridge T
MAREDUDD & RHYS AB OWAIN
Hereford
Northampton
R
N
CADWGAN AP MEURIG
Portskewet
Gloucester
G
LEOFWINE
Oxford
London

Sandwich
Salisbury
Canterbury
Winchester
Dover
HAROLD
Hastings

Exeter

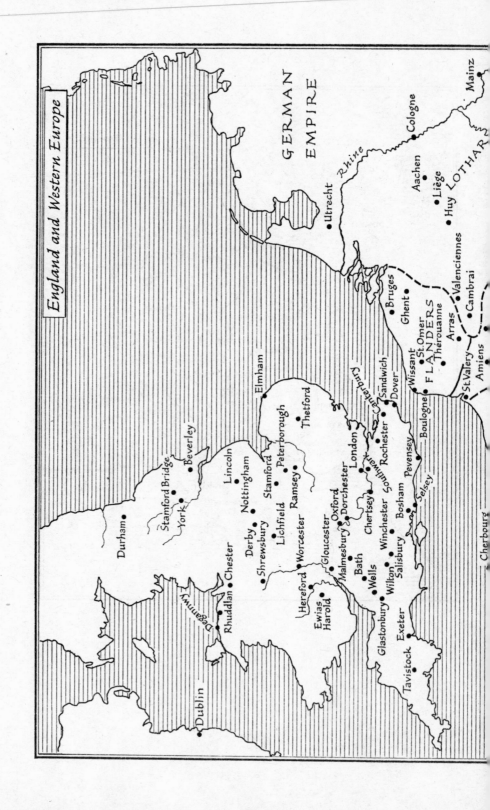

England and Western Europe

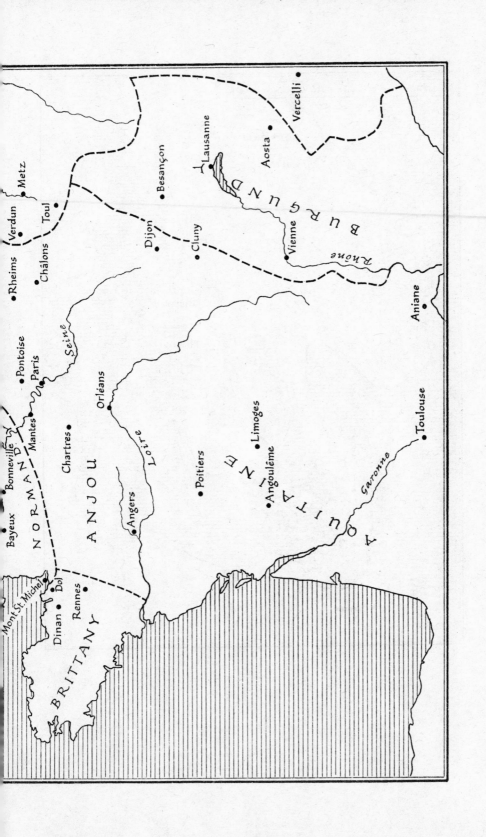

Vercelli

Aosta

Lausanne

Metz
Verdun
Rheims
Toul
Châlons
Besançon

Dijon

Cluny

BURGUND

Vienne

Rhône

Aniane

Pontoise
Paris

Seine

Orléans

Bonneville
Mantes
Chartres

ANJOU

NORMAN

Loire

Limoges

Poitiers

Angoulême

Toulouse

Garonne

AQUITAINE

Bayeux

Mont St. Michel

Dinan
Dol
Rennes

BRITTANY

Angers

England's Relations with Scandinavia

INDEX

persons are indexed under their first name
* indicates that the person appears on Genealogical Table I
† indicates that the person appears on Genealogical Table II

Aachen, 215

Abingdon (Berks), abbey of, xxi, xxii, 9, 33, 53, 85, 135–6, 250n.
  abbots of, *see* Rothulf, Siward, Spearhavoc

Achard, bishop of Avranches, 283

Adam of Bremen, xxv

Adela, countess of Flanders, 301

Adelidis, abbess of Barking, 280n.

Adeline of Beaumont, 301

Aelis, countess of Burgundy, 41

Agatha, wife of Edward the Exile,* 19, 215–216, 218

Agnes, countess of Anjou, 98

Ailred of Rievaulx, xxiv, 101, 131–2, 216n., 264, 277, 281–4, 288, 344

Alan III, count of Brittany, 40, 41n.

Alberic, cardinal-bishop of Ostia, 274–6

Alcuin, 12

Alexander III, pope, xix, 278–81, 284, 309 ff., 325, 344

Alfred, aetheling,* 27, 30, 31, 34, 37, 39, 40, 44–6, 89, 106, 114, 117, 137, 257, 308, 339–40

Alfred, king of Wessex, 3, 9, 14, 17, 26, 30, 32, 128, 162, 287, 336

Alfred, Edward's equerry, 125

Amesbury (Wilts), 151

Amiens, bishop of, *see* Guy

Anagni, 280

Andover (Hants), 6

Andrew, king of Hungary, 216–17

Anfrid Cocksfoot, 125

Anglo-Saxon Chronicle, xxi–xxii, 4, 5, 11, 46, 96–7, 118, 188, 219, 342–3

Anjou, 98
  count of, *see* Geoffrey Martel

Anselm, archbishop of Canterbury, 268, 284

Anund, king of Sweden,† 52, 58, 377

army, 94, 111–13, 123–4, 145, 169–76, 191, 198–9, 202, 205–6, 237–8, 246

Arnulf I, count of Flanders, 98n.

Arnulf, bishop of Lisieux, 283, 325

Arthur, king, 286

Ashdon (Essex), *see* Assandun

Ashingdon (Essex), *see* Assandun

Asmund, Svein's foster-son, 200

Assandun, battle of (1016), 11, 339
  church of, 229n.

Asser, 26

Athelstan, king of Wessex, 26–7, 192, 201, 336; *see also* Æthelstan

Athulf, bishop of Hereford, 30n., 329; *see also* Æthelwulf

Attila, king of the Huns, 23

Audemer, St, 71, 128

Augsburg, bishop of, *see* Bruno

Aust (Glos), 208

Avranches, abbey of, 230

Axmouth (Devon), 100n.

Azur, royal steward, 164

Ælfgar, earl of E. Anglia, Mercia, 20, 88–9, 106n., 115, 119, 127, 189n., 193–7, 206–10, 243, 297, 335, 342

Ælfgar, thegn, 75, 88, 333

Ælfgifu, King Æthelred's wife,* 28–30, 32

Ælfgifu of Northampton,* 37–9, 42, 43n., 44

Ælfgifu, named on Bayeux Tapestry, 222n.

Ælfgifu, abbess of Wilton, 271n.

Æfheah (St), archbishop of Canterbury, 5, 6, 10, 29n., 329

Ælfhelm, earl, 43

Ælfhun, bishop of London, 30n., 34, 329

Ælfleda, countess of Northumbria, 194n.

Ælflida, King Magnus's reputed mother, 58n.

Ælfmaer, bishop of Selsey, 30n., 329

Ælfmod, thegn, 29n.

Ælfric, Wihtgar's son, 77n.

Ælfric 'the Homilist', abbot of Eynsham, 9

Ælfric Puttoc, archbishop of York, 61, 104, 331, 333

Ælfsi, abbot of Peterborough, 34

Ælfsige, bishop of Winchester, 30n.

Ælfstan, abbot of St Augustine's, Canterbury, 77

Ælfstan, thegn, 75, 88n., 156, 164, 333

Ælfswith, the aetheling Æthelstan's foster-mother, 34